Family Stories and the Life Course

Across Time and Generations

Family Stories and the Life Course

Across Time and Generations

Edited by

Michael W. Pratt
Wilfrid Laurier University

Barbara H. Fiese
Syracuse University

LEA LAWRENCE ERLBAUM ASSOCIATES, PUBLISHERS
2004 Mahwah, New Jersey London

Lawrence Erlbaum Associates, Inc., Publishers
10 Industrial Avenue
Mahwah, New Jersey 07430

Cover design by Kathryn Houghtaling Lacey

Library of Congress Cataloging-in-Publication Data

Family stories and the life course : across time and generations /
edited by Michael W. Pratt, Barbara H. Fiese.
p. cm.
Includes bibliographical references and index.
ISBN 0–8058–4282–9
1. Family—Psychological aspects. 2. Developmental psychology.
3. Intergenerational relations. I. Pratt, Michael W. II. Fiese, Barbara H.
HQ728.F32443 2004
306.85-dc22 2003049447

Books published by Lawrence Erlbaum Associates are printed on acid-free paper, and their bindings are chosen for strength and durability.

Printed in the United States of America
10 9 8 7 6 5 4 3 2 1

To Helen and Adelle, and to the many generations gone before and to come.

—MWP

To all those who have shared and been part of our family stories.

—BHF

Contents

Preface

This book tells the tale of recent psychological research and theory on family stories. Family stories are broadly defined as narrative accounts of personal experiences that have meaning to individuals and to the family as a whole. These chapters draw on work that focuses on the act of telling family stories, as well as the *content* and *coherence* of family narratives. The process of telling family stories is linked to central aspects of development, including language acquisition, affect regulation, and family interaction patterns. The messages inherent in these stories serve to socialize children into gender roles, reinforce moral lessons, consolidate identity, and connect generations. Thus the topic of this book extends across traditional developmental psychology, personality theory, and family studies.

Drawing broadly on the epigenetic framework for individual development articulated by Erik Erikson, as well as on conceptions of the family life cycle and the family as a dynamic system of interacting roles and relations, we bring together contemporary examples of psychological research on family stories and their implications for development and change at different points throughout the life course. The book is divided into sections that focus on family stories at different points in the life cycle, from early childhood, through adolescence and identity formation, young adulthood and the establishment of intimacy, midlife and parenting, and finally mature adulthood and its intergenerational meaning in the roles of partner and grandparent. During each of these periods of the life cycle, research focusing on individual development within an Eriksonian framework of ego strengths is highlighted.

The dynamic role of family stories is also featured here, with work exploring the links between storytelling, family process, intergenerational attachment, and development. We hope that our broad developmental focus can serve to integrate the exciting diversity of this work, and foster further questions and research into the emerging field of family narrative.

Researchers use family narratives in a range of different ways, and the book attempts to illustrate the diversity of these analytic and conceptual approaches. In early development, the research focus in much of the narrative work on the family has been on children's initial acquisition of narrative styles and competencies as well as the development of attachment within the family context. Work on adolescent and young adult narratives in the family has often investigated stories as reflecting, even constituting, patterns of identity and intimacy development during this crucial period of the life span. In mid- and later adulthood, family stories have been explored as important in the representation and transmission of family and personal values to children and to the outside world. Both the process and the meaning of storytelling are our central concerns. As well, the comparative cultural context of family storytelling is explored in several of the chapters.

Throughout the book, narratives also are central as a method for exploring questions of individual and family development, as analyzed through the use of a variety of both quantitative and qualitative methods. While the history of this work in psychology is not long, the authors of these chapters are some of the leading contemporary experts in the field of family narrative, and the range of theoretical and methodological approaches here exemplifies the potential of this rapidly expanding topic area.

ACKNOWLEDGMENTS

As authors concerned with the dynamics of family stories, we must recognize, more than most, the contributions of our own families to everything that we have written here. Mike Pratt wishes to acknowledge the legacy of early family stories from his own parents and grandparents, Ted and Louise Pratt, Carrie Ann Gibson, Florence and William Pratt, whose tales of earlier lives, times and places meant much to his own sense of family, and nurtured a long-lasting interest in family narratives that has spanned his career in the study of developmental psychology. His wife and daughter, Helen and Adelle, have helped him to continue and enrich this early legacy by bringing their own lives into the scope of a new family, and he is grateful for their support and care in all the work that he does. As this book goes to press, he welcomes a new member, Bob Wickett, into his family as Adelle's partner, undoubtedly the source of many new tales and pleasures in extending the tapestry of his family's life.

Mike feels mentored and encouraged in this work by a variety of colleagues, most particularly by Philip and Carolyn Cowan, who have fostered his interest in family research for many years, and provided him with opportunities to share these interests with them and their students, and by Dan McAdams, whose research on generativity and on narrative has been a true inspiration for him both before and throughout the work on this book. He also thanks his long-time research collaborators, Bruce Hunsberger, Mark Pancer, Joan Norris, and Mary Louise Arnold, for their support and collegiality in the undertakings that have led in these directions. Many students, both graduate and undergraduate, over the years at Wilfrid Laurier have contributed much to this enterprise, and brought their own interests and questions to his family research. For all this, and the pleasures of learning together, he thanks them.

Barbara recognizes the continued support from the Family Narrative Consortium: Arnold Sameroff, Harold Grotevant, Frederick S. Wamboldt, Susan Dickstein, and Deborah Fravel. Each in their own way, and through their own stories, have provided invaluable opportunities to explore the multi-faceted nature of family narratives and the encouragement to pursue this work. The members of the Family Heritage Project, Nicole Bickham, Chris Chance, Kimberly Howell, Kathleen Marjinsky, Gemma Skilllman, Tom Tomcho, and John Wilder were exemplary in connecting with families and creating an atmosphere of collaboration in the Family Research Lab. Countless undergraduates at Syracuse University have spent painstaking hours transcribing, coding, and recoding family stories over the past several years. Barbara hopes that they have gone on to create family stories of their own.

Finally, the opportunity to work with so many fine chapter authors in doing this book has made the sometimes taxing task of shepherding such an edited undertaking a genuine pleasure. We also appreciate the faith in this book shown by our editor at Lawrence Erlbaum Associates, Bill Webber, and the excellent support the staff at Erlbaum has provided during its production.

—Michael W. Pratt
—Barbara H. Fiese

1

Families, Stories, and the Life Course: An Ecological Context

Michael W. Pratt
Wilfrid Laurier University

Barbara H. Fiese
Syracuse Unviersity

> *All happy families resemble one another, but each unhappy family is unhappy in its own way.*
>
> —Tolstoy, *War and Peace*

This is a book about families and the stories they tell. Because all families are unique, they each have their own distinctive stories (even the happy ones, despite Tolstoy's famous remark), stories that express the lives of their individual members, but that are also something more than simply the sum of those individual lives. In this opening chapter, we trace a psychological perspective on how the stories of individuals and their families are intertwined across the life course, setting this tale within the larger ecological context of understanding that psychological research has begun to contribute to thinking about the family across the life course. In particular, we identify three properties of stories that broaden our understanding of their role in family development. First, story telling is an *act,* through the process of which children learn to become competent narrators. Second, stories also have a *message,* such that children and adults may receive valuable lessons from them, often ones consistent with cultural mores. Finally, stories aid in the creation of a personal *identity* that evolves over time and integrates lived experiences with meaning-making processes. These three ideas are key elements in all of the discussion that follows.

The chapter begins by addressing the family, and its ecological and developmental contexts in the human life cycle. We then turn to a discussion of narrative as a way of thinking and knowing, and as a core element in the individual's growth and change across the life course. Finally, we articulate models of how the family and narrative intersect in development, and then introduce the chapters to follow.

THE FAMILY AND ITS CONTEXTS

Bronfenbrenner (1979) first clearly drew the attention of psychologists to the fact that the individual's development is embedded in a widening circle of environments and influences, from the most immediate settings of the child's life to the broadest influences of the surrounding culture and society. These broader influences, such as the legal system or society's socioeconomic institutions, act much more indirectly, because the child typically does not actually interact with their representatives. Their influence is instead felt through the shaping that they exert with respect to the child's own personal "microenvironments," of which the central one, particularly in early life, is the family. In Jerome Bruner's (1985) elegant image, parents and other guiding adults represent the "vicars of culture," who interpret for the child the wider world, and bring him or her into society's byways.

In this sense, the family plays a pivotal role in socialization, as an intermediary between the individual and the wider cultural context. The family provides the earliest physical and relational settings in which the child learns to grasp the wider universe of objects and events, and the complexities of human emotion and behavior. Parents and their children talk about everyday, mundane family experiences, such as a trip to the park or a visit to grandparents, constructing accounts of what these experiences were like and what they may mean (e.g., Fivush, 1994; McCabe & Peterson, 1991). Children thus first hear and ultimately learn to recount stories of their personal past in the context of such family interactions. In this book, we aim to explore this role of the family, and in particular, to study the ways that families are part of the child's development of storytelling skills, of value acquisition, and the socialization of beliefs and behavior.

Families are also the setting where much of individual development happens across the life course. While we readily acknowledge the role of the family in the lives of the youngest generation, development occurs in all family members, throughout the life course (e.g., Baltes, 1987). In this sense, families serve as a place for the individual to find and explore new senses of the self and others at all ages, from early childhood into late adulthood. Family stories are one way in which individuals connect across generations and create a sense of family history and identity (Martin, Hagestad, & Diedrick, 1988). Families are thus stage, company, and audience for us all across the life cycle, and stories are an intimate part of that process. So Shakespeare's Hamlet, the prototype for humankind's identity search (Bloom, 1998), as he dies asks Horatio to tell of his life, bound as it is so intensely to his own troubled family history: "Things standing thus unknown shall live behind me. If thou didst ever hold me in thy heart, absent thee from felicity awhile, and in this harsh world draw thy breath in pain, to tell my story." In this book, we want to describe how families support, guide, or sometimes stifle, the growth of their members and their personal sense of self and identity, through the stories they share and shape.

Families are distinctive in another way from other ecological influences in the individual's life, not only as a special place, but also across time. Of all the relationships into which the individual child enters, the bonds of the family are most enduring. The relationships we have with kin are complex and variable, but they are also life-long and indeed enduring across generations; families are the places where these enduring bonds grow, develop, and are often tested. We may choose and then reject our friends, our associates, even our spouses, but the bonds of parents and children, or those of siblings, even if troubled, are not so voluntary or so easily discarded, as Shakespeare's *King Lear* finds to his sorrow (and ultimately, relief). In the midst of trying to disown his children, Lear reminds us how impossible this really is to do: "How sharper than a serpent's tooth it is to have a thankless child." Families endure, even as they come to include new members through birth, adoption, marriage or remarriage, and their perspectives and stances with respect to the wider world may echo across the generations in the kinds of stories they tell to new members (e.g., Fiese, Hooker, Kotary, Schwagler, & Rimmer, 1995). In this book, we explore these intergenerational functions of family stories too.

The Ecological Context of the Family

In understanding and elaborating the role of the family in lifespan development, we will find it useful to take a systems perspective. Parke and Buriel (1998) make the valuable point that such a perspective leads us to a consideration of both the overlapping sets of dyadic relationships (e.g., parent-child, marital, sibling) that are the building blocks of the family, and also of the entire "family unit" per se, and its possible effects on the lives of individual family members. To date, however, most family research has concentrated on roles and (at most) dyadic relationships, and has neglected to explore ways in which the family as a whole may be characterized, and may serve to influence individual child and adult development (Norris, Pratt, & Kuiack, 2003).

Reiss (1989) is one theorist who has directed attention to this issue. He has suggested the importance of the role of family paradigms, myths, stories, and rituals, each of which represent ways through which the family organizes and communicates perceptions of the world to its members. For example, families may have particular traditions or routines for daily events, such as dinnertime or bedtime, and these routines may include special stories or rituals. These family processes convey important and enduring views and values about how the world should be understood, and these views and values may be passed down through the generations as a result of such family interaction (Fiese, Wilder, & Bickham, 2000; Parke & Buriel, 1998). Though our focus in this book is specifically on family stories, it seems obvious that Reiss's various constructs are overlapping, and that stories are embedded within family rituals, like sharing meals or bedtime, and serve to convey family belief systems.

As noted, the family "micro-system" (to use Bronfenbrenner's term) is itself surrounded by wider social contexts that influence the developing individual, both directly and indirectly, through their roles in influencing the family's other members (Bronfenbrenner, 1979), all the way up to the broadest, cultural factors that shape the individual and the family through basic values and views (the "macrosystem"). Several of the chapters in the current volume focus on what may be conveyed about the self and the world in different cultures through the kinds of stories that families tell and the storytelling patterns in which they engage (see chapters 12 and 13).

How are these various ecological levels involved in shaping family stories? McAdams (2001) argues that individual life stories, which in his theory are the core components of identity at least in modern societies, are constructed based on the shaping context and resources provided by the wider culture. Thus, one of the commonest of life stories available in North American society is an "individual success" script, the "rags to riches," self-made millionaire of Sunday morning telemarketing fame. In a broader sense, such an individualism theme has been a pervasive strain in American culture for centuries (e.g., Bellah, Madsen, Sullivan, Swidler, & Tipten, 1985), and individuals may readily adapt it in recounting their own life histories. The Bronfenbrenner ecological model indicates, however, that intermediate levels such as the family and the subculture will likely be important in this process of formulating the individual life story as well (e.g., McGoldrick, Heiman, & Carter, 1993), through the mediating role they play in individual socialization as embedded in the wider society. So, for example, grandchildren may, with pride and a sense of family connection, tell stories of the ambitious and resourceful immigrant generations that preceded them and widened their current opportunities (Hilbers, 1997).

Cultural-Historical Context of the Life Course and the Family

As Erikson (1963) recognized, the human life cycle has a basic, evolutionarily constructed pattern that is built into the ground plan of our species (obviously shared generally with other mammals, see Hrdy, 1999). Children are born dependent and in need of extensive care. If they receive this care, they grow toward puberty, and sexual and reproductive maturity. After a period of adult reproductive potential, their fertility is over or reduced, and they ultimately reach old age and death. This basic, if stark, outline is biologically guided and universal, and it entails the central role of the family (or at least some caretaker) in enabling the child's growth and development. However, it was also Erikson's (1963) genius to acknowledge, much more than his mentor Freud, the richness and complexity of ways in which human social life, itself sprung from this biological potential, can organize the processes of development across the life cycle.

Erikson's (1963) well-known model of eight stages in the individual's life course is closely keyed to the developmental history of the family. The initial five stages constitute a first, childhood act in this play of life, with scenes depicting the struggle of trust versus mistrust, autonomy versus shame, initiative versus guilt, industry versus inferiority, and identity versus confusion. These are enacted typically within the family of our birth. The second act, consisting of scenes of intimacy versus alienation, generativity versus stagnation, and integrity versus despair, takes place within the context of a more extended and reconstituted family during the long period of human adulthood. Erikson (1963) described, with an anthropologist's appreciative eye, the ways in which different cultures patterned these basic building blocks of the human life span differently, and sought to trace the possible implications of such differences.

Interestingly, the ways in which these stages or periods of the life course are marked also appear to have been historically variable. In the past century, for example, the average human life span in technologically developed countries has increased substantially (perhaps 20–25 years), and this change, along with many other cultural and societal changes, has had a large influence on how scholars (and others) describe the life course. The terminology of development in later life has thus become increasingly differentiated as researchers have pursued these questions (e.g., into young-old versus old-old, Smith &

Baltes, 1997). Similarly, the transition from adolescence to adulthood has been lengthening in modern societies, due to vocational and technological changes, and a new period of "emerging adulthood" has recently been suggested (Arnett, 2000).

What are the implications of such historical changes for the intergenerational family? As adults live longer, family ties of course become more enduring as well as complex, but they generally do not seem to be weakening. Putney and Bengtson (2001), writing about midlife and the family, conclude: "Findings from empirical research show that while families are more diverse in structure and process, intergenerational attachments remain strong. Our review here suggests that individuals need the solidarity of the multigenerational family and will go to great efforts to preserve it" (pp. 562–563). We believe that stories can play a central role in establishing and maintaining these family bonds, and some of the chapters in this volume are testimony to the ways in which researchers are attempting to study these intergenerational issues (e.g., chapters 11, 15, and 16).

Practicing and Representing Aspects of the Family

Fiese et al. (2000), drawing on the work of Reiss (1989), have articulated a key distinction between the practicing and representing aspects of family life. These two concepts are meant to capture the contrast between the family's *behavioral* interactions, on the one hand, and the *beliefs* of its members that both shape and respond to these practices, on the other. These two aspects of family life are seen as mutually interactive and transactional in a dynamic sense. However, they are exemplified for research purposes by contrasting types of constructs, notably "family rituals" in the case of practices, and "family stories" for beliefs (Reiss, 1989; Sameroff & Fiese, 2000).

Despite this clear and useful conceptual divide, it is apparent that the study of these two aspects of family life can each involve both practicing and representing aspects. For example, family rituals, such as dinnertime, involve ongoing, patterned social interactions that serve to stabilize the family and provide meanings and expectancies for its members. These practicing aspects of dinnertime rituals also can be studied in terms of the beliefs and values of the family's members regarding their structure and purposes (e.g., Fiese & Marjinsky, 1999). Most germane to the current volume, family stories have both representing and practicing characteristics (Fiese et al., 1999). The content, themes, and coherence of specific family stories may be studied as reflective of the family's view of the world and its values and expectations for its members (Sameroff & Fiese, 2000). The process of a story's actual telling may also be studied, as a practicing aspect of the family, and this may reflect much about the interpersonal climate and relationships within the family. Stories are always *for someone,* as McAdams (1999) points out, always inherently social and dialogical, like other aspects of discourse (e.g., Bakhtin, 1981), and the ways in which they are negotiated between family tellers and listeners are revealing and important to examine. For example, there may be cultural differences in the extent to which young children are expected to be attentive listeners, with Asian parents more likely than their North American counterparts to tell stories of moral "lessons" to the young child. These cultural differences may be construed as reflecting different conceptions of the child listener across these cultures, which in turn translate into different associated parental storytelling practices (chapter 13, this volume).

Fiese et al. (2000) go on to describe how the practicing and representing aspects of the family are instantiated at the various levels of the family discussed above. Marital, parent-child, and sibling dyads, as well as triadic connections within the boundaries of the family, all have both behavioral and representational aspects that have been studied in family research. For example, at the level of triadic interaction, marital alliances in husbands and wives, as well as parent-child alliances, have been compared during videotapes of dinnertimes (Vuchinich, Emery, & Cassidy, 1988), indicating that mothers and fathers are more likely to side with each other than with children, overall. The importance of these kinds of triadic relationship patterns is suggested by the work of Katz and Gottman (1995), who found that families in which husbands tend to withdraw from conflicts with their wives also tend to exhibit more intrusive mother-child interactions and associated higher levels of child problems. McHale further calls to our attention how mothers and fathers create co-parenting alliances that can either support healthy child emotional development or disrupt the family system as a whole (McHale & Rasmussen, 1998).

As suggested by Parke and Buriel (1998), the "whole-family" level is crucial to conceptualize and understand, in addition to these multiple interactive levels of the dyad and the triad within the family unit. Family rituals and stories are valuable ways of investigating this broadest level of analysis (Fiese et al., 2000). Thus, family stories may vary in content as well as in their coherence and depiction of the social world. For example, Oppenheim, Wamboldt, Gavin, Renouf, and Emde (1996) showed that couples whose conjoint narratives of their child's birth were more emotionally coherent and expressive subsequently showed greater levels of marital satisfaction. Given what we know of the couple system and the family, these family-level representations might be expected to be linked to child adaptation as well (Cowan, Powell, & Cowan, 1998).

Despite the fact that rituals and stories are useful and important as indicators of whole family patterns and meanings, it also seems clear that they can be studied with respect to dyadic or triadic aspects of family relationships, and be informative in that regard. For example, a number of studies have now investigated the relations between children's narrative representations of the parent's caregiving and children's own adaptation. It has been shown, for example, that young children's stories of the mother as responsive are associated with fewer behavioral problems in the child (Oppenheim, Nir, Warren, & Emde, 1997; Sher-Censor & Oppenheim, chapter 4, this volume), and that adolescents' greater openness to their parents' perspectives or "voices" in stories of parent-child value teaching is associated with better subsequent adjustment and a clearer sense of identity (e.g., chapter 7, this volume). Such parent-child research reflects the fact that stories can be used to explore the entire gamut of family relationships and their implications for growth and development. There has also been considerable research on couple stories and their relations to child outcomes (e.g., Fiese & Marjinsky, 1999). Interestingly, however, there has been little work on siblings' stories and their potential implications to date. Also, current research in this domain as in others too often has been focused on mothers, and has failed to investigate the stories told by fathers (Cowan, 1999; Parke & Buriel, 1998).

STORIES AND THE INDIVIDUAL LIFE CYCLE

So far, we have used the term "narrative" loosely and quite interchangeably with respect to the everyday term "stories." In this section, we provide more context for the definition of narrative, as a particular modality of human thought (Bruner, 1986), and explain its background in recent theory and research within the field of psychology.

Understanding Narrative

Bruner (1986, 1990) has made a key distinction between different ways of knowing or thinking in human experience, contrasting the "paradigmatic mode," on the one hand, with the "narrative mode" on the other. Bruner argued that these two distinctive ways of thinking are both widely available to humans, yet are fundamentally distinct and not reduceable to one other. Paradigmatic thinking is exemplified by classification of objects or events as fitting within a particular category; such thinking about these objects or events (e.g., an orange) is governed by category membership, and all examples within the categories are treated as equivalent based on this shared property (Polkinghorne, 1996). This sort of paradigmatic cognitive activity allows the individual to draw upon general knowledge and reasoning skills based in abstract formulations about object properties (e.g., the skins of such fruits need to be peeled before they are eaten). The criteria by which such reasoning is evaluated include systematic logic and "truthfulness," or correspondence with a shared, objectified reality (Bruner, 1990).

In contrast, the narrative mode treats individual experiences as unique historical events, and involves thinking about these events in terms of their organization into meaningful temporal episodes based on human motives or intentions, actions, and outcomes. These organizations in time are the prototypic "plots" for understanding everyday human activity, and for stories of such activity, which children learn very early to grasp through the development of a gradually elaborated "theory of mind" in interpreting the behavior of others (McAdams, 2001). Intentional human actions are thus seen as categorically distinct from the body's physical movements, even by the youngster of 4 or 5 (Smith, 1978). It is the meaningful "gestalt" of such events that forms the basis for reasoning about them in the narrative mode, implying that they have a particular order and organization, and that they are linked through the intentional quality of human activity (Polkinghorne, 1996). The criteria for evaluating such narrative knowing are quite different from those for paradigmatic reasoning, involving plausibility and coherence as aspects of a "good story," instead of logic and truth (Bruner, 1990).

These characteristics of the narrative mode of knowing mean that stories and narratives are not simple reproductions of personal life experiences, but rather are *reconstructions* of the past, through the use of interpretive "plots" that are adapted from the repertoire of stories available and learned from the culture (Polkinghorne, 1996). Interestingly, the forms for understanding intention and everyday activities may differ in some respects across cultures, as work on the theory of mind in different cultural contexts suggests (e.g., Vinden, 1996). If this is so, then available story plots or forms may differ for different cultures, and families may play an important role in displaying these cultural modalities to the developing individual (Miller, 1994). Narratives also reflect past events in the light of current understandings and interpretations of their meanings and outcomes. In other words, narrative knowing as a process is in some deep sense a creative act, and involves the possibility of reconstruction of personal experiences differently at different points in the life course, depending on the individual's perspective and maturity (Polkinghorne, 1996). For example, Pratt, Norris, Arnold, and Filyer (1999), following earlier work by McAdams, Diamond, St. Aubin, & Mansfield (1997) on the "generativity script" in midlife, reported that highly generative adults across the life span commonly tell life stories that are seen as much more positive and "redemptive" in current telling than they were during their original experience. And, as the enduring popularity of Dickens' *A Christmas Carol* attests, life stories with these redemptive types of structures were preferred over those of other types by a panel of uninstructed raters (Pratt et al., 1999).

Past Psychological Research on Narrative

McAdams (2001) has reviewed the history of narrative research in the field of personality psychology, documenting how the concept of life stories moved from the position of an exotic, somewhat speculative backwater earlier in the 20th century, to a dynamic and much more central position within the field in the 1980s and 1990s. As he notes, this transformation in the role of narrative was paralleled in many other areas of psychology, such as clinical and developmental, and indeed in the broader domains of history and the social sciences as well (e.g., Habermas & Bluck, 2000). For example, there has been a 500% increase in the use of "narrative" as a keyword when comparing citations in the psychological literature from 1991–2001 to 1980–1990. The idea of narrative, with its focus on the historical life context, and the construction of an individual narrator's perspective or "voice," has become a potential post-modern grounding metaphor for the fields of the human sciences as a whole (Sarbin, 1986).

As a part of this program of work, new narrative theories of individual development have been advanced, particularly by Hermanns (1996) and by McAdams (2001). Hermanns' (1996) framework emphasizes the dialogical nature of the self, that it is constructed from multiple life "stories" and "voices" that are constantly in dialogue and response with one another, as the person seeks to interpret the diverse experiences of the past across many contexts. These ideas are similar to Gergen's (1992) model of the self as shifting and in flux, as meaning in the postmodern world is not in the text itself, but relative and constantly renegotiated by the listener and speaker. Consequently, the self is understood as dialogical in nature, and is not seen as a unitary, coherent whole.

McAdams's (2001) most recent formulation of his theory provides a comprehensive overview of the development of narrative skills in childhood toward the core of modern identity formation, the "life story," in adolescence and young adulthood. This life story is for McAdams the center of the individual's personality, which serves to give coherence and meaning to the adult's sense of self. While McAdams (2001) accepts that there is a degree of ongoing revision and change in the life story, he is more sanguine about the possibilities of formulating a unitary, coherent identity across the diverse experiences and contexts of life than many of the post-modern theorists such as Gergen (1992) or Hermanns (1996). In the next section, we follow McAdams (2001) outline in discussing the development of narrative capacities in the individual's life context.

Narrative and the Life Course

Important cognitive developments provide the constituents that enable narrative skills to grow and develop across the life course. During the first 2 years of life, as Piaget (1970) documented, infants' symbolic capacities develop markedly, and their capacity to understand and represent the self emerges as well. Toward the end of the second year, with the emergence of language and its implications for memory, a capacity for a personalized autobiographical memory begins to develop (Howe & Courage, 1997). Over the course of the next several years, parents and other adults help children learn to formulate stories of their past experiences for telling, and generate a limited sense of the self and its past through these processes. Based in these interchanges with parents and the print and visual media of books, television, now the Internet as well, children also become acquainted with the conventional forms of stories in our culture, with orderly elements or episodes that involve a problem, attempts to deal with it, and an outcome or ending (Mandler, 1984). Children come to rely on such structures in processing and remembering their own and others' experiences, and find that information that diverges from this framework is more difficult to store and remember. Many other developments, such as children's understanding of the goals and intentions of others, are also critical during the preschool and early school years, as documented through study of the emergence of the "theory of mind" in childhood (e.g., Wellman, 1993). Everyday storytelling activities are also a medium for socializing perspective taking, critical thinking, and other intellectual achievement prior to the onset of formal schooling (Ochs, Taylor, Rudolph, & Smith, 1992). Indeed, the ways in which cultures support storytelling prior to formal schooling suggest its central role in cognitive development in the formative early years (Rogoff & Toma, 1997). These core elements of the autobiographical memory system have been called "personal event memories" (Pillemer, 1998).

Despite these important cognitive advances, however, the capacity to represent the self through a complex life story that traces personal memories within the context of an autobiography still is not readily apparent until adolescence

(Habermas & Bluck, 2000). It is only with the development of cognitive capacities for formulating systematic causal explanations that link inner qualities of the self and past events and experiences that a personal "life story" can develop. For example, adolescents for the first time become capable of understanding an inner self that is distinct from its outer behaviors, and that such inner qualities can provide thematic coherence which links together superficially different behaviors in a complex and systematic way (e.g., Selman, 1980). Advances in socio-cognitive capacities are thus seen as necessary for development of a life story in adolescence (Grotevant, 1993; Habermas & Bluck, 2000; McAdams, 2001).

Throughout the extended period of midlife and adulthood, the personal life story continues to be elaborated and extended, as the individual, to some degree, reworks and re-visions experiences to fit current concerns and issues, particularly those focused around identity issues (McAdams, 2001). Contrary to the emphasis in Erikson's (1963) original formulations, identity in modern societies continues to be a matter of importance and concern across the life course, rather than being "settled" by young adulthood. People's life stories are likely to be highly variable, but some evidence suggests that the coherence of the life story may continue to develop even into mature adulthood, perhaps through practice and systematic experiences of the retelling of central life events to others (e.g., Kemper, 1992; Pratt & Robins, 1991).

FAMILIES AND STORIES: AN INTIMATE RELATIONSHIP

In this section, we turn from the individual's development to an examination of the place of narrative within the family life cycle, and consider what some of the most important questions and issues may be that family narrative research can address, as well as the role of the wider culture in relation to family narrative. Finally, we discuss the various ways in which narratives have been used so far in family research.

In thinking about the role of family in relation to narrative across the life course, and within the culture, we have been guided by two distinct perspectives on individual development: the epigenetic framework of Erikson (1963) and the sociocultural framework of Vygotsky (1978). While the Eriksonian view is relatively familiar, and was described earlier in this chapter, the second perspective may be less generally known. Vygotsky and others in his Russian sociocultural school (e.g., Bakhtin, 1981) viewed development as a social process of the individual child adapting interpersonal interactions with others, especially adults, to private, intrapersonal cognitive ends (Wertsch, 1991). Vygotsky's most elaborated application of his theory was to language and its role in thinking. Thus, he held that the child first learns to communicate interpersonally with others, and then gradually adapts this social process to the service of his or her own internal thinking and cognitive self-regulation. The self as thinker becomes both speaker and addressee in a fundamentally dialogical relationship, first in the "private speech" phenomenon of talking aloud to the self in the preschool years, and later as the "inner speech," or covert verbal thought of maturity (Vygotsky, 1978). We believe this sociocultural framework is of interest across the life course with regard to narrative and its development.

Stories and the Study of the Family Life Cycle

In Erikson's (1968) conception, identity is the central element in life course development, joining childhood and adulthood through the gateway of adolescence. In such a metaphor, the family becomes the key element of the wider field on which this gateway is constructed. McAdams's theory (2001), as discussed earlier, grounds identity development, in the Eriksonian sense, through the development of a personal life story during adolescence and young adulthood. During childhood, the young person first becomes skilled in telling stories about personal experiences within the nurturing confines of the family, through the supportive activities of parents, who encourage the child to practice and develop these skills through shared recountings of past experiences (e.g., Fivush, 1994). However, it is not until adolescence that these sorts of "personal event memories" become organized into a coherent life story (Habermas & Bluck, 2000). And even into later life, the family retains its central importance in life narratives (Coleman, Ivani-Chalian, & Robinson 1998). Here we trace the family's role in these major developments.

Childhood for Erikson (1963) represents the period when a basic sense of self and of relationships, and a variety of skills important to the culture, first must be acquired. As noted, one of the most important of these skills is narrative, as the child learns to tell about, and indeed, to create, an autobiographical past through the experience of joint storytelling with the parent about his or her own everyday experiences (Fivush, 1994; McCabe & Peterson, 1991). The social context of this activity is centrally important, as the parent or guiding adult initially provides almost complete "scaffolding" of the young child's verbal memories, as Fivush and McCabe and Peterson have demonstrated. Consistent with the ideas of the sociocultural perspective on development (Rogoff, Baker-Sennett, Lacasa, & Goldsmith, 1995; Vygotsky,

1978), the child gradually acquires the skills to tell about personal experiences by adapting the parental supports of this social context to his or her own individual narrative efforts. In essence, this process suggests that the child internalizes the parent's guiding and organizing model for retelling, and makes it his or her own. This retelling also may aid in the construction of "the" family story as a condensed and complex marker for family beliefs and values. Variability in mother-child dyads in how this is carried out suggests that family environments may shape some differences in the patterning of this skill with implications for the child's own later narrative development (e.g., Peterson & McCabe, 1994; chapter 2, this volume).

From the sociocultural perspective, then, families are the mediators of culture (Bruner, 1985), and they can be expected to foster differing patterns and styles of storytelling within the context of family life (e.g., Miller, 1994; Wang, 2001). For example, Chinese parents are more likely to utilize shared family narratives as an opportunity to teach lessons to the child, whereas North American families are likely to emphasize instead the child's creativity and autonomy in these family stories (Miller, Wiley, Fung, & Liang, 1997). The broad distinction between a more collective and a more individuated self in maturity across cultures (Markus & Kitayama, 1991) may be to some degree reflected in and traceable to these different patterns of narrative interaction in childhood.

Adolescence and young adulthood are the key periods for the acquisition of a sense of identity, which involves both an understanding of the self through time and of the self's distinctiveness from others (Erikson, 1968). These two components of identity serve to create both temporal and personal coherence within modern adulthood. The individual life story, according to McAdams (2001), provides these critical elements of identity in modern societies. The personal life events that young children have learned to recall through experiences with parents now become integrated into a larger, coherent life story. As Thorne (2000) points out, however, these narratives are fundamentally interpersonal, being told and retold for others as the individual seeks to construct a sense of self in a social world. Again, then, the essentially social nature of these developments is highlighted, consistent with the sociocultural perspective.

Is the family in some sense a key setting for this development? Certainly a consensus has developed that one of the essential tasks for the adolescent in North American culture is to establish a sense of autonomy or independence, while simultaneously maintaining a sense of connectedness to parents and the extended family (Grotevant & Cooper, 1998). Adolescents' stories of important issues in their lives commonly involve family relationships, as well as peers, and as noted, adolescents typically tell these life stories to families or friends, who collaborate in the co-construction of these stories as they are told and re-told (Grotevant, Dunbar, Kohler, & Esau, 2000; Thorne, 2000). Indeed, stories of the family dominate mid-adolescents' descriptions of key "turning points" in their lives (Mackey, Arnold, & Pratt, 2001).

Are there cultural differences in the family's role in the formation of the life story? There is certainly evidence that parents in some cultures are less likely to be engaged as listeners to their children's talk than those in other cultures (e.g., Schieffelen, 1990). It would seem likely that there are variations in the ways in which parents respond to their adolescents' recountings of life events, in terms of how the self is to be construed as more or less autonomous or embedded in family relationships, as noted previously for cross-cultural research on childhood, though we are not aware of such work on adolescents to date.

The long period of adulthood and maturity within the human life cycle, largely ignored by Freud in a developmental sense, was described by Erikson as involving a sequence of three distinct stages: intimacy, generativity, and ego integrity. The construction of a new family and the relationships that this engenders in the individual's life are key elements in personal development in the midlife period, and these networks of family continue to increase in some ways in complexity as individuals grow older and further intergenerational links develop. Indeed, midlife adults may play a central role in fostering such linkages across generations within the family (Putney & Bengtson, 2001).

Contemporary research on the "intergenerational stake" in relations of the family in Western societies at least suggests that older adults have a particularly strong investment in solidarity across the generations, as opposed to the adolescent and young adult individual's stronger investment in establishing personal autonomy (Putney & Bengtson, 2001). Concomitant with this, older adults in mid- and later life, particularly women, are often the "kin-keepers" of the family, investing considerable time and energy in maintaining family relationships and connections (Oliveri & Reiss, 1987). Is this role particularly associated with family storytelling? We do not know, but both men and women in later life are prone to discuss the family as the central continuity in their life stories (Coleman et al., 1998). And, as Pratt and Norris (1999) have noted, the life stories of older adults are often given coherence by their sense of having learned important lessons from a more mature family member or other adult figure from their earlier lives.

What is known about culture differences in the role of the family in later life, and its impact on the life story? There is certainly indication that the status of older adults within the society and the family varies considerably across cultures and over historical time (e.g., Hareven, 1977). It seems likely that this may be associated with different messages within these cultures that have distinct implications for the treatment and functioning of older adult family members. For example, Ryan (e.g., 1991) has shown, in her work on the "communication predicament" model of aging in North American cultures, that everyday discourse and forms of address with the elderly are exquisitely sensitive to these sorts of social status issues. Older adults in nursing homes are typically addressed with "baby talk," in ways that appear to outsiders both warm and at the same time demeaning and that may undermine these adults' sense of competence. It seems likely that these practices may be quite different in some Asian cultures, characterized by stronger norms of filial piety (Levy & Langer, 1994). In what ways might this be reflected in the stories told by and about the oldest family members of different societies? Though little has been done on this topic, this question promises to be of interest for future study.

The Multiple Roles of Family Stories in Research

Stories play a number of different roles in the research that makes up this book, and in the field of psychology in general. The role of narratives as a research tool varies on a continuum of centrality, from their use as simply one of a number of techniques for obtaining data on aspects of individual motivation or personality, to a theory-driven conception of their role as a central component in the individual's or family's sense of identity (McAdams et al., 1997). In this section, we briefly review three important uses of narrative that can be documented in previous research, as well as in the chapters of the present volume: narratives as *method,* as *medium,* and as *meaning-making.*

Historically, narratives were first used as *methods* of obtaining information on various aspects of individuals' personalities and qualities. In the tradition of this sort of research (e.g., McClelland, 1961), people are asked to tell stories in response to a stimulus (such as an ambiguous figure) or about a personal life event, and then these stories are coded as revealing a range of different levels of some quality (e.g., level of intimacy or achievement motivation). In such work, the use of narrative as a method is less focal, and stories are not conceived as playing any special or unique role in the development or personality of the individual, but perhaps as simply reflecting one mode of everyday thinking and communication which can be revealing of the individual's personal qualities. Of course, stories about the family also can be used in just such a manner, as a way of exploring the family members' or relationships' characteristic qualities or dynamics, and such usage continues to be an important research strength.

Stories can also be studied as an important *medium* of socialization within social groups, and perhaps particularly within families. Because narrative is a universal mode of communication about everyday events, storytelling is often an important practice in the lives of families (Fiese et al., 1999). Parents tell stories to their children about their own past experiences, and they teach children, collaboratively, to develop the skills of telling and retelling stories about their own current experiences, as we noted earlier (see also Fivush, 1994). Following Reiss (1989), the ways in which stories are told and shared in the family are an important aspect of "practicing," and can reflect interesting variations in the style of family life and relationships (e.g., Fiese et al., 1999; Gould & Dixon, 1993). Of course, the kinds of stories told, specifically differences in story content, can also tell us about the "representing" aspects of family life. For example, males and females may select different kinds of stories to tell their sons and daughters about their past family experiences (Fiese et al., 1995; Pratt, Arnold, & Hilbers, 1998), and these differences may reflect broader issues in gender socialization within the culture.

Finally, stories clearly represent the individual's efforts at *meaning-making*. The act of story telling requires that the teller describe a set of experienced events for the audience, as well as taking a stance regarding the evaluation and implications of these events, even, perhaps, a stance that necessarily carries moral implications (e.g., Tappan, 1991). Furthermore, stories are seen by many narrative theorists as the mechanism by which individuals constitute a sense of the self and its identity (e.g., Gergen, 1992; McAdams, 2001). As noted, McAdams' theory explicitly recognizes this role of the life story in modern society, as providing the developing adolescent or young adult with a sense of personhood that is at the core of personality (McAdams, 2001). Individuals are seen as drawing on the cultural reservoir of stories to provide elements from which the person's sense of self is constructed. Thus, the self as reflected in these life stories would be expected to differ across different cultures (e.g., Miller et al., 1997; Wang, 2001).

This constitutive function for stories with respect to individual identity has its parallels within the context of the family. Families can be said to have their own "identities" too, and family stories serve as an important way of communicating, negotiating, and re-negotiating that identity among their members. Families are a central audience for their individual members, and their representations within personal stories can be revealing of individual and family functioning. For example, Thorne (2000) has argued that important personal memories are always social in fundamental respects, in that they are not generally kept to the self, but shared with family or close friends. These remembered tellings are often linked to the personal memory itself, but also register novel understandings and meanings that reflect distinctive audience reactions. At any rate, the role of the family as audience, as stage, and sometime as director for the retellings of personal memories is implicit in many of the chapters that follow.

THE CHAPTERS IN THIS VOLUME

Shakespeare, in *As You Like It,* described the life course as seven acts ("All the world's a stage, and all the men and women merely players. They have their exits and their entrances; and one man in his time plays many parts, his acts being seven ages.") Simplifying the bard a little, though always a risky proposition, the story of family narrative told in this volume is organized into six sections, following loosely the life and role course of the individual through the family system: childhood, adolescence, young adulthood, mid-life and parenthood, later life and grandparenthood, and finally a more integrative coda that summarizes and comments on the preceding chapters, and extends the prospects for future research.

In Part I, on childhood, our authors focus on the development of both linguistic and social competence. Carole Peterson and Allysa McCabe (chapter 2) describe their research on the ways that parents appear to be involved in young children's acquisition of narrative competence. Robyn Fivush and her colleagues (chapter 3) then discuss research on family narrative processes and children's adaptation, both in linguistic and especially in social modalities. Sher-Censor and David Oppenheim's chapter (chapter 4) focuses on preschool children's social attachment development and its relation to narratives. Finally, JoAnn Robinson and Michael Eltz (chapter 5) describe how more standardized narrative data, drawn from the MacArthur Story Stem battery widely used in the attachment literature, can be used to explore the relations between patterns of early care giving in impoverished families and children's subsequent empathic and agonistic representations of relationships at age 6.

In Part II, covering adolescence and young adulthood, three chapters focus on adolescent narratives and the central issues of identity development within the context of the family. Nora Dunbar and Hal Grotevant (chapter 6) report narratively based research on identity development in early to middle adolescence for a large sample of adopted children. Mary Louise Arnold and colleagues (chapter 7) then describe methods and conceptualizations of older adolescents' representations of their parents' views and voices in their stories, and the ways these are related to adolescent adaptation and identity over time. Finally, Avril Thorne and her colleagues (chapter 8) report on a study of a particular context, parents' decisions about how to discuss their own past drug usage with their teenage children, and the ways that both adolescent and parent identity issues may surface and interact in these decisions.

Part III focuses on the issues of intimacy and romantic relationship development, highlighted in chapter 9 by Susan Dickstein, which draws on the attachment perspective to examine narrative measures and approaches to the investigation of marital and couple functioning in conjunction with individual attachment.

Following this, Part IV includes four chapters that examine parenting and socialization processes from a narrative perspective during the midlife period of adult development. This section begins with a chapter by Dan McAdams (chapter 10) on the Eriksonian construct of generativity and its family and wider societal implications. This is followed by a chapter on parents' stories of their own families of origin and their potential role in socialization processes within the young family by Barbara Fiese and Nicole Bickham (chapter 11). Two chapters then cover the cross-cultural literature on parent-child joint story telling (and listening) and their possible implications for cultural patterns of differences between North American and Chinese societies. Chapter 12, by Qi Wang, focuses on the possible differential socialization of memory functions across cultures that may be rooted in variations in early parent-child dialogue. Heidi Fung and her associates (chapter 13) then discuss East–West cultural differences in the pervasive but neglected role of child *listener.*

Part V covers the role of older adults' family narratives, both within the couple relationship and in the context of grandparenting. Chapter 14, by Odette Gould, describes a cognitive perspective on aging and narrative function in the context of couple and wider social interaction. Chapter 15, by Joan Norris and associates, discusses functions of grandparent narratives in family socialization processes, as well as the role of generativity within this later period of the life course. Ellen Ryan and her associates (chapter 16) then describe work on the functions and processes of intergenerational story writing that bridges the grandparent and grandchild generations.

The final chapter, by Barbara Fiese and Michael Pratt (chapter 17), is a summary and discussion of the previous chapters in the context of two key questions: What do family stories tell us about personal development, and what do narratives tell us about families and the family system? We attempt a beginning integration of life course and systems perspectives on narrative in the family, and suggest some directions for future work in this burgeoning field.

ACKNOWLEDGMENTS

Preparation of this manuscript was supported, in part, by a grant from the Social Sciences and Humanities Research Council of Canada, and by the University Research Professorship Award from Wilfrid Laurier University for 2001–2002 to the first author. The authors thank Bruce Hunsberger for his comments on an earlier draft.

REFERENCES

Arnett, J. J. (2000). Emerging adulthood: A theory of development from the late teens through the twenties. *American Psychologist, 55,* 469–480.

Bakhtin, M. (1981). *The dialogic imagination.* Austin, TX: University of Texas Press.

Baltes, P. B. (1987). Theoretical propositions of life-span developmental psychology: On the dynamics between growth and decline. *Developmental Psychology, 23,* 611–626.

Bellah, R., Madsen, R., Sullivan, W., Swidler, A., & Tipten, S. (1985). *Habits of the heart.* Berkeley, CA: University of California Press.

Bloom, H. (1998). *Shakespeare: The invention of the human.* New York: Riverhead Books.

Bronfenbrenner, U. (1979). *The ecology of human development.* Cambridge, MA: Harvard University Press.

Bruner, J. (1985). Vygotsky: A historical and conceptual perspective. In J. Wertsch (Ed.), *Culture, communication and cognition: Vygotskian perspectives.* Cambridge, UK: Cambridge University Press.

Bruner, J. (1986). *Actual minds, possible worlds.* Cambridge, MA: Harvard University Press.

Bruner, J. (1990). *Acts of meaning.* Cambridge, MA: Harvard University Press.

Coleman, P., Ivani-Chalian, C., & Robinson, M. (1998). The story continues: Persistence of life themes in old age. *Ageing and Society, 18,* 389–419.

Cowan, P. A. (1999). What we talk about when we talk about families. In B. H. Fiese et al., The stories that families tell: Narrative coherence, narrative interaction, and relationship beliefs. *Monographs of the Society for Research in Child Development, 64* (Serial No. 257).

Cowan, P. A., Powell, D., & Cowan, C. P. (1998). Parenting interventions: A family system perspective. In W. Damon (Ed.), *Handbook of child psychology* (5th ed., Vol. 4., pp. 3–72). New York: Wiley.

Erikson, E. H. (1963). *Childhood and society* (2nd ed.). New York: Norton.

Erikson, E. H. (1968). *Identity, youth and crisis.* New York: Norton.

Fiese, B. H., Hooker, K., Kotary, L., Schwagler, J., & Rimmer, M. (1995). Family stories in the early stages of parenthood. *Journal of Marriage and the Family, 57,* 763–770.

Fiese, B. H., & Marjinsky, K. (1999). Dinnertime stories: Connecting family practices with relationship beliefs and child adjustment. In B. H. Fiese et al., The stories that families tell: Narrative coherence, narrative interaction, and relationship beliefs. *Monographs of the Society for Research in Child Development, 64* (Serial No. 257).

Fiese, B. H., Sameroff, A., Grotevant, H., Wamboldt, F., Dickstein, S., & Fravel, D. (1999).

The stories that families tell: Narrative coherence, narrative interaction and relationship beliefs. *Monographs of the Society for Research in Child Development, 64* (Serial No. 257).

Fiese, B. H., Wilder, J., & Bickham, N. (2000). Family context in developmental psychopathology. In A. Sameroff, M. Lewis, & S. Miller (Eds.), *Handbook of developmental psychopathology* (2nd ed., pp. 115–134). New York: Kluwer Academic.

Fivush, R. (1994). Constructing narrative, emotion, and self in parent-child conversations about the past. In U. Neisser & R. Fivush (Eds.), *The remembering self* (pp. 136–157). New York: Cambridge University Press.

Gergen, K. J. (1992). *The saturated self: Dilemmas of identity in contemporary life.* New York: Basic Books.

Gould, O., & Dixon, R. (1993). How we spent our vacation: Collaborative storytelling by young and old adults. *Psychology and Aging, 8,* 10–17.

Grotevant, H. D. (1993). The integrative nature of identity: Brining soloists to sing in the choir. In J. Kroger (Ed)., *Discussions in ego identity* (pp. 121–146). Hillsdale, NJ: Lawrence Erlbaum Associates.

Grotevant, H., & Cooper, C. (1998). Individuality and connectedness in adolescent development: Review and prospects for research on identity, relationships, and contexts. In E. Skoe & A. von der Lippe (Eds.), *Personality development in adolescence: A cross national and life span perspective.* London: Routledge & Kegan Paul.

Grotevant, H. D., Dunbar, N., Kohler, J. K., & Esau, A. M. (2000). Adoptive identity: How contexts within and beyond the family shape developmental pathways. *Family Relations, 49,* 379–387.

Habermas, T., & Bluck, S. (2000). Getting a life: The emergence of the life story in adolescence. *Psychological Bulletin, 126,* 748–769.

Hareven, T. (1977). Family time and historical time. *Daedalus, 106,* 57–70.

Hermanns, H. J. M. (1996). Voicing the self: From information processing to dialogical interchange. *Psychological Bulletin, 119,* 31–50.

Hilbers, S. (1997, April). *Adolescents' narratives of parent and grandparent value socialization: Stories of kindness and care.* Poster presented at the biennial meetings of the Society for Research in Child Development, Washington, DC.

Howe, M., & Courage, M. (1997). The emergence and early development of autobiographical memory. *Psychological Review, 104,* 499–523.

Hrdy, S. B. (1999). *Mother nature: A history of mothers, infants, and natural selection.* New York: Pantheon.

Katz, L., & Gottman, J. (1994). Patterns of marital interaction and children's emotional development. In R. D. Parke & S. Kellam (Eds.), *Exploring family relationships with other social contexts* (pp. 49–74). Hillsdale, NJ: Lawrence Erlbaum Associates.

Kemper, S. (1992). Language and aging. In F. Craik & T. Salthouse (Eds.), *The handbook of aging and cognition.* Hillsdale, NJ: Lawrence Erlbaum Associates.

Levy, B., & Langer, E. (1994). Aging free from negative stereotypes: Successful memory in China among the American deaf. *Journal of Personality and Social Psychology, 66,* 989–997.

Mackey, K., Arnold, M. L., & Pratt, M. W. (2001). Adolescents' stories of decision-making in more or less authoritative families: Representing the voices of parents in narrative. *Journal of Adolescent Research, 16,* 243–268.

Mandler, J. (1984). *Stories, scripts and scenes: Aspects of schema theory.* Hillsdale, NJ: Lawrence Erlbaum Associates.

Markus, H., & Kitayama, S. (1991). Culture and the self: Implications for cognition, emotion, and motivation. *Psychological Review, 98,* 224–253.

Martin, P., Hagestad, G. O., & Diedrick, P. (1988). Family stories: Events (temporarily) remembered. *Journal of Marriage and the Family, 50,* 533–541.

McAdams, D. P. (1999). Personal narratives and the life story. In L. Pervin & O. John (Eds.), *Handbook of personality: Theory and research* (2nd ed., pp. 478–500). New York: Guilford Press.

McAdams, D. P. (2001). The psychology of life stories. *Review of General Psychology, 5,* 100–122.

McAdams, D. P., Diamond, A., St. Aubin, E. de, & Mansfield, E. (1997). Stories of commitment: The psychosocial construction of generative lives. *Journal of Personality and Social Psychology, 72,* 678–694.

McCabe, A., & Peterson, C. (Eds.). (1991). *Developing narrative structure.* Hillsdale, NJ: Lawrence Erlbaum Associates.

McClelland, D. (1961). *The achieving society.* Princeton, NJ: van Nostrand.

McGoldrick, M., Heiman, M., & Carter, B. (1993). The changing family life cycle: A perspective on normalcy. In F. Walsh (Ed.), *Normal family processes* (2nd ed., pp. 405–443). New York: Guilford Press.

McHale, J. P., & Rasmussen, J. L. (1998). Coparental and family group-level dynamics during infancy: Early family precursors of child and family functioning during preschool. *Development & Psychopathology, 10,* 39–59.

Miller, P. (1994). Narrative practices: Their role in socialization and self-construction. In U. Neisser & R. Fivush (Eds.), *The remembering self* (pp. 158–179). New York: Oxford University Press.

Miller, P., Wiley, A., Fung, H., & Liang, C-H. (1997). Personal story-telling as a medium of socialization in Chinese and American families. *Child Development, 68,* 557–568.

Norris, J. E., Pratt, M. W., & Kuiack, S. (2003). Parent-child relations in adulthood: An intergenerational family systems perspective. In L. Kuczynski (Ed.), *The handbook of parent-child relations* (p. 325–344). Thousand Oaks, CA: Sage.

Ochs, E., Taylor, C., Rudolph, D., & Smith, R. (1992). Story-telling as a theory building activity. *Discourse Processes, 15,* 37–72.

Oliveri, M., & Reiss, D. (1987). Social networks of family members: Distinctive roles of mothers and father. *Sex Roles, 17,* 719–736.

Oppenheim, D., Nir, A., Warren, S., & Emde, R. (1997). Emotion regulation in mother–child narrative co-construction: Associations with children's narratives and adaptation. *Developmental Psychology, 33,* 284–294.

Oppenheim, D., Wamboldt, F., Gavin, L., Renouf, A., & Emde, R. (1996). Couples' co-constructions of the story of their child's birth: Associations with marital adaptation. *Journal of Narrative and Life History, 6,* 1–21.

Parke, R. D., & Buriel, R. (1998). Socialization in the family: Ethnic and ecological perspectives. In W. Damon (Ed.), *Handbook of child psychology* (5th ed., Vol. 3., pp. 463–552). New York: Wiley.

Peterson, C., & McCabe, A. (1994). A social interactionist account of developing decontextualized narrative skill. *Developmental Psychology, 30,* 937–948.

Piaget, J. (1970). Piaget's theory. In P. M. Mussen (Ed.), *Carmichael's manual of child psychology* (3rd ed., pp. 703–732). New York: Wiley.

Pillemer, D. (1998). *Momentous events, vivid memories.* Cambridge, MA: Harvard University Press.

Polkinghorne, D. (1996). Narrative knowing and the study of lives. In J. Birren, G. Kenyon, J-E. Ruth, J. Schroots, & T. Svensson (Eds.), *Aging and biography: Explorations in adult development* (pp. 77–99). New York: Springer.

Pratt, M. W., Arnold, M., & Hilbers, S. (1998). A narrative approach to the study of moral orientation in the family: Tales of kindness and care. In E. E. Skoe & A. L. von der Lippe (Eds.), *Personality development in adolescence: A cross-national and life span perspective* (pp. 61–78). London: Routledge.

Pratt, M. W., Norris, J., Arnold, M. L., & Filyer, R. (1999). Generativity and moral development as predictors of value socialization narratives for young persons across the adult lifespan: From lessons learned to stories shared. *Psychology and Aging, 14,* 414–426.

Pratt, M. W., & Norris, J. (1999). Moral development in maturity: Lifespan perspectives on the processes of successful aging. In T. Hess & F. Blanchard-Fields (Eds.), *Social cognition and aging* (pp. 291–317). New York: Academic Press.

Pratt, M. W., & Robins, S. (1991). That's the way it was: Age differences in the structure and quality of adults' personal narratives. *Discourse Processes, 14,* 73–85.

Putney, N., & Bengtson, V. (2001). Families, intergenerational relationships, and kinkeeping in midlife. In M. E. Lachman (Ed.), *Handbook of midlife development* (pp. 528–570). New York: Wiley.

Reiss, D. (1989). The practicing and representing family. In A. J. Sameroff & R. Emde (Eds.), *Relationship disturbances in early childhood* (pp. 191–220). New York: Basic Books.

Rogoff, B., Baker-Sennett, J., Lacasa, P., & Goldsmith, D. (1995). Development through participation in sociocultural activity. In J. Goodnow, & P. Miller (Eds.), *Cultural practices as contexts for development* (pp. 45–65). San Francisco, CA: Jossey-Bass.

Rogoff, B., & Toma, C. (1997). Shared thinking: Community and institutional variations. *Discourse Processes, 23,* 471–497.

Ryan, E. B. (1991). Language issues in normal aging. In R. Lubinski (Ed.), *Dementia and communication: Clinical and research implications* (pp. 84–97). Toronto: B. C. Decker Publishing.

Sameroff, A., & Fiese, B. H. (2000). Transactional regulation and early intervention. In S. J. Meisels & J. P. Shonkoff (Eds.), *Handbook of early childhood intervention* (2nd ed., pp. 119–149). New York: Cambridge University Press.

Sarbin, T. (1986). The narrative as root metaphor for psychology. In T. Sarbin (Ed.), *Narrative psychology: The stories nature of human conduct* (pp. 3–21). New York: Praeger.

Schieffelen, B. (1990). *The give and take of everyday life: Language socialization of Kaluli children.* Cambridge, UK: Cambridge University Press.

Selman, R. (1980). *The growth of interpersonal understanding: Developmental and clinical analyses.* New York: Academic Press.

Smith, J., & Baltes, P. B. (1997). Profiles of psychological functioning in the old and oldest-old. *Psychology and Aging, 12,* 458–478.

Smith, M. C. (1978). Cognizing the behavior stream: The recognition of intentional action. *Child Development, 49,* 736–743.

Steinberg, L., & Morris, A. (2000). Adolescent development. *Annual Review of Psychology, 52,* 83–110.

Tappan, M. B. (1991). Narrative, authorship, and the development of moral authority. *New Directions for Child Development, 54,* 5–25.

Thorne, A. (2000). Personal memory telling and personality development. *Personality and Social Psychology Review, 4,* 45–56.

Vinden, P. G. (1996). Junin Quechua children's understanding of mind. *Child Development, 67,* 1707–1716.

Vuchinich, S., Emery, R., & Cassidy, J. (1988). Family members as third parties in dyadic family conflict: Strategies, alliances, and outcomes. *Child Development, 59,* 1293–1302.

Vygotsky, L. S. (1978). *Mind in society.* Cambridge, MA: Harvard University Press.

Wang, Q. (2001). Culture effects on adults' earliest childhood recollection and self-description: Implications for the relation between memory and the self. *Journal of Personality and Social Psychology, 81,* 220–233.

Wellman, H. (1993). Early understanding of mind: The normal case. In S. Baron-Cohen, H. Tager-Flusberg, & D. Cohen (Eds.), *Understanding other minds: Perspectives from autism* (pp. 10–39). New York: Oxford University Press.

Wertsch, J. (1991). *Voices of the mind.* Cambridge, UK: Cambridge University Press.

PART I

Child Narratives: Competence and Attachment Development

2

Echoing Our Parents: Parental Influences on Children's Narration

Carole Peterson
Memorial University of Newfoundland

Allyssa McCabe
University of Massachusetts–Lowell

INTRODUCTION

There is no such thing as a born storyteller. Rather, narrative skills are shaped by many influences, and one of the most important is the sort of habitual verbal interaction that takes place between parents and children. From the time they are born, children are immersed in a world of narration (Miller, 1994). Parents frequently tell narratives to each other about themselves and about their children. In fact, probably everyone in the child's environment exchanges stories every day about themselves and other people, both present and absent. And as other authors in this book make clear, narratives are characteristic of every stage of a person's life, from early childhood to old age. But parents in particular have an important influence on children's narrative skills because of how much time they spend with their children as well as how strongly attached they are to each other.

One of the most notable observations of those who study narratives is the enormous variation that exists in narrative structure. For example, large differences have been documented in the sorts of stories that are told by people who belong to different cultures, including those of different cultural heritages who reside in the same country (McCabe, 1996). Large differences have also been documented for ethnically similar but economically disparate groups (Peterson, 1994). Of most interest to us in this chapter is the large individual variation that can be found even within ethnically, culturally, and economically similar groups.

Such large individual variation is not simply of academic interest; evidence is accumulating that narrative skill is one of the most important predictors of children's school success and literacy acquisition (Paul & Smith, 1993). Those who competently construct narratives that are consistent with the expectations of teachers are less likely to be defined as learning disabled (Roth, 1986) and more likely to make the transition to literacy readily (Snow, 1983). In fact, in one large-scale longitudinal study, kindergarten narrative production significantly predicted fourth- and seventh-grade reading comprehension (Tabors, Snow, & Dickinson, 2001).

For more than two decades, we have been studying the development of narrative skills in children, and for much of this time we have attempted to understand and explain individual variation in narrative skill. In this chapter, we first provide examples of the enormous variability that can exist in the narrative skills of preschoolers and then summarize a research program that has attempted to explain such variation. We have focused on the role of parents in fostering their children's narrative skills, and to do this, we studied a group of children (and their parents) longitudinally when children were between 2 and 6 years of age. Relationships between the ways parents engaged their children in narrative conversations and their children's developing competence in a number of narrative skills were explored, including the overall complexity of children's narratives and the development of a number of narrative components, such as contextual orientation, causality, and evaluation. Then we turn to theoretical explanations of why parent-child conversations can play such an important role in fostering the development of child narrative skill, based on Vygotskian theoretical constructs such as scaffolding. Finally, we present an intervention study that explicitly tested the importance of Vygotskian scaffolding in altering children's narrative skills.

Variability in Child Narrative Skill

To provide a sense of how substantial such individual variation can be, we present one of the most sophisticated narratives produced by each of three children at age 3½ years. These children were part of a sample of 10 children whose narrative development was followed longitudinally from age 2 (beginning at 25–27 months of age) until age 6. All of the children were White middle-class children with well-educated parents, living in an ethnically homogeneous community in Canada.

Example 1: Cathy

Researcher: Have you ever gotten stung by a bee?
Cathy: But Mark [her brother] got a big sting when he was just first born.
R: Well, tell me about it. What happened?
C: I, I was walking with him and, and I just and he falled and he didn't know that he falled right on a bee. And he, and his knee was on a bee and stung, he got stung on a bee.
R: He got stung on a bee?
C: Uh-huh. And then I was walking another baby, Randy, and you know what?
R: What?
C: I heard him and me and Randy came running. And you know what?
R: What?
C: Paul, Paul Smith came too.
R: Paul Smith came too.
C: I tried to pick him up but, but he didn't want me to but I had to call my Mommy.
R: You had to call your Mommy, uh-huh?
C: My Daddy and everybody who I knowed who was a grown-up. And then everybody who I knowed and who was a grown-up came.
R: They all came, uh-huh.
C: From my house. And I was walking in the park. They came over after Mark and they wanted, they wanted to see what happened to Mark.
R: They wanted to see what happened to Mark? Uh-huh?
C: And then I, I told them and I looked down at his knee and there it was, stung.
R: And there it was, stung. Looked at his knee and there it was stung, uh-huh?
C: And I tried to pick him up and he wanted me to pick him up right at that minute.

Example 2: Helen

Researcher: After that happened I had to go to the hospital. Have you ever been hurt like that?
Helen: We didn't go to the hospital. Cause cause whenever Ward [her brother] gets hurt he cries and cries and one bad one was on on and and and and there was a bee after him and he can't walk very good and he had a fever.
R: There was a bee after him and he can't walk very well and he had a fever?

H: Yeah. At at Nana's country place. And we were going in the floor like that and that bee came up and running after Ward.
R: A bee came along and was running after Ward?
H: Yeah. We going home and then the bee came along. I think that bee was terrible. I think that bee is a bite bee.

Example 3: Terry

Researcher: Have you ever caught a fish?
Terry: Yes.
R: Oh, you did?
T: It was a great big one, and I, and I lifted 'em off and I lifted 'em up in the boat.
R: And you lifted them off and you lifted them up in the boat?
T: Yes!
R: And you lifted them up in the boat. Uh huh. And?
T: I lift them at the boat.
R: You lift them in the boat?
T: Yes!
R: Uh huh?
T: Lift them at the boat.
R: Yeah?
T: I lift them in the boat.
R: Yeah?
T: And he's a great big one.
R: Uh huh?
T: And he's a yuck one.
R: He's a yuck one?
T: Yes and I sawed him.
R: Uh huh?
T: Purple.

The stories from these three children differ dramatically. Cathy's narrative is well-structured according to the widely recognized tenets of good structure proposed by Labov and Waletzky (1967/1997). She provides orientation to the context of her narrative, that is, the who, where, and when of the story. She develops the action of the story, that is, the succession of events that communicate what happened. She builds her story around an emotional or evaluative high point or crisis event, that is, her brother's bee sting, and she resolves the crisis event before ending the narrative. She also provides considerable emotional evaluation throughout the narrative so that her attitude about the events, her perspective and feelings, are evident to the listener.

This organization of a narrative, based on the prototype described by Labov and Waletzky (1967/1997) was termed a "classic" narrative by Peterson and McCabe (1983), who traced the development of this structural pattern in a large group of 3½–9½-year-old children. They also described several developmental precursors of this sophisticated pattern, such as an "end-at-the-high-point" narrative which has all of the other components of a classic narrative except that the narrator cuts the story off at the high-point or crisis event and omits a resolution. "Chronological" narratives are lists of successive events, rather like a laundry list of things that happened, with no overall coherent organization. These are often produced when children list the various things they did at a party or on a trip. "Leapfrog" narratives leap around from event to event in a confusing fashion, and "impoverished" narratives have too few events to be described structurally. These are minimal narratives that provide little information.

In comparison to the "classic" narrative provided by Cathy, Helen's narrative about a virtually identical event is confusing. Although Helen orients the listener to important contextual information (where events occurred), she doesn't develop the action or build her story around an evaluative high point or crisis event. In fact, she never explicitly states the crisis event, that is, whether or not her brother actually got stung by the bee or merely chased. Her narrative is an example of a "leapfrog" narrative.

Terry's narrative is quite different again; it is simply "impoverished." During this narrative (one of the longest he produced), he provides no contextual information and describes only one actual event or action which he repeats five times, namely lifting a fish into the boat. Although he provides a bit of description of the fish and an evaluation of it, there is little else in this minimal narrative. Thus, these three narratives, one showing idealized "classic" form, one a "leapfrog" narrative and one a "one-event impoverished" narrative, from children who have similar cultural and economic backgrounds and who are the same age, illustrate the sorts of differences in narrative skill that piqued our interest.

How can one account for such divergent narrative skills? In our research we have been focusing on parent-child interactions that revolve around narrative talk. Most parents reminisce with their children about events that have occurred in the children's lives—what they did that morning, their visit to a friend's the previous day, their trip to their grandparents' last week, and so on. Considerable variation has been documented in how parents engage in narrative talk with their children, not only cross-culturally (McCabe, 1996; Minami & McCabe, 1995), but also within culturally and economically homogeneous samples.

For example, Fivush and Fromhoff (1988) described differences in how White middle-class mothers structure conversations about past events with their preschool-aged children that they termed *elaborative* versus *repetitive.* Elaborative mothers talk more about past events, and provide considerable elaborative detail as well as prompt their children for the provision of such detail. In contrast, repetitive mothers talk less, ask fewer questions, and are more likely to simply repeat prior questions if they did not get an answer. McCabe and Peterson (1991) also found substantial differences in parental styles of conducting conversations about past events. One style (similar to the elaborative style of Fivush and Fromhoff) was termed a *topic-extending* style. These parents extended their children's talk about each past event by means of additional questions and comments, and they attempted to elicit from their children a lot of information about each event being recalled. *Topic-switching* parents, in contrast, asked a few, often formulaic, questions about each past event and then abruptly changed the topic to another event. Thus, their children were given little opportunity to construct an extensive narrative or to elaborate on what they did recall. In addition, McCabe and Peterson described a repetitive style that is similar to that described by Fivush and Fromhoff.

Given the substantial differences in parental styles of narrative elicitation, the next question is whether such differences are predictive of children's development of narrative competence. So we began a longitudinal project with parents and children. Ten middle-class children were recruited at 25–27 months of age and their parents (both mothers and fathers) were provided with a tape recorder at 1- or 2-month intervals for 18 months (until their child reached 3½ years) and asked to record conversations in which they talked to their children about past events. In order to have an independent measure of children's narrative skill, a researcher also regularly interviewed children in a standardized way. They were given art materials or other similar activities in order to minimize self-consciousness, and the researcher told a number of short narratives and then prompted the child to provide ones too ("Did anything like that ever happen to you?"). While the child was telling a narrative, the researcher only responded with simple encouragement like "uh huh," or "really?" rather than asking specific questions that might affect what the child said next. Thus, the narratives children told were self-structured rather than structured by listener questions. These techniques have been found to be very successful at eliciting narratives from children (Peterson & McCabe, 1983). Children were interviewed monthly during the first 18 months of the study and every 6 months thereafter when they were 3½ to 6 years of age.

COMPLEXITY OF CHILDREN'S NARRATIVES

Although all parents agreed to participate, they differed substantially in how much data they provided. Table 2.1 presents the number of tapes provided by the parents, combining those from both mothers and fathers (taken from McCabe & Peterson, 1990). The parents who provided us with the most tapes were those of Cathy, one of whose narratives can be found in Example 1 above. The two families who provided us with the least included that of Terry (who produced Example 3 above). We had to help Terry's parents figure out times for taping, because they claimed that they seldom engaged in narrative conversations, and even so, we got few tapes. Another child from whose parents we got few tapes was Sally; her mother said that she almost never talked to Sally one-on-one, as we required. She even rejected our offers to babysit her other children so that she could talk with Sally by herself because she didn't engage in such conversations with Sally. We assume that both the willingness parents had of talking with their children one-on-one and their cooperation in providing tapes of those conversations reflect habitual parent-child interaction in the home.

The differing parental styles of talking with their children about past events were related to what children produced. First, we selected two time periods in which we had tapes from all of the parents, namely when their children were 27 months and 31 months of age. The type of narrative questions and comments that are most helpful for children is what has been termed *topic-extension* by McCabe and Peterson (1991) or *elaboration* by Fivush and Fromhoff (1988). The number of these utterances in the parental tapes from these two ages was tabulated and related to how long children's self-structured narratives were (i.e., elicited by a researcher) at the end of the parent-taping sessions, namely when the child was 3½ years old. There was a significant ($p < .05$) positive relationship between the number of propositions in the longest three narratives that 3½-year-old children told to the researcher and the number of topic-extending statements made by parents when the children had been 27 months ($r = .66$) and 31 months ($r = .53$), as well as the number of one form of topic-extending question asked by parents at 31 months ($r = .63$). In contrast, the number of parental questions introducing new topics at 27 months was inversely correlated with the length of their child's three longest narratives at 3½ years ($r = -.60$—data from McCabe & Peterson, 1991). Thus, children told longer narratives to a researcher if their parents, many months earlier, had engaged in topic extension and minimized topic-switching. These results are similar

TABLE 2.1
Number of Tapes Provided by Parents When Children Were 2–3½ Years Old, and Frequency (and Percentage) of Each Narrative Structural Pattern Produced by Children at Younger (Y = 3½–4½ Years) and Older (O = 5–6 Years) Ages

		Parent Tapes	*Structural Patterns of Child Narratives*										Total Child Narrs.
			Impoverished		*Leapfrog*		*Chronology*		*End-at-hi-pt*		*Classic*		
Child		#	*M*	%	*M*	%	*M*	%	*M*	%	*M*	%	*Narrs.*
Cathy	Y	18	25	53	7	15	9	19	2	4	4	8	47
	O		14	34	5	12	11	27	1	2	10	24	41
	total		39	44	12	14	20	23	3	3	14	16	88
Carl	Y	11	28	80	3	9	0	0	0	0	4	11	35
	O		13	41	2	6	11	34	1	3	5	16	32
	total		41	61	5	7	11	16	1	1	9	13	67
Paul	Y	16	22	73	2	7	2	7	2	7	2	7	30
	O		13	38	1	3	8	24	5	15	7	21	34
	total		35	55	3	5	10	16	7	11	9	13	64
Leah	Y	8	28	70	2	5	6	15	1	2	3	7	40
	O		26	50	8	15	12	23	0	0	6	12	52
	total		54	59	10	11	20	22	1	1	9	10	92
Ned	Y	11	23	57	3	7	11	27	1	2	2	5	40
	O		15	38	1	3	18	46	1	3	4	10	39
	total		38	48	4	5	29	37	2	2	6	8	79
Helen	Y	11	29	74	5	13	5	13	0	0	0	0	39
	O		17	41	2	5	16	39	2	5	4	10	41
	total		46	58	7	9	21	26	2	2	4	5	80
Kelly	Y	10	20	80	2	8	2	8	0	0	1	4	25
	O		11	33	2	6	16	48	2	6	2	6	33
	total		31	53	4	7	18	31	2	3	3	5	58
Sally	Y	3	28	87	0	0	4	13	0	0	0	0	32
	O		17	65	2	8	6	23	0	0	1	4	26
	total		45	78	2	3	10	17	0	0	1	2	58
Gary	Y	8	34	85	3	8	3	8	0	0	0	0	40
	O		22	81	0	0	3	11	2	7	0	0	27
	total		56	84	3	4	6	9	2	3	0	0	67
Terry	Y	4	21	75	6	21	1	4	0	0	0	0	28
	O		15	88	1	6	1	6	0	0	0	0	17
	total		36	80	7	16	2	4	0	0	0	0	45

to those of a longitudinal study by Fivush (1991). She found that the degree of topic elaboration by parents (measured by the number of propositions per turn at talk) when their children were 2½ years of age was highly correlated with how elaborative their own children were when they talked with a researcher a year later.

But more than narrative length and elaboration are important. Table 2.1 also shows the number of narratives of each structural pattern that children produced when they talked with a researcher at biannual intervals between 3½ and 6 years of age (data from McCabe & Peterson, 1990). There was a strong relationship between the number of tapes provided by parents when their children were between 2 and 3½ years of age, and the structure of their children's narratives over the successive 3 years. The more tapes parents provided, the higher the percentage of their children's narratives that were classically structured ($r = .84$, $p < .01$) and the lower the percentage of impoverished narratives ($r = -.79$, $p < .01$). In addition, the total number of topic-extending questions and statements made by parents in all of their tapes was positively related to the number of classic narratives their children produced ($r = .79$, $p < .01$). Thus, it seems that more parental input in terms of engaging the child in narrative conversations, and more utterances that extend or elaborate topics, are related to children developing more advanced narrative skill. In contrast, the differences between children in narrative competence were not related to their syntactic competence or verbal intelligence, as measured by their Mean Length of Utterance at 27 and 31 months of age and their scores on the Peabody Picture Vocabulary Test (PPVT) at ages 4 and 5 years ($p > .4$).

There is another striking pattern in Table 2.1. If one compares the narratives of each child at younger (Y) and older (O) ages, namely at 3½–4½ years versus 5–6 years, there is substantial developmental progression for most children. In particular, the proportion of primitive narratives that fit the impoverished pattern decreases, and the proportion of the most sophisticated pattern, the classic one, increases. Notably, only three children's narratives at 5–6 years are still mostly impoverished: Terry and Sally (whose parents provided few tapes), and Gary. Although Gary's parents provided more tapes, they were extremely short, seldom even 5 minutes in length. Gary and Terry showed no developmental improvement over this 3-year time span in narrative structure and still produced no classic narratives by the end of the study. Sally produced only one classic narrative. In contrast, fully 24% of Cathy's narratives conformed to the classic narrative pattern and only a third of her narratives were impoverished when she was 5–6 years of age.

THE DEVELOPMENT OF NARRATIVE COMPONENTS

Narratives consist of a number of components, all of which must be knitted together into coherent wholes. We have explored the development of many of these narrative components, including the provision of contextual information, such as where and when events took place, the identification of causal relationships among events, and children's evaluation of narrative events. We turn to these next.

Orientation to Context

Narratives are fundamentally a verbal recounting of past experiences, but in order for such accounts to be comprehensible to a listener, they must be embedded within a spatial-temporal context. Such orientation to context plays a key role in making narratives comprehensible to listeners (Labov & Waletzky, 1967/1997; Polanyi, 1985). Eisenberg (1985), among others, has suggested that one reason the narratives of children are often so difficult to understand is that they lack such contextual embedding. Furthermore, the ability to provide context for there-and-then events is an important component of the decontextualized language skills that seem to be so essential for literacy acquisition (Snow, 1983).

Earlier, we stressed the importance of a topic-extending or elaborative parental style of reminiscing with children, but parents who are classified similarly as topic-extending may nevertheless differ in their emphasis on contextual orientation. For example, two mothers in our longitudinal sample were classified as highly topic-extending or elaborative, and Table 2.2 shows how many utterances they provided per narrative topic before changing to a different topic (data taken from Peterson & McCabe, 1992). The data are broken down into the first 6 months of the longitudinal collection of data from parents (when children were 27–32 months), the second 6 months (33–38 months), and the last months (39–44 months). Although both mothers were topic-extending, they differed in the techniques they used and in what they were elaborative about. Helen's mother was very concerned about her daughter providing the context for the events that were being talked about, and her conversation was filled with questions about *who, where, when, why,* and *what object.* Cathy's mother, although she also asked questions about context, was relatively more concerned about the action of the events being related, that is, *what happened.* The ratio of questions that request context information from their daughters versus questions requesting information about action is

TABLE 2.2
Properties of Mothers' Narrative-elicitation Style
and the Percentage of their Children's Self-Structured Narratives
to a Researcher that Provide Orientation to Context

	Cathy			*Helen*		
	27–32 mo	*33–38 mo*	*39–44 mo*	*27–32 mo*	*33–38 mo*	*39–44 mo*
Mother's narrative elicitations						
Utterances/narrative	16.7	16.5	19.4	25.8	26.6	14.7
Ratio of context questions to action questions	1.4:1	1.6:1	1.5:1	2.7:1	2.6:1	2.6:1
Ratio of content questions to yes/no questions	2.8:1	4.0:1	4.4:1	1.5:1	2.2:1	1.6:1
Children's self-structured narratives						
% clearly specified *who*	85%	90%	88%	83%	92%	95%
% with *where* (all narratives)	40%	43%	46%	25%	42%	58%
% *where* (away-from-home narrative)	24%	47%	54%	38%	56%	70%
% with *when*	19%	38%	40%	0%	19%	60%
% with *why*	2%	5%	12%	0%	7%	21%

Note. Table adapted from Peterson and McCabe (1992).

shown in Table 2.2 (adapted from Peterson & McCabe, 1992), and Helen's mother asks almost twice as many context questions relative to action questions as does Cathy's mother. There is another difference between the mothers: Throughout the 18 months, Helen's mother asked a large percentage of yes/no questions. These make few demands on children in that they do not require an elaborated, content-rich answer. Cathy's mother, in contrast, asked relatively few of these non-demanding yes/no questions, except early on when Cathy's inability to answer a content-rich question often led to rephrasing the question into a simplified yes/no format. As Cathy's ability to answer content-rich questions increased, the frequency of yes/no questions decreased.

Also shown in Table 2.2 are the percentages of children's self-structured narratives that included clear specification of *who* and identification of *where, when,* and *why* events took place (from Peterson & McCabe, 1992). For *where,* narratives are further broken down into those that describe events taking place at locations other than home (where specification of location is essential for comprehension of the story) as well as in all narratives regardless of location. Although both children are comparable during the first 6 months of the study, Helen's likelihood of providing contextual embedding is considerably higher a year later. Because Helen's mother stresses the importance of contextual orientation in her questions, Helen has learned that this is important information that should be included in her narratives.

But contextual embedding is not enough. A narrative that is well-structured, conforming to the classic narrative pattern, must have a cogent development of the action of the narrative, which Cathy's mother emphasizes. Cathy's mother also demands more elaborative and information-rich responses to her questions. As Table 2.1 shows, this emphasis on action or on *what happened,* as well as on content information, is reflected in Cathy's earlier mastery of classic narrative structure.

The case study of two mothers just described was extended to an analysis of the types of questions asked by all of the parents in our longitudinal study (Peterson & McCabe, 1994, 1996). Questions were classified as context questions (divided into wh-context and yes/no-context) or questions about other content, such as actions. These questions about other content were also divided into wh- questions and yes/no questions. As well, clarifying questions and statements were tabulated. This was done for the recorded parent-child conversations that took place during the three 6-month periods of our 18-month collection of taped parent-child conversations, that is, when children were at Age 1 (26–31 months), Age 2 (32–37 months) and Age 3 (38–43 months old). In addition, the provision of *when* and *where* context was assessed in the children's self-structured narratives elicited by a researcher during these same three periods.

There was little relationship between the types of questions parents asked in the first or second time period and the child's provision of spatial-temporal context in the same time periods. That is, almost all correlations between parent and child at Age 1 or Age 2 were nonsignificant. However, there were a number of significant relationships between the sorts of questions parents emphasized during the first year of the study and the amount of contextual orientation that children provided in the last 6 months of the study. These significant correlations are shown in Table 2.3 (taken from Peterson & McCabe, 1996). Note that there are a total of eight correlations between earlier parental context questions at Ages 1 and 2 and child performance at Age 3, and of these, fully seven were significant. That is, the number of context questions that parents asked both a full year, as well as half a year, earlier predicted how well their children provided spatial-temporal context when they were 3 years of age. An interesting comparison is the contrast between these earlier parental context questions (of which seven out of eight were significant) and synchronous context questions, that is, context questions asked by parents at Age 3 and their children's contextual orientation at Age 3. Only two of the four synchronous correlations between parent and child at Age 3 were significant. Thus, it seems that parents' context questions at an earlier point in time are more important than those questions asked concurrently, despite the fact that common sense would have predicted a relationship between questions asked and information provided at any given point in time. Another important contrast is between the role of parental context questions and other sorts of parental questions and utterances. There was virtually no relationship between the number of other sorts of parental questions during the first year of the study and children's later propensity to include spatial-temporal information in their narratives during the final 6 months of the study. Of a total of 72 possible correlations between questions about other

TABLE 2.3
Significant Correlations Between Frequencies of Questions About Context and Children's Provision of Where and When

	Child Performance		
Parent Behavior	*Age 1*	*Age 2*	*Age 3*
Wh-context questions			
		where	
Age 1	−.65, $p = .020$	—	—
Age 2	—	—	.54, $p = .024$
Age 3	—	—	.68, $p = .015$
		when	
Age 1	—	—	.57, $p = .042$
Age 2	—	—	.69, $p = .013$
Age 3	—	.74, $p = .007$	.66, $p = .019$
Yes/no context questions			
		where	
Age 1	—	—	.76, $p = .005$
Age 2	—	—	.57, $p = .042$
Age 3	—	—	—
		when	
Age 1	—	—	.64, $p = .022$
Age 2	—	—	.78, $p = .004$
Age 3	—	—	—

Note. Table reprinted from Peterson and McCabe (1996).

content (both wh- and yes/no questions), clarifying questions, or statements and children's provision of either *where* or *when* context, only three were significant—a result that is probably due to chance.

These data argue strongly that it is not simply talking with children about past events nor asking questions about any sort of content that is important for children to learn how to embed their narratives within a spatial-temporal context; rather, children who are asked a lot of questions about context come to increasingly include contextual information in their self-structured narratives. In other words, children learn the components of a narrative that are important because of what parents emphasize in parent-child conversations about past events. Similar relationships between earlier parental questions about orientative context and later child skill in providing such contextual embedding have been found by others as well (e.g., Fivush, 1991).

General Evaluation

From the beginning, narrative researchers have emphasized the importance of emotional evaluation (Labov & Waletzky, 1967/1997). A good story not only tells a listener what happened, it also tells the listener what those events meant to the narrator. That is, it embeds the events within a context of personal meaning, of emotional reaction. It informs the listener about the narrator's perspective on those events. In essence, evaluation is the heart of narration.

There are a number of ways in which narrators can evaluate the events in their narratives, including specifying affect ("I was sad"), their cognitions or perceptions ("I got confused"), repetition for effect ("The needle went up and down and up and down"), elaboration of details ("My chin bleeded. It bleeded on my mitten."), gratuitous terms ("very," "really," "some," as in "I was some happy"), negation ("I didn't do it"), exclamation ("Was I mad!"), attention getters ("And then know what?"), comparison ("Crying like a madman"), intensifiers and qualifiers ("stupid," "fun," "silly"), reported speech ("She said that she was happy"), compulsion words ("Mommy made us come in then"), words that are evaluative per se ("squished," "finally" as in "We finally got him to do it"), exaggeration ("I ran as fast as a deer"), objective judgments ("Ten dollars is a lot of money for a kid"), and subjective judgments ("That was okay").

In longitudinal assessments of parental evaluation in parent-child reminiscing, parents have been shown to be relatively consistent (Haden, 1998; Reese, Haden, & Fivush, 1993). That is, some parents are highly evaluative and others are much less so during parent-child conversations about past events. Parents also seem to be more evaluative when talking with their girls than boys, in that they talk more about emotions (and a wider variety of emotions) to daughters (Cervantes & Callanan, 1998; Dunn, Bretherton, & Munn, 1987; Fivush, 1998). Some researchers have found gender differences in children's presentation of emotion in their narratives (Buckner & Fivush, 1998; Haden, Haine, & Fivush, 1997); others have found few differences in children's use of most other forms of evaluation (Peterson & McCabe, 1983; Peterson & Biggs, 1998, 2001) with the exception of the evaluative device of reported speech. Girls include more reported speech than do boys (Ely & McCabe, 1993).

Parents who have an elaborative reminiscing style are likely to use more evaluation (Reese & Fivush, 1993), and we were curious about whether there are more specific relationships between parental and child evaluation. That is, does evaluation show the same sort of specificity effect that has been previously found for orientation? To answer this, we assessed total parent evaluative input in our longitudinal sample when children were 27, 31, and 34 months, as well as total child evaluative output in their researcher-elicited narratives at 27, 31, and 34 months, as well as at 4½ years (McCabe & Peterson, 2000). In addition, we assessed the role of overall topic-extending input by parents in all of the tapes that they provided us.

Two major findings emerged from this study. First, there was no direct relationship between parental and child evaluation. The rank of parents in terms of the evaluative input they provided at 27, 31, and 34 months did not correlate with the rank of children in terms of providing narrative evaluation to an experimenter at those ages and when 4½ years old. On the other hand, there was a relationship between how topic-extending a parent was and how much evaluation children provided. That is, when parents were ranked, those who were more topic-extending during parent-child reminiscing had children who had higher ranks in terms of how much evaluation they included in their self-structured narratives ($rho = .52$, $p < .05$). Thus, it seems that it is general parental interest in extending discussion about the past that is important, not specific parental attention to evaluation. Parents who are interested in a child's past experiences, and who are elaborative and topic-extending during parent-child reminiscing, have children who are more likely to evaluate their experiences when narrating.

Our sample size was small, however, and this may well be the reason that relationships between parental and child use of evaluative talk did not prove to be significant. Several studies with sample sizes over 40 found concurrent relationships between parent and preschooler emotion language in picture description (Denham, Cook, & Zoller, 1992) and autobiographical narration (Farrar, Fasig, & Welch-Ross, 1997) and longitudinal relationships in parent and toddler references to feeling states in non-narrative free conversations recorded at home (Dunn et al., 1987). Most relevant is work by Haden, Haine, and Fivush (1997) that found a longitudinal relationship between maternal emphasis on evaluations in personal narrative talk at 3½ and child provision of such evaluation at 5 years, although the child's inclination to provide relatively more evaluative information to a neutral experimenter at 3½ years was also predictive.

The fact that we found significant componential relationships in a small sample for orientation but not for general evaluation may mean that the strength of the relationship in the latter case is weaker than that of the former, something less likely to be detected in a small sample. Provision of information about what a personal experience means is complex and, by definition, subjective, and parents are often quite surprised to find out that, for example, the favorite part of a child's trip to Disneyland was not seeing Mickey Mouse or any particular ride but rather finding real geode rocks in a planter outside the rest rooms. In other words, parents are less able to directly scaffold children in articulating what an event meant than they are when and where it happened. This interpretation is bolstered by the finding we report later in this chapter that an intervention experiment had a significant impact on provision of orientation but not of evaluation.

Causal Relationships

Events in our lives are often highly inter-related, and one important form of inter-relationship is causality. Some events cause other events to happen or set up necessary preconditions. For example, falling on a nail can cause a cut on the leg, pulling on a cat's tail can cause the cat to scratch, or hitting another child can cause that child to hit back. Explicitly informing a listener about causal relationships in narrated events leads to narratives about those events being perceived as more coherent and comprehensible (Buckner & Fivush, 1998; Fivush, 1991). Thus, learning to describe causal relationships between events is another component skill involved in competent narration.

An important question is whether parental practices during narrative elicitation vis-à-vis specifying causality are related to children's acquisition of skill in describing causal relationships between events. To answer this, we first combed through the researcher-elicited narratives of children in our longitudinal sample and we found that the age when children first included a spontaneous expression of causality varied widely, from 30 to 66 months of age (McCabe & Peterson, 1997). Next, we analyzed the parent-child conversations, and we found remarkable consistency in parental behavior. In conversations that took place more than 6 months prior to children's first spontaneous expression of causality, parents almost never mentioned causality. For example, at 7 months prior to a child's first independent causal statement, there were 0.08 mentions of causality per narrative topic by parents. However, parents consistently increased their discussion of past causality with their child approximately 6 months prior to their child's first spontaneous production of causal language. At 6 months prior to a child's first causal expression (regardless of the child's age at that time), parents talked about causality 0.21 times per narrative, and at 5 months prior, there were 0.52 causal mentions per narrative, and in the next few months it remained equivalently high. Thus, a half year prior to a child's first spontaneous expression of causality, parents began to emphasize causality in their narrative conversations. Children began responding to these parental prompts about causality, and all children were able to respond to at least some parental scaffolds about causality at least a month prior to the time when they could produce causal language spontaneously, and on average 5 months prior. Thus, a consistent pattern was found: rare references to causality by parents, a sudden increase in parental prompts about causality 6 months prior to children's first spontaneous production of causal language, children increasingly responding to scaffolded interactions about causality, and finally, spontaneous production of causality by children.

Other investigators have also found a relationship between parental conversations about causality and children's inclusion of causality in their narratives. For example, in a longitudinal investigation, Fivush (1991) assessed the number of references to causal or conditional relationships in maternal language and the number of such references in their children's narratives to a researcher a year later. There was a strong positive correlation between the two frequencies ($r = .78$); mothers who talked about causality more when their children were 2½ years old had children who talked more about causality a year later, at age 3½.

Reported Speech

Causal linkage between events has often been considered to be one form of evaluation (Labov & Waletzky, 1967/1997), and as we have seen, it shows specific parent-child effects. But another form of evaluation, other than causality, also has been found to yield specific effects. In a different study in which dinnertime conversations were recorded for 22 middle-class families that had a child between 2 and 5 years of age, Ely, Gleason, Narasimhan, and McCabe (1995) found that mothers used more of the evaluative device of reported speech than did fathers. Of most interest here is that there was a significant correlation between the amount of reported speech by mothers and children ($r = .63$, $p < .005$), but not between fathers and children ($r = .16$). Thus, children seem to resemble their mothers in the use of this device. When reported speech was investigated in the Peterson and McCabe (1992) longitudinal study, mothers of 2- to 3½-year-old children again were found to use substantially more prompts for reported speech (i.e., 100 of 107 observed prompts for reported speech were made by mothers), and mothers themselves made almost all observed reports of past speech (50 of 55 observations). By the time their children were 5, girls' attention to past speech was double that of boys' (Ely, Gleason, & McCabe, 1996).

The value of reporting speech has been documented to be gendered. Tannen (1990) put it best when she quoted one very representative complaint by a woman about her husband, "Men don't tell the whole story—who said what," and another who said, "It's like pulling teeth to get him to tell me, 'What did she *say*,' 'What did he *say*?'" (p. 116). She goes on to note that men see such emphasis on reported speech as attention to unimportant details. Tannen was writing about adults, of course, but what we have seen is that such divergent values have a very early onset in the preschool years.

Gender

The eventual impact of such gender differences in adult preferences for narrative components eventuates in replication of gender differences in their offspring. Moreover, parents of both sexes may set aside their own preferences in the interest (albeit probably not conscious) of fostering what they see as gender-appropriate narration. For example, both fathers and mothers alike talk in distinctively different ways to their young daughters versus their young sons (see Fivush, 1998, for a review).

Gender differences in adults' narrative preferences added to increasingly observable gender differences in children, and the well-known fact that mothers tend to talk substantially more with their children than do fathers can be fit into the sociocultural framework that we have adopted. Such a sociocultural framework would lead us to expect more congruence between the narrative styles of mothers and their daughters than between any other pairing (e.g., fathers and daughters or mothers and sons), and we have found evidence that such is the case.

Recently, we have independently collected self-structured narratives from both parents and children about the same events. This research differs from prior research in our laboratory in that parents narrated to a researcher rather than engaged in parent-child reminiscence, and they were asked to narrate about a target event, the same one as the child. This event was a highly salient one in children's lives, namely an injury serious enough to require hospital emergency room (ER) treatment. Families were recruited from the ER and visited at home several days later, and their memory for the injury and subsequent hospital treatment was assessed as part of other research. Prior to memory probing, self-structured narratives were elicited ("Tell me about when you/your child got hurt."). There were 137 preschool-aged children (2–5 years) and 98 school-aged children (8–13 years) and their parents (154 mothers and 81 fathers) who participated.

The parents' and children's narratives were assessed on a range of narrative measures, including two measures of *length* (number of words and number of clauses), two measures of *elaboration* (number of descriptors and number of new units of information), one measure of *cohesion* (number of inter-clausal connectives), two measures of *coherence* (number of temporal and of causal/conditional linguistic links), and two measures of *contextual embedding* (number of references to time context and spatial context). As well, new units of information were sub-categorized in terms of whether they referred to people, location, activities, objects, or attributes. In all, there were 14 measures of narrative properties.

There is, of course, enormous individual variation in the narratives of both parents and children, with some individuals stressing the importance of contextual embedding, others stressing the importance of descriptive elaboration, and so on. We computed correlations between parents and children, with children categorized as preschool- or school-aged, and both parents and children separated by gender. The patterns of correlations that we found are shown in Table 2.4 (taken from Peterson & Roberts, 2003). Strikingly, the narratives of older daughters and their mothers are highly similar in at least one measure of all five narrative properties, that is, length, elaboration, cohesion, coherence, and context-setting. Specifically, fully 10 of the 14 measures comparing mothers and older daughters are significant at the $p < .004$ level. In contrast, none of the correlations between older daughters and their fathers are significant. There is no relationship between older sons' narrative measures and those of either parent. (Very few of the correlations between preschoolers and their parents were significant, probably because their narratives were so short.)

The high degree of similarity in how mothers and their school-aged daughters linguistically represent events in their narratives supports suggestions of a special status for mother-daughter dyads, in comparison with mother-son, father-daughter, or father-son dyads (Russell & Saebel, 1997). In their review of research regarding the distinctness of the four types of parent-child dyad, Russell and Saebel stated that although evidence was limited, there seemed to

TABLE 2.4
Significant Correlations Between Child-Parent Dyads, with Bonferroni Correction ($p < .004$)

	Parent-Daughter Dyads				*Parent-Son Dyads*			
	Younger Kids		*Older Kids*		*Younger Kids*		*Older Kids*	
	Mom	*Dad*	*Mom*	*Dad*	*Mom*	*Dad*	*Mom*	*Dad*
Measure	$N = 51$	$N = 15$	$N = 25$	$N = 16$	$N = 48$	$N = 23$	$N = 30$	$N = 27$
Length:								
Clauses	—	—	0.76*	—	—	—	—	—
Words	—	—	0.72*	—	—	—	—	—
Elaboration:								
Descriptors	—	—	0.74*	—	—	—	—	—
Unique units	—	—	0.64*	—	0.41*	—	—	—
Person	—	—	0.52*	—	—	—	—	—
Location	—	—	0.54*	—	—	—	—	—
Object	—	—	—	—	—	—	—	—
Activity	—	—	—	—	—	—	—	—
Attribute	—	—	0.74*	—	—	—	—	—
Cohesion:								
Connectives	—	—	0.77*	—	—	—	—	—
Coherence:								
Causal/cond.	—	—	0.66*	—	—	0.82*	—	—
Temporal	0.39*	—	—	—	—	0.69*	—	—
Context:								
Time context	—	—	—	—	—	—	—	—
Spatial context	—	—	0.77*	—	0.47*	—	—	—

Note. Table from Peterson and Roberts (2003). Copyright © 2003 by the American Psychological Association. Adapted with permission.
*$p < .004$.

be greater affective closeness or emotional cohesion between mothers and their daughters than between parents and children in other dyad compositions. We suggest that narrative exchanges between mothers and their daughters are a key aspect of such affective closeness and emotional cohesion, and that the correspondence in narrative structure embodies both.

THEORETICAL CONSIDERATIONS

To reiterate, we and others have shown repeatedly that there is a relationship between how parents reminisce with their children and their children's development of narrative skills. Parents who use a topic-extending, elaborative style have children who become skilled narrators at earlier ages. Topic-extending, elaborative parents have children who tell longer narratives and who are likely to demonstrate more sophisticated narrative structure such as the classic narrative pattern. But there are more direct relationships than this between what parents do and how child narrative skill develops. For example, the sort of questions that seem to be crucial for children's developing skill at embedding their narratives within an appropriate spatial-temporal context are those that specifically prompt the child to provide contextual information. Asking any sort of question will not do; rather, context orientation skill in children is related to parental questions specifically about context orientation. Furthermore, there seems to be a time-lagged relationship between such parental prompts and child skill development.

Data such as these support a Vygotskian theoretical framework. Vygotsky's (1978) theory proposes that social interactions (i.e., inter-psychological processes) give rise to internal (intra-psychological) processes. In particular, the theory emphasizes the importance of adults or other knowledgeable individuals scaffolding the early attempts of a beginner who is acquiring a new skill. Adults regulate how a task is done as well as provide extensive guidance and feedback to a child learner, thus providing the structure and much of the content of the task. Essentially, adult feedback and questions serve as a scaffold for the child's skill acquisition. The repeated information about what to do that is contained in the scaffold becomes internalized over time, and thus the child's own inner speech takes over the functions that previously were filled by the external scaffolds provided by parents and others. Another important concept is the zone of proximal development. This is the difference between what children can do on their own and what they can accomplish with adult scaffolding. Good scaffolding by an adult is sensitive to the child's level of accomplishment in a particular type of task, and as children become more proficient, the scaffold is decreased. Some recent formulations, however, have emphasized the bidirectionality of parent and child influences, proposing a spiral model of increasing task sophistication by parents as child competence increases (Haden et al., 1997; Reese et al., 1993). Specifically, these authors suggest that adult scaffolds may be primitive when child skill levels are very low, and as children become more competent at the task, the adult scaffold increases in sophistication. Essentially, feedback from children about increasing skill competence leads to more elaborate concepts being scaffolded, so that both partners are engaged in increasingly complex task-related behavior. Children have been shown to acquire many cognitive skills through the help of adults' provision of effective scaffolds (McLane, 1987; Rogoff & Gardner, 1984).

Parent-child discourse has been highlighted as an important source of parental scaffolding (Peterson & McCabe, 1994), and in terms of children's acquisition of narration, Vygotskian theory would hypothesize that the specific sorts of narrative interactions engaged in by parents and children would play a key role in facilitating children's narrative skills. Parents who provide a narrative scaffold that is rich in questions and statements about orientative context essentially teach their children the importance of including this sort of information in their narratives, as well as show them how it should be incorporated. Thus, over time children begin to spontaneously provide contextual information *in anticipation of habitual parental prompts for it.* We have also seen that parental prompts about causality precede in a regular way children's ability to linguistically express such relationships spontaneously. That is, there is a progression from little prompting for causality in adult narrative scaffolds to increasing questions about *why* by parents accompanied by an increasing incidence of children responding to such prompts appropriately, and finally children being able to spontaneously produce linguistic causal connections in their self-structured narratives. This is consistent with Vygotsky's zone of proximal development: Parents provide virtually no prompting about causality when children are not yet capable of appropriate response, but as children acquire the ability to respond to causal prompts, their frequency increases sharply even though children still cannot provide causal information unassisted by parental prompting. Finally, children are able to independently include causality in their narratives. Vygotsky's theory would posit that through parental scaffolding, children learn narrative properties, and that variation in the scaffolds that parents construct vis-à-vis narration will be related to variation in child narrative skill.

An Intervention Study: Teaching Effective Scaffolding

Although there have been numerous demonstrations of time-lagged relationships between earlier parental reminiscing style and later child narrative skill, these have been correlational in nature. And, of course, even time-lagged correlation does not mean causation. A more powerful research design is required, namely an experimental intervention. This has been done (Peterson, Jesso, & McCabe, 1999). We recruited 20 economically disadvantaged families with 3½-year-old children, all of whom were on Canadian social assistance (equivalent to welfare in the U.S.), and randomly assigned them to either an intervention or a control group. The mothers' styles of eliciting narratives from their children were assessed at the beginning of the study by leaving a tape recorder with them to record reminiscing, as was the children's skill at constructing self-structured narratives to a researcher using our standard narrative-eliciting procedures. Children's language skills were also assessed by the PPVT. Subsequently, a researcher talked with the intervention mothers about the sorts of narrative interactions that seem to foster children developing the narrative skills that help them to "fit in" with school.

The intervention emphasized the following points (from Peterson et al., 1999):

1. Talk to your child frequently and consistently about past experiences.
2. Spend a lot of time talking about each topic.
3. Ask plenty of "wh" questions and few "yes/no" questions. As part of this, ask questions about the context or setting of the events, especially where and when they took place.
4. Listen carefully to what your child is saying, and encourage elaboration.
5. Encourage your child to say more than one sentence at a time by using backchannel responses or simply repeating what your child has just said.
6. Follow your child's lead. That is, talk about what your child wants to talk about.

The researcher illustrated each of these points and both showed the parent transcripts of other parents reminiscing with their children and played them tapes of these interactions. These provided concrete examples of parents using or failing to use the types of prompts and interaction style we were fostering. Then the researcher engaged in role playing with the parent, to help them learn these techniques. Subsequently, families were visited every other month and interim telephone calls were made to remind and encourage the mothers. The intervention lasted for a year. Control mothers were told that we were interested in learning more about how children develop narratives. At the end of the year-long intervention, post-test data were collected: Parents were again given tape recorders and asked to record parent-child reminiscing, children were interviewed again by a researcher, and the PPVT was re-administered. A year later, when the children were approximately 5½ years old, 14 of the children (half in each group) were found and a researcher elicited more narratives from the children for a follow-up assessment. Comparisons of families who could not be found with those that remained in the study showed that these two groups did not differ in parental or child variables in pretesting. Attrition was attributed to families in poverty being more likely to move or have disconnected telephones.

TABLE 2.5
Mean Number of Parent Measures
(and Standard Deviations) at Pre-Test and Post-Test

	Time of Test	
Measure	*Pre-Test*	*Post-Test*
Open-ended prompts		
Control Group	11.3 (6.4)	11.7 (4.1)
Intervention Group	9.7 (5.5)	14.4 (4.2)
Wh-context questions		
Control Group	6.4 (4.2)	6.8 (4.1)
Intervention Group	4.5 (3.5)	8.5 (2.6)
Back-channeling		
Control Group	3.8 (2.9)	3.2 (2.7)
Intervention Group	3.0 (1.8)	4.9 (2.5)
Total of above 3		
Control Group	21.5 (7.2)	21.7 (6.9)
Intervention Group	17.2 (5.8)	28.2 (4.0)*
Yes/no questions		
Control Group	9.2 (3.2)	10.2 (3.2)
Intervention Group	7.5 (3.7)	8.8 (2.7)

Note. Table reprinted from Peterson et al. (1999).
*$p < 0.05$ for the Group × Time interaction.

An analysis of the parental tapes showed that the intervention mothers indeed altered their reminiscing style in ways consistent with our intervention. Table 2.5 (from Peterson et al., 1999) shows that intervention-group mothers, relative to controls, increased the number of open-ended prompts, context-eliciting questions using wh- questions, and back-channel supportive responses over time. If one combined these three types of utterances, there was a significant Group × Time interaction. Specifically, the two groups did not differ at the pre-test assessment, but intervention mothers significantly improved and included more of these in their conversations than did control mothers by the time of the post-test assessment. There was little difference between the two groups of parents in the frequency of yes/no questions.

In terms of child changes, intervention children's PPVT scores significantly improved over the course of the 1-year intervention, relative to the control children's scores (see Table 2.6, adapted from Peterson et al., 1999). But there was as yet limited change in children's narrative skills. It seems that vocabulary can be influenced over the course of relatively short-term intervention (consistent with the findings of others such as Whitehurst & Valdez-Menchaca, 1988), but more complex narrative skills may take longer to influence.

The story was different a year later, however, during the follow-up assessment. Two important characteristics of narratives are orientation to spatial-temporal context and informativeness. Table 2.6 shows the total amount of spatial and temporal context-setting information and the number of new or unique units of information, that is, how informative the narratives were, for each child's three longest narratives during pre-test, post-test, and follow-up assessments. Intervention children substantially increased the amount of spatial-temporal context as well as the informativeness of their narratives. Control children, in comparison, showed no improvement in context-setting and less dramatic improvement in informativeness.

Overall, this study lends strong support to the important causative role of parental reminiscing styles. Parents who were taught to scaffold contextual information in their narrative interactions had children who substantially improved in their skill at embedding their narratives within a spatial-temporal context. Parents who were taught to encourage children to provide more information and to elaborate on what they had said had children who produced more informative, elaborated narratives. In other words, teaching parents different ways of scaffolding their children's narratives worked.

TABLE 2.6
Outcome Language (PPVT) and Narrative Measures (Amount of Context-Setting Information and Unique Units of Information) for Children at Pre-Test, Post-Test, and Follow-up Assessments

	Time of Test		
Measure	*Pre-test*	*Post-test*	*Follow-up*
PPVT			
Intervention group	52.5	59.0	—
Control group	54.1	55.5	—
Total context-setting information			
Intervention group	11.0	11.7	25.8
Control group	9.1	13.5	11.3
Unique units of information			
Intervention group	31.4	27.9	170.4
Control group	33.6	36.1	117.9

Note. Table adapted from Peterson et al. (1999).

CONCLUSIONS

In conclusion, children's narratives reflect numerous aspects of their lives. Children echo their parents in a general predilection for talking at length about past events (or not), but also in many specific ways. Parents' concern for descriptive detail predicts their children's provision of such detail. Parents' discussion of what causes what predates children's provision of such information by half a year. Parents' general interest in what has happened to a child, as indicated by their tendency to talk at length about this, predicts a child's evaluation of such experience, though the nature of that evaluation very much derives from the child's own perspective. Not only does parental interest in the past predict children's narrative ability, it also causes such ability to develop, as we demonstrated in an experimental intervention that involved random assignment of parents and successful increment in vocabulary and, eventually, narrative ability in the experimental group. Through parents, children learn general values regarding the form of narrative valued by the culture. Finally, daughters, especially, mirror their mothers when talking about traumatic events. In all these ways, then, storytellers are made, not born.

REFERENCES

Buckner, J. P., & Fivush, R. (1998). Gender and self in children's autobiographical narratives. *Applied Cognitive Psychology, 12,* 407–429.

Cervantes, C. A., & Callanan, M. A. (1998). Labels and explanations in mother-child emotion talk: Age and gender differentiation. *Developmental Psychology, 34,* 88–98.

Denham, S. A., Cook, M., & Zoller, D. (1992). "Baby looks *very* sad": Implications of conversations about feelings between mother and preschooler. *British Journal of Developmental Psychology, 10,* 301–315.

Dunn, J., Bretherton, I., & Munn, P. (1987). Conversations about feeling states between mothers and their young children. *Developmental Psychology, 23,* 132–139.

Eisenberg, A. R. (1985). Learning to describe past experiences in conversation. *Discourse Processes, 8,* 177–204.

Ely, R., Gleason, J. B., Narasimhan, B., & McCabe, A. (1995). Family talk about talk: Mothers lead the way. *Discourse Processes, 19,* 201–218.

Ely, R., Gleason, J. B., & McCabe, A. (1996). "Why didn't you talk to your mommy, Honey?" Parents' and children's talk about talk. *Research on Language and Social Interaction, 29,* 7–25.

Ely, R., & McCabe, A. (1993). Remembered voices. *Journal of Child Language, 20,* 671–696.

Farrar, M. J., Fasig, L. G., & Welch-Ross, M. K. (1997). Attachment and emotion in autobiographical memory development. *Journal of Experimental Child Psychology, 67,* 389–408.

Fivush, R. (1991). The social construction of personal narratives. *Merrill-Palmer Quarterly, 37,* 59–81.

Fivush, R. (1998). Gendered narratives: Elaboration, structure, and emotion in parent-child reminiscing across the preschool years. In C. P. Thompson, D. J. Herrmann, D. Bruce, J. D. Read, D. G. Payne, & M. P. Toglia (Eds.), *Autobiographical memory: Theoretical and applied perspectives* (pp. 79–103). Mahwah, NJ: Lawrence Erlbaum Associates.

Fivush, R., & Fromhoff, F. A. (1988). Style and structure in mother-child conversations about the past. *Discourse Processes, 11,* 337–355.

Haden, C. A. (1998). Reminiscing with different children: Relating maternal stylistic consistency and sibling similarity in talk about the past. *Developmental Psychology, 34,* 99–114.

Haden, C. A., Haine, R. A., & Fivush, R. (1997). Developing narrative structure in parent-child reminiscing across the preschool years. *Developmental Psychology, 33,* 295–307.

Labov, W., & Waletzky, J. (1967/1997). Narrative analysis: Oral versions of personal experience. In J. Helm (Ed.), *Essays on the verbal and visual arts* (pp. 12–44). Seattle: University of Washington Press. Reprinted in *Journal of Narrative and Life History, 7,* 3–38.

McCabe, A. (1996). *Chameleon readers: Teaching children to appreciate all kinds of good stories.* New York: McGraw-Hill.

McCabe, A., & Peterson, C. (1990, July). *Keep them talking: Parental styles of interviewing and subsequent child narrative skill.* Paper presented at the fifth International Congress of Child Language, Budapest, Hungary.

McCabe, A., & Peterson, C. (1991). Getting the story: A longitudinal study of parental styles in eliciting narratives and developing narrative skill. In A. McCabe & C. Peterson (Eds.), *Developing narrative structure* (pp. 217–253). Hillsdale, NJ: Lawrence Erlbaum Associates.

McCabe, A., & Peterson, C. (1997). Meaningful "mistakes": The systematicity of children's connectives in narrative discourse and the social origins of this usage about the past. In J. Costermans & M. Fayol (Eds.), *Processing interclausal relationships: Studies in the production and comprehension of text* (pp. 139–154). Mahwah, NJ: Lawrence Erlbaum Associates.

McCabe, A., & Peterson, C. (2000, July). *An effort after meaning: Parental influences on children's evaluations in narratives of past personal experiences.* Paper presented at the seventh International Pragmatics Association Conference in Budapest, Hungary.

McLane, J. B. (1987). Interaction, context, and the zone of proximal development. In M. Hickmann (Ed.), *Social and functional approaches to language and thought* (pp. 267–285). New York: Academic Press.

Miller, P. J. (1994). Narrative practices: Their role in socialization and self-construction. In U. Neisser & R. Fivush (Eds.), *The remembering self: Construction and accuracy in the self-narrative* (pp. 158–179). Cambridge: Cambridge University Press.

Minami, M., & McCabe, A. (1995). Rice balls versus bear hunts: Japanese and Caucasian family narrative patterns. *Journal of Child Language, 22,* 423–446.

Paul, R., & Smith, R. L. (1993). Narrative skills in 4-year-olds with normal, impaired, and late developing language. *Journal of Speech and Hearing Research, 36,* 592–598.

Peterson, C. (1994). Narrative skills and social class. *Canadian Journal of Education, 19,* 251–269.

Peterson, C., & Biggs, M. (1998). Stitches and casts: Emtionality and narrative coherence. *Narrative Inquiry, 8,* 51–76.

Peterson, C., & Biggs, M. (2001). "I was really, really, really mad!" Children's use of evaluative devices in narratives about emotional events. *Sex Roles, 45,* 801–825.

Peterson, C., Jesso, B., & McCabe, A. (1999). Encouraging narratives in preschoolers: An intervention study. *Journal of Child Language, 26,* 49–67.

Peterson, C., & McCabe, A. (1983). *Developmental psycholinguistics: Three ways of looking at a child's narrative.* New York: Plenum.

Peterson, C., & McCabe, A. (1992). Parental styles of narrative elicitation: Effect on children's narrative structure and content. *First Language, 12,* 299–321.

Peterson, C., & McCabe, A. (1994). A social interactionist account of developing decontextualized narrative skill. *Developmental Psychology, 30,* 937–948.

Peterson, C., & McCabe, A. (1996). Parental scaffolding of context in children's narratives. In J. H. V. Gilbert & C. E. Johnson (Eds.), *Children's language* (Vol. 9, pp. 183–196). Mahwah, NJ: Lawrence Erlbaum Associates.

Peterson, C., & Roberts, C. (2003). Like mother, like daughter: Similarities in narrative style. *Developmental Psychology, 39,* 551–562.

Polanyi, L. (1985). *Telling the American story.* Norwood NJ: Ablex.

Reese, E., & Fivush, R. (1993). Parental styles of talking about the past. *Developmental Psychology, 29,* 596–606.

Reese, E., Haden, C. A., & Fivush, R. (1993). Mother-child conversations about the past: Relationships of style and memory over time. *Cognitive Development, 8,* 403–430.

Rogoff, B., & Gardner, W. P. (1984). Adult guidance in cognitive development: An examination of mother-child instruction. In B. Rogoff & J. Lave (Eds.), *Everyday cognition: Its development in social context* (pp. 95–116). Cambridge, MA: Harvard University Press.

Roth, F. P. (1986). Oral narrative abilities of learning-disabled students. *Topics in Language Disorders, 7,* 21–30.

Russell, A., & Saebel, J. (1997). Mother-son, mother-daughter, father-son, and father-daughter: Are they distinct relationships? *Developmental Review, 17,* 111–147.

Snow, C. E. (1983). Literacy and language: Relationships during the preschool years. *Harvard Educational Review, 53,* 165–189.

Tabors, P. O., Snow, C. E., & Dickinson, D. K. (2001). Homes and schools together: Supporting language and literacy development. In D. K. Dickinson & P. O. Tabors (Eds.), *Beginning literacy with language* (pp. 313–334). Baltimore, MD: Brooks.

Tannen, D. (1990). *You just don't understand.* New York: Ballantine.

Vygotsky, L. S. (1978). *Mind in society.* Cambridge, MA: Harvard University Press.

Whitehurst, G. J., & Valdez-Menchaca, M. C. (1988). What is the role of reinforcement in early language acquisition? *Child Development, 59,* 430–440.

3

Family Narratives and the Development of Children's Emotional Well-Being

Robyn Fivush
Jennifer Bohanek
Rachel Robertson
Marshall Duke
Emory University

> *After the good times were over, as we grew older, we were to tell each other stories about the past, each adding his or her own fragments of pleasurable detail, until the joint memory became something larger than each single memory, and yet became something that each of us possessed fully, as if it were solely our own.*
>
> —Wilson (1998, p. 142)

Much of family interaction focuses on telling family stories; in everyday interactions, over the dinner table, in the car, across the television dialogue, and in more formal, ritualized interactions, at holiday dinners, family reunions, weddings, and funerals, family members engage in co-constructing the events they have shared together in the past. These narratives, often told again and again, define the shape of each family's emotional life. The way in which individual family members participate in the recreation of the family's shared past modulates an evolving self-understanding both as an individual and as a member of the family. In this chapter, we examine the ways in which families co-construct narratives. Our focus is on individual differences in the process of family reminiscing, and we argue that the way in which families co-construct their shared past has implications for children's developing emotional well-being and resilience. More specifically, families that are able to talk about emotionally complex and difficult events in more open, integrated, and coherent ways may help provide children with the resources to cope with and resolve aversive experiences.

In the first section, we present evidence of individual differences in parental reminiscing style that emerge very early in development, and we demonstrate how these differences influence both autobiographical memory and emotional development across the preschool years. Although most of the research focuses on emotionally positive experiences, we discuss the limited research on parent-child narratives of more stressful events as well, and how this may be related to the parent-child emotional relationship. We then turn to a study currently in progress targeting pre-adolescent children, in which we are exploring family narratives about both positive and negative shared experiences, and we discuss relations between individual differences in the process of narrative interactions and children's emotional well-being.

EARLY PARENT-CHILD REMINISCING

Children are surrounded by family stories virtually from birth. Parents begin telling family stories to their children during infancy, well before children can understand, let alone participate in, these narrative retellings (Fiese, Hooker, Kotray, Schwagler, & Rimmer, 1997). As children grow older and become more capable participants, parents begin to encourage and expect children to engage in joint reminiscing (Eisenberg, 1985; Miller, 1994). Several researchers have described the ways in which families discuss past events with and around children in everyday contexts (Fiese & Marjinsky, 1999; Miller, 1994; Ochs & Capps, 2001). Most of these studies collect spontaneous family conversations and examine the ways in which narratives of past events emerge within everyday activities such as chatting with family and friends, or family talk over the dinner table. The resulting narrative descriptions highlight ways in which individual identities and family relationships are defined and clarified within these conversational interactions.

In addition to revealing how families communicate, family narrative interactions are also related to child outcome. For example, Fiese and Marjinsky (1999) rated family dinnertime narratives on coherence and emotional modulation. Parents' appropriate modulation of affect, but not overall conversational coherence, was linked to fewer behavior problems in children. Ochs, Taylor, Rudolph, and Smith (1992) have further argued that family storytelling is a site for the socialization of self and other (see also Miller, 1994). They examined the ways in which families re-tell the same stories, reworking the narrative to explain and clarify. Their descriptions illuminate how these give-and-take interactions go beyond influencing memories for the events; they encourage perspective taking, critical thinking, theory building, and relationship roles within the family.

Importantly, a great deal of research confirms that there are individual differences in the ways in which parents reminisce about shared past experiences with their young children (Fivush & Fromhoff, 1988; Hudson, 1990; McCabe & Peterson, 1991). Many of these studies use a more directed elicitation of parent-child reminiscing and often focus on one parent and child conversing about shared events. Level of elaboration has emerged as a critical factor in differentiating individual styles of reminiscing (Farrant & Reese, 2000). Some parents show a highly elaborative style, frequently talking about the past, and describing past experiences in rich and embellished detail. These parents also encourage and affirm their children's participation in reminiscing. In contrast, other parents are less elaborative, talking about the past less frequently, and when reminiscing, giving sparse detail about what happened, often asking the same question over and over until the child responds. Less elaborative parents do not try to elicit their children's participation in reminiscing to the same extent as more elaborative parents, nor do they provide as much feedback to their children during the conversation.

Critically, parental reminiscing style is not related to sheer amount of talk in other contexts. Highly elaborative parents are not necessarily more talkative in a free play context with their young children (Haden & Fivush, 1996) or more elaborative when reading stories together (Haden, Reese, & Fivush, 1996). Thus it seems that parental reminiscing style is specific to the goals and functions of sharing the past. One of the central functions of reminiscing about shared experiences is to create and maintain social and emotional bonds (Fivush, Haden, & Reese, 1996; Bluck & Alea, 2002). Through co-constructing shared experiences together, parents and children are creating shared histories that provide a sense of self in relation to others through time. Parents who engage in more elaborated reminiscing provide a richer and more detailed narrative of the shared past, thus facilitating a more differentiated and nuanced sense of self in their children. And, in fact, children of more elaborative parents begin to tell more detailed and elaborated stories of their own personal past than children of less elaborative parents by the end of the preschool years (Harley & Reese, 1999; Reese, Haden, & Fivush, 1993).

Provocatively, there are gender differences in early parent-child reminiscing. Whereas there are few stylistic differences between mothers and fathers in the way in which they discuss past events with their preschool children, both mothers and fathers talk in greater detail and encourage and affirm their daughters' participation in shared reminiscing to a greater extent than their sons'. In turn, girls tell more elaborated and detailed narratives of their own past than do boys (Reese & Fivush, 1993; Reese, Haden, & Fivush, 1996).

Most important, when we share the past together, we move beyond recalling what happened and provide information about our emotional reactions and feelings about the event (Labov, 1982). Parent-child reminiscing is rich in emotional detail, although again, there are individual differences in the extent to which parents and children share their past emotions, and these differences are related to gender. Some research has found that mothers talk in more emotionally elaborated ways about the past than fathers (Fivush, Brotman, Buckner, & Goodman, 2000), but other studies have not found differences between parents (Reese et al., 1996). However, a great many studies have now confirmed that both mothers and fathers include more emotional detail when reminiscing with daughters than with sons (Adams, Kuebli, Boyle, & Fivush, 1995; Fivush, 1989, 1991; Fivush et al., 2000; Fivush, Berlin, Sales, Mennuti-Washburn, & Cassidy, 2003; Kuebli & Fivush, 1992). And by the end of the preschool years, girls are talking about their past experiences in more emotional ways than are boys.

These patterns indicate that children are learning to tell the stories of their lives through participating in early parent-child reminiscing. Parents who reminisce in more elaborated ways, studding their conversation with rich detail and emotional nuances, have children who develop more elaborated and more emotional narratives of their personal past. But why are some parents more elaborative than others? If it is the case that parent-child reminiscing functions to create and maintain social and emotional bonds, then we would expect differences in parental reminiscing style related to the parent-child emotional relationship. Through co-constructing the events of our lives, we create emotional attachments that bond us together through time and allow us to anticipate a shared future.

REMINISCING AND ATTACHMENT

One of the core constructs in conceptualizing parent-child emotional relationships is attachment. The mother-child attachment bond develops over the first year of the child's life, based on the kinds of social and emotional interactions experienced (see Cassidy & Shaver, 1999, for an overview). Mothers who are more sensitive and emotionally open to their children's needs have children who develop a secure sense of self in the world. In contrast, mothers who are less sensitive and less emotionally open have children who feel more insecure. Securely attached infants are able to explore the physical and social world more easily and comfortably than insecure infants. Although these early attachment relations are assumed to be nonconscious, as children grow older, they develop working models of their relationships with others (Bowlby, 1988; Bretherton, 1996). These working models are assumed to be expressed and modulated through parent-child communication (Thompson, 2000). Securely attached dyads are theorized to be able to converse in more emotionally open, integrative and coherent ways than insecurely attached dyads.

If a principal function of parent-child reminiscing is to create and maintain social and emotional bonds, then we would expect a relation to attachment status such that more elaborative parents would facilitate a more secure attachment. Further, if attachment status allows for differential communication, then more secure attachment should facilitate more elaborative parent-child reminiscing. Thus, attachment and reminiscing style should be dialectically related across development. There is some emerging evidence that this is the case. Both Fivush and Vasudeva (2002) and Farrant and Reese (2000) have found that more securely attached dyads reminisce in more highly elaborated ways than less securely attached dyads.

A limitation of this research, however, is the focus on reminiscing about mostly positive, child-centered events. Parent-child reminiscing about emotionally negative experiences is of great theoretical interest for several reasons. First, whereas it seems obvious that reminiscing about emotionally positive events facilitates emotional bonding, it is not at all clear that reminiscing about negative events serves this same function. Instead, it seems that parents may discuss negative experiences with their young children for very different reasons, including helping their children to understand how and why aversive events occurred, how to understand and cope with these kinds of experiences in order to alleviate negative affect, and to teach children about how to avoid such experiences in the future. Second, within attachment theory, it has been hypothesized that security of attachment may be particularly important when families confront negative experiences; a secure attachment relationship may allow families to discuss stressful events more openly, leading to a greater sense of social support in coping with these kinds of events (Bowlby, 1988; Bretherton, 1996; Pillemer, 1998). Thus, the way in which families are able to co-construct emotionally negative and stressful experiences during reminiscing may be related to children's ability to cope with aversive events; those families that are able to discuss past negative experiences in more emotionally open and coherent ways may facilitate resilience in their children.

PARENT-CHILD REMINISCING ABOUT NEGATIVE EVENTS

Only a few studies have explicitly examined parent-child reminiscing about emotionally negative and stressful events. In Fivush et al. (2003), mothers reminisced with their 4-year-old children about everyday events in which the child experienced sadness, anger, and fear. Events discussed included such things as losing a prized toy, having a conflict with a sibling or peer, and being left at the babysitter's—clearly, events that all children experience on a regular basis. Conversations were coded for both style, along a dimension of elaboration, and content. Content included mentioning the cause of the emotional experience (e.g., "Were you sad when Daddy went on a business trip?"), attributions of emotional reactions (e.g., "I know you were sad. I was sad, too.") and resolutions (e.g., "But then we talked about it and you felt better, right?").

Overall, mothers were more elaborative with daughters than with sons, and girls were more elaborative than boys. Across all three types of emotional experience discussed, mothers focused more on causes than attributions or resolutions, indicating that mothers are concerned with helping their children understand how and why they experience negative emotion. But when discussing fear and sadness, mothers focus on resolving the negative affect. When discussing anger, in contrast, mothers focus on attributions of the emotional state itself and talk little of resolution. These patterns suggest that mothers are concerned with helping their children understand and cope with fear and sadness more than anger. Moreover, sadness and fear are socially sharable; through discussing resolutions of negative affect, parents and children negotiate and resolve these feelings in a supportive conversational context. Although anger is acknowledged, parents and children do not co-construct narratives of anger that validate and resolve this emotion. Thus mother-child reminiscing about everyday emotional experiences is a rich context for the development of children's emotional understanding and well-being. Through participating in adult-structured reminiscing, children are developing a sense of self as an emotional being, and learning how to evaluate, resolve, and share everyday emotional experiences with others.

But what of more stressful, or even traumatic experiences? How might mothers discuss truly aversive events with their children, and how might this help young children to understand and resolve negative affect? To date, only two studies have examined this question. In Sales, Fivush, and Peterson (2003), mothers reminisced with their preschool children about an injury requiring outpatient emergency room treatment and about an emotionally positive event. Parental reminiscing style was consistent across the two events; those parents who were highly elaborative when discussing a positive event with their children were also highly elaborative when discussing a negative event, but the content differed. Parents focused more on emotion overall, and especially positive emotion, when discussing the positive event, and on causal explanations when discussing the negative event. Similarly, Ackil, Waters, Dropnik, Dunisch, and Bauer (1999) asked mothers and their 8- to 12-year-old children to discuss a tornado that had devastated their town a few weeks earlier, as well as an emotionally positive event, and also found a focus on causal explanation for the negative event. In this study, however, they found more emotion talk overall about the negative than positive event. Again, however, positive emotion was discussed more during the positive event and negative emotion during the negative event. Not surprisingly, then, parents discuss emotions consonant with the valence of the event. More interesting, the focus on discussing causes in both studies confirms that when discussing emotionally negative events, parents are concerned with helping their children understand how and why such events happen, and possibly to help them resolve these difficult emotional experiences.

Across studies, the focus on discussing causes and resolutions of emotionally negative experiences and the relation between parental reminiscing style and attachment status suggest that individual differences in family narrative interactions may be critical in children's developing emotional well-being. Children whose families are better able to discuss their shared past experiences in more elaborative and emotionally open ways may help provide their children with the tools necessary for understanding and resolving aversive affect.

FAMILY NARRATIVES AND EMOTIONAL RESILIENCE

We are currently examining relations between family narratives and children's resilience more explicitly. Our focus is on working families with at least one preadolescent child. As family structure becomes more complicated, with both parents working in and out of the house, and negotiating more complex parent and child schedules, the ways in which families reconstruct their shared experiences together becomes a critical juncture for families to recreate themselves as an emotionally cohesive unit (Fiese & Marjinsky, 1999; Ochs & Capps, 2001).

We targeted families with a preadolescent child because the clinical literature suggests that the teenage years are particularly rife with family conflict and this is the developmental period when children are most likely to begin to have problems with identity that can lead to serious outcomes such as delinquency, depression, and substance abuse (Carr, 1999; Lerner & Lerner, 2001). Our goal is to establish family patterns of communication that may buffer children from the difficulties of navigating the teenage years, and our plan is to follow these families over the next several years to assess long-term relations among family narratives, family functioning, and individual outcome. Forty two-parent families with a target child between the ages of 9 and 12 years are participating. Thirty-three are dual-earner families, and 7 are single-earner families. Half of the families have a preadolescent daughter, 29 families are Caucasian, 5 are African-American, and 5 are of mixed race. Thirty of the families are traditional nuclear families, 8 are blended families, and 2 are extended families with at least one additional adult living with them.

Here we present a subset of the data collected in the larger project: elicited family narratives of shared positive and negative events. During a home visit, a research assistant asked the family to discuss one emotionally positive event that the family enjoyed together and one emotionally negative event, something stressful that the family experienced together. The families were free to select the events, and to discuss the events in whatever fashion for whatever length of time they chose. Although families were instructed to discuss the nominated events as they normally would amongst themselves, some families occasionally spoke to the experimenter and provided background information during the narrative. However, despite these digressions the conversations would always return to a family discussion. Conversational length varied widely among families, with some families discussing these events for 40–45 minutes and others only discussing the events for 5 minutes. Despite this, the range of events was not that variable from family to family. Almost all of the positive events selected were family vacations or holiday gatherings, and most of the negative events were relatively normal stressors that all families face, such as death of a grandparent, death of a pet, or a serious illness or accident of a parent or child, as described in Table 3.1. Thus the negative events were within the range of normative experience and represent the kinds of stressful events that virtually all families must deal with over time.

We are in the beginning stages of coding and analyzing these narratives. Our initial coding focuses on how the family negotiates the telling of the story. Based on previous research (Fiese & Marjinsky, 1999), but most impor-

TABLE 3.1
Description of Events

	Number of Families	*% of Families*
Positive Events:		
Family vacations	31	78%
Sibling birth	3	8%
Sports/tournaments	3	8%
Visits to/from relatives	2	5%
Ceremony	1	1%
Negative Events:		
Death of friend/family	12	30%
Death of pet	8	20%
Child's illness/injury	5	13%
Accident/disaster	5	13%
Family conflict	3	8%
Move to new city	3	8%
Mishap during vacation	3	8%
Parent's illness	1	1%

tant, emerging from the narratives themselves, we developed five characteristics that describe how families co-construct these narratives: collaborative, cooperative, child-centered, facilitated/moderated, and disharmonious, as summarized in Table 3.2. Note that the characteristics are not mutually exclusive. Because these are long and complex conversations, families may display several of these characteristics in the course of sharing the event together. Thus, we scored each conversation along each characteristic on a 0 to 3 scale, such that 0 indicated the characteristic was not represented at all, 1 indicated the characteristic was represented in a limited way, 2 indicated that the characteristic was well represented but not dominant, and 3 indicated that it was the dominant characteristic represented in the narrative interaction. Thus, conceptually, a family can be high on both collaborative narrative interaction and also be child-centered, or high on facilitated/moderated narrative interaction but still disharmonious.

Two coders independently listened to each conversation as they read through the transcripts and assigned each narrative a score of 0 to 3 on each of the narrative characteristics. Across the five characteristics, coders agreed 93% of the time for both positive and negative events (range = 88% to 98%). Disagreements were within one point an additional 6% of the time, with disagreements of two points or more only occurring 1% of the time. All discrepancies were then resolved through discussion. Table 3.3 shows the

TABLE 3.2
Description of Narrative Characteristics

Narrative Characteristic	*Description*	*Indicators*	*Instance Criteria*
Collaborative	The narrative unfolds as the family members each add small bits of information; the narrative is being told by all the participants simultaneously, as if they are all of one mind.	Family members finish each other's sentences, say the same thing simultaneously, or interrupt without changing the topic.	Must include three conversational turns, one indicator and two new pieces of information.
Cooperative	Family members take turns telling the story, each telling their own point of view.	Family members listen to each other and are allowed to finish their own thoughts without interruption.	Must include either one speaker giving several pieces of information on one topic or several speakers giving small pieces of information on one topic.
Child-centered	Parents try to elicit information from the children by asking leading questions, prompting them, and giving them cues.	The conversation is dominated by questions from parents and responses by the children.	An instance includes the parent's question and the child's response; or if the child does not answer, the question alone can be counted as an instance.
Facilitated/ Moderated	The conversation is moderated and facilitated primarily by one parent.	A single moderator initiates topics, chooses speakers, gives extended monologues, or ignores other family member's input.	A parent must exhibit two of the indicators, or one indicator two times.
Disharmonious	Family members appear to be disconnected, are not like-minded, and/or don't have a shared understanding of events.	Mild disagreements, denial of feelings, little shared affect, put-downs, complaining, and parental lecturing.	One occurrence of any of the indicators.

Table 3.3
Mean Scores on Each Characteristic for Positive and Negative Events

Dimension	*Pos. Event Score*	*Neg. Event Score*	*Correlation betw/ Pos. and Neg. Scores*
Collaborative	1.35	.73	.56*
Cooperative	2.05	2.13	.52*
Child-Ctrd	2.17	2.07	.49*
Facilitated-Mod.	.12	.20	.54*
Disharmonious	.10	.30	.43*

$^*p < .01$

mean scores on each characteristic for the positive and negative events, as well as the correlations between the two characteristics across the two event types. As can be seen, families most often displayed cooperative and child-centered characteristics in these narratives, with little evidence of facilitated/moderated or disharmonious interactions. Further, families showed similar characteristics of narrative interaction across positive and negative events. Still, there was a great deal of individual variation from family to family in how they co-constructed the narratives.

In the following sections, we provide more detailed descriptions and examples of each of these characteristics. In the following excerpts, "TC" stands for target child, the preadolescent child that is the focus of our assessment. Other children in the family are indicated as "Sib1," "Sib2," and so on. Not surprisingly, it was fairly common for family members to speak over one another. Because this kind of information was important for coding the narrative characteristics, we adopted notation to indicate overlapping speech. The symbol < was used to indicate the moment when a second speaker began talking and the symbol > was used to indicate the moment when the second speaker was no longer speaking over the initial speaker. Thus, the speech that was spoken at the same time was enclosed in the symbols across conversational turns.

COLLABORATIVE INTERACTIONS

In conversations with collaborative characteristics, family members each added different pieces of the story and expanded on what others contributed. All of the conversational turns fit together as an integrated whole, which resulted in a conversation that was richer and more complex than any of the individuals could have told on their own. Laughing, good-natured joking and teasing, and requests for telling the story were also present. The following is part of a collaborative exchange between the mother and the preadolescent son about the younger daughter being burned by hot food:

Mom: We <were at Auntie Mona's house.

TC: We> were at Auntie Mona's house.

Mom: Because I wasn't going over <there

TC: And>

Mom: I was dropping y'all off. I, I was leaving y'all over there, I think or <something.

TC: I think> And um so there w- were these gr-grits Gabrielle was gonna eat for breakfast and so and, and um <so

Mom: They> were sitting on the table.

TC: So, they were very hot and then,

Mom: I guess, well Auntie Mona had Michael put them in the microwave. <They were those instant (unintelligible) microwaves.

TC: And > sh-she, I think she overcooked them.

TC: So they were very <hot,

Mom: She> was letting them cool off.

TC: And then and she was letting them cool off, and I had a um, magnifying glass and I um there was, they had the light and so it was under the light and I put the magnifying glass, um right on the um, on the <um

Mom: over> the bowl, the grits,

TC: over the bowl and for um, a couple of seconds and then David called me downstairs and, and um,

Mom: No, <she accidentally,

TC: We>

Mom: And then she

TC: and then she accidentally

Mom: and then she <um

TC: touched it>

Note how the mother and child both finished each other's sentences and continued to add new information while the story developed into an integrative account of what happened. Neither dominated the story, but each added additional details in a coherently evolving narrative. Overall, in collaborative interactions family members create a shared narrative in which they agree on what happened and what it meant. When there is confusion about what happened, they work through the details and come to a shared understanding and perspective.

COOPERATIVE INTERACTIONS

In narratives typified by this characteristic, family members take turns telling the story and encourage each other to contribute. Family members engage in polite turn-taking (waiting their turn instead of talking over one another), asking each other questions ("How did you feel about . . ."), and verifying information ("yeah," "mmm-hmm"). They listen to each other and are allowed to finish their own thoughts. In this excerpt, the family is discussing when the family pet died:

Mom: That's because he was sick. You know and there was that big cancerous spot <there.
TC: And I > remember sitting on couch back there watching you all cry (unintelligible)
Mom: Yeah. Do you remember how old you were?
Sib1: But I remember you didn't cry because you weren't that close <to him.
Dad: I bet> Eric (the target child) was in first grade then.
TC: Hmmm.
Mom: Yeah, yeah and then we had ah. Daddy and I brought Max in the car so that the veterinarian could put Max to sleep.
TC: Mmm.
Mom: And I think I took it the hardest because Max was in our lives since Stacy (the daughter), I was pregnant with Stacy.
Sib1: Before.
Mom: And Max was our first baby, Daddy and I.
Sib1: Because I, I looked in the photo albums and saw a picture of you and Dad both holding Max by the balloons saying that you were going to have a baby, which was me.
Mom: Yeah. And that's why Max was in our life all that time and it was real sad when we had to put him in the car. And Daddy remembers this cuz I don't think, Daddy, Keith you haven't uh was that the first dog you put to sleep?
Dad: Yeah, it was horrible. It was not . . . it wasn't . . . it was horrible. Um Max, Max tolerated me. Max was a real good dog and he tolerated me. . . .

Note how family members are encouraged to give their own perspective, and nearly every new piece of information was verified by another family member. But in contrast to a collaborative interaction, new contributions do not build a coherent story, but rather each expresses the speaker's individual role and perspective.

CHILD-CENTERED INTERACTIONS

In child-centered narrative interactions, parents help their children tell the story by asking leading questions, prompting them, and giving them cues. Parents ask questions intended to solicit responses from the children and not to learn new information; parents often know the answers to these questions. In this excerpt, the family is recalling their vacation in Europe:

Mom: What did you like the most about the trip to Europe?
TC: I liked it when we went to uh (unintelligible) Castle.
Mom: Why did you like that?
TC: It was really fun. It was just fun.
Dad: What did you like the most?
Mom: In the castle?
TC: I liked the food.
Mom: You liked the food? <Just like your brother, huh? (Laughs)
Dad: Yeah.> What did you like the most?
Sib 1: I liked the castle.

At the beginning of the conversation, both parents encourage the children to participate by asking broad, open-ended questions. Parents confirm the children's answers, and then ask for elaboration. The parents obviously wanted the children to do the talking; they did not interact much between themselves, and they focused their attention on the children. After asking a few very broad questions, more specific questions were intended to elicit as much information from the children as possible—both factual and emotional. Here is a conversation about another family's trip to Brazil:

Dad: Was it a vacation or was it something you had to do?
TC: Vacation.
Dad: So what do you remember about the trip out there?
TC: <Uh . . .
Sib 1: That we would have to run around and eat some French-fries.
Dad: That's all you remember that you ate some French-fries <and . . .
Sib 1: We went scuba diving.
Dad: You went scuba diving.
TC: And then we got to get really close to fish and we got to um, we went down water slides on tubes.

Parents ask open-ended questions, allowing their children to chose among multiple possible topics, and then encourage their children to continue to tell the story by repeating and confirming their responses. Through this kind of questioning, parents provide a loose organization within which the children tell the story. It is possible that families demonstrated this characteristic because of the nature of the task; families knew we were interested in their preadolescent child (this is how they were recruited into the study) and therefore they may have interpreted the task as one in which they were suppose to elicit their children's memories of these family events. Still, not all families engaged in this kind of interaction, and most who did showed other narrative characteristics as well.

FACILITATED/MODERATED INTERACTIONS

A narrative dominated by this characteristic was moderated and facilitated primarily by one parent. Other family members did little to initiate topics of conversation, but rather followed the lead of the moderator. In contrast to child-centered interactions, the questions are not open-ended, allowing children to tell the story in their own way. Rather, the parent asks pointed questions to lead the narrative in a particular direction. In the following narrative, the father orchestrated the entire conversation. As he initiated the conversation about the target child's participation in a baseball league, he introduced a theme which he continued throughout the narrative:

Dad: . . . And what was remarkable about the experience for us is that Kyle (target child) was unknown, untested and new at this. And what position did you start off uh batting order?
TC: Uh, second?
Mom: <No, no, no.
Dad: No, no, no.> At the beginning of the year, what . . ?
TC: Eighth.
Dad: Eighth. You were eighth batting order, which means you were one of the worst hitters there. And then how did you move up during the year?
Mom: By hitting. (Laughs) <By hitting the ball.
TC: Uh, the best>, then to second.
Dad: Second.
TC: Then back to second.
Dad: Then back to second. And, in the beginning of the year, you started off playing what position?
TC: Left field.
Dad: And then what position did you finish at the end of the year?
TC: First base.
Dad: First base! From the outfield to the infield and from eighth in the batting order to second.

The father continues to lead the other family members throughout the conversation to tell a particular story about the son's improvement over the season that culminated in the playoffs. Importantly, when other family members contribute, their contributions, and especially their evaluations of the event are re-interpreted by the father:

Dad: Kyle, why don't you take the story from here about the playoffs since you were in 'em.

TC: We started off with six teams then three of the teams played each other and then there's four teams watching. And um then two of the teams . . . one team plays another team and then another team plays another team and uh . . . Well, everyone goes to the championship and we won one of those and we went to the championship and we won the championship.

Dad: You won three straight playoff games and so, for us, it was remarkable to see a team that finished in the middle of the standings sweep at the end. And there was much excitement and much joy and Kyle contributed a lot to the team's winning.

Even when he explicitly asks for his son's contribution to the story, the father takes back the floor, and re-narrates the events to conform to his own perspective. Thus in facilitated/moderated interactions, one parent takes on the role of the narrator, and scaffolds the family's narration. In addition to providing the storyline, the parent also provides a particular perspective on why this event was memorable and important, and may even impose this perspective on other family members.

DISHARMONIOUS INTERACTIONS

During disharmonious exchanges, family members appeared to be disconnected, not like-minded, and did not have a shared understanding of the event. It must be emphasized that instances of this characteristic were isolated, and did not dominate the entire conversation. In this example, the mother and child are discussing a friend who had been living with them moving away, and they have a disagreement about the daughter's emotional reaction:

Mom: Does it make you sad?

Sib 1: No.

Mom: You're not sad any more?

Sib 1: No.

Mom: You were sad this afternoon.

Sib 1: No I wasn't.

Mom: Yes you were.
Sib 1: I wasn't.
Mom: What were you?
Sib 1: Happy.
Mom: You were happy? You're happy she's moving?
Sib 1: Yeah.
Mom: You get more space in the house?
Sib 1: Yeah.

Rather than accepting the child's assertion that she was not sad, the mother insists that she was sad that afternoon. Disharmonious exchanges can also include name-calling. Many families did tease each other or call each other names in a joking manner. However, in disharmonious interactions, participants were serious as they put down other members of their family. Finally, some families also used their conversation time to lecture their children. These exchanges were counted as disharmonious when either the parent or the child showed some negative affect while lecturing or being lectured to (frustration, anger, sadness, exasperation). Again, these exchanges were not conducted in a teasing manner; the parents wanted the children to realize what they did wrong. In this example, the event involved the child crashing his bike through a window just as the family was leaving for vacation.

Dad: Seems I recall asking him to put the scooter in the garage.
(3 exchanges take place in between)
TC: It was leaning this way and I was going to make it lean this way but I didn't catch it and it went through. So I was gettin' ready to go put it up.
Mom: But if you had put it up when you were told to put it up in the first place, do you think that would have happened?
TC: No. (long pause) No. (louder, again a pause) No! (child almost yells this last response).
Mom: Okay.

The mother wanted to make the point that if the child had listened to his stepfather and put the bike away when he was supposed to, this incident would not have happened. When she asked him whether or not he thinks the incident would've taken place if he had listened, she waits for several seconds each time the child says "No." The child became frustrated (or angry), and raised his voice each time he repeated his answer. Once the mother thought she adequately made her point, she says "okay," and the conversation changes direction. Again, no family was disharmonious across the entire conversation, but a few families displayed these disharmonious characteristics at several points during the interaction.

IMPLICATIONS AND FUTURE DIRECTIONS

As already discussed, we argue that the ways in which families reminisce about the events of their lives has implications for children's developing sense of self and emotional well-being. How might these different narrative characteristics be related to these issues? Families that narrate the past in collaborative ways weave stories that are mutually shared. Most important, family members build the narrative together, each additional piece of information contributing to a coherent narrative told from a shared, unified perspective. In this way, collaborative narratives may help children to understand themselves as part of a cohesive family unit that shares a mutual understanding of important events. Cooperative interactions, in contrast, do not build a unified narrative, but rather form individual but still validated narratives. Family members actively solicit and confirm each other's versions of what happened, leading to a narrative told from multiple individual perspectives. Cooperative interactions may help children build a sense of self as an individual, separate from but still supported by other family members, as well as helping children learn how other family members react to and evaluate events. Both collaborative and cooperative interactions are emotionally open and involve sharing among all family members, but each focus on a different sense of self-construal.

Child-centered interactions also solicit and validate the child's view of the event, but, whereas in cooperative interactions all members of the family share their perspective, in child-centered interactions the parents do not present their own view. The child's perspective is accepted and validated but is not shared by or interweaved with other family member's perspectives. Thus, in child-centered interactions, children are learning to define self as separate but, unlike in collaborative and cooperative interactions, they are not simultaneously learning how others may think about the past. In this way, children are learning about self as an individual but may not be learning how to place their own individual perspective in the context of the family. The mirror image of this style is facilitated/moderated, in which the child's perspective may be solicited but is not validated. Instead, the parent imposes a particular form on the narrative and even a particular perspective. Children are learning that self is defined as a part of the family and this is further defined as having a specific, imposed perspective (as opposed to a negotiated, shared perspective as in collaborative interactions). Finally, disharmonious interactions lead to a fragmented sense of self; the child is defined in opposition to rather than as a part of the family unit, and interactions are emotionally negative. The child's perspective is not validated; indeed, it is often explicitly contradicted.

Again, we emphasize that most families show elements of many characteristics, and therefore, not surprisingly, children's' sense of self emerging from these interactions is complicated and multilayered. Indeed, it may be the case that families that show a balanced use of all five characteristics lead to the most differentiated sense of self and the greatest sense of emotional well-being in their children. Further analyses on our data set will hopefully answer some of these questions.

From a clinical perspective, researchers have expanded their focus in recent years from intervention and prevention only to also consider the ways in which children and adults overcome adversity in their private and public lives. Practicing clinicians, for example, have reported a significant increase in cases dealing with family stress, childhood fears, and general adjustment problems. In addition, several books have appeared which have as their main focus the topics of increasing resilience (e.g., Brooks & Goldstein, 2002; Reivich & Shatte, 2002) and of the salutary effects of storytelling on well-being and adjustment in adults and children (Smith, 1990). Finally, one cannot ignore the potential immunizing effects (though not yet documented) of works such as the books by Lemony Snicket in which the child protagonists demonstrate resilience by overcoming terrible situations (Snicket, 2001).

In addition to examining the relation between family reminiscing interactions and well-being, our project will also delve into the ameliorative or immunizing benefits of narrative content. This component reflects clinically derived "hunches" that the telling of family stories appears to mediate the development of resilience in children. While not systematic, there is much experiential data to suggest that children raised in families that tell stories about themselves—family histories, family "legends"—seem to raise children that have a lower incidence of maladjustment as well as better prognoses for recovery. Through clinical interviews and other diagnostic techniques and through case studies, clinicians and educators have long known the benefits of the sense of stability, continuity, and strength that seems to arise when children know of their background, the good things as well as the bad. Again, we hope to address these issues in further analyses of the family narratives and relations between the narratives and standardized measures of family and child functioning.

CONCLUSIONS

In this chapter, we reviewed individual differences in how families co-construct shared experiences and how these differences are related to various aspects of children's social and emotional well-being. During the preschool years, when children are just beginning to share their experiences with others, more elaborative parents facilitate the development of narrative skills, such that children of highly elaborative parents come to tell more detailed and embellished narratives of their personal past. Moreover, parents who reminisce in more emotionally elaborative ways have children who come to tell more emotionally rich narratives of their own past. Intriguingly, elaborative reminiscing is related to attachment, suggesting that parents and children who are co-constructing more embellished narratives of their shared past are creating and maintaining strong and secure emotional bonds. Our current research with families with preadolescent children extends these findings. Our preliminary analyses of these conversations focuses on individual differences in the ways in which families co-construct stories of emotionally positive and negative events, and reveals intriguing differences in this process. Most important, this research illustrates that family narratives are not simply about what has happened in the past; they are very much a part of the way in which families recreate themselves as a social and emotional unit in the present.

ACKNOWLEDGMENTS

Some of the research reported in this chapter was supported by a grant from the Sloan Foundation supporting the Emory Center for Myth and Ritual in American Life. We would like to thank Justin Rowe, Stacy Zolondek, Carla Gober, Jean Mennuti-Washburn, Deborah Yunker and Amber Lazarus for help in data collection and preparation.

REFERENCES

Ackil, J., Waters, J., Dropnik, P., Dunisch, D., & Bauer, P. (1999, April). *From the eyes of the storm: Mother-child conversations about a devastating tornado.* Poster presented at the biennial meetings of the Society for Research in Child Development, Albuquerque.

Adams, S., Kuebli, J., Boyle, P., & Fivush, R. (1995). Gender differences in parent-child conversations about past emotions: A longitudinal investigation. *Sex Roles, 33,* 309–323.

Bluck, S., & Alea, N. (2002). Exploring the functions of autobiographical memory. In J. D. Webster & B. K. Haight (Eds)., *Critical advances in reminiscing work: From theory to application* (pp. 61–75). New York: Springer.

Bowlby, J. (1988). *A secure base: Clinical applications of attachment theory.* London: Routledge.

Bretherton, I. (1996). Internal working models of attachment relationships as related to resilient coping. In G. G. Noam & K. W. Fischer (Eds.), *Development and vulnerability in close relationships* (pp. 3–27). Mahwah, NJ: Lawrence Erlbaum Associates.

Brooks, R., & Goldstein, S. (2002). *Nurturing resilience in our children.* New York: NTC Publishing.

Carr, A. (1999). *Handbook of child and adolescent psychology.* London: Routledge.

Cassidy, J., & Shaver, P. R. (1999). *Handbook of attachment: Theory, research and clinical applications.* New York: Guilford.

Eisenberg, A. (1985). Learning to describe past experience in conversation. *Discourse Processes, 8,* 177–204.

Farrant, K., & Reese, E. (2000). *Attachment security and early mother-child reminiscing: A developmental exploration.* Manuscript submitted for publication.

Fiese, B. H., Hooker, K. A.., Kotray, L., Schwagler, J., & Rimmer, M. (1997). Family stories in the early pages of parenthood. *Journal of Marriage and the Family, 57,* 763–770.

Fiese, B. H., & Marjinsky, K. (1999). Dinnertime stories: Connecting family practices with relationship beliefs and child adjustment. *Monographs of the Society for Research in Child Development, 64* (2, Pt. 3), 52–68.

Fivush, R. (1989). Exploring sex differences in the emotional content of mother-child talk about the past. *Sex Roles, 20,* 675–691.

Fivush, R. (1991). Gender and emotion in mother-child conversations about the past. *Journal of Narrative and Life History, 1,* 325–341.

Fivush, R., Berlin, L., Sales, J. M., Mennuti-Washburn, J., & Cassidy, J. (2003). Functions of parent-child reminiscing about negative events. *Memory, 11,* 179–192.

Fivush, R., Brotman, M., Buckner, J. P., & Goodman, S. (2000). Gender differences in parent-child emotion narratives. *Sex Roles, 42,* 233–254.

Fivush, R., & Fromhoff, F. (1988). Style and structure in mother-child conversations about the past. *Discourse Processes, 11,* 337–355.

Fivush, R., Haden, C., & Reese, E. (1996). Remembering, recounting and reminiscing: The development of autobiographical memory in social context. In D. Rubin (Ed.), *Reconstructing our past: An overview of autobiographical memory* (pp. 341–359). New York: Cambridge University Press.

Fivush, R., & Vasudeva, A. (2002). Remembering to relate: Maternal reminiscing style and attachment. *Journal of Cognition and Development, 3,* 73–90.

Haden, C., & Fivush, R. (1996). Contextual variation in maternal conversational styles. *Merrill-Palmer Quarterly, 42,* 24–51.

Haden, C., Reese, E., & Fivush, R. (1996). Mother's extratextual comments during storybook reading: Maternal style over time and across texts. *Discourse Processes, 21,* 135–170.

Harley, K., & Reese, E. (1999). Origins of autobiographical memory. *Developmental Psychology, 35,* 1338–1348.

Hudson, J. A. (1990). The emergence of autobiographic memory in mother-child conversation. In R. Fivush, & J. A. Hudson (Eds.), *Knowing and remembering in young children* (pp. 166–196). New York: Cambridge University Press.

Kuebli, J., & Fivush, R. (1992). Gender differences in parent-child conversations about past emotions. *Sex Roles, 12,* 683–698

Labov, W. (1982). Speech actions and reaction in personal narrative. In D. Tannen (Ed.) *Analyzing discourse: Text and talk.* Washington, DC: Georgetown University Press.

Lerner, J., & Lerner, R. (Eds). (2001). *Adolescence in America.* Santa Barbara, CA: ABC-CLIO

McCabe, A., & Peterson, C. (1991). Getting the story: A longitudinal study of parental styles in eliciting narratives and developing narrative skill. In A. McCabe, & C. Peterson (Eds.), *Developing narrative structure* (pp. 217–253). Hillsdale, NJ: Lawrence Erlbaum Associates.

Miller, P. J. (1994). Narrative practices: Their role in socialization and self-construction. In U. Neisser & R. Fivush (Eds.), *The remembering self: Construction and accuracy in the life narrative* (pp. 158–179). New York: Cambridge University Press.

Ochs, E., & Capps, L. (2001). *Living narrative: Creating lives in everyday storytelling.* Cambridge, MA: Harvard University Press.

Ochs, E., Taylor, C., Rudolph, D., & Smith, R. (1992). Storytelling as a theory-building activity. *Discourse Processes, 15,* 37–72.

Pillemer, D. (1998). What is remembered about early childhood events? *Clinical Psychology Review, 18,* 895–913.

Reese, E., Haden, C., & Fivush, R. (1993). Mother-child conversations about the past: Relationships of style and memory over time. *Cognitive Development, 8,* 403–430.

Reese, E., Haden, C., & Fivush, R. (1996). Mothers, father, daughters sons: Gender differences in reminiscing. *Research on Language and Social Interaction, 29,* 27–56.

Reese, E., & Fivush, R. (1993). Parental styles for talking about the past. *Developmental Psychology, 29,* 596–606.

Reivich, K., & Shatte, A. (2002). *The resilience factor: Seven essential skills for overcoming life's obstacles.* New York: Broadwat Books.

Sales, J. M., Fivush, R., & Peterson, C. (2003). Parent-child conversations about positive and negative events. *Journal of Cognition and Development, 4,* 185–210.

Smith, C. (1990). *From wonder to wisdom: Using stories to help children grow.* New York: New American Library.

Snicket, L. (2001). *A box of unfortunate events.* New York: Harper Collins.

Thompson, R. (2000). The legacy of early attachments. *Child Development, 71,* 145–152.

Wilson, B. (1998). *Blue windows: A Christian Science childhood.* New York: Picador.

4

Coherence and Representations in Preschoolers' Narratives: Associations With Attachment in Infancy

Efrat Sher-Censor
David Oppenheim
University of Haifa

Discussions of oral narratives often distinguish between the organization and the content of narratives—what some refer to as the "how" versus the "what" of the narrative. This distinction refers to two levels of analysis: The first looks at the coherent link between the elements of the narrative—the "how," and the second looks at the narrative themes and the way story protagonists are portrayed—the "what." The central discovery from recent attachment research, and particularly from the work of Main involving adults' narratives regarding their childhood attachment experiences (Hesse, 1999; Main, Kaplan, & Cassidy, 1985), is that the individual differences most pertinent for assessing attachment representations are revealed in the *coherence* of the narratives adults tell about childhood relationships, and that the content, "what" interviewees describe, is less relevant. The goal of this chapter is to describe a study that applied this critical distinction to the narratives of preschoolers by assessing separately the coherence and the content of such narratives, and linking these assessments to the preschoolers' attachments to their mothers as measured when they were infants. Before we describe the study, we open with a review of the main concepts of attachment theory, emphasizing attachment behavioral strategies in infancy and their assessment, as well as Internal Working Models (IWMs) of attachment and their influence on children's information processing. This is followed by a review of previous attachment/narrative studies, as well as the hypotheses that guided the present study.

ATTACHMENT THEORY—INTRODUCTION

According to attachment theory (Bowlby, 1967/1982), infants are pre-adapted to seek their caregivers' proximity in order to receive comfort, soothing, and protection. Depending on the caregivers' sensitivity in responding to these needs, infants develop, toward the end of their first year of life, behavioral strategies designed to manage their distress (Ainsworth, Blehar, Waters, & Wall, 1978; Bowlby, 1967/1982; De Wolff & van IJzendoorn, 1997). These strategies can be assessed using the *Strange Situation Procedure* (SSP; Ainsworth et al., 1978), a validated laboratory procedure (van IJzendoorn & Kroonenberg, 1988) that involves a series of increasingly stressful episodes, including short separations between the infants and their caregivers. In assessing infants' strategies, special emphasis is given to their behaviors towards their caregivers during the reunion episodes.

In an optimal attachment relationship, referred to as *secure* attachment, infants express their attachment needs freely and expect to receive sensitive and responsive reactions from their caregivers (Bowlby, 1967/1982). In the SSP such infants, referred to as *securely attached* and designated "B," seek their caregiver's physical or psychological proximity and calm down quickly (Ainsworth et al., 1978). When the caregivers are less sensitive, *insecure attachment* relationships develop: Infants whose attachment behaviors are usually ignored or rejected by their caregivers learn to *avoid* expressing their attachment needs. In the SSP such infants, designated "A," turn or walk away from their caregivers or refuse to interact with them (Ainsworth et al., 1978). When the caregivers are inconsistently sensitive to their infants' bids for comfort and soothing, infants learn to maximize their attachment signaling. This strategy is displayed in the SSP by infants' *ambivalent* behaviors (e.g., a desire for proximity mixed with angry behavior) or prolonged expressions of distress (Ainsworth et al., 1978). These infants are designated "C." Finally, when caregivers behave incoherently or in frightened or frightening ways towards their infants, the infants might have transient breakdowns in their behavioral strategy (Main & Hesse, 1990; Main & Solomon, 1986). This *disorganized* strategy, designated "D," is displayed in the SSP through contradictory features of attachment strategies (e.g., combination of resistance and avoidance) or through showing odd behaviors, such as freezing or showing stereotypic movements (Main & Solomon, 1986).

INTERNAL WORKING MODELS OF ATTACHMENT

With development, children's attachment patterns become internalized as *Internal Working Models* (IWMs) that include representations of the attachment figures' availability and responsiveness in particular contexts and also complementary representations of how worthy the children are of receiving care. In addition, IWMs also consist of rules that guide children's processing of attachment-related information and their regulation of affect and behavior (Bowlby, 1967/1982; Bretherton, 1985). Secure children develop flexible, open, and free access to their thoughts, feelings, and memories related to attachment. In contrast, insecurely attached children's access to attachment-related thoughts, feelings, and memories are limited, distorted, or biased, with different types of insecurity associated with different types of information-processing biases (Bretherton & Munholland, 1999).

Children with *avoidant* attachments are prone to use defensive exclusion of their rejection experiences due to the anxiety they cause. Thus, alongside the IWMs of the rejecting or disappointing aspects of the attachment figure and the unworthy or incompetent child, which may be inaccessible to consciousness, avoidant children may develop another, incompatible positive set of IWMs which are accessible to awareness. To maintain the separation between these incompatible IWMs, avoidant children distance themselves from negative affect, emotional needs, and closeness (Bowlby, 1967/1982). *Ambivalent* children construct IWMs of their caregiver as inconsistently available and responsive (Ainsworth, 1984), leading to biased information processing toward frightening aspects of the environment and to heightening negative emotional expression (Cassidy, 1994; Kobak & Sceery, 1988). Finally, *disorganized* children have "fragile" IWMs that appear to break down under stress (Cassidy, 1988; Solomon & George, 1999.)

This aspect of IWMs, namely, the way they shape information processing regarding attachment related issues, is of critical importance for studies involving the assessment of attachment using narrative approaches (Oppenheim & Waters, 1995). Children's narrative productions are probably not simple reflections of their representations of the other and the self (e.g., a secure child portraying a parent showing nurturance and sensitivity in response to the child's distress vs. a child with avoidant attachment portraying a parent ignoring or rejecting the child's bids for closeness). Rather, their narrative productions will be significantly shaped by the rules that govern access to attachment-related information. Thus, we might expect secure children's narratives to openly, coherently, and in an emotionally regulated way include nurturance as well fear, sadness, and anger themes in their narratives. Insecurely attached children's narratives, in contrast, might be characterized by lack of openness and coherence, involving overemphasis of either positive or negative themes, and by difficulties in maintaining regulation and flexibility when narrating about such themes. In sum, we might expect differences not only in the *content* of these children's narratives but also in the *coherence* of their narratives. These ideas have received some support from studies of children's IWMs of attachment assessed through the narratives they produce, and we review these next.

RESEARCH ON INTERNAL WORKING MODELS USING NARRATIVE TECHNIQUES

Two narrative techniques have been employed to study preschoolers' attachment representations. The first was an adaptation of the *Separation Anxiety Test* (SAT; Klagsburn & Bowlby, 1976), which consists of a set of pictures showing parents and children in a series of increasingly stressful attachment-related scenes (e.g., a child watches a parent leave). Preschoolers were asked to respond to the SAT pictures by describing how the child in the picture feels and what he will do and what they themselves would do in similar situations (Slough & Greenberg, 1990). The second, which was also used in the study described in this chapter, involved story-completion tasks in which children were asked to construct narratives about attachment related themes (Bretherton, Ridgeway, & Cassidy, 1990; Oppenheim, 1997; Solomon, George, & DeJong, 1995; Waters, Rodrigues, & Ridgway, 1998) as well as other affective themes (Cassidy, 1988; Green, Stanley, Smith, & Goldwyn, 2000) in response to story stems presented to them using a family of dolls. The dolls were used in order to facilitate the narrative production of younger children for whom a purely verbal task might be too difficult. Findings from studies using these techniques have shown that children's attachment as assessed in infancy (Bretherton, Ridgeway, & Cassidy, 1990; Main et al., 1985) or concurrently (Cassidy, 1988; Shouldice & Stevenson-Hinde, 1992; Slough & Greenberg, 1990; Solomon et al., 1995) was meaningfully related to their narrative productions.

Secure children tended to construct coherent stories (Solomon et al., 1995). They also tended to express emotional openness and describe the protagonist's negative feelings, or volunteer information about their own separation experiences (Main et al., 1985; Slough & Greenberg, 1990; Shouldice & Stevenson-Hinde, 1992). In their narratives they portrayed emotionally available caregivers and children who are cooperative, worthy of the caregiver's support and capable of dealing constructively with the problems presented in the story stems (Bretherton Ridgeway, & Cassidy, 1990; Cassidy, 1988; Solomon et al., 1995; Waters et al., 1998). In contrast, *insecure children* did not complete the task or said they did not know what happened next. Some gave incoherent or unorganized responses and failed to deal with the story stem's main issues, or failed to bring their stories to an integrated resolution (Bretherton, Ridgeway, & Cassidy, 1990; Main et al., 1985; Solomon et al., 1995). Additional features were specific to the type of insecurity characterizing the child.

Insecure-avoidant children tended to avoid discussing attachment issues. They lessened the importance of the relationships between the child-protagonist and his or her mother, denied the separation between them, or described schematic and affectless events during the separation and reunion (Cassidy, 1988; Solomon et al., 1995). Caregivers were described by the preschoolers as unavailable emotionally and the child protagonists as rejected (Cassidy, 1988). *Insecure-ambivalent children* tended to describe enjoyable events during separation stories while including in their narratives many events, and losing the main storyline (Solomon et al., 1995). In the SAT they tended to show mostly anger responses (Shouldice & Stevenson-Hinde, 1992). Children who were classified as *insecure-controlling* (a category which is thought to be related to disorganized classification in infancy; Teti, 1999) tended to show more difficulties in their responses compared to other children. Some of them had difficulties creating a story. Those who succeeded tended to show confusion in feeling or in identification with the child protagonist, and others included illogical elements or destructive and violent themes (Shouldice & Stevenson-Hinde, 1992; Solomon et al., 1995). They also tended to portray children and caregivers who either were helpless or were frightening and abusive (Solomon et al., 1995). Taken together the studies of children's attachment narratives reveal theoretically coherent links between such narratives and independent, observational assessments of children's attachments to their mothers. The findings also raise four issues, and these provide the background for the present study.

The first issue involves distinguishing between the content and the coherence of narratives. The coding systems used in the studies reviewed earlier in this chapter involved assessments of both the content and the coherence of the narratives without a clear distinction between the two. In Cassidy's study (1988), for example, only the content of the stories was examined, and Bretherton, Ridgeway, and Cassidy (1990) examined content as the criterion for security and incoherence as the marker of insecurity. In the Solomon et al. (1995) study the two criteria are combined in one classification system, and this is similar in the SAT scales (Main et al., 1985; Shouldice & Stevenson-Hinde, 1992; Slough & Greenberg, 1990). Because, as reviewed earlier, the content/coherence distinction has emerged as central in the analysis of adult attachment narratives, it seems important to apply it systematically in the study of child narratives as well. Therefore, the present study examined separately the links between attachment in infancy and the *coherence* and *content* of preschoolers' narratives. In examining the coherence of the narratives, we used the Robinson, Mantz-Simmons, Macfie, & The MacArthur Narrative Working Group (1992) Coherence scale. The scale measures the fluency of the narrative as well as the way narrators address the problem in the story stem: their acknowledgment and understanding of the problem and its resolution. In examining the content of children's narratives, we focused on the domains deemed relevant to attachment in previous research (Bretherton, Ridgeway, & Cassidy, 1990): the degree to which children portray the child protagonist and parental figures as competent in dealing with emotionally stressful situations.

The second issue involves the distinction between avoidant and ambivalent attachments. There were only a few infants with ambivalent attachments in the studies reviewed previously, as is typical for studies conducted in North America and Western Europe (van IJzendoorn & Sagi, 1999). Due to this limitation we know much less about the expression of ambivalence in child narratives. Because the emotion and attention regulation strategies characteristic of ambivalent attachments are quite different (and perhaps even opposite) from those characteristic of avoidant attachment (Cassidy & Berlin, 1994; Dozier & Kobak, 1993), there is reason to believe that the expression of ambivalence in child narratives might be quite different from that of children with avoidant attachment. The present study, conducted in Israel where most insecurely attached children have ambivalent attachments, provided an opportunity to examine this issue.

The third issue is that only two of the studies mentioned herein were longitudinal and examined the link between attachment in infancy and later narratives (Bretherton, Ridgeway, & Cassidy, 1990; Main et al., 1985), whereas the other studies used concurrent assessments of attachment and narratives using the Cassidy and Marvin (1989) coding system. The validity of this assessment, particularly in terms of longitudinal links with infant-mother attachment has received little support, however (Bar-Haim, Sutton, Fox, & Marvin, 2000). Therefore an additional goal for this study was to replicate the findings linking attachment as assessed in infancy using the well-validated Strange Situation with preschoolers' narratives.

A final issue was that most of the studies reviewed included only attachment-related stems or did not make clear distinctions between these stems and stems about other emotional issues. Thus it is unclear whether the findings are specific to narratives about attachment issues, which would be consistent with the idea that narrative methods assess IWMs of *attachment,* or whether the findings are more general and involve children's narration about a wider range of affective themes. Therefore, The MacArthur Story Stem Battery (MSSB; Bretherton, Oppenheim, Buchsbaum, Emde, & MacArthur Narrative Group, 1990), which includes story stems that cover a range of emotional issues, was used in the present study, and a distinction was made between stories about attachment themes and stories about other emotional themes. We describe the MSSB next.

THE MSSB

The MSSB is a structured story-completion task in which children are presented with story beginnings, or "stems," and are asked to complete the stories. The development of the MSSB was influenced by psychoanalytic play therapy (e.g., Erikson, 1950; Freud, 1946) as well as by research on early emotional (e.g., Wolf, Rygh, & Altshuler, 1984) and cognitive development (e.g., Nelson & Gruendel, 1981). The MSSB was designed to gain insight into children's inner worlds, including their representations of interpersonal relationships with family and peers and their moral understanding (for review, see Bretherton & Oppenheim, in press). Therefore, the story beginnings portray a variety of emotional issues drawn from children's everyday life, including family conflicts, transgressions, and attachment-related interactions in which children are in need of comfort and security.

The story stems begin with a background setting, followed by a complication or a problem that the protagonist has to face. The stems are enacted using a standard doll family in a dramatic and playful way designed to engage the child. The examiner ends the enactment at the climax of the drama, leaving room for the child to decide how to deal with the presented problem and in which direction to lead the story. The MSSB is the most commonly used story-stem assessment of children's emotion narratives, and there is considerable evidence regarding its validity: MSSB narratives have been linked to parent-child narrative co-constructions (Oppenheim, Emde, & Wamboldt, 1996; Oppenheim, Nir, Warren, & Emde, 1997), children's social competence (Page & Bretherton, 2001), behavioral problems (Oppenheim, 2003; Oppenheim, Emde, & Warren, 1997; Toth, Cicchetti, Macfie, Rogosch, & Maughan, 2000; von Klitzing, Kelsay, Emde, Robinson, & Schmitz, 2000), and emotional dysregulation (Robinson, Herot, Haynes, & Mantz-Simmons, 2000). The MSSB was also found to be associated with measures reflecting the child's immediate environment, including parental psychological distress (Oppenheim, 2003) and child maltreatment (Buchsbaum, Toth, Clyman, Cicchetti, & Emde, 1992; Macfie et al., 1999; Toth et al., 2000). Nine of the 14 MSSB story stems that appeared to be most productive in previous studies were used in the current study. The story stems were grouped according to their content: Three stories involved attachment themes, three described emotional conflicts, and three involved transgression themes.

In sum, our hypotheses were: (a) The narratives of children who were securely attached to their mothers as infants would be more coherent than the narratives of children who were insecurely attached (ambivalent or disorganized); (b) children who were securely attached to their mothers in infancy would describe in their narratives more competent children and caregivers compared to children who were insecurely attached (ambivalent or disorganized); and (c) children who were disorganized in their attachment to their mothers in infancy would include more aggressive and destructive themes in their narratives than children who had organized attachments (i.e., secure or ambivalent) in infancy.

METHOD

Participants

One hundred thirteen children and their mothers were selected for longitudinal investigation from a larger sample of 758 infant-mother dyads (Sagi, Koren-Karie, Gini, Ziv, & Joels, 2002). Participants were recruited when the infants were born. Inclusion criteria for mothers were: a nonrisk pregnancy, a minimum of 2 years' residence in Israel, and mastery of the Hebrew language. When children approached the age of 4.5 years, a subsample was contacted again and invited to participate in the follow-up study (Oppenheim, Koren-Karie, & Sagi, 2001). The majority (89%) of mothers with whom successful contact was established agreed to participate in the study. Children in the present study were selected based on their attachment classifications in infancy with the intention to create a sample with a large proportion of insecure children. All ambivalent (C) and disorganized (D) infants whose classifications were available at the time of the follow-up were therefore included in the present study. A group of randomly selected (except for approximately equal representation of both genders) secure (B) infants approximately equal in size to the C group was selected. No avoidant (A) infants were included, since the avoidant classification is extremely rare in Israel (van IJzendoorn & Sagi, 1999).

The present sample constituted 45 B (24 girls, 21 boys), 47 C (24 girls, 23 boys), and 21 D (10 girls, 11 boys) children.[1] Mean age of the children at the follow-up was 54.9 months (range 53–56 months). Mean number of children in the participating families at the time of the follow-up was 2.6 (range 1–5). Twenty-nine percent of the children were first-borns. Mean age of mothers at the time of the follow-up was 33.8 (range 24–45). At the time of recruitment, when the children were infants, all families were intact. At the time of the follow-up, 97% remained intact, 1% was divorced, and 2% were widowed. Maternal education ranged between 10 and 20 years of education (M = 13.6 , SD = 2.07). Comparisons of the participants in the follow-up sample with the larger sample of 758 participants revealed no significant differences in SES, number of children, birth order of the target child, maternal education, and maternal age.

Procedure

Between the ages of 12 and 16 months (M = 12.51) infants and their mothers were invited to a laboratory playroom and were observed in the SSP. The procedure was videotaped. At the age of approximately 4.5 years, the children and their mothers were invited to the laboratory playroom again for a 1.5-hour visit. After several joint tasks for the children and their mothers, they were separated. Subsequently, the children participated in the MSSB. The entire task was videotaped. Following the MSSB, an examiner administered to the child a vocabulary test.

Assessments

Strange Situation Procedure (SSP)

The SSP is a well-known and validated procedure (Ainsworth et al., 1978; van IJzendoorn & Kroonenberg, 1988), and therefore is described in brief:

[1]The original sample included 120 children. Two of them did not engage in the MSSB. The scores of additional five children on the Vocabulary sub-test of the WPPSI-R (Wechsler, 1967/1973) were 1 standard deviation below the mean or lower. Therefore, these seven children were not included in the study.

The procedure involves a series of increasingly stressful episodes (8 episodes, 3 minutes each), observed in a laboratory playroom. The episodes include two separations and two reunions of infant and mother. Based on their behavior, infants are classified into one of four attachment patterns, of which one is a secure pattern and three are insecure patterns: Secure (B)—securely attached infants calm down quickly when their mothers return. Upon reunion they show minimal resistance to the mother or avoidance of her. The three insecure patterns are:

1. Avoidant (A)—avoidant infants do not seek proximity to their mothers upon reunion, but rather avoid them.
2. Resistant/ambivalent (C)—these infants seek contact with their mothers, but at the same time resist them. Some C infants are unable to settle down during the reunion episodes.
3. Finally, Disorganized (D) infants show momentary absence of any particular strategy to deal with the separation stress. They display inconsistent or odd behaviors (Main & Solomon, 1986).

Interrater reliability (kappa) based on 59 participants was .81 on the A/B/C/D classification system. Differences between coders were conferenced, and consensus codes were used.

MacArthur Story-Stem Battery (MSSB)

The MSSB (Bretherton, Oppenheim, et al., 1990) is composed of a series of story beginnings describing a range of emotion-laden family interactions. Story stems are presented to the children using a family of dolls in an animated, dramatic manner, and all of them end with the invitation: "Show me and tell me what happens now." In order to facilitate children's narratives, the examiner uses nondirective comments, such as "Does anything else happen in the story?" If the children do not spontaneously address the main issues of the story, they are asked standard nondirective prompts regarding those issues. For example, in one of the story stems the younger sibling hurts her hand. If the child does not address this theme, the examiner asks him or her: "Does anybody do anything about the hurt hand?" The examiner proceeds from one story stem to the next only after the child deals with the main issues in the story stem or after he or she is given a second chance to do so, using the probes just mentioned. Nine story stems from the battery were translated to Hebrew and used in this study (see Appendix 4.1). The entire episode was videotaped.

Coding Children's Narratives. Children's narratives were transcribed verbatim and were coded from the videotapes and the transcripts. Narratives were rated on three scales:

1. *Coherence.* The scale, developed by Robinson et al. (1992), ranges from 0 to 10. The scale examines three aspects of narratives: their fluency, the child's understanding of the problems presented in the story stems, and the resolution of the problems. The odd scores are: 0—child does not comment about the story stem, 1—fragmented story with shifts in story line, 3—child understands the conflict but does not offer resolution; a portion of the story may be incoherent, 5—child understands the conflict and handles it by using a simplification of the story, 7—child understands the story and offers a resolution; a short story with no embellishment, 9—child understands the conflict and offers a resolution that includes embellishment; there are no incoherent segments. For the purpose of the present study, the original Robinson et al. scale (1992) was elaborated. This included developing specific criteria for *understanding the conflict, simplification, and resolution* for each story stem. In addition, the coding of coherence was aided by two newly developed indexes: *Number of shifts* in the storyline, where "shift" is defined as an illogical change in the story line, and *number of aggressive and destructive themes,* which involved the number of themes in the children's stories that describe severe aggressive acts toward characters in the story (e.g., parents are severely beating each other, father kills the older child, the monster kills the family) or catastrophes (e.g., the house burns, the child drowns in the sea). The "shifts" and "aggressive and destructive themes" indexes were used to fine-tune the coherence rating, so that if a narrative included several shifts or aggressive themes the coherence score was lowered (see Wagner, 2001). The aggressive and destructive themes index was also used as an independent score because Solomon et al. (1995) indicated that such themes may be particularly characteristic of children with disorganized attachments.

Two coders who were blind to children's attachment classifications coded the coherence of children's story completions. Because aggressive and destructive themes were rare, this index was converted into a dichotomous variable indicating presence or absence of such themes in each story group. Interrater reliability (Kappa) of the aggressive and destructive themes index based on 26 participants was 0.91. Interrater reliability (Pearson correlation) of the coherence scale based on 29 participants was 0.75. Differences between coders were resolved by discussion and consensus codes were used.

2. *Competent child representations.* A 5-point scale based on the security criteria in Bretherton, Ridgeway, and Cassidy (1990) assessed the degree to

which the child-protagonist was described as dealing competently with the issues raised in the story stem. The scale ranged from scores of 1 or 2, describing the child protagonist as ignoring the problem, being aggressive, helpless, failing to resolve the issue, or taking the role of the caregiver, to 5, describing the child as directly dealing with the issue at hand in an appropriate way and resolving the issue. As in the coherence scale, specific criteria were developed regarding what are inappropriate, simplified, and competent reactions for each story stem.

3. *Competent caregiver representations.* A 6-point scale, also based on the security criteria in the Bretherton, Ridgeway, and Cassidy (1990) study, assessed the degree to which the caregivers were described as dealing competently with the issues raised in the story stems. The scale ranged from low scores of 1 or 2, describing the parent as getting hurt in the beginning of the story, disappearing, being helpless, or not being able to resolve the main issues of the stem, to 6, describing the caregiver as dealing with the issue in a competent way and being successful in resolving the issue. Here, too, specific criteria were developed for each story stem regarding what are inappropriate, simplified, and competent reactions.

Three coders who were blind to children's attachment classifications coded the two representations scales. Inter-rater reliability (interclass correlation coefficient) based on 40% of the stories was .85 for the competent child representations scale and .86 for the competent caregiver representations scale. Differences between coders were resolved by discussion, and consensus codes were used.

As mentioned previously, the stories were divided into three groups: attachment stories (Monster, Separation, and Reunion); emotional conflict stories (Mother's Headache, Three Is a Crowd, and Lost Keys), and transgression stories (Spilled Juice, Hot Gravy, and The Bathroom Shelf). The scores of each of the scales were averaged across the three narratives within each group.

Child Vocabulary

Children were administered the Vocabulary subtest of the WPPSI-R (Wechsler, 1967/1973), and their scores were calculated using the test's norms.

RESULTS

We begin by examining the relations between the narratives and background variables. Next we present the associations among the three scales within each of the story groups, and then we turn to examine the relations between attachment classifications in infancy and the narrative scales.

Preliminary Analyses

Gender Differences

While gender and coherence in the attachment stories were only marginally associated ($t = -1.72$, $p = 0.09$), associations were found between gender and coherence in the emotional conflict stories and transgression stories. Compared to boys, girls narrated more coherent emotional conflict stories ($M_{girls} = 5.01$, $M_{boys} = 4.25$, $t = -1.11$, $p < 0.02$) and transgression stories ($M_{girls} = 5.61$, $M_{boys} = 5.04$, $t = -1.00$, $p < 0.03$). Gender was also related to the competent child representations scale: Girls described in their emotional conflict and transgression stories more competent children compared to boys ($M_{girls} = 4.48$, $M_{boys} = 3.86$, $t = -1.62$, $p < 0.001$ and $M_{girls} = 4.23$, $M_{boys} = 3.93$, $t = -0.82$, $p < 0.051$ in the two story groups respectively). There were no gender differences on competent child representations scale in attachment stories. Finally, gender was associated with competent caregiver representations scale in the attachment stories: Compared to boys, girls described more competent caregivers ($M_{girls} = 4.56$, $M_{boys} = 4.24$, $t = -0.87$, $p < 0.04$). Consistent with most attachment studies, no association was found between attachment classifications and gender (χ^2 (2, $N = 113$) = .19, ns).

Vocabulary

Positive correlations were found between children's vocabulary and coherence in the attachment stories (r (111) = .17, $p < .04$), emotional conflict stories (r (112) = .27, $p < .002$) and transgression stories (r (112) = .25, $p < .004$). Because gender was also associated with the coherence scale in two of the three story groups, we examined next whether the gender differences we found in coherence were a function of gender differences in vocabulary. ANCOVAs comparing coherence scores of boys and girls while controlling for vocabulary ruled out this possibility: The association between gender and coherence scores in emotional conflict and transgression stories remained significant (F (2, 109) = 6.74, $p < .011$; F (2, 109) = 5.03, $p < .027$, respectively). Children's vocabulary was not associated with the competent child representations or with the competent caregiver representations scales. In addition, children's vocabulary was not associated with attachment classifications (F (2, 109) = .12 , $p > .886$).

Intercorrelations Among Narrative Scales

The narrative scales were positively correlated among themselves and across stories. Specifically, the coherence scale was positively correlated with the competent child representations and with competent caregiver representations scales in all three story groups, with correlations ranging between .23 and .50 (all *ps* $< .007$). The competent child representations scale was positively correlated with the competent caregiver representations scale in all three story groups as well, with correlations ranging between .27 and .33 (all *ps* $< .002$). Most inter-correlations of the scales across stories were positive and significant. More specifically, the inter-correlations of the coherence scale ranged between .64 and .70 (all *ps* $< .001$), the inter-correlations of the competent caregiver representations scale ranged between .23 and .30 (all *ps* $< .01$). The inter-correlation of the competent child representations scale in attachment and transgression stories was not significant ($r(100) = .03$, $p > .39$). The inter-correlations of this scale in the attachment and emotional conflict narratives and in transgression and emotional conflict narratives were positive and significant ($r(98) = .27$, $p < .004$, $r(111) = .25$, $p < .004$, respectively), however. Thus, although there were quite a few significant correlations across the stories, we examined the links with attachment separately for each scale and for each story group for the reasons described earlier.

Attachment in Infancy, Gender, and the Narrative Scales

Because we found significant associations between gender and the narrative scales we first computed five 2-way ANOVAs with attachment classifications in infancy and gender as factors and the dependent variables found to be associated with gender: coherence in the transgression and emotional conflict stories, competent child representations scores in emotional conflict and transgression stories and competent caregiver representations scores in the attachment stories. No significant interactions were found in these analyses. The subsequent analyses were therefore conducted for the sample as a whole.

Attachment in Infancy and Coherence

Following Olds et al. (2002), we transformed the coherence scores into dichotomous variables with scores between 0 and 5 considered incoherent, and scores between 6 and 10 considered coherent. The idea behind this strategy was to highlight the number of incoherent stories children told (i.e., the

TABLE 4.1
Mean Number of Coherent Narratives
According to Attachment Classifications in Infancy

Story Group	*Secure* *M (SD)*	*Ambivalent* *M (SD)*	*Disorganized* *M (SD)*	$t_{(B\ vs.\ C)}$	$t_{(B\ vs.\ D)}$
Attachment	1.73 (.34)	1.49 (.34)	1.62 (.32)	1.7**	.63
Emotional conflict	1.39 (.35)	1.23 (.33)	1.24 (.32)	1.2**	.90*
Transgression	1.52 (.34)	1.49 (.34)	1.44 (.35)	.20	.43

$^{*}p < .05.$ $^{**}p < .01.$

bottom part of the coherence scale) and to de-emphasize individual differences within the coherent range of the scale (i.e., the top part of the scale). The cut-off point was "5," since scores of "6" and above describe stories that have all the required elements of a coherent story—an organized storyline that addresses openly the main problem of the story stem and ends with a resolution of the problem without resorting to a simplified solution. The dichotomized coherence scores were averaged across the three stories within each of the three story groups. Next, we computed three sets of planned comparisons with attachment classifications as the independent variable and the coherence scores as the dependent variables. B children, as hypothesized, had more coherent *attachment stories* compared to C children (see Table 4.1). There was no significant difference between the mean number of coherent attachment stories of B and D children. As hypothesized, B children also had more coherent *emotional conflict stories* compared to C as well as D children. Finally, in contrast to our hypotheses, no significant difference was found in the number of coherent *transgression stories* between B, C, or D children.[2]

Attachment in Infancy and Competent Child Representations

A planned comparison with attachment classifications as an independent variable, and competent child representations in the *attachment stories* as the dependent variable, revealed that, as hypothesized, D children described in their narratives less competent children than B children (see Table 4.2). B and C children did not differ significantly from one another. Contrary to our

[2]We also examined the relations between attachment classifications in infancy and the original coherence scores (i.e., before they were dichotomized). Planned comparisons revealed identical results, with one difference: When considering the full range of the scale, D children did not differ significantly in their coherence from B children in emotional conflict stories.

TABLE 4.2
Competent Child Representations Scores
According to Attachment Classifications in Infancy

Story Group	Secure M (SD)	Ambivalent M (SD)	Disorganized M (SD)	$t_{(B\ vs.\ C)}$	$t_{(B\ vs.\ D)}$
Attachment	4.19 (1.12)	4.19 (1.01)	3.65 (1.11)	.01	.91*
Emotional conflict	4.3 (1.07)	4.16 (1.04)	3.94 (1.03)	.32	.64
Transgression	3.93 (1.06)	4.18 (.98)	4.18 (.74)	−.62	−.49

$^{*}p < .05$.

hypotheses, planned comparisons with attachment classifications as independent variable and competent child representations in both the *transgression* and the *emotional conflict* stories as dependent variables revealed no significant differences.

Attachment in Infancy and Competent Caregiver Representations

A planned comparison with attachment classifications as the independent variable and competent caregiver representations in the *attachment stories* as the dependent variable revealed that, as hypothesized, B children described in their narratives more competent caregivers than C children (see Table 4.3). B and D children did not differ significantly from one another. Contrary to our hypotheses, planned comparisons with attachment classifications as the independent variable and competent caregiver representations scores in the *transgression* and *emotional conflict* stories as dependent variables did not reveal significant differences.

TABLE 4.3
Competent Caregiver Representations Scores
According to Attachment Classifications in Infancy

Story Group	Secure M (SD)	Ambivalent M (SD)	Disorganized M (SD)	$t_{(B\ vs.\ C)}$	$t_{(B\ vs.\ D)}$
Attachment	4.57 (.86)	4.22 (.95)	4.49 (1.05)	.84*	.14
Emotional conflict	3.96 (1.21)	3.65 (1.24)	3.64 (1.26)	.58	.47
Transgression	4.61 (.79)	4.46 (.71)	4.76 (.46)	.51	−.41

$^{*}p < .05$.

Attachment in Infancy and Aggressive and Destructive Themes

Our third hypothesis was that D children would include more aggressive and destructive themes in their narratives compared to children who had organized attachment classifications (either B or C) in infancy. In order to examine this hypothesis we combined the B and C groups into one, non-D group. A one-tailed chi-square test revealed a significant association between the D attachment classification in infancy and aggressive and destructive themes in the *attachment stories* (χ^2 (1, N= 113) = 8.41 , p = .004, Fisher's Exact Test). D children were more likely to show aggressive and destructive themes than non-D children in their attachment stories. One-tailed chi-square tests did not reveal significant associations between the D attachment classification in infancy and aggressive and destructive themes in the *emotional conflict stories* (χ^2 (1, N= 113) = .228, p= .168, Fisher's Exact Test) and the *transgression stories* (χ^2 (1, N= 113) = .16, p= .182, Fisher's Exact Test).

DISCUSSION

The coherence of preschoolers' narratives and, to a certain extent, the content of their narratives as reflected in the representation of competent coping with stress of child and adult protagonists, were found to be linked to child-mother attachment assessed 3.5 years earlier, when the children were infants. These findings are in accordance with Main's work (Main et al., 1985) about adults' attachment narratives. As described earlier, Main as well as other researchers (see van IJzendoorn, 1995) have consistently found that what was most significant in characterizing adults' security was their capacity to talk about their experiences coherently—that is, in an open, objective, succinct, and collaborative manner. Our findings suggest that assessment of coherence can be meaningfully and appropriately applied not only to the narratives of the linguistically competent and mature adult but also to the story completions of young children. In addition, the link between coherence and security found in adults can also be shown with respect to the young child. To our knowledge ours is the first study to examine the coherence and content of child narratives separately and show the specific security–coherence links.

We also found some links between attachment in infancy and the content of children's narratives. Preschoolers who were secure in infancy portrayed more competent caregivers in their attachment narratives than did preschoolers who had ambivalent attachments, and they also described more competent children in these narratives compared to preschoolers who had disorganized attachments. These findings, while somewhat less strong than the coherence findings (at least in terms of the number of the associations), are consistent with previous studies linking preschoolers' narratives and attachment. They indicate that secure preschoolers are more likely to portray caregivers and children as handling attachment-related stressful situations competently. We now continue the discussion by focusing separately on secure, ambivalent and disorganized children.

Secure Attachment and Preschoolers' Narratives

As mentioned previously, children who had secure attachments to their mothers as infants tended as preschoolers to narrate attachment and emotional conflict stories that were more coherent when compared to children who had ambivalent and disorganized attachments in infancy. Faced with story stems describing evocative emotional themes such as separation from parents, being afraid of an imaginary monster, and witnessing an argument between parents, they completed the story stems with a clear narrative that not only openly referred to these themes but also brought them to resolution. Compared to ambivalent children, they also were more likely to portray competent caregivers in their attachment narratives, and compared to disorganized children were more likely to portray competent children in these narratives.

Consider, for example, the story completion of a girl classified secure as an infant. In this story stem the child wakes up during the night hearing a noise, and she cries out: "There's a monster in my room!"

Child as narrator: "Mom and Dad are talking: Did you hear that Hagit (the child protagonist) is crying?"
Child as Hagit: "Mom, Dad, there's a monster in my room."
Child as parents: "What monster?"
Child as Hagit: "Can you hear the noise?"
Child as parents: "Oh! It's behind her!"
Child as mother: "Oh, it's just a spider, a real one . . . Ahh! (feigning fear)"
Child shows mother startling and asking father: "Is this a real spider?"
Child as Hagit: "Yes."
Child as narrator: "The spider went to sleep. It was tired."
Examiner: "Does anything else happen?"

Child as narrator:	"And then Dad . . ." (Child is looking for other dolls in the examiner's box)
Examiner:	"Does anything else happen?"
Child as narrator:	"Now dad took a pistol. He went and searched, and now he found the monster. He shot with the pistol "bang, bang" and it is dead. They threw it away to the garbage can, and then they all lived happily ever after."

As can be seen in this example, this secure child constructs a coherent and fluent story with a well-organized storyline. She clearly understands the problem of the scary monster posed in the stem and addresses it openly. She describes and enacts the protagonist's and the parents' emotional reactions to the source of danger (the protagonist cries, the parents are concerned about her distress, and later mother expresses her fear of the spider). Moreover, she succeeds in finding a resolution. The first solution she develops, in which the spider goes to sleep, appears not to satisfy her, so she moves on to find a better, irreversible solution: The father faces the spider, and kills it. The story ends with closure—the spider is dead, thrown away, and they "live happily ever after." The child's security is also expressed in the competence she attributes to the child and parents. The child protagonist, Hagit, actively seeks help from her parents by calling them and telling them what happened. The parents are responsive to her cry, and the father helps resolve the problem: He searches for the monster-spider and kills it.

This case example is in accordance with the way secure IWMs are conceptualized. The effective responses secure children receive are thought to be internalized (Bowlby 1967/1982), and it is possible that such internalizations were reflected in the descriptions of competent caregivers we discovered in children's story completions. Furthermore, secure children are presumed to develop complementary representations of the self as worthy of care and capable of dealing with problems, and it is possible that these representations were reflected in their descriptions of the child protagonists dealing effectively with the stressful situations or openly communicating their need for help.

The coherence and representations of the narratives of secure children may also be a function of the parent-child communication patterns of which they were a part. As suggested by Fivush and colleagues (chapter 3, this volume) and Peterson and McCabe (chapter 2, this volume), children's narrative skills are shaped by parent-child communication. Furthermore, both theory (Bretherton & Munholland, 1999; Oppenheim & Waters, 1995) and research (Etzion-Carasso & Oppenheim, 2000; Koren-Karie, Oppenheim, Haimovich, & Etzion-Carasso, 2003; Main et al., 1985) have suggested that security of attachment is reflected in open, coherent, and flexible mother-child dialogues. Such dialogues are therefore likely to promote coherence in secure children's independent narration (Oppenheim et al., 1997), such as the narratives provided on the MSSB.

Ambivalent Attachment and Preschoolers' Narratives

Compared to secure children, ambivalent children tended to have fewer coherent attachment and emotional conflict stories. These preschoolers seemed to have difficulties in keeping an organized storyline and/or in openly addressing the themes and bringing them to a resolution. Ambivalent children also tended to describe less competent caregivers when dealing with attachment issues, compared to children who were secure in infancy. The monster story of an ambivalent child can exemplify these difficulties:

Child: "Mother wakes up."
Examiner: "Can you show me how?"
Child: "Like that. And then Gil (the protagonist) told her what was going on."
Examiner: "What did he tell her?"
Child: "That . . . I have to think."
Examiner: "You can think."
Child: "I don't know."
Examiner: "And then what did he tell her? She woke up and came, and then what happened?"
Child: "She told him: What is that noise?"
Examiner doesn't understand the child's words and asks him to repeat.
Child: "Gil said that it was a monster."
Examiner: "And then what happens?"
Child: "He wanted to go and see what was going on."
Examiner: "Yes."
Child: "I don't know."
Examiner: "And then what happened?"
Child: "I don't know."
Examiner: "Try to think."
Child: "But I don't know."
Examiner: "You can make up whatever you want . . . what happened after Gil wanted to know what was going on?"
Child: "I don't know."
Examiner: "What did they do? Let's think, did they do anything else? Did they say anything?"
Child: "I don't know."

Examiner: "So what happened regarding the monster?"
Child: "I don't know."
Examiner: "How does the story end?"
Child: "I don't know."
Examiner: "What happened to the monster?"
Child: "It went away fast."
Examiner: "And the story ends like this?"
Child: "Yes."

The story constructed by this child lacks coherence: It is not fluent, and although the child expresses an understanding of the problem (the mother responds to her child's cry, and both mother and child are aware of the problem), the child does not succeed in developing a story and in finding a way to resolve the problem. Only after many prompts the child brings the story to an end, but he uses a simplified solution—the monster goes away. No explanation is offered regarding the process that led to its leaving. In addition, the maternal figure is not portrayed as competent in a time of need. Although the mother responds to her child (she wakes up and inquires about the noise), she does not face the monster or help in any other way to calm the child down.

These portrayals are consistent with what we know about ambivalent attachments. It has been suggested that mothers of ambivalent children are at times as responsive as the mothers of secure children, but at other times are unresponsive (Ainsworth, 1984). Due to this inconsistency it is hard for ambivalent infants to develop confident expectations of their caregivers, and this lack of confidence is presumed to be reflected in their IWMs. In this study we found that ambivalent children reflect such expectations in their story completions by portraying a caregiver who rejects, ignores, or is incompetent in helping the child protagonist in the stressful attachment situation.

The incoherence of ambivalent preschoolers' narratives might reflect their biased information processing. These children, as already mentioned, are presumed to have a bias toward the frightening aspects of the environment and towards negative emotional expressions (Cassidy, 1994; Kobak & Sceery, 1988). Presented with stressful emotional story stems, such bias might make it difficult for them to construct a narrative with an organized storyline concerning the stressful issue, and to bring the issue to resolution.

As in the case of secure children, children's narratives might also reflect their experiences communicating with their parents about affective issues. Mothers who were classified as preoccupied in the AAI (a classification that parallels the ambivalent classification of infants in the Strange Situation; van IJzendoorn, 1995) have been found in several studies to show difficulties in scaffolding their children and in leading an open and coherent dialogue with them (Crowell & Feldman, 1988, 1991; Kobak, Ferenz-Gillies, Everhart, & Seabrook, 1994). These difficulties in mother-child dialogue might be reflected in the preschoolers' own narration as well, as was seen in this study.

Taken together, these findings suggest that children who were ambivalently attached to their mothers in infancy experience more difficulties as preschoolers in narrating about emotionally laden issues, compared to children who were securely attached in infancy. These findings extend previous narrative work (Bretherton, Ridgeway, & Cassidy, 1990; Cassidy, 1988; Solomon et al., 1995), which focused primarily on discriminating between secure and insecure/avoidant classifications, and rarely had sufficient ambivalent children to examine their narration.

Disorganized Attachment and Preschoolers' Narratives

Infants who were disorganized in infancy seem to continue to show markers of absence or breakdown of their behavioral and regulatory strategies later on in their development (Cassidy, 1988; Lyons-Ruth & Jacobvitz, 1999; Solomon & George, 1999). Based on this argument we expected that preschoolers who had disorganized attachments as infants would be less coherent and portray less competent figures compared to secure children. Also, we expected them to present aggressive and destructive themes in their narratives more often than preschoolers who had organized (secure or ambivalent) attachments as infants. These hypotheses were only partially supported.

Preschoolers who were classified disorganized as infants tended to have fewer coherent emotional conflict stories, compared to secure children. They also tended to portray less competent child figures in their attachment narratives than secure preschoolers. This finding is in accordance with the Solomon et al. (1995) study, in which controlling children (the behavioral pattern thought to reflect disorganization at the preschool years) tended to narrate stories that portrayed child figures as out of control, potentially destructive, or helpless. Also consistent with Solomon et al. is our finding that D-type children expressed more aggressive and destructive themes in their attachment stories. For example, in the separation story stem some of these children described the child protagonists as severely beating each other and the grandmother figure during the separation, while others described an injury or even death of the child who remained under the supervision of grandmother. However, in contrast to our hypotheses and the Solomon et al. study, D-type children did not tend to portray less competent caregivers in their narratives, and their attachment and transgression narratives were not less coherent than B-type children. Also, it should be mentioned that while children classified D had more aggressive and destructive themes than non-D children, only one third of D children included such themes. Thus, such themes are clearly not characteristic of *all* children classified as Disorganized.

D children, in sum, showed some difficulties in their narratives compared to B and C children, but did not emerge in this study as performing consistently worse than all other children, as might be expected. One possible explanation is that the narrative measures we used were not sensitive enough to detect the unique expressions of disorganization. Another possibility is lack of stability of the D classification. Because we did not have a concurrent attachment measure it is possible that the children classified disorganized as infants were no longer disorganized as preschoolers. It should be recalled that only one previous study using narratives found significant differences between the narratives of D and non-D children (Solomon et al., 1995), and in that study the narrative assessments and attachment classifications were concurrent. Moreover, studies of D children's emotional and behavioral adaptation in the years after infancy, particularly when dealing with children from low-risk samples such as ours, are not conclusive (for review of these studies see Lyons-Ruth & Jacobvitz, 1999). Thus, while we found that preschoolers who had disorganized attachments as infants showed markers of difficulties when narrating about attachment and emotional conflict topics, the mixed picture of our findings calls for more research and for caution in reaching sweeping conclusions about the narratives of these children.

"Domain Specificity": Different Findings in Different Stories

The use of the MSSB, which includes not only story stems that target attachment themes but also story stems about other emotionally laden themes, permitted us to examine whether the link between attachment and later narratives is specific to story stems about attachment or is also evident in story stems raising other emotional themes. Our findings indicated that the links were not general, and did not cut across all emotion narratives. In general, and perhaps not surprisingly, attachment narratives were most productive in revealing attachment-related differences. Both the coherence and the content of these narratives were related to attachment in infancy. Emotional conflict narratives were less productive. Their coherence, but not their content, was related to attachment. Last, the transgression narratives were the least productive, revealing no relations with attachment in infancy.

Thus, children's responses to the story stems appear to relate to the specific emotional domain tapped by the stems. Our findings suggest that attachment and transgression are seen by children as, and may very well be, distinct emotional domains. While transgression and morality are clearly very central in the life of preschool children, there are no consistent findings regarding links between these domains and attachment. Although it has been suggested (for review, see Bretherton, Golby, & Cho, 1997) that mothers of secure infants tend more than mothers of insecure children to sensitively combine explanations in their discipline (Stayton, Hogan, & Ainsworth, 1973) and that their children in infancy (Stayton et al., 1973) and toddlerhood (Londerville & Main, 1981) show more signs of internalization of moral values, other studies have shown that toddlers' security of attachment is not related to maternal observed discipline style and is only moderately correlated with maternal self-reports about discipline practices (Kochanska, 1995). Moreover, Kochanska found that although both attachment quality and maternal discipline practices are possible antecedents for socialization, their impact is moderated by child temperament (Kochanska, 1995, 1997).

The results of this study highlight the importance of the specific emotional domains raised in the story stems and suggest that children respond in a discriminated way to the stems based on the emotional domains they tap. We offer two implications for research: First, researchers are advised to select from the MSSB story stems based on their focus of interest (and may also construct additional story stems if the domain is not sufficiently covered in the MSSB; Bretherton & Oppenheim, 2003). Second, while it is common to aggregate measures across story stems in order to increase reliability, this strategy may mask important differences between the stories. Even when measures obtained from the stories are significantly correlated with each other (as were the measures in this study), permitting the creation of an aggregate score, it is quite possible that associations with an external correlate (such as attachment, in this study) are specific to some, but not all, stories.

Gender Differences

Girls described more competent caregivers in their attachment stories and more competent children in their emotional conflict and transgression stories than boys. Gender differences were also found in the coherence of the transgression and emotional conflict narratives, with girls scoring higher than boys. The differences in coherence were present even when gender differences in vocabulary were controlled. This finding is consistent with a few previous studies using the MSSB (Oppenheim, 2003; von Klitzing et al., 2000). Also, studies about preschoolers' autobiographical narratives have found that preschool girls' narratives are more elaborated and show better temporal and causal organization (Buckner & Fivush, 1998; Fivush, 1998; Fivush, Haden, & Adam, 1995), features that are part of our coherence scale. These differences have been linked to gender-related differences in parental style when co-constructing narratives with their children about emotional experiences (e.g., Fivush, 1991; Zahn-Waxler, Ridgeway, Denham, Usher, & Cole, 1993). Parents tend to support their daughters more during conversation and they talk more about emotions, and elaborate and give more explanations about the causes of the emotions when talking with their girls than with their boys. Parents thus appear to encourage in their children gendered communication styles, and these may be manifested in children's own narratives, as was found regarding coherence in this study (Oppenheim et al., 1997).

It is interesting to further speculate about the specific stories in which gender differences were found. Girls' coherence and competent child representation scores were higher in the transgression and emotional conflict story groups. Five of the six story stems included in these groups focus on violation of maternal prohibitions and/or moral dilemmas. In the preschool years, girls have been repeatedly found to be more advanced in their moral development. They are more compliant with rules, and they show more signs of internalization of moral standards in their behavior (Kochanska, Padavich, & Koenig, 1996), as well as in their reactions to hypothetical situations, including narrative completion tasks (Kochanska, 1997; Kochanska et al., 1996). It could be the case, therefore, that this gender difference was also reflected in the higher coherence and the more competent child descriptions of girls identified in the story stems tapping morality, maternal prohibitions, and reactions to transgressions.

ACKNOWLEDGMENTS

Support for the study was provided by grant 812/95 from the Israel Science Foundation to David Oppenheim and by the National Institute of Child Health and Human Development grant number (RO1) #HD25975 to Abraham Sagi-Schwartz. This chapter is based in part on an MA thesis written by Ella Wagner at the Department of Psychology, University of Haifa, Israel. We would like to thank Abraham Sagi-Schwartz for making the sample available for longitudinal investigation. We would also like to thank Rachel Bransky, Yael Cohen, and Galit Gross for their help in administering the MacArthur Story-Stem Battery and Smadar Dolev and Anat Heimberg for coding the story stems. Finally, we would like to extend our thanks to the children and mothers who participated in the study.

REFERENCES

Ainsworth, M. D. S. (1984). Attachment. In N. S. Endler & J. McV. Hunt (Eds.), *Personality and the behavioral disorders* (Vol. 1, pp. 559–602). New York: Wiley.

Ainsworth, M. D. S., Blehar, M. C., Waters, E., & Wall, S. (1978). *Patterns of attachment: A psychological study of the strange situation.* Hillsdale, NJ: Lawrence Erlbaum Associates.

Bar-Haim, Y., Sutton, D. B., Fox, N. A., & Marvin, R. S. (2002). Stability and change of attachment at 12, 24, and 58 months of age: Behavior, representation, and life events. *Journal of Child Psychology and Psychiatry, 41,* 381–388.

Bowlby, J. (1982). *Attachment and loss: Vol. 1. Attachment.* New York: Basic Books. (Original work published 1967)

Bretherton, I. (1985). Attachment theory: Retrospect and prospect. In I. Bretherton & E. Waters (Eds.), Growing points of attachment theory and research. *Monographs of the Society for Research in Child Development, 50 (1–2, Serial No. 209),* 3–38.

Bretherton, I., Golby, B., & Cho, E. (1997). Attachment and the transmission of values. In J. E. Grusec & L. Kuczynski (Eds.), *Parenting and children's internalization of values: A handbook of contemporary theory* (pp. 103–134). New York: John Wiley & Sons.

Bretherton, I., & Munholland, K. A. (1999). Internal working models in attachment relationships. In J. Cassidy & P. R. Shaver (Eds.), *Handbook of attachment: Theory, research, and clinical applications* (pp. 89–111). New York: Guilford Press.

Bretherton, I., & Oppenheim, D. (2003). The MacArthur Story Stem Battery: Development, administration, reliabilty, validity and reflections about meaning. In R. N. Emde, D. P. Wolf, & D. Oppenheim (Eds.), *Making meaning with narratives* (pp. 55-80). New York: Oxford University Press.

Bretherton, I., Oppenheim, D., Buchsbaum, H., Emde, R. N., & the MacArthur Narrative Group. (1990). *MacArthur Story Stem Battery.* Unpublished manual.

Bretherton, I., Ridgeway, D., & Cassidy, J. (1990). Assessing internal working models of attachment relationship: An attachment story completion task for 3-year-olds. In M. T. Greenberg & D. Cicchetti (Eds.), *Attachment in the preschool years: Theory, research, and intervention* (pp. 273–308). Chicago: University of Chicago Press.

Buchsbaum, H. K., Toth, S. L., Clyman, R. B., Cicchetti, D., & Emde, R. (1992). The use of a narrative story stem technique with maltreated children: Implication for theory and practice. *Development and Psychopathology, 4,* 603–625.

Buckner, J. P., & Fivush, R. (1998). Gender and self in children's autobiographical narratives. *Applied Cognitive Psychology, 12,* 407–429.

Cassidy, J. (1988). Child-mother attachment and the self in six-year-olds. *Child Development, 59,* 121–134.

Cassidy, J. (1994). Emotion regulation: Influences of attachment relationships. In N. A. Fox (Ed.), The development of emotion regulation: Biological and behavioral considerations. *Monographs of the Society for Research in Child Development, 59 (2–3, Serial No. 240),* 228–249.

Cassidy, J., & Berlin, L. J. (1994). The insecure/ambivalent pattern of attachment: Theory and research. *Child Development, 65,* 971–991.

Cassidy, J., & Marvin, R. S. (1989). *Attachment organization in three- and four-year-olds.* Unpublished coding manual, University of Virginia and Pennsylvania State University.

Crowell, J. A., & Feldman, S. S. (1988). Mothers' internal working models of relationships and children's behavioral and developmental status: A study of mother-child interaction. *Child Development, 59,* 1273–1285.

Crowell, J. A., & Feldman, S. S. (1991). Mothers' working models of attachment relationships and mother and child behavior during separation and reunion. *Developmental Psychology, 27,* 597–605.

De Wolff, M., & van IJzendoorn, M. H. (1997). Sensitivity and attachment: A meta-analysis on parental antecedents of infant attachment. *Child Development, 68,* 571–591

Dozier, M., & Kobak, R. R. (1993). Psychopathology in adolescent attachment interviews: Converging evidence for repressing strategies. *Child Development, 63,* 1473–1480.

Erikson, E. H. (1950). *Childhood and society.* New York: Norton.

Etzion-Carasso, A., & Oppenheim, D. (2000). Open mother-pre-schooler communication: Relations with early secure attachment. *Attachment and Human Development, 2,* 347–370.

Fivush, R. (1991). Gender and emotion in mother-child conversations about the past. *Journal of Narrative and Life History, 1,* 325–341.

Fivush, R. (1998). Gendered narratives: Elaboration, structure, and emotion in parent-child reminiscing across the preschool years. In C. P. Thompson, D. J. Hermann, D. Bruce, J. D. Read, D. G. Payne, & M. P. Togila (Eds.), *Autobiographical memory: Theoretical and applied perspectives* (pp. 79–103). Mahwah, NJ: Lawrence Erlbaum Associates.

Fivush, R., Haden, C., & Adam, S. (1995). Structure and coherence of preschoolers' personal narratives over time: Implication for childhood amnesia. *Journal of Experimental Cognitive Psychology, 60,* 32–50.

Freud, A. (1946). *The psycho-analytical treatment of children.* London: Imago Publishing Co.

Green, J., Stanley, C., Smith, V., & Goldwyn, R. (2000). A new method of evaluating attachment representations in young school-age children: The Manchester Child Attachment Story Task. *Attachment and Human Development, 2,* 48–70.

Hesse, E. (1999). The adult attachment interview: Historical and current perspectives. In J. Cassidy & P. R. Shaver (Eds.), *Handbook of attachment: Theory, research, and clinical applications* (pp. 395–433). New York: The Guilford Press.

Klagsburn, M., & Bowlby, J. (1976). Responses to separation from parents: A clinical test for young children. *British Journal for Projective Psychology and Personality Study, 21,* 7–27.

Kobak, R. R., Ferenz-Gillies, R., Everhart, E., & Seabrook, L. (1994). Maternal attachment strategies and emotion regulation with adolescent offspring. *Journal of Reasearch on Adolescence, 4,* 553–566.

Kobak, R. R., & Sceery, A. (1988). Attachment in late adolescence: Working models, affect regulation, and the representations of the self and others. *Child Development, 59,* 135–146.

Kochanska, G. (1995). Children's temperament, mothers' discipline, and security of attachment: Multiple pathways to emerging internalization. *Child Development, 66,* 597–615.

Kochanska, G. (1997). Multiple pathways to conscience for children with different temperaments: From toddlerhood to age 5. *Developmental Psychology, 33,* 228–240.

Kochanska, G., Padavich, D. L., & Koenig, A. (1996). Children's narratives about hypothetical moral dilemmas and objective measures of their conscience: Mutual relations and socialization antecedents. *Child Development, 67,* 1420–1436.

Koren-Karie, N., Oppenheim, D., Haimovich, Z., & Etzion-Carasso, A. (2003). Dialogues of seven-year-olds with their mothers about emotional events: Development of a typology. In R. N. Emde, D. P. Wolf, & D. Oppenheim (Eds.), *Making meaning with narratives* (pp. 338–354). Oxford University Press.

Londerville, S., & Main, M. (1981). Security of attachment, compliance, and maternal training methods in the second year of life. *Developmental Psychology, 17,* 289–299.

Lyons-Ruth, K., & Jacobvitz, D. (1999). Attachment disorganization: Unresolved loss, relational violence, lapses in behavioral and attentional strategies. In J. Cassidy & P. R. Shaver (Eds.), *Handbook of attachment: Theory, research, and clinical applications* (pp. 520–554). New York: Guilford Press.

Macfie, J., Toth, S. L., Rogosch, F. A., Robinson, J., Emde, R. N., & Cicchetti, D. (1999). Effects of maltreatment on preschoolers' narrative representations of responses to relieve distress and of role reversal. *Developmental Psychology, 35,* 460–465.

Main, M., & Hesse, E. (1990). Parents' unresolved traumatic experiences are related to infant disorganized attachment status: Is frightened and/or frightening parental behavior the linking mechanism? In M. T. Greenberg, D. Cicchetti, & E. M. Cummings (Eds.), *Attachment in the preschool years: Theory, research, and intervention* (pp. 161–182). Chicago: University of Chicago Press.

Main, M., Kaplan, N., & Cassidy, J. (1985). Security in infancy, childhood, and adulthood: A move to the level of representation. In I. Bretherton & E. Waters (Eds.), Growing points in attachment theory and research. *Monographs of the Society for Research in Child Development, 50 (1–2, Serial No. 209),* 66–104.

Main, M., & Solomon, J. (1986). Discovery of a new, insecure–disorganized/disoriented attachment pattern. In M. Yogman & T. B. Brazelton (Eds.), *Affective development in infancy* (pp. 95–124). Norwood, NJ: Ablex.

Nelson, K., & Gruendel, J. (1981). Generalized event representations: Basic building blocks of cognitive development. In M. E. Lamb & A. L. Brown (Eds.), *Advances in developmental psychology* (Vol. 1, pp. 131–158). Hillsdale, NJ: Lawrence Erlbaum Associates.

Olds, D. L., Kitzman, H., Cole, R., Robinson, J., Sidora, K., Luckey, D.W., et al. (2002). *Enduring effects of nurse home visiting on maternal life-course and child development: Age-six follow-up of a randomized trial.* Unpublished manuscript.

Oppenheim, D. (2003). Children's emotional resolution of MSSB narratives: Relations with child behavior problems and parental psychological distress. In R. N. Emde, D. P. Wolf, & D. Oppenheim (Eds.), *Making meaning with narratives* (pp. 147–162). Oxford University Press.

Oppenheim, D. (1997). The attachment doll-play interview for preschoolers. *International Journal of Behavioral Development, 20,* 681–697.

Oppenheim, D., Emde, R. N., & Wamboldt, F. S., (1996). Associations between 3-year-olds' narrative co-constructions with mothers and fathers and their story completions about affective themes. *Early Development and Parenting, 5,* 149–160.

Oppenheim, D., Emde, R. N., & Warren, S. (1997). Children's narrative representations of mothers: Their development and associations with child and mother adaptation. *Child Development, 68,* 127–138.

Oppenheim, D., Koren-Karie, N., & Sagi, A. (2001). Mothers' empathic understanding of their preschoolers' internal experience: Relations with early attachment. *International Journal of Behavioral Development, 25,* 16–26.

Oppenheim, D., Nir, A., Warren, S., & Emde, R. N. (1997). Emotion regulation in mother-child narrative co-construction: Associations with children's narratives and adaptation. *Developmental Psychology, 33,* 284–294.

Oppenheim, D., & Waters, H. S. (1995). Narrative processes and attachment representations: Issues of development and assessment. In E. Waters, B. Vaughn, G. Posada, & K. Kondo-Ikemura (Eds.), Caregiving, cultural, and cognitive perspectives on secure base behavior and working models: New growing points of attachment theory and research. *Monographs of the Society for Research in Child Development, 60 (2–3, Serial No. 244),* 197–215.

Page, T., & Bretherton, I. (2001). Mother-and father-child attachment themes in the story completions of preschoolers from post-divorce families: Do they predict relationships with peers and teachers? *Attachment and Human Development, 3,* 1–29.

Robinson, J., Herot, C., Haynes, P., & Mantz-Simmons, L. (2000). Children's story stem responses: A measure of program impact on developmental risks associated with dysfunctional parenting. *Child Abuse and Neglect, 24,* 99–110.

Robinson, J., Mantz-Simmons, L., Macfie, J., & The MacArthur Narrative Working Group. (1992). *Narrative coding manual.* Unpublished manual.

Sagi, A., Koren-Karie, N., Gini, M., Ziv, Y., & Joels, T. (2002). Shedding further light on the effects of various types and quality of early child care on infant-mother attachment relationship: The Haifa Study of Early Child Care. *Child Development, 73,* 1166–1186.

Shouldice, A., & Stevenson-Hinde, J. (1992). Coping with security distress: The separation anxiety test and attachment classification at 4.5 years. *Journal of Child Psychology and Psychiatry and Allied Disciplines, 33,* 331–348.

Slough, N., & Greenberg, M. (1990). Five-year-olds' representations of separation from parents: Responses for self and hypothetical child. In I. Bretherton & M. Watson (Eds.), *New directions for child development: No. 48. Children's perspective on the family* (pp. 67–84). San Francisco: Jossey-Bass.

Solomon, J., & George, C. (1999). The place of disorganization in attachment theory: Linking classic observations with contemporary findings. In J. Solomon & C. George (Eds.), *Attachment disorganization* (pp. 3–32). New York: Guilford Press.

Solomon, J., George, C., & DeJong, A. (1995). Children classified as controlling at age six: Evidence for disorganized representational strategies and aggression at home and at school. *Development and Psychopathology, 7,* 447–463.

Stayton, D. J., Hogan, R., & Ainsworth, M. D. S. (1973). Infant obedience and maternal behavior: The origins of socialization reconsidered. *Child Development, 42,* 1057–1070.

Teti, D. M. (1999). Conceptualizations of disorganization in the preschool years: An integration. In J. Solomon & C. George (Eds.), *Attachment disorganization* (pp. 213–242). New York: Guilford Press.

Toth, S. L., Ciccetti, D., Macfie, J., Rogosch, F. A., & Maughan, A. (2000). Narrative representations of moral-affiliative and conflictual themes and behavioral problems in maltreated preschoolers. *Journal of Clinical Child Psychology, 29,* 307–318.

van IJzendoorn, M. H. (1995). Adult attachment representations, parental responsiveness, and infant attachment: A meta-analysis on the predictive validity of the Adult-Attachement Interview. *Psychological Bulletin, 117,* 387–403.

van IJzendoorn, M. H., & Kroonenberg, P. M. (1988). Cross-cultural patterns of attachment: A meta-analysis of the strange situation. *Child Development, 59,* 147–156.

van IJzendoorn, M. H., & Sagi, A. (1999). Cross-cultural patterns of attachment: Universal and contextual dimensions. In J. Cassidy & P. R. Shaver (Eds.), *Handbook of attachment: Theory, research, and clinical applications* (pp. 713–734). New York: Guilford Press.

von Klitzing, K., Kelsay, K., Emde, R. N., Robinson J., & Schmitz, S. (2000). Gender-specific characteristics of 5-year-olds' play narratives and associations with behavior rating. *Journal of the American Academy of Child and Adolescent Psychiatry, 39,* 1017–1023.

Wagner, E. (2001). *"A good story": The relations between attachment patters in infancy and narrative coherence in preschool.* Unpublished masters thesis, University of Haifa.

Waters, H. S., Rodrigues, L. M., & Ridgeway, D. (1998). Cognitive underpinnings of narrative attachment assessment. *Journal of Experimental Child Psychology, 71,* 211–234.

Wechsler, D. (1973). *Manual for the Wechsler Preschool and Primary School Scale of Intelligence* (A. Libliech, Ed. & Trans.). Jerusalem: Hebrew University of Jerusalem. (Original work published 1967)

Wolf, D. P., Rygh, J., & Altshuler, J. (1984). Agency and experience: Actions and states in play narratives. In I. Bretherton (Ed.), *Symbolic play: The development of social understanding* (pp. 195–217). Orlando, FL: Academic Press.

Zahn-Waxler, C., Ridgeway, D., Denham, S., Usher, B., & Cole, P. M. (1993). Pictures of infants' emotions: A task for assessing mothers' and young children's verbal communications about affect. In R. N. Emde & J. D. Osofsky (Eds.), The IFEEL pictures: A new instrument for interpreting emotions. *Clinical infant reports series of the Zero to Three/National Center for Clinical Infants Programs* (pp. 217–236). Madison, CT: International Universities Press.

APPENDIX 4.1
The MacArthur Story-Stem Battery (Stems Used in the Present Study)

Story Stem	*Participants*	*Brief Description*
Attachment story stems:		
Monster	Child, parents	The child wakes up during the night, and thinks there is a monster in his room.
Separation	2 siblings, parents, grandmother	The parents go on an overnight trip while grandmother babysits.
Reunion	2 siblings, parents, grandmother	The parents return from their trip.
Emotional conflict story stems:		
Mom's Headache	Mother, child, child's friend	The mother has a headache, turns the TV off and asks the child to be quiet. A friend comes over and asks to watch an exciting TV show.
Three is a crowd	2 siblings, friend, parents	A child is playing with his or her friend. The child's sibling wants to play too, but the friend says "If you let your little brother play, I won't be your friend any more."
The Lost Keys	Child, parents	The mother accuses the father of having lost her keys, and an argument ensues.
Transgression story stems:		
Spilled Juice	2 siblings, parents	The child accidentally spills a pitcher of juice at the dinner table.
Hot Gravy	2 siblings, parents	A child is warned by his mother not to touch the pot of gravy on the stove, but becomes impatient, touches the pot and gets burned.
The Bathroom Shelf	2 siblings, mother	*Part I:* The mother announces that she has to leave and warns the children not to touch anything on the bathroom shelf. While the mother is gone, one of the children cuts his finger and asks for a Band-Aid. *Part II:* The mother returns.

Source: Bretherton, Oppenheim, et al., 1990.

5

Children's Empathic Representations in Relation to Early Caregiving Patterns Among Low-Income African American Mothers

JoAnn Robinson
University of Colorado

Michael Eltz
E. P. Bradley Hospital, Denver, CO

Children's prosocial and agonistic representations of relationships arise within the context of their experience with caregivers in early childhood. However, little is known about the impact of caregiving that is informally shared within networks of kin and family friends. Shared caregiving of young children is a well-recognized strength of African American women living in poverty, especially among young, single mothers (Brodsky, 1999; Chase-Lansdale, Brooks-Gunn, & Zamsky, 1994; Jackson, 1993; McAdoo, 1995). Extended networks of kin, fictive kin, and family friends are resources that young mothers access in order to gain support both emotionally and in their caregiving responsibilities. Sadly, outside of studies of early child care, research has not considered the impact of these shared caregiving patterns on young children's social emotional development, and specifically the development of empathic attitudes and behaviors. Randolph and Koblinsky (2001) caution that the impacts of multiple care providers of children of low-income African American mothers is not sufficiently studied to state unequivocally that it is generally a positive experience. It is therefore important to study the impacts of caregiving in this context further, because families raising young children in violent inner cities are challenged to protect their children and nurture prosocial behaviors and attitudes.

In this chapter, we consider patterns of early child care responsibility in a large sample of mostly young, low-income African American women during the first 2 years of their first children's lives in relation to the development of prosocial and agonistic representations of relationships when they were between 6 and 7 years of age. We begin our introduction by considering the role of parents in the development of empathy and prosocial behavior in early childhood. Then we discuss empathic and prosocial themes in young children's representations expressed in the MacArthur Story Stem Battery. Finally, we consider what we know about shared patterns of caregiving responsibility as a developmental context.

EMPATHIC DEVELOPMENT

Research on the development of prosocial and empathic attitudes and behaviors in young children emphasizes the importance of parental empathy for the child's needs, sensitive caregiving behaviors, and expectations and instructions by parents for the young child to behave prosocially (Zahn-Waxler & Radke-Yarrow, 1990). Observational studies show that warmth and sensitive interaction styles during non-distress situations also are related to children's empathy and prosocial behavior (Cummings, Hollenbeck, Iannotti, Radke-Yarrow, & Zahn-Waxler, 1986) as well as with change toward greater empathy among toddlers (Robinson, Zahn-Waxler, & Emde, 1994). These findings are based on empirical research with samples that are nearly exclusively middle-class and of European American descent, and where care giving is centered on mothers. However, it is particularly interesting to study the development of prosocial attitudes and behaviors in minority children. Mutuality and communalism are cited as important values that are reflected in the parenting practices and values of many minority groups and undergird relationships among adults and children, including African Americans, Latinos, and Native Americans, and Hawaiians (Genero, 1995; Randolph & Koblinsky, 2001).

The more common methods employed to study parental influence on empathy and prosocial development include responses to interview questions or questionnaires about mothers' own valuing of sympathetic behavior (e.g., Eisenberg, Fabes, Schaller, Carlo, & Miller, 1991) and about their responses to children's intentional or inadvertent behaviors that result in some injury or loss to another child (Eisenberg & Fabes, 1998; Zahn-Waxler, Robinson, & Emde, 1992). Zahn-Waxler and Radke-Yarrow (1982) used a diary method where mothers recorded such naturally occurring instances, including their responses to those instances, finding that greater use of reasoning rather than punishments contributed to greater empathy in their children. These maternal reports were generally concurrent with observations of children's empathy in early childhood. In this study, we examine maternal empathic attitudes during mothers' pregnancy with the focal child.

Disciplinary practices are also considered an important part of the socialization of empathy. Hoffman (2000) has argued that it is the disciplinary interaction between parent and child following a transgression that serves as the behavioral guide toward greater empathy and morality. Therefore, we expected that more consistent (vs. inconsistent) discipline in response to transgressions would have a positive influence on empathy, and included in our study a measure of this when children were 6 years of age.

PROSOCIAL AND AGONISTIC NARRATIVES

In the literature on children's empathy, there is conflicting evidence on whether empathic behaviors are inversely related to agonistic behaviors. Some studies of very young children suggest that they are not correlated because young, sociable children are more likely to engage in both more prosocial and more agonistic acts with peers (Eisenberg & Mussen, 1989). However, as children age, socialization pressures favor the retention of prosocial behaviors and the reduction of agonistic behaviors (Zahn-Waxler & Radke-Yarrow, 1990), leading us to anticipate that similar processes may influence the development of children's ideas or representations about relationships. Eisenberg and colleagues have frequently used children's self-reports of empathic responses, often in response to videotaped segments or imagined situations (Eisenberg et al., 1992). They have found that by early school age children who tend to endorse more empathic behaviors also endorse fewer agonistic actions. Such self-reporting is similar to the story stem narrative, where a story situation is presented that children are invited to complete in whatever way they choose.

Children's narratives have been identified as an important source of information about children's attitudes and representations toward relationships. The MacArthur Story Stem Battery (MSSB) is a method that has been used in numerous investigations of young children's socioemotional development (Robinson, Corbitt-Price, Holmberg, & Wiener, 2002). The story stem method is a non-intrusive assessment that taps into children's understanding and representation of their worlds. Story-stem narratives are cognitively and emotionally accessible to preschoolers, as well as older children, in their portrayal of common human dilemmas. The story-stem technique has been described as "a symbolic means of representing experience" (Buchsbaum, Toth, Clyman, Cicchetti, & Emde, 1992) that may "provide information about children's views of themselves and their world" (Warren, Oppenheim, & Emde, 1996).

Warren et al. (1996) supported the validity of the narrative in capturing meaningful information from young children about aggressive and destructive representations when they found significant positive associations with both parent and teacher reports of behavior problems in the narratives of middle-class children. Buchsbaum and Emde (1990) first reported that empathic and prosocial themes were prevalent in the narratives of 3-year-old children. Oppenheim, Emde, Hasson, and Warren (1997) found a developmental trend for children to resolve story-stem dilemmas with increasingly frequent prosocial resolutions. By age 5, 70% of children resolved dilemmas prosocially. Zahn-Waxler et al. (1994) found in a preschool-age sample that varied in risk for conduct disorder that prosocial resolutions were most frequently observed in females at high risk for conduct problems, suggesting their preoccupation with conflict resolution. In a sample of maltreated preschool children, Macfie and colleagues reported that representations of adults responding to the distress of others were less frequent than for non-maltreated children, while self-responses to distress portrayed in the story were seen more often among maltreated children (Macfie, Toth, Rogosch, Robinson, Emde, & Cicchetti, 1999). Most of these investigations did not find the expected inverse correlation between prosocial and agonistic themes. However, Oppenheim, Nir, Emde, and Warren (1997) reported that children who co-constructed more stories with their mother with prosocial themes tended to have fewer agonistic themes.

An example of a story with extreme levels of aggression and rejecting behaviors is the following, offered by a boy in our sample. In this story, it is noteworthy that the child's inclusion of agonistic themes follows themes that reflect the child's initially attempting to repair a conflict in the story known as "Three's a Crowd." In this story stem, older brother Ronnie and a friend Paul are playing with a ball when Ronnie's little brother, Sean, comes out and asks to play, too. Ronnie agrees, but Paul says, "If you let your little brother play, I won't be your friend anymore."

Child: Oh no. (Ronnie) "Please let him play. I will be your friend. Anyway, I got a football. I don't need to play with your little ball because I got a big football. Come on, Little Brother. Let's go get our own big football. And anyway, I don't want your ball!" (Kicks ball off the table) (Paul) "I want to be your friend." (Ronnie) "No, you're not! (Ronnie hits Paul) "I'm going to go get my ball. I got your ball now! I got your ball now!" (sing-song teasing and taunting voice as Ronnie and Sean kick ball) (Paul) "No, that's not fair. That's not fair. That's my ball!" "Oh shut up!" (destruction sounds as Ronnie hits Paul, knocks him down) "Come on, Brother. Forget him. (Ronnie and Sean play with ball) (Paul gets up and says) "Anyway, I'm not dead now." (destruction sounds as Ronnie hits Paul again.) "But you'll be dead now. Come on. Let's play." (Ronnie and Sean resume playing) I'll beat you up again! (Destruction sounds as Ronnie hits Paul.) Watch me. I'm going to kick you. (explosion sound) And then Mom and Dad come back and see Ronnie's friend on the ground. Ronnie tells the story, but Dad said, "Ronnie, you did it. You did it. You're mad because you had his ball, and he wants his ball." "Shut up!" (Ronnie hits Dad, hits Mom) "You too, Mom!" Come on, Brother. Let's forget these dead people."

Another child, responding to the same stem, is able to respond to the challenge by the friend with prosocial themes, repairing the conflict and including the younger sibling:

Child: And then he said, "That's my brother. If he can't play, I'm not playing." And then he took his ball and went home, and then he thought a minute, and he came back. He (Ronnie) had his arms crossed. He put them down, and he said, "Paul, you came back." Then they faced each other, and then he (Ronnie) put his hand up, and he (Paul) put his hand up (as in High-Fives), and they hugged, and they were best friends again, and then he (Ronnie) asked again, and Paul said, "Okay." And he got his ball, and he (Paul) rolled it to little brother, and he rolled it to Ronnie.

Elsewhere, we have discussed the potential of the MSSB to tap both the symptoms and consequences of parenting dysfunction (Robinson, Herot, Haynes, & Mantz-Simmons, 2000). Oppenheim, Emde, and Warren (1997) provided some evidence for this when they examined children's representations of mothers in their stories. Representations of mothers as warm and nurturing were inversely correlated with mother's self-reports of depressive symptoms as well as her reports of the child's behavior problems. Toth, Cicchetti, Macfie, Maughan, and Vanmeenen (2000) found that parental representations were negatively skewed among maltreated children. We will include positive parental representations in our examination of children's narrative themes.

An example of representations of parents and grandparents as nurturing and affectionate is seen in the following response to the Departure story, where mom and dad leave for a trip and the children stay home with grandmother. As they leave, the younger sister protests, "But I don't want you to go!" This story is presented at the end of the battery, and it is interesting that this child included elements from previous stories:

Child: She starts crying, and then, "Mom, I'm going to miss you." "Thank you, sweetheart." Then she gave Shana a kiss, and then she went over, and grandma put her arm around her. And then she said, "Shana, sometimes mom and your dad have to be alone." And then Rhonda started crying, and she said, "Okay." She went back over to her sister, and they held hands, and then they (Mom and Dad) went in the car.

Examiner: Now show me what the children do while the parents are away.

C: They went in the back yard while grandma, she set the grill, and then they started playing with her ball. They were kicking it to each other, and then Paula. I need Paula.

E: You can just pretend.

C: And then Paula came over. She said, "Hey, can I play?" She said, "No, you can't play," Shana said. "You didn't let me play last time." "But when I came back, I let you play." "Oh yeah, that's right. Come on." Then they started throwing the ball to each other. They were sitting and rolling the ball to each other."

This investigation is the first that focuses on African American children using the MSSB. It is reasonable to assume that their empathic and agonistic representations will be predicted by similar maternal influences as European American children. This is also the first study of children's narratives that has attempted to demonstrate associations between maternal attitudes and behaviors during pregnancy and infancy and the child's narrative representations at age 6. More specifically, the current investigation will allow us to examine how children's narratives may be shaped by maternal attitudes and behavior within the context of specific patterns of shared care of the child.

PATTERNS OF CAREGIVING RESPONSIBILITY

Recent findings from the NICHD Study of Early Childcare (NICHD SECC) indicate that quantity of nonparental care is not in and of itself a significant predictor of a variety of social-emotional outcomes (NICHD Early Child Care Research Network, 1997a, 1998). In-home care by sitters, grandmothers, and fathers was one of the five types of care studied in the NICHD SECC; for toddlers and preschoolers, the highest level of sensitive caregiving was provided by in-home caregivers compared to all other forms of care (NICHD Early Child Care Research Network, 2000). This finding suggests that shared care with family members can often offer a positive and sensitive substitute during mother's absence. This finding was not moderated by either ethnicity or family income, suggesting that among low-income as well as middle-income families, minority as well as nonminority families, relatives and close friends often provide sensitive care. However, the NICHD study sample is also largely middle class and of European American descent (NICHD Early Child Care Research Network, 1998) and the poverty subsample quite small, leading to some uncertainty about the reliability of these findings.

Our sample is comprised of African American mothers living in poverty, many of whom were unmarried teens; a vulnerable segment of society in the United States (McAdoo, 1995). Because sharing care with grandmother and other kin is generally recognized as an important feature of the resiliency of single African American mothers coping with economic adversity, we do not have a priori hypotheses that one pattern of care will be associated with greater prosocialness or less agonistic representations of relationships. However, we do propose that variation in maternal characteristics and mother-child relationship factors may be more strongly associated with children's empathy within the context of exclusive maternal care compared to shared care arrangements.

Specifically, we examine whether children receiving exclusive maternal care or shared care during the first 2 years differ in the frequency of prosocial and agonistic representations in their story completion narratives. Because patterns of care may reflect differing levels of risk (e.g., shared care with grandmother may occur more frequently among very young mothers), we briefly describe demographic differences between women utilizing exclusive versus shared care patterns. Finally, we explore whether there are advantages in exclusive maternal care patterns for the development of empathy and prosociality in their children. Specifically, we ask whether shared care patterns are more likely to dilute the impacts of maternal attitudes that might be associated with children's empathic and agonistic themes compared to exclusive maternal care.

METHOD

Participants

Data for this report were gathered from a sample of low-income, African American, first-time mothers who had been recruited from a public health clinic in Memphis, Tennessee, to participate in the New Mothers Study at the time of their first pregnancy (Kitzman et al., 1997). The original design specified random assignment to one of four treatment conditions:

1. Transportation to prenatal visits.
2. Transportation to prenatal care and postnatal research visits.
3. Transportation to prenatal care and prenatal home visits by a nurse.
4. Transportation to prenatal care and postnatal research visits plus pre- and postnatal home visits by a nurse until the child was 2 years.

Only women and children in Treatment Conditions 2 and 4 were studied beyond the perinatal period ($n = 743$). The women were mostly young (64% were 18 or younger at the time of enrollment), African American (92%), and overwhelmingly poor (85% were living in households with incomes at or below the federal poverty guidelines). However, only data from African American women assigned to Treatment Condition 2, the "control" condition for estimating the impact of the nurse home visiting intervention, are reported ($n = 473$), to control for differences that may have resulted from families receiving intervention. These women were, on average, 17.9 years of age at the time of enrollment, average education was tenth grade, and annual discretionary household income was reported to be $1,349 on average.

Creating Patterns of Caregiving

Mothers reported on the number of days per average week that different caregivers served as the primary provider, to create caregiving percentage values for each child at both the 12- and 24-month time periods. Parents identified the number of days they were the primary caregiver for the child, as well as the number of days other people in the child's life (i.e., grandmother, husband/boyfriend, plus two additional support people) served as the primary provider. The total response was not limited (i.e., total could be more than 7 days), such that parents could identify days in which multiple people had some period of primary caregiving responsibility. Percentages for all caregivers were created by dividing the individual caregiver's total days into the sum of total days. Subsequently, cluster analysis was used to identify patterns of caregiving.

Because cluster analysis is an exploratory methodology, we sought a cluster solution based on theoretical assumptions and then compared it to other cluster analysis techniques. Theoretical decisions were based on research information on caregiving practices and demographic information on living arrangements from several sources including the NICHD SECC (NICHD

Early Child Care Research Network, 1996, 1997a, 2000) where nonmaternal care was most often provided by a father or grandparent during infancy and toddlerhood. Similar patterns have been shown in demographic databases (Federal Interagency Forum on Child and Family Statistics, 1999; United States Census Bureau, 2000, 2003).

Given that the majority of children lived in the same household as the mother, we presumed a strong likelihood that the mother would typically be part of all caregiving compositions. Thus, clusters presented as likely were mother and father/partner together, mother alone, and mother with grandmother, and mother with another relative or nonrelative. Thus, theoretically, we expected four clusters of caregiving constellations. Because cluster analysis is an exploratory methodology, we first tested our theoretical expectations at each time period and then compared it to other possible solutions with fewer or greater number of clusters. In all approaches, the theoretically expected groups were represented at 12 and 24 months.

Combining information from both age points produced a 4 × 4 matrix of care patterns. In order to limit the amount of complexity we consider here, we restricted our examination of the data to children whose mothers reported similar caregiving arrangements across the first 2 years (n = 193 children). Sixty-one children (32%) had exclusive care from their mother; 42 (22%) children had shared care from mother and grandmother; 41 children (21%) had shared care from their mother and her husband/boyfriend; and 49 children (25%) had care distributed across multiple caregivers. See Table 5.1 for distribution of caregivers within each group.

TABLE 5.1
Average Days per Week People Helped Care for Child During First Two Years

Child Age	*Mother*	*Grandmother*	*Husband/ Boyfriend*	*Helper 1*	*Helper 2*
12 mos					
Exclusive maternal care	6.90	0.36	0.22	0.39	0.26
Shared w/ grandmother	6.43	4.83	0.74	0.92	0.79
Shared w/ husband/boyfriend	6.68	1.49	5.22	0.76	0.46
Distributed care	6.39	2.61	2.63	4.94	2.22
24 mos					
Exclusive maternal care	6.95	0.14	0.15	0.48	0.08
Shared w/ grandmother	6.76	4.74	1.00	0.86	0.29
Shared w/ husband/boyfriend	6.44	1.22	5.73	1.15	0.51
Distributed care	6.12	2.43	1.69	4.71	2.88

Procedures and Measures

Children's Prosocial and Agonistic Representations of Relationships. During the year following kindergarten completion, after they had turned 6 years of age, the children and their mothers participated in a follow-up visit at the study offices. Children's narrative representations were elicited using eight story stems from the MacArthur Story Stem Battery (MSSB: Bretherton, Oppenheim, Buchsbaum, Emde, & the MacArthur Narrative Working Group, 1990). Eight stems were selected to elicit themes about relationship conflicts or loss (Lost Dog, Three's a Crowd, Lost Keys, Separation and Reunion, Scary Dog) and/or moral conflicts (Spilled Juice, Stolen Candy). The story stems were administered during a lengthy assessment of the child and were preceded by a 60-minute general abilities test and a 15-minute play break with mom. This had the advantage of facilitating rapport with the examiner, and minimizing problems of reticence for shy children.

Four narrative themes or clusters of themes are considered in our analyses: Prosocial Themes, Verbal Punishments, Parental Warmth, and Agonistic Themes. Prosocial narrative themes that were scored included: empathy/helping, affiliation, affection, and positive ending of the story. Each theme was scored as present/absent in each story. They were averaged within stories and then averaged across all stories (alpha = .51). Discipline themes that included limiting-setting, scolding, or time-out were coded as "Verbal Punishments." They were present or absent within each story and were averaged across stories. Representations of parent figures (mothers, fathers, or grandmothers) as warm and nurturing were also scored as present or absent for each parent figure within each story, and were averaged within and then across stories. Agonistic themes included: refusal of empathy, dysregulated aggression, use of physical punishments, and negative story ending (i.e., someone is in trouble or conflict continues at the end of the story). Refusal of empathy and negative story ending were scored as present/absent in each story; dysregulated aggression included up to four types of themes that were weighted as: 1 = playful/verbal aggression, 2 = hurtful aggression, 3 = unprovoked, poorly controlled aggression, and 4 = assaulting an adult. Each variable was first averaged across stories, standardized, and all variables were then averaged together across all stories (alpha = .42). The relatively low internal consistency is not considered a problem in the methodology since children may include disparate elements to express the prosocial or agonistic thrust of their story.

Parent-child interaction videotaped during the play break was rated with the Emotional Availability Scales–Middle Childhood Version (Biringen,

Robinson, & Emde, 1993). The scales consist of five global ratings including Maternal Sensitivity, which capture information about the mother's flexibility, timing, and responsiveness with the child. For this investigation, we used just the Maternal Sensitivity scale.

Maternal Psychological Characteristics. At the time of enrollment in the study and prior to random assignment, mothers responded to an interview that included several demographic and psychological characteristics. Two questionnaires tapped psychological characteristics: her recalled experience of warmth, rejection, and strictness in her relationship with her parents growing up (Khaleque & Rohner, 2002; Rohner, 1990), and her attitudes toward childrearing from the Adult/Adolescent Parenting Inventory (AAPI: Bavolek, 1989; Lutenbacher, 2001). From the AAPI, we focused only on the subscale tapping lack of empathy toward children. At the 6-year follow-up the mother was asked whether her current male partner (either husband or boyfriend) was involved in providing resources, comfort, or engaging in activities with her child. Yes/no responses to these questions were summed; data were missing if the mother had no current partner. In addition, mothers reported on their current parenting practices through the Alabama Parenting Questionnaire (APQ: Shelton, Frick, & Wooton, 1996); we focused on the Inconsistent Discipline subscale.

RESULTS

Maternal Risks Associated With Patterns of Caregiving

Differences in maternal demographic and psychological characteristics across caregiving groups were tested with ANOVA models. As can be seen in Table 5.2, most differences followed a general pattern that showed significant differences between women sharing care with grandmother and women using exclusive maternal care. Women sharing care with grandmother were less advantaged and showed greater risk characteristics than were women using exclusive care. Women who shared care with grandmother over the first 2 years were younger and had less education than women using exclusive maternal care ($p < .001$), or women sharing care with a husband/boyfriend ($p < .005$), or women using highly distributed care ($p < .06$). Households where mothers had exclusive care had greater discretionary income than those who shared care with grandmother, shared care with the husband/boyfriend, or who had highly distributed care. Differences were also observed in the percent of poverty in their

TABLE 5.2
Differences Between Caregiving Groups on Maternal Characteristics

	Exclusive Maternal Care[a]	*Shared Care w/ Grandmother*[b]	*Shared Care w/ Boyfriend*[c]	*Distributed Care*[d]
Maternal age	18.85[ab]	17.36	18.08	18.00
Education level	10.85	9.38[bacd]	10.59	10.16
Discretionary income	2720[abd]	−173	291	79
Percent poverty neighborhood	39.6[ad]	37.3	33.9	29.5
Recalled warmth	3.69[ad]	3.55	3.73[cd]	3.45
Recalled rejection	1.31	1.46	1.32	1.48
Recalled strictness	2.24	2.33	2.31	2.39
Lack of empathy	2.56[abcd]	2.90	2.94	2.86
Teaching task 2yr	38.37	36.77	37.38	38.75
# mos Birth Interval at 6 yr	42.30[ac]	35.51	31.52	45.35[dbc]
Partner involvement 6yr	1.26	1.09	1.59[cbd]	1.20
Inconsist. discipline 6yr	2.19	2.25	2.41	2.30
Mat. Sensitivity 6yr	5.93	5.84	5.95	6.12

Key to superscripts: First letter significantly different from subsequent letters at $p < .05$.

neighborhood at enrollment. Women using highly distributed care had a lower percent poverty than exclusive maternal care and for shared care with grandmother. Amount of employment did not differ across groups (not tabled).

In the area of attitudes relevant to empathic development, differences were observed in maternal recalled warmth in her own relationship with parents while growing up. Women using distributed care reported less warmth than those using exclusive maternal care ($p < .01$) or women who shared care with a husband/boyfriend ($p < .01$). Mother's nonempathic attitudes toward children also favored women who used exclusive maternal care. They had fewer nonempathic attitudes toward children than those with highly distributed care ($p < .02$), shared care with grandmother ($p < .02$), and shared care with mother's husband/boyfriend ($p < .01$).

At 6 years of age, the average number of months reported until the birth of the next-born child favored women using exclusive maternal care compared to those who shared care with a husband/boyfriend ($p < .02$). In addition, women using highly distributed care had a greater interval than either shared care with grandmother ($p < .05$) or care shared with mother's husband/boyfriend ($p < .01$). The difference between exclusive maternal care and highly distributed care was not significant.

Not surprisingly, there were group differences favoring the women who shared care with their husband/boyfriend on the involvement of these part-

TABLE 5.3
Differences in Narrative Representations Between Caregiving Groups

	Exclusive Maternal Care[a]	*Shared Care w/ Grandmother*[b]	*Shared Care w/ Boyfriend*[c]	*Distributed Care*[d]
Prosocial themes	100.04	99.19	98.89	101.55
Verbal discipline	99.21	99.92	97.80	101.45
Parental warmth	98.86	98.76	98.65	99.41
Aggressive themes	98.61	101.22[ba]	99.11	99.01

Key to superscripts: First letter significantly different from subsequent letters at $p < .05$.

ners with the child at age 6; women who had shared care with a partner in infancy reported greater current partner involvement than either the distributed care group ($p < .05$) or the group sharing care with grandmother ($p < .05$). There were no differences across groups for mother's reported inconsistent discipline or her observed sensitivity at child age 6. In general, these results showed the group sharing care with grandmother to be the most disadvantaged group.

Differences in Prosocial and Agonistic Theme Use Across Caregiving Groups

Analysis of variance was also used to test for difference in narrative themes. As can be seen in Table 5.3, children of women who used highly distributed care created more prosocial/empathic themes than other children, although the differences were nonsignificant trends. Average level of verbal punishment themes also were greater for children who experienced distributed care, but these differences, too, did not reach significance. Children of women who shared care with grandmother created narratives with more aggression and agonistic themes than children of women who had exclusive care ($T_{1,167} = 2.62$, $p < .05$). Nonsignificant trends were also found between children in shared care with grandmother and those whose mothers shared care with a husband/boyfriend or who had highly distributed care. Differences in agonistic themes were not found between children in exclusive maternal care and the other two groups. No differences were found for representations of maternal warmth.

Correlates of Prosocial and Agonistic Narrative Themes Within Caregiving Groups

Correlations between maternal characteristics and children's narrative themes can be found in Table 5.4. Within the exclusive maternal care group, mother's

TABLE 5.4
Correlates of Narrative Themes by Caregiving Pattern

	Lack of Empathy	*Recalled Warmth*	*Recalled Rejection*	*Recalled Strictness*	*Interactive Warmth: 2 yr*	*# mos. Between Births*	*Current Partner Involvement*	*Sensitivity 6 yr*	*Inconsistent Discipline*
Exclusive Maternal Care									
Prosocial Themes	–.20	.24⁺	–.26⁺	–.31*	.30*	.01	.23	.33*	–.17
Warmth	–.15	.23	–.15	–.25⁺	.14	.15	.11	.18	.02
Verbal Punishment	.28*	.09	–.02	–.18	.37*	–.25⁺	.04	.21	.18
Agonistic Themes	.45**	–.09	.07	.10	.06	–.38**	–.22	–.08	.22
Shared w/ Grandmother									
Prosocial Themes	–.04	–.05	–.25	.06	.34*	.02	.30	.23	.05
Warmth	.16	–.19	–.26	.07	.38*	.28⁺	.41*	–.01	–.09
Verbal Punishment	.08	–.12	–.09	–.26	.13	.09	.50**	.00	–.04
Agonistic Themes	.30⁺	–.17	.19	.08	.02	–.01	.08	–.15	.39*
Shared w/ Husb./Boyf.									
Prosocial Themes	–.05	–.06	.23	–.29⁺	.01	.15	–.35*	–.03	.33*
Warmth	–.16	.16	–.05	–.13	.21	–.06	–.49**	–.11	.14
Verbal Punishment	.20	–.17	–.04	–.17	–.11	–.12	–.25	–.18	.28⁺
Agonistic Themes	.02	.37*	–.25	–.07	.01	–.03	.14	–.02	–.16
Distributed Care									
Prosocial Themes	–.25	.02	–.16	–.25	–.17	.17	–.26	–.05	.04
Warmth	–.23	–.03	–.10	–.25	.19	–.11	–.37*	.05	.13
Verbal Punishment	.05	.04	.01	–.03	–.06	–.10	–.16	–.11	.13
Agonistic Themes	.05	–.07	.17	.24	.18	–.12	.12	–.18	.04

⁺$p < .10$. *$p < .05$. **$p < .01$.

lack of empathy reported prior to the child's birth was negatively correlated with children's verbal punishment themes and positively correlated with agonistic themes. Recalled strictness experienced with a mother's parents was negatively correlated with prosocial themes. Mother's observed warmth and skill in interaction with her child at age 2 was positively correlated with prosocial themes and verbal punishment themes, and prosocial themes were correlated with her sensitivity observed at child 6 years. Finally, the interval to the birth of the next child was negatively correlated with children's agonistic themes.

For the group sharing care with grandmother, mothers' teaching task warmth and skill at age 2 were positively associated with their children's prosocial themes and representations of parental warmth. Greater involvement of mother's current partner was positively associated with children's themes of verbal punishment and parental warmth. Mother's self-reported inconsistent discipline when the child was age 6 was positively associated with children's use of agonistic themes. In the group sharing care with a husband/boyfriend, the pattern of correlations did not fit expectations. Greater recalled warmth was positively correlated with agonistic themes. More involvement of her current partner was negatively correlated with children's prosocial themes and representations of parental warmth. Inconsistent discipline reported at 6 years was positively correlated with prosocial themes. Within the group using highly distributed care, only one correlation was significant. Greater partner involvement was negatively correlated with children's representations of parental warmth.

DISCUSSION

Associations between Maternal Characteristics and Child Narratives

We had anticipated finding a stronger pattern of maternal correlates of children's prosocial and agonistic narrative themes among the exclusive care group compared to the other groups, especially the distributed care group, because exclusive care maximized mother's contact with the child and exposure to the maternal attitudes and behaviors we assessed. We found some support for this in the pattern of correlations in this group. Mother's self-reported lack of empathy at enrollment was correlated with aggressive themes. Closer spacing of children also was related to the frequency with which children introduced agonistic themes in their stories. Mothers' recalled strictness at enrollment and observed maternal behaviors at ages 2 and 6 years were correlated with their children's prosocial narrative themes. Children's representations of verbal punishments, which are weakly correlated with both prosocial and agonistic themes (r = .21), were positively correlated with mother's nonempathic attitudes in pregnancy but were also positively correlated with maternal warmth and skill in the teaching task at age 2. These latter correlations suggest that there is an underlying sociability dimension that unites these four themes in the children's narratives. Alternatively, inclusion of verbal punishments in stories reflects the child's impulse to contain aggression but also reflects the use of more nurturing containment, hence the correlation with both prosocial and agonistic themes. Overall, the coherence of the pattern of correlations supports the expected associations between maternal empathy and sensitive interactions and the children's representations of relationships in this group.

Few significant correlations were observed among children whose care was shared with the child's grandmother, although they followed theoretical predictions. Greater maternal skill and warmth observed at age 2 was associated with more prosocial themes and representations of maternal warmth. Mother's report of more inconsistent discipline practices at age 6 correlated with more agonistic themes. Most interesting among children reared by mother and grandmother, however, are the moderately strong correlations between mother's report of her current partner's involvement with the child and the more frequent inclusion of verbal punishments and maternal warmth in the children's narratives. The correlations suggest that for these children, whose mothers were younger and less economically advantaged at the time of their births, greater involvement of a father figure as they enter school supports positive representations of parenting for the child.

However, the pattern of correlations for the group sharing care in infancy with a husband/boyfriend was theoretically *in*consistent. Mothers' recalled warmth from their parents was significantly positively associated with greater *agonistic* themes in their children and greater inconsistent discipline reported by mothers at age 6 was associated with more *prosocial* themes. Further, negative correlations between male partner involvement at child age 6, and children's prosocial themes and representations of parental warmth, were also found and shed some light on these unexpected findings. Perhaps sharing the child's care in infancy with a male partner was not an optimal strategy regarding child development; when partners were more involved at age 6, the children were adversely affected. Including fewer prosocial themes and less parental warmth in their expressed representations of relationships may suggest less trust or safety in their experience. A suggestion of this pattern was also seen in the single significant correlation in the children's representations in the highly distributed care group; when mother's partner was more involved at age 6, children also represented parents warmly less often. The negative association between male partners' involvement and children's parenting representations likely has to do with the historical as well as current greater participation of male partners in these children's lives (see Table 5.1). These findings are in marked contrast to the group of children who were cared for by mothers and grandmothers, where the child may have experienced a history of safety and trust. Given the importance of marriage in African American communities (McAdoo, 1995), this finding deserves serious consideration in other studies of partner involvement and children's socioemotional development.

It is important to note that while there may be associations between certain patterns of caregiving and child narratives, we do not know what these same children might look like in another caregiving style and therefore cannot assume that utilizing multiple caregivers is a maladaptive approach. For example, while children who receive care from both their mother and grandmother show more agonistic themes than children cared for exclusively by their mothers, those same children may show a higher level of agonistic themes if they were to also receive exclusive maternal care, given their mothers' youth and poverty. In that scenario, grandmother may be providing protective effects for a group that would otherwise be severely disadvantaged.

Associations Between Early Care and Child Narratives

We did not hypothesize that children in one group would incorporate more prosocial or less agonistic themes compared to another. We found that agonistic themes were more frequent among children raised by their mothers and grandmothers compared to children whose care was exclusively by mother. We found, however, that children who experienced highly distributed care in their first 2 years tended to have more prosocial themes than children whose care was shared with mother's husband/boyfriend. These findings are not surprising, but we hesitate to interpret them with any confidence. However, children whose care was shared by grandmother were the most disadvantaged socioeconomically, and for this reason, this finding might be expected. Children in the distributed care group were more prosocial in their narratives. It seems plausible that exposure to more models of prosocial behavior from the different caregivers in the distributed care group may offer these children advantages in their developing representations of caring relationships.

Associations Between Early Care and Maternal Characteristics

Women who exclusively cared for their child had many advantages compared to those using other caregiving patterns. They were significantly older, better educated, and had more discretionary income at the time of study enrollment than women who shared care with the child's grandmother. Women with exclusive maternal care also had emotional advantages that might lead to greater prosocialness in their children. They recalled greater warmth in their relationship with their parents compared to women with highly distributed care of their child, and they had fewer nonempathic attitudes for children compared to all other groups. Women using exclusive maternal care had longer intervals to the birth of their next child than did women sharing care with their husband/boyfriend. However, women with exclusive care of their child also lived in neighborhoods with a greater rate of poverty than all others at the time of enrollment. In general, excepting neighborhood poverty, these differences suggest that women with exclusive care of their child had more social advantages and had more attitudes/beliefs supportive of more prosocial and less agonistic behaviors in their children, particularly in comparison with women sharing care with the child's grandmother. No specific investigation was conducted regarding the direction of these effects; consequently it is unclear whether the advantages seen in this group indicate that having more resources makes a mother more likely to utilize exclusive care, as opposed to other possible explanations, for example, they needed to develop more resources because they didn't have any other social supports. Nonetheless, there does appear to be a relationship between maternal resources and exclusivity of care, which may have risk implications for women who share care with grandmothers or husbands/boyfriends.

In some respects, however, the exclusive maternal care group was quite similar to the other care groups. It is important to note that while sharing child care responsibility during the child's first 2 years characterized three of the four groups of women, on average women worked very little during that time. Women in this sample did not experience significant employment rates until children were between 4 and 6 years of age. Exclusive-care mothers were not significantly warmer and more skilled at 2 years or more sensitive with their children at age 6 years. Exclusive-care mothers were also not significantly older or better educated than the group sharing care with their husband/boyfriend. These two groups also did not differ in the recalled warmth, strictness, or rejection in their relationship with their parents. However, these mothers may have differed in other characteristics that were not measured, given the dramatic differences in how their attitudes, behaviors, and life circumstances were associated with their children's development.

CONCLUSIONS

The content of children's representations of relationships likely draws from many sources in their experience. However, the content of the story stems also may draw children into different sectors of their experience. Themes of breaking rules, peer and parent conflict, threat, and separation and loss were reflected in the selected MSSB stories. In exploring early sources of influence on children's prosocial and agonistic representations of relationships, it was impressive to see the span of time these associations covered (up to 7 years) among children exclusively reared by their mothers. Also impressive was the breadth of influences that were significantly associated with children's representations at age 6 among those exclusively reared by their mothers, including maternal lack of empathy in pregnancy, recalled warmth, rejection, and strictness in mother's own parents, mother's interactive style both concurrently and from when the child was age 2, and the spacing of births. The role of fathers and father figures also prominently influenced children's representations of parental warmth, verbal discipline, and prosocial relatedness, but only among children reared jointly by others as well as their mothers.

Our investigation has brought to light the importance of variations in care that children experience in their first years of life for their development of representations of relationships. It also provides some directions for future studies. The NICHD SECC's recent reports on the effects of child care on children's socioemotional development have found that the quantity of care has negative effects, irrespective of the quality of care (Belsky, in press). Quantity of care for children in this study, however, may be a less salient issue than the family risks associated with some types of care. Disentangling this is an important further direction. Doing so may reveal whether there are ways to augment this, such as increasing targeted exposure of other adults to the children cared for by grandmothers. It also would be interesting to see specifically if the nurse visitation intervention impacted the level of prosocial themes in the nondistributed groups or the agonistic themes in the nonexclusive care groups. The study is limited, however, in having no information about the quality of care that was provided by other caregivers, except by the child's own mother. The finding of greater agonistic representations among children whose care was shared by grandmother may be due to the greater socioeconomic disadvantage of their mothers, or it could have been influenced by less sensitive care from grandmothers. We also have little information about the quality of involvement children actually experienced with the male partners who shared in their care with their mothers. However, we do know that only 19% of women were partnered with the child's biological father at age 6, suggesting that less investment in the child by male partners may play a role in the negative consequences for the child's developing representations of parental roles in these families.

Another limitation of this study is the relatively low power to detect differences, since our selected sample was relatively small. We made the decision to focus on women in the control group to avoid any confound with intervention impacts and on women with stable care patterns because more prolonged exposure to these patterns of care were more likely to have an impact on the child. Significant effect sizes were moderate in magnitude in this sample (.4 to .6). Thus, we were unable to address whether child gender moderated any of these effects, an important issue because many studies report girls to be more prosocial than boys and boys more agonistic than girls (Eisenberg & Fabes, 1998).

Despite these limitations, this study carries some important social implications. Families raising young children in a violent inner city (such as Memphis in the early 1990s) are challenged to provide safe, consistent care to their children. Although shared caregiving patterns did not appear to be associated with increased employment of their mothers, economic opportunities for young African American women improved during the decade, and a 50% employment rate was reported by the time the children were 6 years old. Having the exclusive care of one's mother in infancy and toddlerhood may be a way of the past for many poor children in the United States, as welfare reform requires earlier and more extensive employment. This report suggests that there are benefits for children's developing understanding of relationships that will be lost along with the push for greater early maternal employment.

ACKNOWLEDGMENTS

Preparation of this chapter was suported by a grant to the first author from the National Science Foundation (0091430). Data collection for the study was supported by a grant from the Robert Wood Johnson Foundation to David L. Olds, PhD.

REFERENCES

Bavolek, S. J. (1989). Assessing and treating high-risk parenting attitudes. *Early Child Development and Care, 42,* 99–112.

Belsky, J. (in press). Quantity counts: Amount of child care and children's socioemotional development. *Journal of Developmental and Behavioral Pediatrics.*

Biringen, Z., Robinson, J. L., & Emde, R. N. (1993). *Emotional Availability Scales: Middle Childhood Version.* Unpublished scales, University of Colorado Health Sciences Center.

Bretherton, I., Oppenheim, D., Buchsbaum, H., Emde, R. N., & the MacArthur Narrative Working Group. (1990). *MacArthur Story Stem Battery.* Unpublished manual.

Brodsky, A. E. (1999). "Making It": The components and process of resilience among urban, African American, single mothers. *American Journal of Orthopsychiatry, 69,* 148–160.

Buchsbaum, H. K., & Emde, R. N. (1990). Play narratives in thirty-six-month-old children: Early moral development and family relationships. *The Psychoanalytic Study of the Child, 40,* 129–155.

Buchsbaum, H. K., Toth, S. L., Clyman, R. B., Cicchetti, D., & Emde, R. N. (1992). The use of a narrative story stem technique with maltreated children: Implications for theory and practice. *Development and Psychopathology, 4,* 603–625.

Chase-Landale, P. L., Brooks-Gunn, J., & Zamsky, E. S. (1994). Young African American multi-generational families in poverty: Quality of mothering and grandmothering. *Child Development, 65,* 373–393.

Cummings, E. M., Hollenbeck, B., Iannotti, R. J., Radke-Yarrow, M., & Zahn-Waxler, C. (1986). Early organization of altruism and aggression: Developmental patterns and individual differences. In C. Zahn-Waxler, E. M. Cummings, & R. J. Iannotti (Eds.), *Altruism and aggression: Biological and social origins* (pp. 165–188). New York: Cambridge University Press.

Eisenberg, N., & Fabes, R. A. (1998). Prosocial development. In W. Damon (Series Ed.) & N. Eisenberg (Vol. Ed.), *Handbook of child psychology (5th ed.): Vol. 3. Social, emotional, and personality development* (pp. 701–778). New York: John Wiley.

Eisenberg, N., Fabes, R. A., Carlo, G., Troyer, D., Speer, A. L., Karbon, M., & Switzer, G. (1992). The relations of maternal practices and characteristics to children's vicarious emotional responsiveness. *Child Development, 63,* 583–602.

Eisenberg, N., Fabes, R. A., Schaller, M., Carlo, G., & Miller, P. A. (1991). The relations of parental characteristics and practices to children's vicarious emotional responding. *Child Development, 62,* 1393–1408.

Eisenberg, N., & Mussen, P. (1989). *The roots of prosocial behavior in children.* New York: Cambridge University Press.

Federal Interagency Forum on Child and Family Statistics. (1999). America's children 1999. http://www.childstats.gov/ac1999/toc.asp

Genero, N. P. (1995). Culture, resiliency, and mutual psychological development. In H. I. McCubbin, E. A. Thompson, A. I. Thompson, & J. A. Futrell (Eds.), *Resiliency in ethnic minority families: African-American families* (Vol. 2, pp. 31–48). Madison, WI: University of Wisconsin System.

Hoffman, M. L. (2000). *Empathy and moral development: Implications for caring and justice.* New York: Cambridge University Press.

Jackson, J. F. (1993). Multiple caregiving among African Americans and infant attachment: The need for an emic approach. *Human Development, 36,* 87–102.

Khaleque, A., & Rohner, R. P. (2002). Perceived parental acceptance-rejection and psychological adjustment: A meta-analysis of cross-cultural and intracultural studies. *Journal of Marriage and Family, 64,* 54–64.

Kitzman, H., Olds, D. L., Henderson, C. R., Jr, Hanks, C., Cole, R., Tatelbaum, R., McConnochie, K. M., Sidora, K., Luckey, D. W., Shaver, D., Engelhardt, K., James, D., & Barnard, K. (1997). Effect of prenatal and infancy home visitation by nurses on pregnancy outcomes, childhood injuries, and repeated childbearing: A randomized controlled trial. *Journal of the American Medical Association, 278,* 644–652.

Lutenbacher, M. (2001). Psychometric assessment of the Adult-Adolescent Parenting Inventory in a sample of low-income single mothers. *Journal of Nursing Measurement, 9,* 291–308.

Macfie, J., Toth, S. L., Rogosch, F. A., Robinson, J., Emde, R. N., & Cicchetti, D. (1999). Effect of maltreatment on preschoolers' narrative representations of responses to relieve distress and of role reversal. *Development Psychology, 35,* 460–465.

McAdoo, H. P. (1995). African-American families: Strengths and realities. In H. I. McCubbin, E. A. Thompson, A. I. Thompson, & J. A. Futrell (Eds.), *Resiliency in ethnic minority families: African-American families* (Vol. 2, pp. 17–30). Madison, WI: University of Wisconsin System.

NICHD Early Child Care Research Network. (1996). Characteristics of infant child care: Factors contributing to positive caregiving. *Early Childhood Research Quarterly, 11*(3), 296–306.

NICHD Early Child Care Research Network. (1997a). Child care in first year of life. *Merrill-Palmer Quarterly, 43*(3), 340–360.

NICHD Early Child Care Research Network. (1997b). The effects of infant child care on infant-mother attachment security: Results of the NICHD Study of Early Child Care. *Child Development, 68,* 860–879.

NICHD Early Child Care Research Network. (1998). Early child care and self-control, compliance, and problem behavior at twenty-four and thirty-six months. *Child Development, 69,* 1145–1170.

NICHD Early Child Care Research Network. (2000). Characteristics and quality of child care for toddlers and preschoolers. *Applied Developmental Science, 4*(3), 116–135.

Oppenheim, D., Emde, R. N., Hasson, M., & Warren, S. (1997). Preschoolers face moral dilemmas: A longitudinal study of acknowledging and resolving internal conflict. *International Journal of Psychoanalysis, 78,* 943–956.

Oppenheim, D., Emde, R. N., & Warren, S. L. (1997). Children's narrative representations of mothers: Their development and associations with child and mother adaptation. *Child Development, 68,* 127–138.

Oppenheim, D., Nir, A., Emde, R. N., & Warren, S. L. (1997). Emotion regulation in mother-child narrative co-construction: Associations with children's narratives and adaptation. *Developmental Psychology, 33,* 284–294.

Randolph, S., & Koblinsky, S. (2001). The sociocultural context of infant mental health in African American families. *Zero-to-Three, 22,* 29–38.

Robinson, J. L., Corbitt-Price, J., Holmberg, J., & Wiener, P. (2002). *The use of story stems to assess risks in young children: A report on collaborations with the MacArthur Story Stem Battery.* Unpublished manuscript, University of Colorado Health Sciences Center.

Robinson, J., Herot, C., Haynes, P., & Mantz-Simmons, L. (2000). Children's story stem responses: A measure of program impact on developmental risks associated with dysfunctional parenting. *International Journal for Child Abuse and Neglect, 24,* 99–110.

Robinson, J. L., Zahn-Waxler, C., & Emde, R. N. (1994). Patterns of development in early empathic behavior: Environmental and child constitutional influences. *Social Development, 3,* 125–145.

Rohner, R. P. (1990). *Handbook for the study of parental acceptance and rejection.* Storrs, CT: Rohner Research.

Shelton, K. K., Frick, P. J., & Wooton, J. (1996). Assessment of parenting practices in families of elementary school-age children. *Journal of Clinical Child Psychology, 25,* 317–329.

Toth, S. L., Cicchetti, D., Macfie, J., Maughan, A., & Vanmeenen, K. (2000) Narrative representations of caregivers and self in maltreated pre-schoolers. *Attachment and Human Development, 2*(3), 271–305.

United States Census Bureau. (2000). *Household relationship and living arrangements of children under 18 years.* http://www.census.gov/population/socdemo/hh-fam/p20–537/2000/tabC2.txt

United States Census Bureau. (2003). *Living arrangements of children under 18 years old: 1960 to present.* http://www.census.gov/population/socdemo/hh-fam/tabCH-1.pdf

Warren, S. L., Oppenheim, D., & Emde, R. N. (1996). Can emotions and themes in children's play predict behavior problems? *Journal of the American Academy of Child and Adolescent Psychiatry, 34,* 1331–1337.

Zahn-Waxler, C., Cole, P. M., Richardson, D. T., Friedman, R. J., Michel, M. K., & Belouad, F. (1994). Social problem solving in disruptive preschool children: Reactions to hypothetical situations of conflict and distress. *Merrill Palmer Quarterly, 40,* 98–119.

Zahn-Waxler, C., & Radke-Yarrow, M. (1982). The development of altruism: Alternative research strategies. In N. Eisenberg (Ed.), *The development of prosocial behavior* (pp. 109–139). San Diego, CA: Academic Press.

Zahn-Waxler, C., & Radke-Yarrow, M. (1990). The origins of empathic concern. *Motivation and Emotion, 14,* 107–129.

Zahn-Waxler, C., Robinson, J., & Emde, R. N. (1992). The development of empathy in twins. *Developmental Psychology, 28,* 1038–1047.

PART II

Adolescent Narratives: Identity Development and Its Contexts

6

Adoption Narratives: The Construction of Adoptive Identity During Adolescence

Nora Dunbar
Harold D. Grotevant
University of Minnesota

> *I'd like to first of all, be able to make contact with my birthfather. I'd like to know, maybe ethnical background, like where—heritage in particular. Maybe religion if they have any or what sort . . . I know next to nothing about him. I kind of wish the adoption agency would've kept a little better tabs on him so I would know something, because I don't know much at all. . . . I don't know, I think I've got to meet him, just eventually, someday. It's a part of me that's missing; I need to find it, confront it.*
>
> —Hugo, age 15, mediated adoption, Unsettled Identity

> *I think a lot of personality traits I have come, not really unconsciously, I think you do pick up a lot from environment, but I think that there's also a lot, not necessarily chainwise but you know you have and don't really know why, that comes from your parents, well birthparents. Which I think is where I got a lot of mine, 'cause I'm quite different from most of the people in my family, and you know from what I've heard, you know my birth mother, talk about describing her, it sounds a lot similar . . . which is kind of a weird thing.*
>
> —Kelley, age 16, mediated adoption, Integrated Identity

These quotes illustrate the challenge that adopted adolescents face in making meaning of their beginnings, which may be unknown, unclear, or otherwise ambiguous. Meaning-making involves building a story about oneself that attempts to answer many questions: Where did I come from? Who were my parents? Why was I placed for adoption? Do my birthparents think about me now? Do I have siblings? What does adoption mean in my life?

This story is not constructed in isolation. Its elements and affective tone emerge through daily interactions with family members, experiences with peers, and exposure to the media. The ability to construct an integrated, coherent narrative first emerges in adolescence (Habermas & Bluck, 2000). This narrative helps the adolescent make sense of the past, understand the self in the present, and project himself or herself into the future. For the adolescent who has been adopted, this narrative is about the development of adoptive identity, the evolving answer to the question, "Who am I as an adopted person?" (Grotevant, 1997; Grotevant, Dunbar, Kohler, & Esau, 2000). This is part of the larger process of identity development, which is widely recognized as an important task of adolescence because it lays a foundation for adult psychosocial development (Erikson, 1968; McAdams, 2001).

Adoption is recognized as the transfer of parental rights and responsibilities from a child's birth parents to other person(s) who will provide nurturance and guidance. In contemporary Western societies, adoptive relationships are quite varied (Grotevant & Kohler, 1999). Adoption can refer to the infant placed with an infertile couple by birthparents without the financial ability to care for the child, a child brought to a Western nation from an orphanage in a developing country, an abused child removed from his or her birth family and placed with an unrelated adult, a child placed across racial lines, a child with a disability placed into a new family with other children with special needs, and other situations. In our research, adoption arrangements differed in terms of openness, that is, the degree and type of contact occurring between the child's adoptive parents and birth family members. *Confidential* adoptions are those in which no identifying information is shared; parties know only vague general information about each other. In *mediated* adoptions, communication between the adoptive and birth families takes place through a third party (such as an agency social worker) who relays information without identifying details back and forth. *Fully disclosed* adoptions are those in which parties to the adoption have identifying information about one another and typically have ongoing contact of some sort, although it may vary greatly in frequency and intensity.

As adopted children grow up, their adoptive parents help them construct an adoption story that answers concrete questions such as "Where was I born?" and "What does my birth mother look like?" The process evolves in the context of communication between child and adoptive parents—questions are asked, information is shared (Wrobel, Kohler, Grotevant, & McRoy, in press). Over time, the questions become more subtle and existential. The cognitive abilities that emerge in adolescence facilitate the development of an increasingly multifaceted story, but also challenge the young person with contradictions and ambiguities that may emerge. Thus, the development of identity may be more complex for adopted adolescents than for their nonadopted peers (Grotevant, 1997).

Most adopted adolescents experience some degree of differentness (e.g., physical appearance, personality, ethnic or cultural origins, disability) from members of their adoptive families; many face the challenge of constructing an identity from incomplete genealogical information; and all adopted adolescents must undertake coming to terms with themselves in relation to the family and culture into which they were adopted. These additional tasks may result in prolonged identity exploration, the postponement of other identity work until issues regarding adoptive identity are resolved at some level, or perhaps identity confusion.

In our work, adoptive identity is investigated using a narrative approach that highlights the integration and coherence of the self (Grotevant, 1993; McAdams, 1993, 2001, this volume; Polkinghorne, 1991). From this perspective, the adolescent is viewed as creating and recreating a life story that makes meaning of and gives purpose to his or her experience of adoption. This study attempts to categorize the narratives of adopted adolescents into types based on exploration and the narrative attributes of structure and content.

Adolescents' adoptive identity narratives span the intersection of three levels: the intrapsychic, relational, and social. The intrapsychic level includes the individual's internal cognitive and affective processes necessary for constructing an adoptive identity. The relational level includes the birth and adoptive family relationships in which one negotiates and enacts one's adoptive identity. The social level includes interaction in contexts and relationships beyond the family. Adopted adolescents construct their adoptive identity at the intersection of these levels by making meaning of their experiences within and across relationships and contexts.

Narrative approaches highlight the integration and coherence of the self through the evaluation of the structure, content, and function of the narrative (McAdams, 1987). This study attended to the narrative aspects of structure and content. Moshman (1998), who considers identity an explicit theory of oneself as a person, noted that identity "is not just a collection of beliefs about oneself but rather is organized to generate an integrated conception" (p. 3). This definition suggests that one way to conceptualize the structure of the narrative is in terms of coherence, which describes how well the story hangs together. In this study, two rating scales from the Family

Narrative Consortium (Fiese et al., 1999) were used to assess coherence. The first, Internal Consistency, reflects the completeness and development of the theory present in the narrative. The second, Flexibility, refers to the individual's ability to take the perspective of others and to explore new ideas and alternatives. The narrative content of interest in this study includes the degree of salience or importance of the adoptive identity to the adopted adolescent, as well as the level of positive and negative affect expressed about the adolescent's sense of self as an adoptee. In addition to these narrative components, the exploration of adoptive identity was examined as the identity "work" accomplished and then presented through the process of narrative construction (Grotevant, 1993).

In this chapter, cluster analysis is used to derive a typology descriptive of adoptive identity. Profiles of each of the four types are presented, along with a detailed case study of each type. Variations in the types by age, gender, and adoption openness are also discussed.

METHOD

Participants

This examination of adoptive identity development was undertaken as part of the Minnesota/Texas Adoption Research Project, a longitudinal study of variations in openness in adoption arrangements; that is, contact between members of the child's adoptive and birth families (Grotevant & McRoy, 1998). Adoptive families and birth mothers were initially recruited for the study through 35 adoption agencies across the United States. Agencies were instructed to select all previously placed children who were between ages 4 and 12 at the time of the interview and to sample randomly within levels of openness until a set number of families and birth mothers were willing to be interviewed. The sample was limited to children adopted through an agency before their first birthday; in which the adoption was not transracial, international, or special needs; and in which adoptive parents were married. A few families (6.3%) and birth mothers (11.8%) were recruited through newspaper and periodical advertisements. The final Wave I sample included 720 individuals: both parents in 190 adoptive families, at least one adopted child in 171 of the families, and 169 birth mothers. Further details about Wave I may be found in Grotevant and McRoy (1998).

Families were recontacted to participate in Wave II approximately 8 years later, when the adopted children were between the ages of 12 and 20. The final Wave II sample included 177 adoptive families: 173 adoptive mothers, 162 adoptive fathers, 156 adopted adolescents, and 127 birth mothers. Wave II information from 145 adoptive adolescents with complete data was used for this study. Adopted adolescents were primarily Caucasian (92.6%) and included 75 females and 70 males who ranged in age from 11 to 20 years ($M = 15.6$). The adolescents were involved in confidential ($N = 38$), mediated ($N = 36$), and fully-disclosed ($N = 71$) adoptions.

Procedures

Adoptive families were interviewed in their homes in one session that lasted 4 to 6 hours. The session included individual interviews with each parent and adopted adolescent, administration of several questionnaires, and a family interaction task with both parents and the adopted adolescent. Responses of each individual were not disclosed to other family members. Parents were given the opportunity to review the interview protocol and questionnaire booklet prior to our contact with the adolescent. Parents were permitted to strike items if they wished; however, this rarely occurred.

The adolescent interview at Wave II covered the four identity domains of occupation, friendship, religion, and adoption. The questions in the adoption section of the interview tapped adoption-related feelings, beliefs, and knowledge. Most interviews lasted between 1 to 2 hours. Adolescent interviews were transcribed verbatim and coded using an analytic inductive method.

Interview Coding

The first pass of coding assessed the depth of adoptive identity exploration, degree of positive and negative affect regarding the adolescent's adoptive identity, and extent of adoptive identity salience. Afterward, the adolescent's interview was coded for two components of narrative coherence: internal consistency and flexibility. Coding was individually completed by two to five coders. Discrepancies were discussed and consensus achieved for each disagreement. The complete coding manual is available upon request.

Exploration. Exploration assessed how deeply an adolescent had explored his/her adoptive identity and was coded into four levels ranging from *no/minimal* to *great exploration of adoptive identity* (interrater reliability, $M = 85.25\%$). A rating of 1 (no/minimal) indicated the adolescent showed no or minimal evidence of thinking about adoptive identity or meaning of adoption to the self; 2 (low) indicated limited depth in thinking about adoption or adoptive identity with little serious, reflective thinking; 3 (moderate) indicated some depth of exploration with some serious, reflective thinking; and 4 (great) indicated considerable depth in exploration with serious, reflective thinking that showed greater self-awareness and integration.

Salience. Salience assessed the prominence, importance, and meaning of the adolescent's adoptive identity and was coded on a 5-point scale from *no* to *high salience* (interrater reliability, $M = 88.39\%$). A rating of 1 (no) indicated adoptive identity did not matter to the adolescent (e.g., it was not thought about); a 2 (low) indicated a "matter-of-factness" about sense of self as an adopted person (e.g., adolescent may say, "It's not a big deal."); a 3 (moderate) indicated the adoptive identity exists and has meaning for the adolescent, however the adoptive identity may be balanced with other identities; a 4 (moderately high) indicated the adoptive identity is very important to the adolescent, but does not overwhelm the adolescent's sense of self; and a 5 (high) indicated the adoptive identity may consume great psychic and emotional energy and may be the identity that is most prominent or a "leading theme" in the adolescent's sense of self.

The rating of salience of adoptive identity was based primarily on the level of importance and prominence of the identity; the degree to which the adoptive identity influenced behaviors, thoughts, decisions, and feelings; and the adolescent's ranking of the adoptive identity in relation to five other identity domains. However, raters also considered the following in making a coding decision: (a) degree of adoptive identity exploration, (b) level of positive and negative affect associated with adoptive identity, (c) the number of relationships in which the adolescent interacts about adoption related issues (breadth) and the amount of thought and feeling that occurs in these interactions (depth), and (d) adolescent's acknowledgment of differences between adoptive and nonadoptive families.

Internal Consistency. Internal Consistency measured the completeness of the content of the narrative on a 5-point scale, ranging from *no* to a *well-documented theory* (interrater reliability, $M = 85.26\%$). A rating of 1 (no theory) indicated that no theory could be identified in the narrative; 2 (unsupported theory) indicated very little elaboration of examples was present in the narrative; 3 (theory with some support) indicated that personal details and generalizations about one's own experiences were provided, but generally only when prompted by the interviewer; 4 (theory in progress) indicated that statements were consistently supported with evidence and suggested the presence of emerging complexity in the theory; and 5 (well-documented theory) indicated that the theory showed complexity and detailed elaboration.

Flexibility. Flexibility measured the adolescent's ability to view issues as others might see them and to explore new ideas and alternatives on a 5-point scale, ranging from *low* to *high flexibility* (interrater reliability, $M = 86.81\%$). A rating of 1 (low flexibility/rigid) indicated that the narrative strongly adhered to one perspective and that presented issues were all one-sided; 2 (moderately low flexibility) indicated the adherence to one perspective with minimal recognition of alternative views that might be dismissed as invalid; 3 (moderate flexibility) indicated a narrative with clear recognition of more than one perspective; 4 (moderately high flexibility) indicated a narrative that included elaboration of two or more perspectives; 5 (high flexibility) indicated a narrative in which two or more perspectives were integrated and resolved.

Positive and Negative Affect. Degree of affect was coded separately (for positive and negative affect) on two 5-point scales, ranging from *no* to *strong affect* (interrater reliability positive affect, $M = 86.61\%$; negative affect, $M = 87.50\%$). Raters used these codes to evaluate how the adopted adolescent felt about being adopted and/or having an identity as an adopted person. A rating of 1 (no/minimal) indicated no or minimal feelings about adoption or a sense of neutrality; 2 (low) indicated reluctant and/or nondefinitive emotions; 3 (moderate) indicated moderately intense emotions such as liking or disliking; 4 (moderately strong) indicated emotions falling between moderate and strong; and 5 (strong) indicated extreme or intense emotions such as loving or hating.

RESULTS

Cluster analysis by cases (Hair & Black, 2000) was used to classify the adolescents according to the extent to which their narratives about adoption were developed and demonstrated exploration, salience, and affect. Age and gender were left "outside" the clusters rather than incorporated as an intrinsic part of them because identity was thought to vary as a function of these characteristics. Age and gender are considered explicitly in the results and discussion that follow. The following variables were included in the cluster analyses: Adoptive Identity Exploration, Salience of the adoptive identity, Internal Consistency of the narrative, Narrative Flexibility, and Negative and Positive

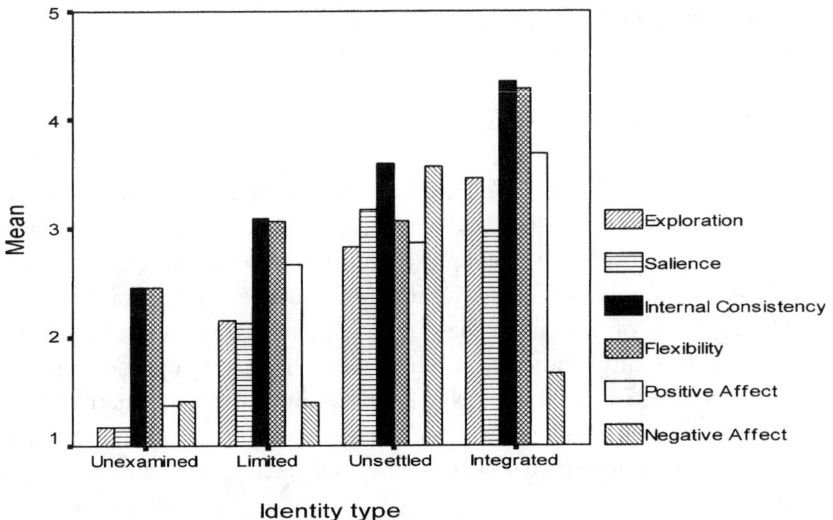

FIG. 6.1. Profile of adoptive identity types.

Affect. Further details about the development of the clusters may be found in Dunbar (2003).

Description and Profile of Identity Types

As seen in Fig. 6.1, the cluster analysis provided convincing evidence of four types of adoptive identity, Unexamined ($n = 24$), Limited ($n = 46$), Unsettled ($n = 30$), and Integrated ($n = 45$). The four types of adoptive identity suggest a progression of increasing exploration and narrative development. The statistical justification for the types and the quantitative data validating the types are presented in Dunbar (2003) and are not repeated here, since the focus of this chapter is on the identity narratives.

The following cases were selected to be representative of the narratives in each identity type. First cases were selected to represent the predominant age, gender, and openness within each type. Then the identity variable scores for these cases were evaluated for closeness to type means and modes. Finally, if more than one possible case was identified, a narrative was chosen that contained themes similar to those found in other narratives within that type.

Unexamined Identity. Trevor,[1] who is almost 13, constructed a narrative characteristic of the Unexamined type. He had not thought much about

[1]All names are pseudonyms.

his adoption, and the ideas he did express had not been examined deeply. He doesn't really remember being told about his mediated adoption, however he thinks it "Didn't really bug me then. Never really does anymore." He doesn't have many feelings about his birth mother, whom he met once when he was 7 (she died shortly thereafter), "I don't know, I didn't really get to know her, so . . . I met her one time, and then she died, so. It was nothing there." He hasn't given much thought to his feelings about his birth father, "Ah . . . I don't know just because I haven't met him, but, I haven't really paid any attention to it."

Conversations with his family about adoption are rare and when he tries to talk with his friends he finds it's too confusing, "I just kind of tell them, like, what happened and stuff like that, nothing, you know, it's not, like, big details and everything, it's just they don't understand mostly . . . it just kind of gets them confused whatever I say, so I just say, 'Don't talk to me about it.'" Views on openness in adoption are only provided when probed by the interviewer, "I don't really know, I haven't really paid attention to anything like that, at all. I just kind of want to meet my birthdad, basically that's really all." He says having contact with his birth family doesn't really matter but also expresses positive feelings about meeting his birth mother, "Well, I thought it was kind of nice to be able to meet her, because most people don't really get to meet their adopted [sic; means birth] parents because some of them don't even want to see them and others do." He declares adoption doesn't enter into his life or decisions, "I think most of the things that I do, just, it's kind of, like, 'No, it doesn't really matter, it's not bad and it's not good.'" However, the strength of this view is compromised by his fairly unarticulated connections between himself as an adopted person and his families of adoption and birth, ". . . just kind of connects, basically, because I'm kind of getting to meet my family and so, we're going to—you know, just going to—going to be able—we're getting together in summer and stuff," and what he does at church, "They just, kind of have a party to get together so, they—other adopted kids get to meet the other ones . . . there's a Christmas party for them and stuff like that. It's nothing, like, really big and not like major group, like, we do activities and stuff like that and it's, you know, fun." The overall impression from Trevor's narrative is that adoption is a minor part of his life that he has not spent much time or energy contemplating.

Many adolescents in this group had not thought about adoption issues raised by the interview and often answered questions with "I don't know," or provided short statements as answers. As seen in Table 6.1, these adolescents exhibited the lowest mean scores on all variables except Negative Affect. Most of these narratives showed no depth in exploration of adoptive identity and

TABLE 6.1
Means (M) and Standard Deviations (SD) of Identity Variables by Adoptive Identity Type

		Type					
Variable		*Unexamined* *24*	*Limited* *46*	*Unsettled* *30*	*Integrated* *45*	F[†]	η^2
							.50
Exploration	M	1.17[a]	2.15[b]	2.83[c]	3.47[d]	113.63	.71
	SD	0.38	0.47	0.65	0.55		
Salience	M	1.17[a]	2.13[b]	3.17[c]	2.98[c]	74.23	.61
	SD	0.38	0.54	0.65	0.62		
Internal consistency	M	2.46[a]	3.09[b]	3.60[c]	4.36[d]	53.33	.53
	SD	0.83	0.46	0.81	0.57		
Flexibility	M	2.46[a]	3.07[b]	3.07[b]	4.29[c]	44.93	.49
	SD	0.78	0.68	0.74	0.63		
Positive affect	M	1.38[a]	2.67[b]	2.87[b]	3.69[c]	49.49	.51
	SD	0.65	0.60	0.90	0.85		
Negative affect	M	1.42[a]	1.39[a]	3.57[b]	1.67[a]	67.19	.59
	SD	0.78	0.58	0.82	0.74		

Note. Pillai's Trace = 1.50, $p < .001$. [†]Reported F values refer to follow-up univariate tests; all F tests significant at $p < .001$; df = 3, 141. Different superscripts in the same row denote significant differences between means, using planned comparisons with Bonferroni adjustment.

revealed no salience of the adoptive identity for the adolescent (see Table 6.2 for details). The internal consistency of most narratives was very low, indicating loose theories with little support. Narrative flexibility followed a similar pattern, with most narratives revealing a low to moderate ability to perspective-take or explore new ideas. Little emotion was displayed in the majority of the narratives. Adolescents with narratives in this type were more likely to be male and more often in confidential adoptions (see Table 6.3).

Several themes emerged from these narratives that provide insight into the evident lack of exploration. Some adolescents' disinterest in understanding more about their adoption and what it means to them seemed tied to their feelings of rejection by their birth parents ("I guess if they sent me up for adoption, they didn't want me then, I don't think they would want me now"; "If they wanted me to live with them then they wouldn't have put me up for adoption"). Other adolescents reported a hesitancy to delve deeper into adoption issues because they were happy with the way their lives were currently ("I'm happy just the way I am . . .") or because they were afraid that exploring

TABLE 6.2
Percentage of Cases for Identity Variables Within Adoptive Identity Types

	Type			
Variable	*Unexamined* *24*	*Limited* *46*	*Unsettled* *30*	*Integrated* *45*
Exploration				
No/minimal	83.3%	4.3%		
Low	16.7%	76.1%	30.0%	2.2%
Moderate		19.6%	56.7%	48.9%
Great			13.3%	48.9%
Salience				
No/minimal	83.3%	8.7%		
Low	16.7%	69.6%	6.4%	17.8%
Moderate		21.7%	66.7%	68.9%
Moderate/high			20.0%	11.1%
High			3.3%	2.2%
Internal consistency				
No theory	8.3%			
Unsupported	50.0%	6.5%	3.3%	
Some support	29.2%	78.3%	50.0%	4.4%
In progress	12.5%	15.2%	30.0%	55.6%
Well-documented			16.7%	40.0%
Flexibility				
Low/rigid	8.3%		3.3%	
Moderate/low	45.8%	19.6%	13.3%	
Moderate	37.5%	54.3%	56.7%	8.9%
Moderate/high	8.3%	26.1%	26.7%	53.3%
High				37.8%
Positive affect				
No/minimal	70.8%	2.2%	6.7%	
Low	20.8%	32.6%	23.3%	2.2%
Moderate	8.3%	60.9%	50.0%	48.9%
Moderate/strong		4.3%	16.7%	26.7%
Strong			3.3%	22.2%
Negative affect				
No/minimal	75.0%	65.2%		46.7%
Low	8.3%	30.4%	3.3%	42.2%
Moderate	16.7%	1.4%	53.3%	8.9%
Moderate/strong			26.7%	2.2%
Strong			16.7%	

TABLE 6.3
Age, Gender, and Adoption Openness Within Adoptive Identity Type

	Type			
Variable	*Unexamined* *24*	*Limited* *46*	*Unsettled* *30*	*Integrated* *45*
Age				
Mean	14.87	15.18	15.21	16.67[1]
Range	12.72–18.11	11.51–20.84	11.10–19.11	12.75–20.56
Gender[2]				
Female (75)	33.3%	47.8%	60.0%	57.8%
Male (70)	66.7%	52.5%	40.0%	42.2%
Openness[3]				
Confidential (38)	41.7%	26.1%	13.3%	26.7%
Mediated (36)	29.2%	32.6%	20.0%	17.8%
Fully disclosed (71)	29.2%	41.3%	66.7%	55.6 %

Note. [1]Integrated adolescents were older than those in all other groups [$F(3,144) = 6.83, p < .001$]. [2]Gender was unequally distributed across types [$\chi^2(3, N = 145) = 5.59, p = .03$]. [3]In openness groups, identity types were unequally distributed within fully disclosed adoptions [$\chi^2(3, N = 145) = 9.85, p = .02$].

adoption issues would be uncomfortable or take them somewhere they didn't want to go ("This is my life and I'm happy with it . . . opening adoption would 'drag something into a hole.' " . . . "Because I feel like it's over and that I'm happy where I am and I just don't want to mess with that other part."). Finally, many narratives were characterized by the minimization of adoption as a relevant issue for the adolescent ("Adoption is irrelevant to everything, it has no part in it really"; "I don't really think about adoption that much so it's just, I probably don't even realize that I am.").

Limited Identity. At 13½, Jason has begun to do some degree of thinking about how adoption relates to who he is. He remembers being told he was adopted by his parents, but his memory is vague and he feels the disclosure had little impact on him: "I know it was when I was young, because I've always known about it, but, I don't really remember what age I was at. I mean it was like, I'm sure it was probably when I was like, 6 or, 5, 6 or 7, but, I may not have understood what it meant then, but I know, I remember being told about it, back then. . . . My mom and dad adopted me in like some court or, something it was, like, I remember being told that my birthmom like had us in a special court and they handled or they, adopted me and I'm really not sure like what I was first told, like, how my mom told me that she wasn't my real mom. . . . It didn't really make any difference to me because I still love my mom and dad because they're the ones who raised me everything and, didn't really make me feel any different than how I already was."

He doesn't feel a strong need to talk about adoption and the conversations that he does have with others are infrequent and unemotional; however, he also recognizes that, "I mean, you have to be like a strong person like, to be able to like take all the questions that people ask you." He doesn't really talk with his parents about it anymore, "I think before, they, I just ask them questions about it, they'd answer me about that . . . we used to talk about it more, like I didn't know as much about everything." When he talks with his friends he just tries to explain adoption as well as he can, but he'd rather "just like to have fun." His interactions with his birth mother are also low-key: "I just talk her sometimes on the phone or I write letters and, pretty much, I don't feel like I really need to have to talk about it like, I'm not happy with myself or something."

His description of his meeting with his birth mother and family is matter-of-fact: "We just, they just came in and we talked for a while and then, my little, half-brother really, really liked balls so, we like played baseball outside with him and, that's what we did most the time and then we ate." He doesn't feel a sense of urgency around needing to see his birth family again, "Whenever we have time to would be nice, like we're going to go down for a basketball tournament this year but, we couldn't go down for that. So, we'll probably make another time sometime, I'm not sure when, though." For him the meetings are enjoyable, although he "Felt nervous before, during it was fun because I got to know them and knew what they liked to do." After the meeting, "I thought, I was like happy that I met them and I thought it was pretty fun that we had done that."

He likes his birth mother and thinks of her as, "just another friend that we can have, that I can have and, I'm not sure really." He doesn't "really get bothered or worried by anything really, about them ever." He believes his birth mother is "Happy, like because I just get to see her and my mom and dad write to her and tell her how I do and everything so. And I don't really know like what she expects from me and I think she's just happy that I, we keep in touch with her and I write letters and stuff." At this point, knowing his birth mother does not have intense emotional meaning for him.

He feels positively about the connections he has with his birth mother and her family, but would like to know more about his birth father, "I'd like to know what my dad looks like, and where he is now. Pretty much, I'd just be able to, I know quite a bit about my mom and I'd be able to find out more about her because I know where she is and, if I really want to get in touch with her, I'd be able to." He enjoys exchanging gifts with his birth family, "I like it because I feel good that I can send or they send stuff to me and I can send stuff to them, it makes me feel good I kind-of like, makes them, I don't know, little kids happy too, and so," and feels lucky that he receives things from them, "I feel like, fortunate that they send stuff to me that they care enough to send stuff."

He reveals some ways that he thinks adoption connects with his life, but he has not thought deeply about these linkages. He has musical talent like his birth grandfather, ". . . he played musical instruments and I do too. So, my mom and dad told me that . . . that I had talents like he did. . . . I just all of a sudden like, was I like wanted to play the cello[2] and stuff and I was pretty good at it, for not practicing very much." Adoption does not affect his future: "marriage any way or having children or adopting and I'm pretty sure we'd try and have children first, but like, and if we wouldn't I'm sure I'd try and adopt some kid." He recognizes his life would be somewhat different if he had not been adopted, but he believes he would not be much different, "Well I know I'd be in a different town. I'd have a stepdad and two, a half-brother and a half-sister. Well, I think I'd be the same kind of person though, because my mom is really nice and friendly and, I don't think it would be too much different from this."

His views about the meaning of adoption and family are tied to religion; however, he has difficulty clearly articulating his beliefs, ". . . my mom has this thing that she says, like when I'm asleep sometimes she like comes in my room and like, says this thing like, it's like, " 'You're flesh in my flesh, no bone in my bone so miraculously of my own, I'll never forget for a single minute you didn't grow under my heart but in it.' But, I like, that's kind-of like spiritual and stuff and has something to do with it." Although the connections he has made are not easily apparent in his narrative, the meaning for him helps to explain extended family ties: "With my extended family, like even though I'm not really blood-related to them I mean, it still feels good to know that they love me even though, I'm not really blood-related to them. And that's like a positive feeling."

Although he has mentioned various ways being adopted is a unique experience (having birth family, not being blood-related) he also believes that being adopted is just like not being adopted, "I would say, I don't know, it's just like being like a real kid and, your parent, you still have like, you still have the right over the kid and like, the parents have the say in everything and it's just like a normal, your own child."

[2] Potentially identifying details have been changed.

Most adolescents in this group were willing to think about and discuss adoption, but did not recognize it as a huge issue in their lives. As seen in Table 6.1, these adolescents exhibited scores in the mid-range on most variables. The narratives of most of these adolescents showed modest depth in the exploration of adoptive identity and revealed little salience attached to the adoptive identity (see Table 6.2 for details). In general, these narratives contained simple theories that had sparse supporting evidence and showed moderate flexibility. Moderately intense expression of positive affect, accompanied by a range of *no* to *low negative affect* was found in over half of the narratives.

Both boys and girls were equally represented in this type and participated in a range of openness contexts (see Table 6.3). In confidential adoptions contact was seen as potentially disruptive and some adolescents reported fear, mostly when they were younger, about birth parents coming to reclaim them. In mediated adoptions most adolescents planned to contact their birthmothers at age 18. In adoptions where contact had stopped, the thought of reinitiating contact brought up feelings of awkwardness, "I don't know what I'd say if I saw her." However, for those who wished to meet birth parents, most desired only to see if there were physical similarities with birthparents; very few wished to establish a relationship or meet birth parents to answer deeper questions about the self. In fully disclosed adoptions, contact was seen as normal, and the relationship with the birth mother was often close.

Adolescents in this group downplayed differences between adopted and nonadopted families. Adoption was presented as being not any different from not being adopted ("There's no difference between whether I was their child, their real child, or theirs like I am now." "You know you're adopted, you're adopted, you know. It's not any different than if you were not adopted."). Perhaps consequently, few discussions about adoption took place within the family. Most of these narratives presented adoption with an air of matter-of-factness and with little emotional charge. Adoption was portrayed as accepted fact that happened in the past and that hasn't had much impact on one's life ("I don't think too much about adoption. It's not a big issue in my life. I feel it's happened, you can't change that." "It's just that it happened. I'm glad it happened instead of abortion, but, you know, besides that, it just happened." "I'm fine with it (adoption) and it's just a thing of the past."). Most adolescents viewed adoption simply as a benevolent act that helps out a child by giving them a chance at a better life, and also by some as helping birth parents to achieve their own goals in life such as finishing an education or eventually obtaining a better job. Adolescents also acknowledged experiencing a fluctuation in the frequency and intensity of thought about adoption over time ("Sometimes it's important to me and sometimes it isn't"). Many reported talking about adoption more in the past and felt that adoption was more important to them when they were younger. Adolescents' mainly positive acceptance of their adoption and denial of differences due to adoption, combined with low levels of curiosity and little emotional involvement, seem to have led to limited exploration about adoption.

Unsettled Identity. Kelsey, who is 16 and in a fully disclosed adoption, tells a story that shows she is working out her adoption-related thoughts and feelings. Throughout her narrative she mentions the emergence of uncomfortable or negative thoughts and feelings that she alternatively ponders for extended periods of time or tries to push out of her consciousness. For example, when describing conversations with others she says, "I don't like to talk about adoption, I don't want to talk about it all the time. . . . If I talk to people it's mostly about the adoption process. . . . Sometimes I open up and talk to people, but it doesn't happen very often. I just think a lot, like, during the conversation and afterwards and I just kind of, I don't know, I feel different because no one else has the experience I have. I always get this weird feeling. And then I have to think forever about it. I'm just better if I don't think about it. I always just wonder, like, little things, like, details about, like . . . people always know, like, what time they were born. That's always bothered me that I don't know that and just, like, I don't know."

She has strong positive and negative feelings about her relationship with her birthparents that she has examined to varying degrees. At one point she declares she knows "as much as I want to know (about my birth parents)." However, she also describes her curiosity about her birthfather, although she limits her thinking about him: "I don't think about my birth dad very often. My (birth) mom has made an effort to try to talk to me, so she should get to know more than he should—he shouldn't get to know anything. . . . I don't know if he'd like to know anything because he hasn't tried. I don't know if he wants to know about me, or . . . I kind of just want to know where he's at or what he's doing with his life, but I don't know if there's a way I can find that out so I don't really think about that." She enjoys exchanging pictures and letters with her birth mother: "I like to have pictures, actually, because then I can show my friends that this is who my mom is, this is who my little brother and sister are (both laugh). And I like getting letters because I like to hear what she has to say. The pictures are my favorite probably." But she continues to speculate about unanswered questions: "I always wonder, like, what she was like when she was my age, what kind of things she did, if we looked alike at all . . . she's always just the person I'd wondered about, I don't ever know about her."

Kelsey feels uncomfortable when she has direct contact with her birth mother but hasn't really examined why she feels this way: "We talked and I felt really uncomfortable. I don't know, she cried, and she was hugging me, it was just weird. You're excited, but and you want to see them, but then as soon as you see them it's . . . it changes all of a sudden. Like, I remember I was so excited, but during it, not excited at all. (laughs) . . . back then I was just, like, "Oh, now I've met my birthmom" no big deal kind of thing, but I didn't really think much afterwards . . . I just told my (adoptive) mom I didn't like it and it was uncomfortable and I probably didn't want to do it again for awhile, so she's waiting." She is angry that her birth mother didn't want to tell her kids about Kelsey. "I think the one thing that bothers me the most is the fact that she wasn't going to tell her kids about me, until we kind of pushed it. And I don't know why she should have to hide that from them . . . I mean they're young and they'll understand it and then they'll grow up knowing. I think that's fair, more fair to them than just popping it up one day. Other than that I respect her wishes. . . . Sometimes I question what she did, but that's her choice." Although these feelings are difficult for her, she continues to feel positively about contact with her birth family in the future, "I've always just wanted to get to spend time with my mom (birth) and my little brother and sister and my grandma and I hope that I'll be able to do that someday without feeling uncomfortable. She is (a part of my life). Not a huge part because I don't see her very often and I don't really talk to her. She's definitely a part."

Kelsey believes adoption is tough. "(Adoption is) a great learning opportunity, I mean, I've learned a lot from it, but it also it has a bad times to it, it's not just perfect, you know, like, it's a lot harder than just having your own kids." She attributes the distance in her relationship with her adoptive mom to adoption, "My mom (adoptive) and I aren't very close and I know that's (adoption) the reason. I mean if, I'm sure if I lived with my real mom we'd be a lot closer, we'd talk about it and that's just hard because all my friends can talk to their moms." And she believes her relationship with her parents would be better and more open if she were their biological child. Due to these beliefs she thinks those considering adoption should, "know what they're getting into before they just go and adopt, I mean I think they should really think about it and I'm sure my parents probably did, but there's always going to be struggles with adoption and people are just going to have to understand that." However, she would hesitate to adopt, herself: "I would probably never adopt. Well, as much as I want to have kids, if I couldn't I don't, I don't know. Just seeing what our family has gone through, I don't think I want to put my family through that. . . . we always get in little fights about, you know, 'I want to go with my mom, I don't want to live here, I hate you guys.' You know, when really we should be thankful for them adopting us, instead of being nowhere. It's just not a perfect scenario."

A high degree of negative affect was attached to the adoptive identity of most adolescents in the Unsettled group. These adolescents were in the process of sorting out their feelings around their adoptions ("I'm still kind of trying to figure out that one (adoption)," "I have questions I know there's no answers for."). As seen in Table 6.1, narratives of adolescents in this group exhibited the highest scores on salience and negative affect. Over half of the adolescents produced narratives showing evidence of the existence of an adoptive identity that mattered to the adolescent and more than one fifth of the remaining narratives displayed higher levels of salience in which the adoptive identity was more prominent or important than all other identities (see Table 6.2 for details). A large range of intensity of affect was present in the narratives. Most narratives included moderate positive affect. With one exception, moderate or greater levels of negative affect were expressed in the narratives, and the expression of negative affect usually either equaled the expression of positive affect ($n = 10$; 33.3%) or outweighed that of positive affect by one or two degrees ($n = 14$; 46.7%). However, in five narratives the expression of positive in comparison to negative affect was more prevalent by one degree. Most narratives revealed some substantial thinking in the exploration of adoptive identity. In general, these narratives contained theories that were either both simple and consistent with some support by limited evidence or in the process of development with emerging complexity. Similar to the Limited type, most narratives showed moderate flexibility. Adolescents with narratives in this type were more likely to be female and participating in fully disclosed adoptions (see Table 6.3).

Most adolescents expressed dissatisfaction about the frequency, consistency, and intensity of contact with birthparents. In general, adolescents in confidential adoptions were bothered by the lack of information about their backgrounds and wanted to search, although they were ambivalent about making contact. Adolescents in mediated and fully disclosed adoptions were troubled by inconsistent contact with their birth mothers. Across all openness levels adolescents expressed frustration with inadequate information about birth fathers and resentment towards those who broke promises, were disinterested, absent, or lied. Adolescents expressed anger and sadness toward birth parents due to feelings of rejection around the initial placement ("She chose not to be a part of my life, so I chose for her not to be a part of mine.") and additional rejection when contact in mediated and fully disclosed adoptions stopped ("I'm glad that she made the right choice with giving us up for adoption, but I'm mad that she hasn't tried to get a hold of us, and then kept in touch with the adoption agency. To see if we could meet her."). Adolescents used phrases such as "thrown out," "gotten rid of," "discarded," and "trashed kid" to describe themselves.

Negative feelings were also expressed around interactions with peers, relationships within the adoptive family, and relationships between the adoptive and birth families. Many adolescents confronted teasing from peers or dealt with conversations where others didn't understand adoption. Almost half of the adolescents mentioned that adoption created some degree of difference in their families ("Sometimes it makes me feel left out . . . like I'm not part of the family or anything," "It will probably be harder for them because, they might not feel like really attached because they're not blood related.") Adolescents also mentioned problems in the adoptive family due to adoption, such as feelings of distance among family members, especially between adoptive mothers and daughters, or conflict between the adolescent and adoptive siblings or cousins. Across openness levels adolescents expressed concern about the relationship between the adoptive and birth families, including anxiety about hurting adoptive parents by initiating a search or becoming too close to the birth mother, distress around hostility between the two sets of parents ("I need to keep them from being mad at each other and stuff"), or feelings that the two families were very different ("I have two separate families," "It's like two different cultures."). In some instances the culmination of multiple negative experiences around adoption resulted in adolescents who had decided never to adopt in the future ("Well, hopefully I won't have to adopt because I know what it's like for kids and the parents. Because, I mean, I feel different than them, and so I don't want my kids to feel different than me. . . . I don't want to have my kids be adopted, because then I guess I would just feel less and less complete."). In summary, adolescents in the Unsettled group were in the process of working through their feelings around their adoption, principally in relation to their birth parents.

Integrated Identity. In her narrative, Jody clearly explained how important her adoption is to her. At 17, she has thought a great deal about her confidential adoption, especially in relation to her birth parents. She has gained an understanding of herself by considering who she is in relation to both her adoptive and birth parents. "My birth father, was like a mechanic or something. And I like, I'm always—my hands are always moving and I'm always wanting to fix things and work with my hands which I don't know if that has anything to do with it (both laugh) but I just think that is kind of neat. And I know that, from the papers, I know that she (birth mother) has like, I think it says she either has blue or grey eyes and I have blue eyes, so it's like—and my dad (birth) has grey eyes. So, I think that that's where I got my eyes from and my hair color, too, because she has the same color hair as me and that (pause) I think that—yeah, she was like five six and I think I'm five six now. . . . I am very thankful that I have, I think some of her characteristics, I don't know. And I think that I have a pretty good personality which, you know, some people say you get your personality from people you are around most like your parents that you grew up with, but I'm nothing like my—NOTHING like my mom (adoptive), nothing at all. And it's, I mean, I guess, I agree with her on some things but I'm more like my dad than her and so I think that if anyone, I got most of my personality from probably, you know, just through my blood or however you get it and from my dad that I live with, also."

Jody has examined how adoption issues relate to her life in many ways. She has considered how her life might have been different if she hadn't been adopted, "Well if I was living with my birth mother still I'm sure it would be—I would be a totally different person because I would either see myself as being a much stronger person for having to deal with the struggles that I'm sure there would be, you know, many of them or I could see myself as being really weak for feeling let down by the life I was living if that's the way it was and if that's the way it wasn't then, I don't know." At one time she felt pressured to be active in the Methodist Church because she knows her birth mother is Methodist and she "felt the only way to relate to her was to go to church." She wants to volunteer to "talk with people who are adopted" and thinks that she gets the strength to "do good" from reflecting on what a tough decision her birth mother made. She is determined to get a good job in the future so she can feel good about herself when she meets her birth mother.

Jody spends a great deal of time and emotional energy thinking about contacting her birth mother. "When I talk to Joel (boyfriend) about it, I just I get off the phone with him whatever and I just, like, bawl my eyes out. I'm just like, 'Ahhhhhh! Do I look like her? Where is she, where is she?' you know, and it's just because I want so badly just a picture or a letter or something. Could be anything. You know, and I've—a lot of times I've thought well maybe if I go to the high school and look in the yearbooks in like '77 and look for somebody who looks like me. I mean, just little daydreams like that that are so dumb just get me so worked up. And I just, you know, talk to people about it and then sometimes I feel better, like, 'Ok, just calm down.' But sometimes I feel like 'Ahhh! What's going to happen in the next few years?' you know, because I don't know."

She wonders if her birth mother remembers her. "My dad (adoptive) and I had a conversation once about if she thinks about me or if she just tried to forget about me. He just told me, he's like, 'don't worry about that. Ninety-five percent of the people that we've talked with still have never forgotten about their kids whether they be eighty years old or whether it just happened a week ago.' So, it makes me feel really good knowing that, you know, maybe she is—and especially right now being my birthday and everything. I wonder if she's thinking about me now because, like, she had me, you know, so."

Meeting her birth mother is Jody's "lifetime dream." She repeatedly tries to get more information about her adoption from her mother and reminds her father that she will begin her search when she turns 18. "Sometimes I talk to her (adoptive mom) about, like, if she knows anything. I try and push things out of her like, 'Are you sure you don't know anything more?' And I get so mad at her, I'm like, 'Are you sure, are you sure?' . . . And my dad and I, we don't really talk about it that much but I told him, I said, 'You know, when I turn eighteen, we are going down to the agency and I'm looking in that file.'" She attributes some of her motivation for searching to the distance she feels with her adoptive mother. She wants to meet her birth mother, not to replace her adoptive mother, but because she wants more of a "mother figure." She has strong feelings for her birth mother and feels connected to her, "Even though I don't know her personally, it's like I'm a part of her, a very big part of her. And so, I like I love her in a way, you know, just for knowing that she's there . . ."

At the core of Jody's narrative are her conflicted and sad feelings about the importance of biological connectedness and belonging. She doesn't feel bad about being adopted but, she is always so "envious of how my step sister and brothers look exactly like my step-mom. . . . So, I mean, I don't feel bad about it but I just—I feel kind of lonely sometimes." These feelings are plainly in her discussion about marriage and children, "I think that for marriage and for having children, I think that having my own kids is like the most important thing that a marriage would bring to me because it would be like children that I'm starting a whole new background with, you know, if I never met my birth mother. . . . Like, because I know that knowing my grandparents now that I have I WISHED that they were my real grandparents because it's like they have such a great background. So that's what I would want to start is just a, you know, a background for my kids, just somebody who I could call my own. My own blood, my own everything, you know."

Jody concludes her narrative by expressing her urgency around contacting her birth mother, "All I can think of is is there is any way possible, like, ever to have contact with like my birth fam—my birth mother. That would just be like. If I ever knew anybody who could help me with that then I want to know who they are because that's like really important to me and I just want somehow for, you know, because I've been told that my birth mother might have moved to the south somewhere to live with her parents or something, or with his parents. So, they might not even be living in California anymore and if they're not then they might not have as easy access into my files."

Adolescents whose narratives showed an Integrated Identity had been able to incorporate negative and positive aspects of their adoption into a serviceable identity for the present and an adaptive sense of self for the future. These adolescents exhibited the highest scores on all variables except for salience and negative affect (see Table 6.1). With one exception, these narratives showed moderate to great depth in the exploration of adoptive identity (see Table 6.2 details). Over three quarters of the adolescents produced narratives with moderate or greater salience showing evidence of the existence of an adoptive identity that mattered to the adolescent; the remainder of the narratives showed lower salience in which the adoptive identity was portrayed with a sense of "matter-of-factness." In general, these narratives contained theories that showed moderately high flexibility and were either in the process of development, with emerging complexity, or well documented, with detailed and synthesizing explanations. All narratives showed at least a moderate degree of positive or negative affect, and were characterized by either balanced levels of positive and negative affect ($n = 5$; 11.1%) or greater positive than negative affect ($n = 40$; 88.9%). With one exception, moderate or greater levels of positive affect were expressed, and the expression of positive affect frequently outweighed that of negative affect by two or more points ($n = 29$; 64.4%). Adolescents with narratives categorized as Integrated were significantly older than adolescents in all other types and were more likely to be female and participating in fully disclosed adoptions (see Table 6.3).

Many adolescents with narratives in this type recalled feeling "special" or "wanted" when told about their adoption, and viewed their adoption as a positive and happy thing ("I kind of felt that it was a blessing . . . like I had more family added to my family tree so I thought it was pretty cool," "a secret family that only I know about but I didn't know who they were, that loved me."). These adolescents had imputed prosocial motives to their birth parents' placement decisions, believing that their birth parents had placed them with the child's best interest in mind, because they were too young to parent and wanted a better life for the child. In addition, birthparents were described with sympathy and compassion, and adolescents were willing to try to understand their actions ("Probably one of the hardest things a person could ever do is give up their child"). Several narratives revealed the importance of God in understanding adoption ("He chose this place, what I needed and was going to need," "He chose for me to be adopted, I think that was part of what He wanted for me," "I thank God for the family I have. I think He put me here so I could grow up to be the person I want to be").

In general, relations with birth family members were depicted as safe, understandable, and rewarding. In circumstances in which little information was known about birth fathers, adolescents were likely to reserve judgment rather than to assume a negative view. Across openness levels, adolescents expressed motivation to further connections to birth family members. In confidential adoptions most adolescents expressed a desire to search for their birth parents. Adolescents in mediated adoptions wanted increased contact or openness. In fully disclosed adoptions, most adolescents either expressed satisfaction with their relationships or wanted more contact currently or in the future. Adolescents described establishing contact or initiating deeper relationships with birth parents as opportunities for self-discovery ("The part that interests me the most about it, it's just discovering why I am the way I am," "I want to see someone who looks like me because it's the sense that 'yes I belong in this family and stuff, but not really that I am connected to the world,'" "Finding a piece of the puzzle, that's what you're doing," "It's neat getting to know them because everything I learn about them, it's something more I learn about me").

Several narratives suggested that the adolescent had worked through challenging feelings about adoption at an earlier time. Some adolescents described how their feelings about being adopted changed as they matured ("As I grew older I realized it was the best thing for me at the time," "When I was little I worried I was placed because she didn't want me, now I know I was placed because she cared enough," "I felt different, then I started to understand and I felt special"). Other adolescents mentioned adoption was a more important issue in the past (it "consumed my childhood") and this was supported by reports that adolescents no longer discussed adoption with their parents, in part because all their questions had been answered ("I mean quite frankly, everything's been said about that that can be said").

DISCUSSION

This chapter has probed the process of meaning-making for adolescents who were adopted and has identified four patterns of adoptive identity based on narrative criteria. Adolescents whose adoptive identities are Unexamined have not very actively considered the meaning of adoption to them. They do not consider adoption to be a very salient issue, and little positive or negative affect is associated with their view of adoption. Although Unexamined identities were found across all groups of adolescents, those in this category were most often younger, male, and in confidential adoptions. Adolescents in the Limited group had explored adoptive identity to a modest degree but did not feel that it was very important in their lives. They downplayed the difference between adoptive and nonadoptive families, but generally viewed adoption as positive for all concerned. This group included both males and females from different openness arrangements. Adolescents with Unsettled identities had thought a great deal about adoption and typically harbored feelings of rejection and anger. They tended to be females and in fully disclosed adoptions. Finally, adolescents with an Integrated adoptive identity had typically thought a great deal of adoption and had developed a coherent, positive view of adoption and what it meant in their lives. In comparison to the other participants in the study, these adolescents tended to be older, female, and from fully disclosed adoptions.

The patterns revealed in this narrative analysis are consistent with an Eriksonian perspective on identity development. The most extensive research in the Eriksonian tradition has identified four identity statuses, which are based on combinations of identity exploration and commitment (e.g., Marcia, Waterman, Matteson, Archer, & Orlofsky, 1993). Our Unexamined and Integrated types fit most clearly within the identity status framework because these types vary most obviously along the dimensions of exploration and commitment. Diffusion is a pattern characterized by minimal consideration of alternatives for one's identity and minimal commitment to a life choice. Our Unexamined type is similar to diffusion, in that these adolescents have thought little about their adoptive identity and consider it unimportant in their lives. Identity achievement is noted when the adolescent has explored a number of alternatives and has made a commitment in that domain. This is consistent with our Integrated type, in which the adolescent has explored the meaning of adoptive identity and can articulate it in the context of positive and negative affect. Our other two types, Limited and Unsettled, fit less clearly within an identity status framework because adolescents within each of these types varied to a greater extent in the amount of exploration they had undertaken. In addition, in mapping these types to the identity status framework, our narrative variables of internal consistency and flexibility provide only a loose proxy for the dimension of commitment. In our typology, adolescents with foreclosure status can be found in the Limited type, as demonstrated by narratives with key themes of acceptance of adoption as a little explored and unchangeable fact that happened in the past (like an ascribed identity). Adolescents in the moratorium status, who are actively engaging identity options but have not yet made commitments, can be located mostly within the Unsettled type.

Despite the similarities between the identity statuses and the narrative adoptive identity patterns revealed in this chapter, the two systems differ in significant ways because they use different metaphors to characterize identity and identity development. The identity statuses are based on adolescents' actions: to what degree have ideas been considered and have commitments been made? These particular actions are paramount during adolescence because they are stage-specific responses to the challenges adolescents experience to their developing sense of competence (Côté & Levine, 2002).

The narrative approach uses a different metaphor: that of the story. The adolescent's task is to construct a story that gives meaning to his or her life—in this case, specifically about adoption—considered in light of the adolescent's expanding abilities to understand adoption in all its social, legal, ethical, and biological complexity. Although identity exploration is common to the Eriksonian and narrative systems, the narrative patterns also focus on coherence of the story, the narrator's flexibility in articulating it, the salience of adoptive identity among other identity domains, and the affect in which it is embedded.

Future research should address potential developmental pathways in identity formation. The presence of a developmental progression through the four identity statuses of Marcia and colleagues (i.e., diffusion, moratorium, foreclosure, identity achievement) has been vigorously debated (e.g., van Hoof, 1999; Waterman, 1999). Some statuses appear to be less "mature" than others when judged by certain criteria. For example, identity achievement implies extensive exploration of options for one's identity and commitment to a clear choice, whereas diffusion implies absence of both exploration and commitment. However, longitudinal research has revealed that identity development can be cyclical rather than linear. Marcia (1993) noted the discovery of cycles of moratorium-achievement-moratorium-achievement, wherein adolescents move from a state of indecision to one of commitment, but then later move back to a position of indecision, albeit usually at a more sophisticated developmental level. Adolescents do not follow a single developmental progression from one of the identity patterns to another. However, longitudinal analysis of the narrative data should provide new insights into alternative developmental pathways and the more general developmental process of identity development.

This research has implications for professionals who work with adopted adolescents. First, it acknowledges the complexity of the identity development process and implies that parents, teachers, and mental health professionals need to understand and accept the diversity of ways in which adolescents construct their adoptive identities. Second, it suggests the importance of providing an information-rich environment for adolescents so that their sense of adoptive identity is based on fact rather than fantasy or assumption. Third, the insights generated by the narrative approach reinforce the usefulness of tools such as "life books" in working with children and adolescents who are actively exploring identity issues. Finally, these results suggest that resolution of identity issues takes time and the willingness to engage the topic (Grotevant, 1987). Although adolescents with Unexplored identities tended to be younger and those with Integrated identities tended to be older, there was considerable variation across the sample.

In the next stage of our longitudinal work with these adolescents, we will be able to examine continuities and discontinuities in adoptive identity development. Which of the four groups was most likely to show change from adolescence to young adulthood? What happened to the adolescents with negative, unsettled identities when we first interviewed them? Were they able to step back from their pain and anger and develop integrated identities with a different balance of positive to negative affect? Or did their negativity harden over time? How stable were integrated identities? Under what circumstances did adolescents with integrated identities during adolescence reconsider their views and move into a phase of unsettledness or negativity? We will be able to answer these and related questions when we embark on the next phase of our research, which follows up these participants in young adulthood.

REFERENCES

Côté, J. E., & Levine, C. G. (2002). *Identity formation, agency, and culture.* Mahwah, NJ: Lawrence Erlbaum Associates.

Dunbar, N. (2003). *Adoptive identity: A narrative approach.* Unpublished doctoral dissertation, University of Minnesota, St. Paul.

Erikson, E. H. (1968) *Identity: Youth and crisis.* New York: Norton.

Fiese, B. H., Sameroff, A. J., Grotevant, H. D., Wamboldt, F. S., Dickstein, S., & Fravel, D. L. (1999). The stories that families tell: Narrative coherence, narrative style, and relationship beliefs. *Monographs of the Society for Research in Child Development, 64*(2, Serial No. 257).

Grotevant, H. D. (1987). Toward a process model of identity formation. *Journal of Adolescent Research, 2,* 203–222.

Grotevant, H. D. (1993). The integrative nature of identity: Bringing the soloists to sing in the choir. In J. Kroger (Ed.), *Discussions on ego identity* (pp. 121–146). Hillsdale, NJ: Lawrence Erlbaum Associates.

Grotevant, H. D. (1997). Coming to terms with adoption: The construction of identity from adolescence into adulthood. *Adoption Quarterly, 1*(1), 3–27.

Grotevant, H. D., Dunbar, N., Kohler, J. K., & Esau, A. L. (2000). Adoptive identity: How contexts within and beyond the family shape developmental pathways. *Family Relations, 49,* 379–387.

Grotevant, H. D., & Kohler, J. K. (1999). Adoptive families. In M. Lamb (Ed.), *Nontraditional families: Parenting and child development* (2nd ed., pp. 161–190). Mahwah, NJ: Lawrence Erlbaum Associates.

Grotevant, H. D., & McRoy, R. G. (1998). *Openness in adoption: Connecting families of birth and adoption.* Newbury Park, CA: Sage.

Habermas, T., & Bluck, S. (2000). Getting a life: The emergence of the life story in adolescence. *Psychological Bulletin, 126,* 748–769.

Hair, J. F., & Black, W. C. (2000). Cluster analysis. In L. G. Grimm & P. R. Yarnold (Eds.), *Reading and understanding more multivariate statistics* (pp. 147–205). Washington, DC: American Psychological Association.

Marcia, J. E. (1993). The identity status approach to ego identity. In J. E. Marcia, A. S. Waterman, D. R. Matteson, S. L. Archer, & J. L. Orlofsky (Eds.), *Ego identity: A handbook for psychosocial research* (pp. 1–21). New York: Springer-Verlag.

Marcia, J. E., Waterman, A. S., Matteson, D. R., Archer, S. L., & Orlofsky, J. L. (1993). *Ego identity: A handbook for psychosocial research.* New York: Springer-Verlag.

McAdams, D. P. (1987). A life-story model of identity. In R. Hogan & W. Jones (Eds.), *Perspectives in personality* (Vol. 2, pp. 15–50). Greenwich, CT: JAI Press.

McAdams, D. P. (1993). *The stories we live by: Personal myths and the making of the self.* New York: Morrow.

McAdams, D. P. (2001). The psychology of life stories. *Review of General Psychology, 5,* 100–122.

Moshman, D. (1998). Identity as a theory of oneself. *The Genetic Epistemologist, 26*(3), 1–16. [available online: www.piaget.org/GE/1998/GE-26–3.html]

Polkinghorne, D. E. (1991). Narrative and self-concept. *Journal of Narrative and Life History, 1*(2–3), 135–153.

van Hoof, A. (1999). The identity status field re-reviewed: An update of unresolved and neglected issues with a view on some alternative approaches. *Developmental Review, 19,* 497–556.

Waterman, A. S. (1999). Identity, the identity statuses, and identity status development: A contemporary statement. *Developmental Review, 19,* 591–621.

Wrobel, G. M., Kohler, J. K., Grotevant, H. D., & McRoy, R. G. (in press). The family adoption communication model (FAC): Identifying pathways of adoption-related communication. *Adoption Quarterly.*

7

Adolescents' Representations of Parents' Voices in Family Stories: Value Lessons, Personal Adjustment, and Identity Development

Mary Louise Arnold
University of Toronto

Michael W. Pratt
Cheryl Hicks
Wilfrid Laurier University

> *I remember when I was little once, I was making fun of this little girl. She was, like, weird looking. I was just, like, "Oh, my God, she's so weird." And my mom was, like, "Don't do that. You should, like, everybody's the same on the inside. They just may look different." My mom was just saying, like, you shouldn't make fun of people because they're different, that they're just like us. I was just like a little geek. Like, I was making fun of somebody. . . . I was a mean little kid. . . . She said it, like, she didn't say it yelling at me and stuff. She just said it so that I understood that she was being serious. Because I don't think she likes it when people make fun of other people. . . . She just doesn't like seeing that. . . . I just really, I didn't really think about it when I was little. I just really didn't think about it.*
>
> —Kevin, age 14

As this adolescent's story so vividly confirms, parents play a defining role in their children's value socialization. For most children, it is the beliefs and values first experienced within the context of family life that shape their character and lay the foundation for healthy psychosocial functioning in adulthood (Grusec & Kuczynski, 1997; Kagan & Lamb, 1987; Walker, 1999). Although the influence of parents on a child's value socialization undoubtedly begins in early childhood, it is perhaps especially critical during the adolescent years. For it is during this period, with its striking advances in biological, cognitive, and social development, that the child often begins to explore and question familial norms and values in the quest for greater autonomy over his or her own life (Erikson, 1968; Hill & Holmbeck, 1986; Holmbeck, Paikoff, & Brooks-Gunn, 1995; Smetana, 1995, 1997; Silverberg & Gondoli, 1996; Steinberg & Silverberg, 1986).

Not surprisingly, the parental task of value socialization is therefore also particularly challenging during these years, as the adolescent cited at the beginning of this chapter intimates (i.e., ". . . she didn't say it, like, yelling at me and stuff. She just said it so that I understood that she was being serious."). Typically, the parent-child relationship undergoes sensitive renegotiation during adolescence, with parents granting greater freedom and independence to the child while also maintaining consistent support and encouragement (e.g., Collins, Gleason, & Sesma, 1997; Grotevant, 1998; Grotevant & Cooper, 1998; Smetana, 1995, 1997). Despite the likelihood of increased conflict with parents and a shifting of allegiance toward peers, research shows that adolescents do customarily maintain close relationships with their parents, actively seeking advice and guidance from them on important life issues (Allen & Land, 1999; Claes, 1998; Steinberg, 1990). And, even if parental relations do become somewhat testy for a time, by early adulthood most adolescents do subscribe to the values they were originally taught within the family (Offer & Schonert-Reichl, 1992) and show a sense of obligation to it (Fuligni & Pedersen, 2002). The developmental processes by which value socialization occurs within the family, however, remain obscure. What are the interpersonal dynamics of value teaching within the family? How do adolescents interpret and come to understand their parents' value lessons and, ultimately, appropriate (or reject) these beliefs and values as their own?

For several years now, we have been addressing questions such as these in a longitudinal study of adolescent value socialization within the family. In this chapter, we describe a narrative approach we have adopted to investigate adolescents' responsiveness to parental beliefs and values—a construct we call "parent voice"—as it is reflected in the adolescents' stories of important value learning experiences. We share with the proponents of narrative analysis represented in this volume a view that stories provide a powerful qualitative lens through which to observe and document child development, for us illuminating the way the adolescent constructs an autonomous sense of his or her own values in the context of parental influence. We begin with a brief overview of the theoretical framework of our work, before describing our methodological approach. We then summarize some of our recent research findings and their implications for our understanding of parent-adolescent relations and moral socialization more generally. Throughout the chapter, we provide illustration of the parent voice construct through excerpts from the adolescents' narratives of value learning experiences within the family.

THEORETICAL PERSPECTIVES ON THE ROLE OF NARRATIVE IN DEVELOPMENT

As illustrated in the introductory excerpt from our data, adolescents' narratives provide colorful snapshots of family life—in this instance, providing a glimpse of the way a mother taught her young son (now a reformed "little geek") the importance of fairness to others (or not making fun of "weird looking" little girls). Our research on the use of such stories to better understand the family dynamics of value socialization is just one example of a growing interest in the role of narrative within psychology. Described by Bruner (1986) as a distinctive mode of thought, a way of representing the social world and one's personal position and experiences within it, narrative is now widely acknowledged as a viable and constructive means of understanding and documenting human development (e.g., Day & Tappan, 1996; Fiese et al., 1999; Hermans, 1996; McAdams, 2001). Narrative techniques are being used to study an ever-widening range of developmental issues across various contexts, as is well illustrated in this volume (e.g., Pratt & Fiese, this volume).

Within the field of moral development, more particularly, a number of psychologists have recently turned to narrative techniques in an effort to more effectively account for the contextual particularities of moral experience believed to be neglected in the traditional paradigm of Piaget (1965) and Kohlberg (1984). In their work on moral commitment, for example, Colby and Damon (1992) provide an important example of the use of life histories as a way of describing the integration of the self and morality in exemplary social activists. Similarly, Tappan and his colleagues (Day & Tappan, 1996; Tappan, 1991; Tappan & Brown, 1989) have described the development of the moral self as reflected in the construction of a sense of personal "authorship" of moral stances and experiences through narrative analysis. More generally, narratives in the form of fables and epics have been used throughout history to provide rich and meaningful accounts of moral character and to inspire virtue in others (e.g., Coles, 1989; Vitz, 1990).

Our own perspective on the study of value socialization has been influenced by a number of contemporary psychologists whose work provides conceptual illumination of the role of narrative in human development (e.g., Bruner, 1986; Habermas & Bluck, 2000; Hermans, 1996; McAdams, 1990, 2001; Tappan, 1991). From McAdams' perspective, for example, it is narrative itself—a self-defining life story—that constitutes the essential element of the individual's construction of a sense of self or personal identity. In keeping with Erikson's (1968) concept of ego identity, McAdams (1990, 2001; see also Habermas & Bluck, 2000) theorizes that it is in adolescence, with its developmental advances in cognitive and psychosexual growth, that the child is first capable of adopting an historical, or autobiographical, perspective on life. During these years, he argues, adolescents typically achieve a biographical coherence such that personal characteristics and beliefs can be understood in terms of life experiences that may have precipitated them (Haberman & Bluck, 2000). In McAdams' (1990, p. 191) view, throughout this process they "rearrange and remythologize" their past experience, highlighting certain key scenes—"nuclear episodes"—or critical events that mark the self's continuity and change over time. Thus, adolescents gradually undergo a developmental process of "putting their lives together" (McAdams, 2001, p. 117) by integrating past, present, and future into a coherent narrative of the self, which provides psychosocial unity and purpose in life.

As subjective a process as it may seem, adolescent identity and value development does not take place in psychological isolation, however (Erikson, 1968; Penuel & Wertsch, 1995). The adolescent is exposed to and influenced by a range of significant others in the context of cultural and social life, all of whom contribute in varying ways and to varying degrees to his or her construction of a personal belief system. As emphasized in the work of other narrative theorists (e.g., Day & Tappan, 1996; Hermans, 1996; Sarbin, 1986), self or identity development is therefore essentially a "dialogical" process—that is, a process characterized by "an interchange between mutually influencing voices" or perspectives of others (Hermans, 1996, p. 31). In elucidating a more "voiced conception of the self" within narrative psychology, Hermans (1996, p. 43) argues that the self is inevitably aware of the perspectives of others, and these external views are represented in the self as "voiced positions" that dynamically interact within a person's mind as he or she faces decisions and constructs a sense of self through such choices.

From a more purely developmental, yet strikingly complementary, perspective, our narrative approach to adolescent value acquisition is also grounded in the traditional sociocultural framework of Vygotsky (1978) and Bakhtin (1981), as more recently articulated by Wertsch (1991). From Vygotsky's (1978) perspective, the development of mature thought is a gradual process of the appropriation of the social speech of childhood onto the inner mental plane of verbal self-regulatory thinking. It is the phenomenon of private or "inner speech," the child's use of overt self-directed language to regulate thought and behavior, through which this process occurs (e.g., Duncan & Pratt, 1997). According to Vygotsky, the legacy of this developmental process in the thought of the older individual is the dialogical nature of all such thinking based in the gradual internalization of social interaction (Wertsch, 1991). In keeping with the views of Hermans (1996), therefore, the mind is always "in conversation" with previous utterances—or voices—of the self and of important others in the person's life experience. As described by Bakhtin (1981), these interpolated voices of others are thus "ventriloquated" through the individual's own voice.

PARENTING AND THE DEVELOPMENT OF DIALOGICAL VOICE

Most audible among the developing child's "inner voices" undoubtedly will be those of parents, who typically play a dominant role in his or her personal belief and value development. Conceivably, the expression of parental voices in a child's thinking could take various forms, depending on developmental and family contexts. For instance, and perhaps most often, the parent's voice is likely to be concretely historical in nature, to be representative of past advice or admonitions to the child (Day & Tappan, 1996; Ely & McCabe, 1993). An adolescent might recall an occasion when the parent has provided direction or guidance in the past, which is then echoed in his or her inner dialogues about a current situation. However, we would certainly expect that parental voice might become anticipatory as well. In facing a novel problem, an adolescent might imagine how a parent would likely respond to his or her choice of action, thus reflecting this voice of endorsement or disapproval in inner thought (e.g., Pratt & Norris, 1999). In turn, then, we would expect these inner voices to be represented—or "ventriloquated" (Bakhtin, 1981)—in the overt narratives that adolescents tell about their value learning experiences. Recall, for example, the representation of a parental perspective in the mind of the adolescent cited at the outset of the chapter: "I don't think [my mother] likes it when people make fun of other people. . . . She just doesn't like seeing that." For this adolescent, a mother's voice is clearly audible as he shares with us his current thinking about the importance of being respectful of others.

As this excerpt suggests, the adolescent's sense of a parentally mediated ideal, and the parental perspective that emanates from it, have a strong impact on the beliefs and values that characterize his or her emerging identity. Thus, we would expect the quality of parent-child relations and family life to inevitably affect a child's receptivity or responsiveness to such parental influence, and longer-term psychosocial adaptation and adjustment as well. Darling and Steinberg (1993), for example, have suggested that an openness to parental perspectives should be associated positively with the emotional climate of the family, specifically with the degree to which the family is experienced by the child as "authoritative" in nature. Authoritative parenting is a broad style of parental interaction that is characterized by the provision of both guidance and structure, as well as warmth and responsiveness to the child's individuality (Baumrind, 1991; Maccoby & Martin, 1983). In adolescence, such family authoritativeness is associated with more opportunities for parent-child give and take, and with a greater reciprocity between parent and child (Grotevant, 1998; Steinberg, 2001).

Considerable research has shown that authoritative parenting, as defined earlier, is predictive of better adolescent adaptation and adjustment (e.g., Steinberg, 2001; Steinberg, Lamborn, Darling, Mounts, & Dornbusch, 1994). This is presumably because such parenting provides for greater adolescent responsiveness to the parent, and the gradual growth of feelings of mutuality within the relationship (Grotevant, 1998; Maccoby, 1992; Youniss & Smollar, 1985; Wintre & Yaffe, 2000), which in turn encourage a guided sense of autonomy and mature decision-making on the part of the adolescent (Grotevant & Cooper, 1998; Hauser, Powers, & Noam, 1991), key adaptive tasks during this period of development in the life course (e.g., Erikson, 1963).

A NARRATIVE APPROACH TO THE STUDY OF VALUE SOCIALIZATION WITHIN THE FAMILY

The central goal of our narrative research program has been to investigate the processes by which adolescent value socialization occurs within the family—that is, how the developing adolescent constructs a personal belief and value system through parental influence. Drawing directly from both narrative (e.g., Hermans, 1996) and sociocultural (e.g., Wertsch, 1991) theory, we use the term *voice* to depict the adolescent's representation of the views of influential others—in this instance, parents—as reflected in their stories about important value learning experiences within the family.

Although there would likely be several possible dimensions on which the child's representation of parental voice might vary, to date our work has focused on two of these in particular—the clarity of the adolescent's perspective on this voice and the extent to which he or she is responsive to the voice in his or her narrative representations of it. These dimensions, however, are naturally somewhat confounded with each other. Whereas the parent's voice may be clearly audible in an adolescent's story, but not necessarily listened to or respected, it is highly improbable that parental voice could be uncertain or vague, but strongly responded to by the adolescent.

An adolescent's representation of the parent voice, it seemed to us, might range from absent to minimal, on the one hand, up to the most sophisticated level of "reconstruction" and "appropriation" for the self (e.g., Rogoff, 1990) on the other. At these most advanced levels, our derivation of the voice construct has been informed by the distinction Bakhtin has made between two types of dialogical discourse, which we believe may be generally representative of two developmental steps in the internalization process (e.g., Tappan, 1991). The first is a form of externalized discourse in which the child's speech reflects an unconditional allegiance to a voice of authority. This is characterized by a more detached "recitation" or parroting of parent beliefs that have yet to be internalized and appropriated as one's own. In the second type, the child engages in what Bakhtin has called "internally persuasive dialogue." Here, the voice of others is not only audible in the child's speech, but it has also been assimilated and reconstructed by the child himself or herself, as appears to be the case for the adolescent cited at the outset of the chapter (i.e., the reformed "little geek"). In such instances, the child may be said to be "claiming authority and responsibility . . . and authorizing [his or her] own moral perspective" (Tappan, 1991, p. 17).

To capture and depict these variations in adolescents' responsiveness to parental influence in a systematic way (and to enable us to relate these representations to standard quantitative measures of personal and family characteristics), we have developed a technique to assess "parent voice" as reflected in adolescents' narratives of important value learning experiences (Mackey, Arnold, & Pratt, 2001; Pratt, Arnold, & Mackey, 2001). We categorize the adolescent's appropriation of parent voice on an ordered, 5-point scale (see Table 7.1). Each level reflects the adolescent's responsiveness to parental beliefs and values and their integration into his or her own self-regulative belief system. As described earlier, the central components of our measure include the clarity of the adolescent's representation of the parent voice and the extent to which this influence has been appropriated and reconstructed in his or her own thought. Possible indicators of parent voice include literal evidence of parents' speech within the adolescent's thought (e.g., "My dad says . . ."), statements corroborating or contradicting parents' views ("My parents are on the wrong track when . . ."), and emotional or affective overtones

TABLE 7.1
Levels of Parent Voice

1. Parent voice is absent or is summarily dismissed by the child.
2. Parent voice is only minimally present and/or may be passively complied with or questioned by the child.
3. Parent voice is clearly present, but it is "recited" or "parroted" rather than being truly internalized by the child.
4. Parent voice is clear and accepted by the child, but it is not convincingly "owned" or "internally persuasive" to the child.
5. Parent voice is clear, authored in the child's own terms, and respected by the child, though he/she may differ from it.

that imply evidence of responsiveness ("I felt lousy because I knew my parents thought . . .").

For example, at the lowest level, Level 1, the parents' voice either cannot be heard at all in the adolescent's story—perhaps because it is not available to the child, or the child has "tuned it out" of his or her thoughts—or, it is acknowledged, but summarily dismissed or rejected by the child. In one of our more striking cases of the absence of parental voice, a 19-year-old adolescent described for us her parents' reaction to a frightening episode she had recently experienced. She explained that she had been pretty well "sloshed" one night and narrowly escaped sexual assault after accepting a ride from a stranger:

> What really surprised me was that they [her parents] didn't seem all that shocked. They were like, "Oh, really." I felt like I was all alone when that happened, like I was really upset and I really felt like I didn't have anybody to talk to. . . . I told my parents and they said, "Oh, well, if you want to call the cops, that's fine and, if you don't, well, that's fine too." I was like . . . "Are you listening, didn't you hear what I just said?" So it was really, really weird.

In our interpretation, this adolescent badly needed and wanted her parents' support, and the absence of it has left her with a sense of betrayal, making her experience all the more difficult to overcome.

In contrast, at Level 3—the mid-point on our scale—the parents' voice is clearly audible in the adolescent's narrative, but it is "recited" by the adolescent as opposed to being truly owned and internalized. Typically, the child's responsiveness to parental influence takes the form of behavioral compliance, rather than a clear formulation of their beliefs and acceptance of (or at least respect for) them. For instance, one adolescent told us of a time when his parents taught him the importance of being "hard-working." However, despite the clarity of their "voice" in his thoughts, it is doubtful that he has truly appropriated this value as his own. He explained:

> There was a time in French where I was going into the final exam . . . I had 50 right on the nose. I wasn't really keen on French . . . but I buckled down . . . and I just like studied super hard . . . because I didn't want to fail . . . 'cause my French teacher, she called my house and she told my parents . . . [and] they talked to me about it and they said if I don't pass then I'm gonna have to pay for summer school. So that's what really made me buckle down and get going. . . . To tell you the truth, I've never done that much work on one subject. . . . I just knew everything off by heart. I couldn't tell you now, though. That's a different story.

Finally, at Level 5, the highest level on our scale, there is clear evidence that the parental voice is not only audible in the adolescent's story, but it has also been appropriated and "authorized" or reconstructed by the adolescent in his or her own terms, in keeping with Bakhtin's (1981) notion of "internally persuasive" dialogue. One of the stories that conveys this most clearly (and that we enjoy most) comes from a 14-year-old adolescent who told about his earlier efforts to become accepted by a peer group, indicating he had since come to value his independence through the guidance of his parents:

> Ok, there was a big group of people who were like in my class, and they called themselves the good people, like they were all supposed to be cool and everything. And I wasn't in that group and I wanted to be, so I did all sorts of like little things for them. I like practically became their slave. And this came to my parents' notice, and they told me not to bother with those people, to like start my own group and stuff like that. At first I didn't listen, because I thought they didn't know what they were talking about. But after a while I began to see that these guys were just using me, and from then on I've never cared what other people think about me—I just do what I think is right. . . . My parents told me I should think for myself; I shouldn't follow what other people do, and kiss these people on their butts because I want to join the group. . . . I should do what I think is good, no matter what anyone else thinks.

In our view, this adolescent illustrates a strong example of the constructive appropriation of his parents' beliefs and values. The parents' injunctions about independence of thought are not just echoed by this adolescent, but also appear to have been digested and appropriated for the child himself in graphic adolescent ("kiss their butts") terminology.

EMPIRICAL RESEARCH ON PARENT VOICE

Over the course of the past several years, we have been engaged in research on the topic of parent voice. Our work has now involved several studies, most particularly a longitudinal study of adolescent value socialization with a sample of 40 Canadian families, including the mother, father, and adolescent child (Pratt, Arnold, Pratt, & Diessner, 1999). The families are all intact, primarily Caucasian, working- to middle-class, and they represent a range of educational backgrounds and religious ideologies. We have now visited with family members in their homes on three occasions: initially, when the adolescents were age 12–16 (mean age of 14), again at age 14–18 (mean age 16), and most recently when they were 18–22 years of age (mean age 20).

On each occasion, we have asked family members to tell us stories about various value lessons within the context of their daily life and to complete standard questionnaire and interview measures, including indices of parent-child relations and adolescent psychosocial development. Our narrative measures have comprised a range of elicitations across a variety of contexts. One set of stories, for example, has been elicited by asking adolescents (and parents, as well) to tell us about times when their parents have tried to teach them important, self-identified values, such as "honesty" and "kindness" (e.g., Pratt & Arnold, 1995; Pratt, Arnold, & Hilbers, 1998; Pratt, Norris, van de Hoef, & Arnold, 2001). In other work, we have asked adolescents (and young adults) to describe a time when their parents helped with their decision making by offering advice about an important personal issue (e.g., Mackey et al., 2001). Conversely, on another occasion we have asked adolescents to tell us about times when they experienced problems or disagreements with their parents. In several studies we have asked participants to relate stories about a "critical incident" in their lives, an event or experience that has had a strong impact or influence on their development (e.g., Pratt, Arnold, & Mackey, 2001). And, finally, in our most recent work, we have also asked our participants—now young adults—to tell us stories about times when they have felt particularly good or proud of themselves.

In all instances, our analyses of parent voice in the adolescents' narratives have provided support for the validity of the voice construct as an indicator of adolescent responsiveness to parent influence. Most significantly, we have been struck by the extent to which parental views—or voices—could be heard within the adolescents' stories, sometimes as guiding frameworks, and sometimes sounding like foils for the adolescents' own, emerging voices. Despite differences among story contexts, we have found that the parental perspective was typically available to our participants and readily elicited by simple probing (e.g., "What did your parents think?" Mackey et al., 2001), a finding that is consistent with the idea that voices of others are often anticipated in thinking, and function as "sounding boards" in consideration of personal decisions (Day & Tappan, 1996). As one might expect, the adolescents' narratives reflect the commonalities, as well as specific differences, in the ways that parent voices are represented in the thinking of adolescents. Nevertheless, we have consistently found the five levels of parent voice (as described previously) to be reasonably discriminable across varied elicitation contexts, and we have achieved generally high standards of inter-rater reliability in our analyses of them (correlations between independent raters typically in the .80s, e.g., Mackey et al., 2001). It is also noteworthy that parent voice generally has been independent of standard family demographic measures, including family size, parent age, education, and religiosity, throughout our analyses, leading us to believe it is a reasonable reflection of the unique particularities of individual family life and process.

Moreover, we have observed a number of interesting patterns and themes that help to illuminate various aspects of the value socialization process in our analyses of this voice construct. For example, we have found parent voice scores to be moderately positively correlated across the narrative elicitation contexts described above (i.e., average intercorrelations in the .30s and .40s). This suggests that adolescents' responsiveness to parental influence is partly story-specific, as might be expected, but also somewhat generalized across stories, perhaps a reflection of broader family styles such as those described by Darling and Steinberg (1993). These consistent, moderate positive correlations suggest the appropriateness of constructing an overall summary index of voice scores at each age, which is the measure generally discussed hereafter.

Analyses of these summary parent voice scores over time (i.e., at ages 14, 16, and 20) imply varying degrees of consistency in our participants' responsiveness to parental influence as they mature. Perhaps not surprisingly, the greatest stability was observed between parent voice scores at mid-adolescence and early adulthood, that is, at ages 16 and 20 ($r = .65$); a moderate relation existed between scores at early and mid-adolescence, or ages 14 and 16 ($r = .42$); and a relatively weak association was observed between voice scores at the extremes of our developmental time frame, from ages 14 to 20 ($r = .16$). This variation in responsiveness to parental influence across the adolescent years is much in keeping with the parenting literature that highlights the vicissitudes of parent-adolescent relations over time (e.g., Grotevant, 1998; Smetana, 1997; Steinberg, 1990).

PARENT VOICE AND PARENT-CHILD RELATIONS

As discussed earlier, in our derivation of the parent voice construct it has been our assumption that adolescents who represent parental beliefs and values at more sophisticated levels of appropriation will be reflective of families who enjoy positive parent-child relations and a family climate conducive to healthy development. In our more recent work, therefore, we have examined the legitimacy of this assumption. Accordingly, our analyses have included a range of more established indices of parenting styles and of family climate, as reported by the adolescents themselves. These have included their perceptions of family authoritativeness, cohesion, and autonomy encouragement, which we assessed concurrently with parent voice in mid-adolescence (i.e., age 16). In early adulthood (i.e., age 20), we obtained adolescents' assessment of parent-child attachment, as well as reassessing their perceptions of parent authoritativeness.

Adolescents' perceptions of family authoritativeness were assessed on a measure adapted from Dornbusch, Ritter, Leiderman, Roberts, and Fraleigh (1987), and also included a scale of parent discussion and influence ratings across four topics: schools, peers, family issues, and activities/hobbies. In the latter case, each topic was rated on 5-point Likert-type scales for frequency of discussion and for level of parent influence (see Pratt, Danso, Arnold, Norris, & Filyer, 2001, for further description).

Adolescents' perceptions of parental autonomy encouragement were assessed by asking them to describe problems they had experienced with each of their parents, to explain both their own and their parents' views regarding these issues, and their perception of how they had been (or were being) resolved. On the basis of a reading of these responses, autonomy encouragement was rated on a 3-point scale, ranging from 1 (parent actively interferes with the child's autonomy), through 2 (mixed pattern of interference/encouragement or no autonomy issues discussed), to 3 (parent actively supports child's autonomy and/or decision-making). Scores were summed across the two problems to obtain an overall score (see Pratt, Danso, et al., 2001).

In addition, the mid-adolescents' perceptions of family cohesion and emotional closeness were assessed using the index of General Family Functioning (Morris, 1990), a standard 15-item scale. Finally, when our participants were in early adulthood (i.e., mean age 20) we also assessed their perceptions of parent attachment (for both mother and father), using the Index of Parent and Peer Attachment scale (Greenberg, Siegel, & Leitch, 1983). This is a widely used standard questionnaire index of attachment in adolescence and young adulthood.

Results of these analyses have confirmed that parent voice, scored independently from adolescents' narratives, is generally reflective of the quality of family life, at least as perceived by the adolescents themselves on these various standard measures. For example, we have found that families in which the adolescents were more responsive to the parent voice in mid-adolescence (i.e., age 16) were also more likely to be seen by the adolescents as authoritative in their parenting style ($r = .60$), to experience a greater degree of family cohesion ($r = .57$), and to be more encouraging of the adolescent's autonomy ($r = .56$ for mother; $r = .34$ for father).

Moreover, parent voice in mid-adolescence appears to be predictive of longer lasting positive parent-child relations as well. Our participants' perceptions of parent authoritativeness at age 20, for example, continued to be strongly related to their earlier representation of parent voice at age 16, this time when assessed for each parent individually ($r = .63$ for mother; $r = .67$ for father). Similarly, their perceptions of parent attachment in early adulthood were related to parent voice in mid-adolescence ($r = .56$ for mother; $r = .37$ for father). The consistency of this pattern of associations with more generalized or "context-free" assessments of family life supports the validity of our parent voice construct and its usefulness in enhancing our understanding of some of the ways that value socialization may occur within the family (see Mackey et al., 2001; Pratt, Arnold, & Mackey, 2001).

PARENT VOICE AND ADOLESCENT PSYCHOSOCIAL DEVELOPMENT OVER TIME

On the assumption that parental influence typically has a lasting effect on children's adaptation, in our most recent work we have examined relations between adolescents' responsiveness to parent voice and their longer term psychosocial development. Of particular interest to us have been links between representations of parent voice in the formative years of mid-adolescence and standard indicators of adolescent adjustment and adaptation, identity development, and social responsibility in early adulthood (Arnold & Hicks, 2001; Pratt, Arnold, & Mackey, 2001).

In our latest session of family interviews, therefore, conducted when the adolescents were age 18–22 (mean age 20), we collected data on a series of established indices of adjustment and adaptation (in addition to continued use of our narrative measures described previously). These included standard measures of self-esteem (Rosenberg Self-Esteem Scale, 1979), loneliness (UCLA Loneliness Scale, Russel, Peplau, & Cutrona, 1980), depression (CES-D Scale; Radloff, 1977), and dispositional optimism (Life Orientation Test; Scheier & Carver, 1985). In addition, as a measure of identity development in early adulthood, we used a questionnaire assessment of identity status, the Objective Measure of Ego Identity Status (Adams, Bennion, & Huh, 1989). This is a 24-item measure with four subscales of six items each, each measuring levels of one of the four statuses of Marcia (1980): identity achievement, moratorium, foreclosure, and diffusion.

As noted previously, a great deal of evidence has indicated that positive parent-child relations in adolescence predict better subsequent adjustment (e.g., Steinberg et al., 1994). In keeping with our own previous research on concurrent relations between parent voice and adolescent adjustment (Pratt, Arnold, & Mackey, 2001), we made the longitudinal prediction that mid-adolescents who expressed more positive relations with their parents on our narrative voice measure—that is, those who represented and had appropriated parental views on a more sophisticated level—would also display stronger evidence of more mature psychosocial characteristics in later years than adolescents who were less responsive to parental influence. Indeed, these expectations were consistently supported. Correlations across time showed robust relations between parent voice from stories in mid-adolescence (at age 16) and all our examined indicators of psychosocial development in early adulthood (at age 20). On average, mid-adolescents who represented the parent voice at a more sophisticated level also had higher self-esteem ($r = .48$) and sense of optimism ($r = .40$) and reported fewer feelings of loneliness ($r = -.42$) and depression ($r = -.38$) as they approached adulthood 4 years later. Moreover, regression analyses indicated that higher early parent voice scores predicted increments, or growth, in positive adjustment and adaptation over the 4-year span from ages 16 to 20 for self-esteem and loneliness, the two measures available at both these points in our participants' development (Arnold & Hicks, 2001). That is, high scorers on parent voice at 16 showed gains from age 16 to 20 in self-esteem, and declines in loneliness over this time period, whereas low scorers at age 16 did not. In addition, mid-adolescents who were more responsive to parental influence in their stories were also less likely to show the immature forms of identity achievement status in early adulthood (sum of foreclosure and diffusion scores at age 20, $r = -.36$, with parent voice at 16). Clearly, then, adolescents' responsiveness to parents' perspectives in their stories at mid-adolescence was generally predictive of more positive trajectories of adaptation in the period of what Arnett (2000) has called "emerging adulthood." Certainly prediction is not causation in an observational study such as the present one. Even though these are only correlational patterns over time, however, they do begin to speak to the potential power of a narrative methodology in the study of family life and adaptation during this period of adolescent development (e.g., Cowan, 1999).

The potential implications of this pattern of relations between adolescents' responsiveness to parental influence and longer-term psychosocial adjustment were reflected in a number of family stories told by our research participants. For example, having identified with the personal value "independent," Emily recounted the following story of a significant turning point in her early adolescence, when she struggled to overcome a debilitating shyness and became "a whole new person" with the support and encouragement of her mother:

> When I moved to Grade 8, like, that was one of the most important times in my life so far. I was very shy . . . and I had people tease me because I was so shy. I was feeling really, really bad about myself. I felt very depressed and there were times when I just wanted to stay home, and I spent whole days not talking to anybody. . . . When I look back, it's like I'm a whole new person. I have a lot of friends. Um, I actually laugh. I didn't laugh at all before—that's how big a change it's been . . . like it was a whole new beginning. I thought about what I wanted to be like, and it was just like a dream come true sort of thing, because I was worried that the rest of my life would probably be a write-off because I wouldn't be happy. It's very hard to change. . . . In Grade 7 I realized that I was too far along to be able to change. . . . [But] I wanted to make myself, make it better. It took a while to figure out what it was, except my mom, my mom and I talked it through, and we just figured out together what it was gonna be, what I wanted it to be. . . . I wasn't quite sure, um, what I wanted to be like, and how to go about doing that. . . . She agreed with changing completely. . . . We both talked together and decided what I wanted to be like. . . . I got involved in a lot more things, and I got different sorts of clothes than I was wearing before, and I made a big effort to talk to people a lot more, and so I made a lot of friends. I made a few really good friends which I still have. . . . [It was] to do with what I believe and what I wanted people to think of me, and how, how I wanted to be for the rest of my life, that sort of thing.

Of course, not all the narratives of our participants' lives with parents have been as positive. Jeff, for instance, recounted quite discouraging stories of his strained relationships with both of his parents, as he struggled in mid-adolescence with issues of identity and independence. Having previously told us of communication problems with his mother—frequent "little tiffs" that left him "frustrated inside" and wondering "what's going through her head"—here, he narrates a "problem situation" he experienced with his father.

> Okay, I'm gonna tell you about my dad. This is how it goes. . . . My father would come in and he would of course take my mother's side, in other words, team up on me. He wouldn't really listen to all the facts before he jumped in. You know what I mean? We went on a trip . . . and we were driving home, and I wanted to sit in the front. . . . Like, I drove about 12 hours or so, and then from there I sat in the back. We slept at a hotel, and then the next day my dad drove, and then the next day my mother drove, and then the next day my dad drove, and they were both sitting in the front seat. And we were getting on [a major highway] when we had that big, bad winter storm kind of deal, and I just wanted to sit in the front, because I hadn't been, you know. . . . So, I asked my dad if I could sit in the front, and he said, "fine." So my mom had gone to get coffee, and when she came back . . . she's like, "Why are you sitting in the front? You know I have a bad back." And I said, "Well, everything's comfortable. If you want to lie down, we've got blankets and stuff like that. I've been back there for two days, and I'd just like to sit up at the front for a while." And then she started arguing, "Blah, blah, blah." One thing led to another, and she asked my dad, and she goes, "Do I have to put up with this?" And then my dad says, "No." So I go in the back.

These quarrels were predictive of longer term problems. Jeff's outcomes at age 21 were in fact very poor, with significant psychosocial problems of adjustment and substance abuse, though he and his parents both continued to make efforts towards improving their troubled relationship.

In the most recent phase of our longitudinal study, we have also been interested in examining relations between our participants' responsiveness to parental beliefs and values in mid-adolescence and sociomoral dimensions of their longer term development. Previous research in moral development has shown that children raised in more authoritative family environments, where they are encouraged to think autonomously, are more advanced in their moral reasoning and behavior than those raised in more restrictive family contexts (e.g., Boyes & Allen, 1993; Hart, Atkins, & Ford, 1999; Pratt, Arnold, et al., 1999; Walker & Henning, 1999; Walker, Henning, & Krettenaur, 2000). If our parent voice construct is a valid indicator of parent-child relations, as our earlier findings suggest, we anticipated that adolescents who previously responded more positively to parental influence would also be more likely to assume active social responsibility in early adulthood.

To investigate this, our participants' social commitment at age 20 was assessed using the Youth Involvement Inventory (Pratt, Hunsberger, Pancer, & Alisat, 2003). This is a recently developed, 30-item self-report measure of the frequency of involvement in several types of voluntary activity, including helping activities such as visiting those in hospitals, political activities such as collecting signatures on a petition, community activities such as working in a neighborhood organization, and responding activities such as giving money to a cause. All items were reported on a 0 ("you never did this") to 4 ("you did this a lot") scale and summed to provide an overall score.

Adolescents who were more responsive to parent influence at age 16 also displayed a significantly greater sense of social responsibility in early adulthood at age 20, reporting being more socially involved through volunteer work in their communities ($r = .35$). Pancer and Pratt (1999) have suggested that parents frequently play a large role in supporting the involvement of youth in community prosocial activity. Indeed, this suggestion that the family context has implications for the adolescent's relationships in the larger social world is illustrated by the stories that several of our participants told. For example, describing an occasion when her parents taught her the importance of being "kind and caring" to others, Karen shared with us the following story of her experience mentoring an adolescent far less fortunate than herself:

> There was this lady that I baby-sat for, and she had a daughter that was maybe about two years younger than me. . . . Her mom was an alcoholic and had four children and, like, that family was a mess. Her mom wasn't married . . . and she would bring men home and have sex with them while I baby-sat. So it was pretty brutal. But, like, I felt sorry for the children. And the one girl just didn't know how to act. Do you know what I mean? She just didn't know how to act . . . she didn't have any social skills basically. And so she was very annoying, but she also needed friends. She needed someone that was like a big sister to say, you know, "Okay, that's not the way you act and this is the way you act," and just, you know, start teaching her right from wrong 'cause her mother had not. . . . And so, like, I was talking to my parents about her, and stuff like that, and my parents were going to invite her to church . . . and I'm like, "Invite her to church? She's so annoying." But eventually they convinced me that it was the right thing to do, and I did. I don't know that it did that huge of a difference, but I know that she now knows that there's someone that cares about her. . . . So I guess [my parents] taught me just to be kind and caring and just to listen to her problems, 'cause she talked to me a lot about her problems. . . . I feel good about it. I'm glad that my parents convinced me to do that. . . . I think a lot of the time [there's] a comfort zone, you know, I'm comfortable with my friends, I'm comfortable doing what I'm doing, and I don't want to have to step out of it. It's like we're living in a bubble . . . so you just don't want to step out. But, like, my parents were basically pushing me to step out, and once I stepped out I felt good about it. . . . And now she at least knows there's someone else that cares about her, and stuff like that. . . She started noticing that I accepted her no matter what, and she started acting like herself more. It taught me a big lesson, definitely.

Our most compelling example of parental influence on adolescents' sense of social responsibility is presented by Sandra, who explained to us how her parents had taught her the importance of being "fair and just."

> I know I've been taught to be fair and just all my life. . . . But I remember one time when my parents came home with this movie, and it was called *Mahatma Ghandi*. . . . I was quite young, like under 10, and I was like, "What's that?" . . . "No, I don't want to see this. This isn't something I'm interested in. . . ." This was, you know, a movie that was quite, whatever, sophisticated . . . but they wanted me to watch it with them, and I was really affected by it, by the racism in India, I believe it was, yeah, in India. And that really taught me sort of the . . . equality sort of lesson . . . not just the racism, basically human being, dignity, that sort of justice, I guess. . . . I'm glad they did teach it to me . . . because it's a really important lesson to learn. . . . Justice is a thing you encounter every single day of your life, whether you know it or not.

Indeed, Sandra showed she has learned this parental lesson well in a later narrative she recounted of a critical incident in her life, an experience that epitomizes McAdams's (1990) notion of a "nuclear episode" in an adolescent's emerging life story:

> You know in school there's always the cool group and then like the not so cool, well, the losers or whatever, the rejects. . . . I was always part of the little cool crowd. And then all of a sudden . . . there came this girl named "S" into my class. And she was Indian . . . and she was made fun of so much and she was put down about everything. . . . I believe it was a real racial issue. . . . I felt so badly for her because she did not stand up for her rights at all . . . she would smile or brush it off as if everything was okay. But I knew that it wasn't okay. . . . She was such a nice person, so kind and sweet and gentle, and there was nothing wrong with her, she was just so frail . . . I looked at the situation and I said, "Look, if she couldn't stand up for herself, she needs someone else to stand up for her, because what is happening here is not right, and this isn't good." So I started becoming her friend, and all the members of the cool group, they totally ditched me, and they just turned their backs on me and they became so cool and inhumane, you wouldn't believe. . . . It really hurt a lot, because all I wanted was for everyone to be friends. . . . I remember one specific time . . . I was just shocked . . . I was like, "Okay, this has gone way too far" . . . and something inside of me just burned and stinged (sic) and I just couldn't control it. . . . [T]his has been going on for three years now, and you know puberty just kicking in, and I just stood up and I just like burst out and I just started yelling. . . . I don't even remember what I said, but I remember after that I just felt so good, and all the cool girls . . . just stood around us in a circle, and it was totally silent. It was such a moment . . . really weird. It was a day I'll never forget. . . . Why are people so cruel? I mean, we were only little girls.

CONCLUSIONS

In this chapter, we have presented an overview of our narrative approach to the study of adolescent value socialization within the family. In our adoption of this framework, we have attempted to complement more traditional approaches to this important aspect of family life through an analysis of adolescents' responsiveness to parental influence, as represented in their stories of important value learning experiences. Our narrative assessment of parent voice has provided a fruitful means of understanding family dynamics and their implications for adolescent psychosocial development. In particular, the parent voice construct has proved to be a sensitive and reasonably stable index of family climate. As illustrated in our case material, the adolescents' stories reveal compelling instances where parent-child relations are mutually harmonious and fulfilling and those where they are strained, as adolescents and their parents redefine their roles during these critical years. More importantly, adolescents' representations of their parents' voices have also foreshadowed their patterns of psychosocial development in later years. We have found that mid-adolescents who are more responsive to their parents' influence are also more likely to show signs of healthy adaptation, displaying stronger self-esteem, optimism, and identity achievement and fewer feelings of loneliness and depression in early adulthood, and to experience more growth in these respects over this time. In addition, such adolescents also are more likely to display evidence of the longer term impact of parental influence outside the family in their commitment to social service and community action.

Our research, therefore, provides a convincing example of some of the ways narrative techniques can provide insight into adolescent experience and development within and beyond the family context. The use of narrative has enabled us to systematically assess the diverse ways adolescents interpret their family beliefs and values and to identify meaningful distinctions in their appropriation, or rejection, of them as their own. Inevitably, positive parent-child relations provide a source of strength and support to adolescents coping with the vicissitudes of value socialization. In these instances, adolescents' representations of their parents' voices serve as a protective factor as they face the challenging complexities of extra-family influences. Such was the case, for example, of the adolescent we cited earlier who had learned to resist the negative influence of his peers (or not "to kiss these people on their butts") and, rather, to value his own emerging sense of independence through the supportive guidance of his parents. Our focus on a range of standard measures of adolescent adaptation and adjustment has provided potential evidence of how variations in the quality of such family narratives can contribute to the prediction of adolescent outcomes in development. This is an important aspect of criterion validity that narrative family research is just beginning to address (e.g., Cowan, 1999; Fiese et al., 1999). We believe our results point to ways that such narrative analyses can be integrated with more traditional quantitative research in the study of child and family development (Pratt, Arnold, & Mackey, 2001).

If these points are indeed reasonable ones, then the clinical implications of this work are worth pursuing as well. People in their descriptions of family life and experiences in therapeutic contexts inevitably provide a wealth of narratives such as the ones we have described—in fact, this is just what people always do in all kinds of talk about their personal lives (Polkinghorne, 1996). Clinicians also inevitably listen with an ear attuned to the "voices" of parents in the stories of their patients, as they seek to understand process and relationships in the individual's past and current development. Research such as this may provide some insights into how best to frame the meaning of differences across patterns of varied parent-adolescent relationships. More ambitiously, based on data such as ours, one might argue that helping individuals and families to reframe problematic stories about their family lives could indeed prove therapeutic. Such ideas surely deserve careful study using tools like the present ones to test such claims (Cowan, 1999).

Finally, our application of a narrative framework to the study of adolescent value socialization has been consistent with McAdams' (1990, 2001) construal of narrative as a medium for personal identity development. By all accounts, our participants genuinely engaged in the experience of storytelling, often leaving us with the impression that the opportunity itself was personally fulfilling, and perhaps even educational, for them as well. Over the course of their adolescent years, they willingly and enthusiastically shared their perspectives and experiences with us, and we have heard the emergence of their own voices while they grappled with the challenges of constructing a personal belief system. Thus, through their narrative accounts of personal struggle and triumph, they have presented colorful portraits of adolescent lives in the making, as they prepare to embark on their larger life stories.

ACKNOWLEDGMENT

The research reported in this chapter was supported by grants from the Social Sciences and Humanities Research Council of Canada to authors Pratt and Arnold, and Joan Norris.

REFERENCES

Adams, G. R., Bennion, L., & Huh, K. (1989). *Objective measure of ego identity status: A reference manual.* Unpublished manual, University of Guelph, Guelph, Ontario.

Allen, J., & Land, P. (1999). Attachment in adolescence. In J. Cassidy & P. R. Shaver (Eds.), *Handbook of attachment: Theory, research, and clinical applications* (pp. 319–335). New York: Guilford.

Arnett, J. J. (2000). Emerging adulthood: A theory of development from the late teens through the twenties. *American Psychologist, 55,* 469–480.

Arnold, M. L., & Hicks, C. (2001, April). *A narrative approach to studying parent-adolescent relations: Parental influence and adolescent adjustment over time.* Poster presented at the biennial meeting of the Society for Research in Child Development, Minneapolis.

Bakhtin, M. (1981). *The dialogic imagination.* Austin: University of Texas Press.

Baumrind, D. (1991). Effective parenting of adolescents. In P. Cowan & E. M. Hetherington (Eds.), *The effects of transitions on families* (pp. 111–163). Hillsdale, NJ: Lawrence Erlbaum Associates.

Boyes, M., & Allen, S. (1993). Styles of parent-child interaction and moral reasoning in adolescence. *Merrill-Palmer Quarterly, 39,* 551–570.

Bruner, J. (1986). *Actual minds, possible worlds.* Cambridge, MA: Harvard University Press.

Claes, M. (1998). Adolescents' closeness with parents, siblings, and friends in three countries: Canada, Belgium, and Italy. *Journal of Youth and Adolescence, 27,* 165–184.

Colby, A., & Damon, W. (1992). *Some do care: Contemporary lives of moral commitment.* New York: Free Press.

Coles, R. (1989). *The moral life of children.* Boston: The Atlantic Monthly Press.

Collins, W. A., Gleason, T., & Sesma, A. (1997). Internalization, autonomy, and relationships: Development during adolescence. In J. E. Grusec & L. Kuczynski (Eds.), *Parenting and children's internalization of values* (pp. 78–99). New York: John Wiley & Sons.

Cowan, P. A. (1999). What we talk about when we talk about families. In B. H. Fiese, A. Sameroff, H. Grotevant, F. Wamboldt, S. Dickstein, & D. Fravel, The stories that families tell: Narrative coherence, narrative interaction, and relationship beliefs. *Monographs of the Society for Research in Child Development, 64* (2, Serial No. 257), 163–176.

Darling, N., & Steinberg, L. (1993). Parenting style as context: An integrative model. *Psychological Bulletin, 113,* 487–496.

Day, J., & Tappan, M. (1996). The narrative approach to moral development: From the epistemic subject to dialogical selves. *Human Development, 39,* 67–82.

Dornbusch, S., Ritter, P., Leiderman, P., Roberts, D., & Fraleigh, M. (1987). The relation of parenting style to adolescent school performance. *Child Development, 58,* 1244–1257.

Duncan, R., & Pratt, M. (1997). Microgenetic change in preschoolers' private speech: Effects of task difficulty, task novelty, and task repetition. *International Journal of Behavioral Development, 20,* 367–383.

Ely, R., & McCabe, A. (1993). Remembered voices. *Journal of Child Language, 20,* 671–696.

Erikson, E. (1963). *Childhood and society.* New York: Norton.

Erikson, E. (1968). *Identity, youth and crisis.* New York: Norton.

Fiese, B. H., Sameroff, A., Grotevant, H., Wamboldt, F., Dickstein, S., & Fravel, D. (1999). The stories that families tell: Narrative coherence, narrative interaction, and relationship beliefs. *Monographs of the Society for Research in Child Development, 64* (2, Serial No. 257]).

Fuligni, A. J., & Pedersen, S. (2002). Family obligation and the transition to young adulthood. *Developmental Psychology, 38,* 856–868.

Greenberg, M. T., Siegel, J. M., & Leitch, C. J. (1983). The nature and importance of attachment relationships to parents and peers during adolescence. *Journal of Youth and Adolescence, 12,* 373–386.

Grotevant, H. D. (1998). Adolescent development in family contexts. In W. Damon (Series Ed.) & N. Eisenberg (Vol. Ed.), *Handbook of child psychology: Vol. 3. Social, emotional, and personality development* (5th ed., pp. 1097–1150). New York: Wiley.

Grotevant, H. D., & Cooper, C. R. (1998). Individuality and connectedness in adolescent development: Review and prospects for research on identity, relationships, and context. In E. Skoe & A. von der Lippe (Eds.), *Personality development in adolescence: A cross national and life span perspective* (pp. 3–37). London: Routledge.

Grusec, J. E., & Kuczynski, L. (Eds.). (1997). *Parenting and children's internalization of values* (pp. 78–99). New York: John Wiley & Sons.

Habermas, T., & Bluck, S. (2000). Getting a life: The emergence of the life story in adolescence. *Psychological Bulletin, 126,* 748–769.

Hart, D., Atkins, R., & Ford, D. (1999). Family influences on the formation of moral identity in adolescence: Longitudinal analyses. *Journal of Moral Education, 28,* 375–386.

Hauser, S. T., Powers, S., & Noam, G. (1991). *Adolescents and their families: Paths of ego development.* New York: Free Press.

Hermans, H. J. M. (1996). Voicing the self: From information processing to dialogical interchange. *Psychological Bulletin, 119,* 31–50.

Hill, J., & Holmbeck, G. (1986). Attachment and autonomy during adolescence. *Annals of Child Development, 3,* 145–189.

Holmbeck, G. N., Paikoff, R. L., & Brooks-Gunn, J. (1995). Parenting adolescents. In M. H. Bornstein (Ed.), *Handbook of parenting: Vol. 1. Children and parenting* (pp. 91–118). Mahwah, NJ: Lawrence Erlbaum Associates.

Kagan, J., & Lamb, S. (Eds.). (1987). *The emergence of morality in young children.* Chicago: University of Chicago Press.

Kohlberg, L. (1984). *Essays on moral development: Vol. II. The psychology of moral development: The nature and validity of moral stages.* San Francisco, CA: Harper & Row.

Maccoby, E. E. (1992). The role of parents in the socialization of children: An historical overview. *Developmental Psychology, 28,* 1006–1017.

Maccoby, E., & Martin, J. (1983). Socialization in the context of the family. In P. H. Mussen (Series Ed.) & E. M. Hetherington (Vol. Ed.), *Handbook of child psychology: Vol. 4. Socialization, personality and social development* (4th ed., pp. 1–101). New York: Wiley.

Mackey, K., Arnold, M. L., & Pratt, M. W. (2001). Adolescents' stories of decision making in more and less authoritative families: Representing the voices of parents in narrative. *Journal of Adolescent Research, 16,* 243–268.

Marcia, J. E. (1980). Identity in adolescence. In J. Adelson (Ed.), *Handbook of adolescent psychology* (pp. 159–187). New York: Wiley.

McAdams, D. P. (1990). Unity and purpose in human lives: The emergence of identity as a life story. In I. A. Rabin, R. A. Zucker, R. A. Emmons, & S. Frank (Eds.), *Studying persons and lives* (pp. 148–200). New York: Springer.

McAdams, D. P. (2001). The psychology of life stories. *Review of General Psychology, 5,* 100–122.

Morris, T. M. (1990). Culturally sensitive family assessment: An evaluation of the Family

Assessment Device used with Hawaiian-American and Japanese-American families. *Family Process, 29,* 105–116.

Offer, D., & Schonert-Reichl, K. A. (1992). Debunking the myths of adolescence: Findings from recent research. *Journal of the American Academy of Child and Adolescent Psychiatry, 31,* 1003–1014.

Pancer, S. M., & Pratt, M. W. (1999). Social and family determinants of community service involvement in Canadian youth. In M. Yates & J. Youniss (Eds.), *Community service and civic engagement in youth: International perspectives* (pp. 32–55). Cambridge, UK: Cambridge University Press.

Penuel, W. R., & Wertsch, J. V. (1995). Vygoysky and identity formation: A sociocultural approach. *Educational Psychologist, 30,* 83–92.

Piaget, J. (1965). *The moral judgment of the child.* New York: Free Press. (Original work published 1932)

Polkinghorne, D. E. (1996). Narrative knowing and the study of lives. In J. Birren, G. Kenyon, J. E. Ruth, J. Schroots, & T. Svensson (Eds.), *Aging and biography: Explorations in adult development* (pp. 77–99). New York: Springer.

Pratt, M. W., & Arnold, M. L. (1995). Narrative approaches to moral socialization across the lifespan. *Moral Education Forum, 20,* 13–22.

Pratt, M. W., Arnold, M. L., & Hilbers, S. M. (1998). A narrative approach to the study of moral orientation in the family: Tales of kindness and care. In E. Skoe & A. von der Lippe (Eds.), *Personality development in adolescence: A cross national and life span perspective* (pp. 61–79). London: Routledge.

Pratt, M. W., Arnold, M. L., & Mackey, K. (2001). Adolescent representations of the parent voice in stories of personal turning points. In D. P. McAdams, R. Josselson, & A. Lieblich (Eds.), *Turns in the road: Narrative studies of lives in transition* (pp. 227–251). Washington, DC: American Psychological Association.

Pratt, M. W., Arnold, M. L., Pratt, A. T., & Diessner, R. (1999). Predicting adolescent moral reasoning from family climate: A longitudinal study. *Journal of Early Adolescence, 19,* 148–175.

Pratt, M. W., Danso, H., Arnold, M. L., Norris, J., & Filyer, R. (2001). Adult generativity and the socialization of adolescents: Relations to mothers' and fathers' parenting beliefs, styles and practices. *Journal of Personality, 69,* 89–120.

Pratt, M. W., Hunsberger, B., Pancer, S. M., & Alisat, S. (2003). A longitudinal analysis of personal value socialization: Correlates of a moral self-ideal in adolescence. *Social Development, 12,* 563–585.

Pratt, M. W., & Norris, J. (1999). Moral development in maturity: Lifespan perspectives on the processes of successful aging. In T. Hess & F. Blanchard-Fields (Eds.), *Social cognition and aging* (pp. 291–317). New York: Academic Press.

Pratt, M. W., Norris, J. E., van de Hoef, S., & Arnold, M. L. (2001). Stories of hope: Parental optimism in narratives about adolescent children. *Journal of Social and Personal Relationships, 18,* 603–623.

Radloff, L. S. (1977). The CES-D Scale: A self-report depression scale for research in the general population. *Applied Psychological Measurement, 1,* 385–401.

Rogoff, B. (1990). *Apprenticeship in thinking: Cognitive development in social context.* New York: Oxford University Press.

Rosenberg, M. (1979). *Conceiving the self.* New York: Basic Books.

Russel, D., Peplau, L. A., & Cutrona, C. (1980). The revised UCLA Loneliness Scale: Concurrent and discriminant validity evidence. *Journal of Personality and Social Psychology, 39,* 472–480.

Sarbin, T. (1986). The narrative as root metaphor for psychology. In T. Sarbin (Ed.), *Narrative psychology: The storied nature of human conduct* (pp. 3–21). New York: Praeger.

Scheier, M. M., & Carver, C. S. (1985). Optimism, coping and health: Assessment and implications of generalized outcome expectancies. *Health Psychology, 4,* 219–247.

Silverberg, S. B., & Gondoli, D. M. (1996). Autonomy in adolescence: A contextualized perspective. In G. R. Adams, R. Montemayor, & T. P. Gullotta (Eds.), *Psychosocial development in adolescence* (pp. 12–61). Thousand Oaks, CA: Sage.

Smetana, J. (1995). Context, conflict, and constraint in adolescent-parent authority relationships. In M. Killen & D. Hart (Eds.), *Morality in everyday life: Developmental perspectives* (pp. 225–255). New York: Cambridge University Press.

Smetana, J. (1997). Parenting and the development of social knowledge reconceptualized: A social domain analysis. In J. E. Grusec & L. Kuczynski (Eds.), *Parenting and children's internalization of values* (pp. 162–192). New York: Wiley.

Steinberg, L. (1990). Interdependency in the family: Autonomy, conflict, and harmony in the parent-adolescent relationship. In S. Feldman & G. Elliot (Eds.), *At the threshold: The developing adolescent* (pp. 255–276). Cambridge, MA: Harvard University Press.

Steinberg, L. (2001). We know some things: Parent-adolescent relationships in retrospect and prospect. *Journal of Research on Adolescence, 11,* 1–19.

Steinberg, L., Lamborn, S., Darling, N., Mounts, N., & Dornbusch, S. (1994). Over-time changes in adjustment and competence among adolescents from authoritative, authoritarian, indulgent, and neglectful families. *Child Development, 65,* 754–770.

Steinberg, L., & Silverberg, S. B. (1986). The vicissitudes of autonomy in early adolescence. *Child Development, 57,* 841–851.

Tappan, M. (1991). Narrative, authorship, and the development of moral authority. *New Directions for Child Development, 54,* 5–25.

Tappan, M. B., & Brown, L. (1989). Stories told and lessons learned: Toward a narrative approach to moral development. *Harvard Educational Review, 59,* 182–205.

Vitz, P. (1990). The use of stories in moral development: New psychological reasons for an old educational method. *American Psychologist, 45,* 709–720.

Vygotsky, L. S. (1978). *Mind in society.* Cambridge, MA: Harvard Press.

Walker, L. J. (1999). The family context for moral development. *Journal of Moral Education, 28,* 261–264.

Walker, L. J., & Henning, K. H. (1999). Parenting style and the development of moral reasoning. *Journal of Moral Education, 28,* 359–374.

Walker, L. J., Henning, K. H., & Krettenaur, T. (2000). Parent and peer contexts for children's moral reasoning development. *Child Development, 71,* 1033–1048.

Wertsch, J. V. (1991). *Voices of the mind: A sociocultural approach to mediated action.* Cambridge, MA: Harvard University Press.

Wintre, M. G., & Yaffe, M. (2000). First-year students' adjustment to university life as a function of relationship with parents. *Journal of Adolescent Research, 15,* 9–37.

Youniss, J., & Smollar, J. (1985). *Adolescent relations with mothers, fathers, and friends.* Chicago: University of Chicago Press.

8

When Parents' Stories Go to Pot: Telling Personal Transgressions to Teenage Kids

Avril Thorne
Kate McLean
Anna Dasbach
University of California, Santa Cruz

"Tell me a story about when you were young" is a familiar refrain to parents, and also is beginning to be heard by family narrative researchers. Parents in many cultures tell family stories in an effort to guide their children's conduct and convey important values (Fiese, Hooker, Kotary, Schwagler, & Rimmer, 1995). Personal stories lie at the heart of "opportunity education" (Fung, 1999), emerging at moments when the parent's own past experience seems to connect with the concerns of the child. Parents tend to *believe* that the stories they tell their children about their past lives can influence their children's behavior and values, and communities differ with regard to the kinds of parental stories that are told and not told to children (Miller, Sandel, Liang, & Fung, 2001; Miller, Wiley, Fung, & Liang, 1997).

The present study builds on past studies of an important domain of parental storytelling, stories of personal transgressions. Peggy Miller and her colleagues have contributed much of the foundational ethnographic work on how and why parents tell stories of their own transgressions to their children. Miller et al. (2001) found that White middle-class American mothers felt that telling their personal transgressions to their children created closeness by placing the parent at a more equal level with the child. This "self-lowering" parental strategy has also been identified in other studies of narrative socialization practices in White middle-class America (e.g., Ochs & Schieffelin, 1984). In contrast to Chinese mothers, who felt that exposing parental misdeeds would grant permission for transgressive behavior, American mothers emphasized a distinction between the behavior and the person. In narrating their own transgressions, American mothers espoused the view that bad acts do not make a bad person, that bad behavior can be redeemed, and that people are "complex, protean, and flawed" (Miller et al., 2001, p. 178).

The present study explored a specific kind of parental transgression: smoking marijuana in one's teenage years. Although the dilemma of how to talk to one's teenagers about one's own experiences with marijuana is very specific, it is also a fairly common predicament within the community that we studied and in the United States overall. An estimated two thirds of the parents of today's teenagers experimented with marijuana at some point in their youth (Johnston, O'Malley, & Bachman, 1986). Nevertheless, there appear to have been no systematic studies of whether and how parents disclose these youthful experiences to their children. Prior research has focused on relatively innocent parental misdeeds as told to young children. Because marijuana use is illegal and emerges later in adolescence, we turned to the larger family narrative literature to anticipate potential age-developmental changes with regard to transgressive experiences, and the role of marijuana in the development of American adolescents. In this chapter, we tell the story of the beliefs and practices that emerged.

AGE-DEVELOPMENTAL CHANGES IN PERFORMING AND EXPLAINING TRANSGRESSIONS

Adolescents, by virtue of having lived longer than young children and having broader social networks, are likely to be exposed to a varied array of transgressions on the part their families, their peers and the families of their peers. Because transgressive acts breech community norms and tend to require narrative justification (Bruner, 1990), adolescents can also be expected to hear a larger variety of beliefs and values with regard to transgressive behavior. Teenagers are also cognitively more sophisticated than children, and more interested in comparing one value with another in pursuit of an ideology to live by (Goodnow, 1992; Habermas & Bluck, 2000; McAdams, 1993). In White, middle-class America, adolescence is not only an era for exploring alternative practices and values, but also for developing a more egalitarian relationship with parents (e.g., Collins, 1997; Grotevant & Cooper, 1985). This greater mutuality includes more open disclosures on the part of parents than would occur with younger children, such as revealing the true reason that the children were sent away to live with relatives, or the mother's mastectomy scars (McLean & Thorne, 2003). However, parents may be less willing to disclose parts of their past which, if emulated, could put the teenager at risk.

Although children eventually reach an age in which their own transgressions can potentially match those of the parent, parent and teen *values* about transgressive conduct may be slower to coincide. Part of the divergence concerns differences in time perspective, with adolescents more likely to live in the present (Burton, Sussman, Hansen, Johnson, & Flay, 1989). Collins and Repinski (1994) suggested that adolescence is a period in which parents and children may be especially likely to misunderstand each other because the adolescent is changing more rapidly than the parent. Disparity between teens' and parents' views of the child has been found to be highest in early adolescence; by late adolescence, there is likely to be more convergence between parents' and teens' views (Alessandri & Wozniak, 1989).

In considering how and why parents tell transgressive stories to their teens, it is important to consider that for the parent, adolescence is a bygone era, whereas for the teen, adulthood is unknown. Parents know the consequences of their own teenage misdeeds, whereas teens and parents can only guess about the eventual consequences of transgressive conduct on the part of the teen. To encourage responsibility in their adolescent children, should parents refrain from disclosing their own transgressions, or if they do, should they emphasize the negative consequences and forgo the parts of the story that suggest there was anything positive about the experience? Although the Miller et al. (2001) study understandably focused on relatively innocent misconduct, the mothers of the preschoolers described themselves as "wary of a too-ardent adherence to the letter of the law," and felt that there was "much to be learned by experimenting"; there was a value in transgressive selves (Miller et al., 2001, p. 181). Some parents may be willing to tolerate at least some of their teenagers' illicit misdeeds. Under-age drinking, for example, may be allowed in the home under parents' supervision. But what about behaviors that do not become legal, for which one does not legally come of age?

MARIJUANA, ADOLESCENT EXPLORATION, AND RISK TAKING

In a longitudinal study of Northern California residents, Shedler and Block (1990) found that 18-year-olds who had experimented with drugs, mostly marijuana, were better adjusted than were adolescents who were frequent drug users, or who had never experimented with drugs. In explaining their findings, the authors suggested that occasional use of marijuana can be understood as "developmentally appropriate experimentation" in the context of American adolescent culture; in former generations, alcohol primarily served that function.

Marijuana use is not illegal in all cultures, and even in the United States occupies a distinctive niche among illicit transgressions because it is prohibited by the official macro-culture but is visibly tolerated in some communities within the larger culture. In the latter communities, including the Northern California county from which we drew our informants, the values of the official macro-culture reach deeply into the school system and the home. Ex-drug addicts visit schools to tell stories about their personal struggles with drug abuse, and the DARE program teaches children how to identify the smell of marijuana. Recently the television news showed footage of federal raids on local medical marijuana growers, juxtaposed with footage of civic leaders approving the defiant distribution of medical marijuana on the steps of the county courthouse.

Compared to some illicit misdeeds, marijuana use may seem relatively minor. Nonetheless, value conflicts about marijuana use appear to be widespread, diversely managed, and rarely exposed to public view. The value conflicts can be expected to be especially intense for parents of teenagers, not only because marijuana is a prominent vehicle for adolescent exploration but also because adolescence is the period in which parents may be most likely to be asked to disclose and justify their own adolescent risk taking to their children. At that point, parents may feel pressed to "come clean" to their teens not only about their own *use* of marijuana, but also about the *meaning* of such use in their own lives. Full discussion of personal values with regard to marijuana use, if it occurs at all, may not be appropriate until late adolescence, when the child can better understand the parent's point of view. Stated another way, the act of smoking marijuana may emerge developmentally earlier than a mature understanding of the values that may protect children from compromising their future.

HOW TO TALK TO TEENS ABOUT ONE'S OWN MARIJUANA USE: THE OFFICIAL CULTURAL LINE

There is an official cultural line about how parents should protect their children from illicit drug use: "Talk to your kids about drugs." This advice is dispensed in public service television advertisements and on billboards and bumper stickers across America. But how, exactly, should parents talk to their teens about drugs, particularly when the parent has had personal experience with marijuana? Should the conversation focus on impersonal drug facts and on the teen's drug experience, or should the parents also disclose their own personal experience with drugs?

The most accessible source for educating parents about how to talk to their children about drugs is Drug Free America, a nonprofit organization whose website draws from guidelines provided by the U.S. Department of Education. The Drug Free America website (http://www.drugfreeamerica.org/Templates/Help-For-Parents) advises parents to begin to talk early to their children about drugs, to be a good listener, to give a clear no-use message, and to model honest behavior that the child can emulate. The advice to parents who have used drugs in the past is to go slow in the disclosure in an effort to determine the child's readiness for an open answer. In 1999, as we were conceiving the present study, we discovered a script on the Drug Free America website tailored for such occasions:[1]

> The 12-year-old you care for comes home from school and says, pretty matter-of-factly, "I learned about drugs today. The teacher said that lots of people your age used to do drugs. Did you?"
>
> You: "Wow, you're learning about drugs already? What are they teaching you?"
>
> Child: "Well, just about drugs and alcohol, and the teacher said a lot of people your age used drugs when they were young."
>
> You: "Well, I'm not sure what your teacher meant to say, but I can tell you what I know about those times. Would you like me to?"
>
> Child: "Sure."
>
> You: "Well, many people my age, who were young adults back then, tried marijuana. We mostly called it pot. But we didn't know as much about it as we do now. It was the same with cigarettes. We didn't think smoking was very harmful either. So do you still want to know if I smoked marijuana? Think. . . ."
>
> Child: "Are you just trying not to tell me?"
>
> You: "No, I'm trying to be thoughtful about how I answer you so I'll know more about what you think about my drug usage."
>
> Child: "So you did?"
>
> You: "Yes, I tried it. A couple of times because friends of mine were doing it. And then I stopped because I decided it just wasn't a good thing to do."

The above script provided a useful point of departure for our study because it was so vague; the script seemed to end just at the point that the parent was

[1]This script is no longer featured on the website, which now contains more general advice for parents of children at different ages. The source of the advice is the U.S. Department of Health and Human Services (1998, pp. 8–9).

beginning to tell a personal story. The cautionary tone of the script may have been due to its being addressed to a 12-year-old. Is such a script appropriate for older adolescents, or should parents respond more directly and, if so, with how much detail? If parents have smoked pot in the past, should they openly share their stories with their teenagers, or should parents speak with the voice of the parent self, and downplay their teenage selves in an effort to emphasize the role of caregiver?

Responding to the question "Did you ever smoke pot when you were younger?" raises serious issues that lie at the heart of parenting, and at the heart of making sense of one's life in a way that is both honest and responsible. In answering what we will henceforth refer to as *the Question,* one must answer to oneself as well as to one's child. The ideals of personal integrity and responsibility would seem at odds for parents who smoked marijuana in their younger years, and who seek an optimal way to reconcile those values.

THE STUDY

To explore the parameters of this sensitive case of family narratives, we interviewed 17 parents (75% females) and 18 teens (60% females). The large majority of our informants were White, middle-class, and American born, and had at least some college education. The informants all resided in a county of Northern California, an area of the United States known for politically liberal values and which, along with California at large and seven other states, voted in the late 1990s in favor of the medicinal use of marijuana. The parents in the sample ranged in age from 40 to their early 50s, and the average number of children was two. Most of these children were currently in their mid- to late teens, although a few were preteens and several were in their 20s. The parents heard about our study by word of mouth; this is not an optimal method for sampling the community, but we felt it was a useful way to begin to explore the parameters of a very sensitive topic. Most of the teens whom we interviewed were 18 years of age and in their first months of living away from home at college, a time when exposure to alternative lifestyles is in high gear. Most of the teens were recruited from the research participation pool at a local college for a study of "family stories." All informants were promised anonymity.

Initially we intended to interview parents and their own teenage children. However, we found during pilot interviews that the topic could be invasive in its impact on the relationship between the parent and child. Privacy issues were one consideration, for although we assured informants that we would not reveal what they had said to the parent and vice versa, we sensed some hesitation on the part of each. We also heard a few stories about the impact that anticipation of the interview had upon family discussions of the topic, an interesting issue in its own right but one that goes beyond our current scope. Because we were not sure how these family discussions might impact what parents and teens said about the topic, we decided to switch to the safer ground of non-related parents and teens. A woman in her late 40s, with grown children, interviewed most of the parents, and a 20-year-old female college student interviewed most of the teens. The interviewers, like most of the respondents, were White and middle class, and had some college education.

We emphasized to the informants that our intention was not to cast one particular narrative practice as better than another. We don't know enough about how these practices work in the context of particular families, and we have not independently assessed antecedents or outcomes of the practices. Ideally, we would like to capture these narrative practices "on the hoof," as they spontaneously emerge in everyday discourse, and to collect a much larger and more representative sample. But at this stage of the project, we were simply interested in exploring how parents and teens talked about this particular transgression and the range of practices and values that emerged.

Informants' Histories of Marijuana Use

To enhance rapport with the informants, we did not directly ask about their own past and current levels of marijuana use or that of their families. Instead, we waited for them to volunteer this information, and it usually emerged in the course of the interview. Approximately one third of the parents said they had never smoked marijuana, explaining that it was not available when they were growing up or that alcohol was the drug of choice in their family and peer group. Another third of the parents said they had used marijuana along with other illegal drugs and alcohol in the past, but stopped permanently when their children were young; most of these parents regarded themselves as reformed, ex-drug abusers. The final third of the parents described themselves as recreational pot smokers in the past and present.[2] This felicitous distribution of parental drug use (similar proportions of non-users, ex-abusers, and recreational users) allowed us to compare practices of parents with different

[2]Our proportion of parents who had smoked marijuana in the past year, about one third, was larger than the 10% of parents who, in national surveys, report occasional marijuana use (Cass, 2002), but is not surprising given the community in which they resided.

transgressive histories.[3] With regard to the marijuana use of the 18-year-olds, 75% said they had smoked pot; of these, half said their own parents had smoked pot while the others either said their parents had not, or did not mention their parents' marijuana history.[4]

The Interview

In the pilot phase of the study, we used open-ended interviews. However, it soon became clear that teenage marijuana smoking is a topic that merges with other kinds of risky behaviors in adolescence, particularly sex, alcohol, and other drugs. Furthermore, the discourse was not confined to one's own behavior and that of one's children, but also included the behavior of grandparents, other family members, and friends. A few public figures also got referenced with a fair degree of regularity, such as Bill Clinton ("I didn't inhale"), and George W. Bush ("Maybe I did, maybe I didn't"). In an effort to get the informants on track, we would ask, "Did your child ever ask you if you have smoked pot?" To our surprise, we found that answers to this question were usually not straightforward. We got few spontaneous narratives of specific incidents in which parents disclosed their pot experiences to their children. Because the parents appeared to be forthright with us about the extent of their past marijuana use, and because rehearsal aids memorability, we surmised that specific episodes of disclosing their drug use to their children tended to be historically rare and/or subsequently forgotten.

Although vivid stories of parent-child disclosure were not very prevalent in the pilot interviews, opinions abounded about how parents *should* respond to the Question. In most cases, the opinions reportedly were based on one's own experience as a parent and/or a child, and observations about siblings, neighbors, and friends. On the basis of the variety of responses we obtained in the pilot interviews, we developed brief scripted responses that parents said they themselves, their parents, or teens said their parents used to answer the Question. We added to these a scripted response that paraphrased the advice from the aforementioned Drug Free America website, although we did not reveal this source to the informant.

---

[3]One father described himself as a chronic drug abuser all his life; we excluded him from the study because he was atypical of our informants, and because his narrative was so impersonal; he attributed his own drug use and that of his kids' to the pressures of modern life and the permissiveness of the media.

[4]Although a 75% base rate is higher than the 54% of American high school seniors who reportedly have experimented with drugs (Johnston, O'Malley, & Bachman, 1998), it is not surprising for first-year college students in this Northern California community.

The interview protocol shown in Table 8.1 was the basis for the interviews that are the focus of the present study. During the interview, the informant was asked to comment on the appropriateness of each hypothetical script, with minimal intrusion on the part of the interviewer. Parents generally were more voluble than the teens with regard to their personal experiences, and seemed more emotionally engaged by the posed parenting predicaments. The interviews were transcribed, and tallied with regard to which hypothetical scripts the informant viewed as appropriate, which yielded mixed or ambivalent responses, and which were viewed as inappropriate.

TABLE 8.1
Interview Protocol for Parents and Teens

In our past interviews with parents and teens, a number of responses were offered with regard to how parents should talk to their kids about their personal experiences with marijuana. We've listed some of the responses on these cards. We're interested in knowing which responses seem to be appropriate, and which seem inappropriate. Since there are no correct answers to this question, we're interviewing parents [teens] to see what they can tell us.

I'd like you to read the first response out loud, and to tell me whether you think it's something a parent should say to their kid, and why or why not. We're especially interested in the "why or why not" part. Then we'll move on to the next response. Before I read each parental response, I'd like you to pretend to be the kid. Each time, you'll ask the same question: "Some of my friends are talking about smoking pot. Did you ever smoke pot?" I'll then read the response on the card. Then I'd like you to tell me if you think the response is the right thing to say to one's kid, and why or why not. Then we'll proceed to the next card and repeat the process. Do you have any questions? . . . OK let's begin.

Kid says:

"Some of my friends are talking about smoking pot. Did you ever smoke pot?"

Parent responds:

1. "Do you really want me to tell you whether I smoked pot as a kid? Think about how you would feel if I said no, and think about how you would feel if I said yes. Do you really want to know?

[Is this something you think a parent should say to their kid? Why or why not? Interviewer repeats after reading each hypothetical response.]

2. "No, I didn't. That stuff rots the brain and makes people stupid. People start with pot and then go on to harder stuff. It's really dangerous. I hope you never do it."
3. "Yes, I smoked some pot when I was a teenager and I regret it now. It didn't help me do better in school, and I could have gotten into a lot of trouble. I hope you learn from my experience and don't try it."
4. "A lot of kids smoked pot when I was a teenager, and a lot of them smoke it now. At some point someone is going to offer you some and I worry that it will be too strong, or that you'll get arrested. If you do experiment with it some time, I hope you will do it in a safe place and that you will call me if you need me to come get you."

We found that the first two scripts shown in Table 8.1 were unanimously rejected by all of the parents and all of the teens. The third script was endorsed to some degree by all the parents and all of the teens, and the fourth script was endorsed by all of the teens and only some of the parents. In the following sections, we elaborate the parents' and teens' reactions to each script, focusing on the values that emerged for informants with different histories of marijuana use.

Unanimous Endorsement of Honesty

Script 1. *Do you really want me to tell you whether I smoked pot as a kid? Think about how you would feel if I said no, and think about how you would feel if I said yes. Do you really want to know?* All of the parents and teens, who ranged from claimed abstainers to current users, were troubled by the evasiveness of the first script because it seemed deceptive. The importance of giving a straightforward answer to the Question was endorsed by every parent and teen in the study. Parents emphasized the virtue of being forthright and not beating around the bush, as exemplified by three mothers' narratives: "I would never say that to my kid. It seems argumentative, avoids the question, seems deceptive." "If they asked me I figure they do really want to know. This answer makes it seem like I have something to hide, that I'm afraid I would hurt them with the truth." "That's avoiding the issue."

Teens also endorsed the virtue of parental honesty, viewing the script as dodging the question and implying that the parent had something to hide. Understandably, teens more often took the child's perspective, saying that the evasion would make the child feel bad for asking the question and unwilling to confide in the parent. These consequences for the child were volunteered by teen informants who described themselves as having dabbled in pot, and by a teen who said she would never smoke pot, nor would her parents. Here are responses from four teens: "It's vague, general, threatening, leaves the kid in the dark. Makes him feel bad for asking the question. It will make him unwilling to confide in the parent since the parent isn't willing to confide in the kid." "I think the parent is just trying to be cautious, but the kid would clam up if the parent said this; the kid wants something a little more definite." "That's really bad. The parent might as well say, 'Do you want me to lie or do you want me to tell you the truth?' They must think the kid is an idiot." "The kid will think the parent smoked pot and is uncomfortable talking about it."

One of the most vivid stories with regard to evasion came second-hand, from a mother who reported the following conversation with the daughter of a friend. This narrative emphasized the humanizing virtues of parental stories of misdeeds that were cited by parents of preschoolers in prior research (Miller et al., 2001). Italics are added to emphasize the part of the narrative that we found particularly interesting:

> My friend's daughter [Alice] was staying overnight because she and her mom were having battles, having problems and stuff. And [Alice] said, "You know, *my mom acts like she's an angel, she's never done anything like smoke pot, which isn't true. And um, I know it and I think she knows it too.*" And I said, "Well, would you rather have her be open and talk to you, you know talk like we're talking?" And she said, "Yes I would because then at least I'd know my mom is human." And you know, as far as, you know, her mom is some *goody two-shoes* that never did anything and duh-de-duh-de-duh. And I said, "Well, you know a lot of times parents don't want to tell you these things 'cuz they think they'll give you, you know, ideas." And what she said to me was she said, "*How could I possibly get more ideas than I already have?*"

This informant felt that the mother's failure to disclose her own transgressions contributed to the rift between the mother and the child. The informant, who cast herself and Alice's mother as having smoked pot as teens, then added, "If you don't talk to them about it, I think you're setting them up to get into trouble. I think you're setting yourself up for having problems with your kid, bigger problems to deal with." Lying about the transgression was viewed as more grievous than the transgression itself.

Unanimous Endorsement of Personal Integrity, and of Knowing Drug Facts

Script 2. *No, I didn't. That stuff rots the brain and makes people stupid. People start with pot and then go on to harder stuff. It's really dangerous. I hope you never do it.* This script was double-barreled because it included the claim that the parent had not smoked marijuana, and the claim that pot rots the brain and leads to harder drugs. A double-barreled response is not ideal for a questionnaire item, but this sort of response was prominent in our pilot interviews, in which a parent's denial of having ever smoked pot was reportedly followed by a dire warning about the dangers of marijuana. Very few of our informants, either parents or teens, believed that smoking marijuana usually leads to harder drugs, reflecting empirical research (e.g., Gabany & Plummer, 1990; Kandel, 1975). Teens appeared to be more aware of this research than parents, referring to Script 2 as propounding the erroneous "gateway theory" of drugs. The teenage informants had been reared in an era in which drug education was formally dispensed by experts, in contrast to their parents and grandparents, for whom drug education was much more informal.

The grandparents were cast as the most ignorant of drug facts. A number of the parents said that their own parents believed that pot was a gateway to harder drugs, and that dire warnings about pot were a familiar refrain in their family of origin. Their parents were viewed as not only naïve about pot, but also as hypocritical because alcohol was normalized while marijuana was demonized. In one case, this perceived parental hypocrisy was used to justify the daughter's own excessive use of pot in adolescence. The daughter, a former heavy drug user who is now "clean and sober," recounted the following story:

> In my own family there was so much drinking on the part of adults that when I was experimenting with drugs and they told me, "Don't smoke marijuana, it's a dangerous drug," I said, "Well, you're doing your drugs." And I really remembered this hypocrisy and I didn't wanna be that way with our kids. That was real important to me, to not be hypocritical. But then I felt really struck by the fact that I had done things that I had to in order to not be a hypocrite. I had to 'fess up. I wish very strongly I could have led a better example.

The above mother, angry at her own parents' hypocrisy with regard to alcohol, became a heavy drug user. She used drugs with abandon in front of her very young children, just as she said her parents had used alcohol. She now sees the irony of her response to her parents' hypocrisy, and wishes she had set a better example.

Overall, parents were skeptical about Script 2 because someone who had never used pot was unlikely to be knowledgeable about its effects. Parents who had no exposure to pot and endorsed the gateway theory seemed naïve to their children, and parents who condemned pot but were sanguine about the use of alcohol seemed hypocritical.

Teenagers also attributed the naïvité of Script 2 to parental inexperience, but some of the teens also intimated that the experience of smoking pot itself, not just its long-term consequences, could not be understood by inexperienced parents. For example one teen said of the script, "My mom said that to me and it makes me think she's naïve and biased because she never smoked pot and doesn't know the whole story." Several teens said that Script 2 would create a barrier to open communication and might even boomerang:

> Yes, my parents said that to me. In my family, drugs were bad, period. It was ok to drink but not to use pot. It's a very lame answer because there's no exchange allowed; the parent makes it a closed issue. It's too black and white. The kid will feel he can't talk to his parents about it.

Unanimous Endorsement of Expressing Some Degree of Regret

Script 3. *Yes, I smoked some pot when I was a teenager and I regret it now. It didn't help me do better in school, and I could have gotten into a lot of trouble. I hope you learn from my experience and don't try it.* In this script, the parent forthrightly confessed to smoking pot, an admission quickly followed by an expression of regret. The presumed honesty of the admission, the realism of the consequences, and the gentle suggestion that the child learn from the parents' experience were all praised by various informants. A reformed former heavy drug user, the mother of a 16-year-old son, emphasized regret in this bitter account:

> I have to keep drilling the regret into my son's head. . . .I hope he can learn from my experience, but there's pressure from peers, and from his dad [her ex-husband, a chronic pot grower], and I have to be realistic. He's going to experiment. I don't think it's gonna stop him from smoking but I hope it helps him be aware of what's happening to him. He did see me when I first started in recovery; he felt a great relief and we talked a lot about it, the downside and how it made him feel vulnerable because of being raised a pot baby. I had to apologize to him, when he was 10 or 11. But now he's 16 and seems to think it's cool having been a pot baby, it's culturally sanctioned. . . .I do have so many regrets, I look back and go, God I was such a mess.

Another self-identified former heavy drug user whose grown children have "drug problems of their own" reported an episode in which she and her grown son openly exchanged their regrets. Her account suggested the interesting possibility that a parent's regrets can only be fully understood by someone who shares the same experience, in this case, one's grown child.

Whereas the preceding two informants voiced considerable regret about their past drug use, the regret was not transformed into a hopeful vision for the future. Rather, the mothers seemed to feel helpless with regard to their own and their children's future, and their difficulties were compounded by a spouse or ex-spouse who was a heavy drug user. Clearly, parents' stories of regret draw from and influence other family members; regret does not exist in isolation, although we are far from understanding the impact of regret on families and lives.

Recreational pot smokers who endorsed the regret script did so half-heartedly, as if they were drawing from a dominant cultural narrative that might serve as a protective device, but which they did not fully embrace. For example, one such mother endorsed Script 3 because it seemed to be a gentle way to try to deter her children from using drugs. She said, "Yes, I said it that way. It's more honest than lying and saying I didn't smoke pot, but I don't really regret having smoked it. I didn't know what else to say to make them think twice about smoking pot."

Teens liked the script because it seemed more credible than the prior scripts, even if one's parent would never say it. Teens seemed very able to differentiate between what their parents would say and what seemed to be an optimal response:

> It's personal, which is good, and honest about the effects, not an exaggeration, and it's good because you're still being the parent. But my parents wouldn't say this—I'd be shocked! They've never smoked pot.

Some of the teens' parents had reportedly used Script 3, apparently to good effect: "Yes, my dad said this. I really like it. It's honest and states risks, and I've never smoked pot." "Yes, that's what my mom said, 'I'm trusting you to learn from my experience.'" Several teens emphasized the value of giving the teen some leeway; the script seemed to do that by making the child "think twice," instead of prohibiting experimentation: "It's really good. Emphasizes moderation, illegality, and makes the kid think twice." "It's good because it's honest and they're trying to deter you from something they think is bad for you. It makes the kid think."

A few teens questioned whether the regret script would be effective because the child might not be satisfied living vicariously through the parent's experience, or because regret should be an equal opportunity: if a parent could smoke pot and regret it, then a teen could, too. "It's honest and informative about possible consequences, but the mom's experience may not be the kid's experience. Sometimes kids need to experience stuff for themselves." "It's good because she's telling the truth. But it could backfire, the kid might think 'Well, you did it so I'll do it and learn for myself.' It's better to say this to a college student, a kid who's older."

Divergence Between Parents and Teens: Providing a Safety Net for Experimentation

Script 4. *A lot of kids smoked pot when I was a teenager, and a lot of them smoke it now. At some point someone is going to offer you some and I worry that it will be too strong, or that you'll get arrested. If you do experiment with it some time, I hope you will do it in a safe place and that you will call me if you need me to come get you.* This final script emphasized the inevitability of the temptation, the potential physiological and legal dangers, and the importance of being cautious and calling the parent for help, if need be. Although the script did not reveal the parent's own marijuana history, this omission did not seem to trouble the informants. Instead, informants focused on the delicate balance that was conveyed between allowing the teen freedom and responsibility in an era in which exposure to marijuana was viewed as inevitable.

The teens, regardless of their own marijuana history and the attitudes of their parents toward marijuana, were uniformly enthusiastic about the trust and responsibility that was conveyed by Script 4. Teens felt that the script would encourage honesty and openness on the part of the child, as well as responsible experimentation. The enthusiasm for this script was apparent in the response of a young woman who had never smoked pot, nor had her parents. Despite the fact that she could not imagine her parents voicing the script, she thought it was a good way to handle it:

> I think this one is great. The parent is taking responsibility and giving the kid responsibility but also saying "I'll be there for you." The parent is understanding. My parents would never say this, though. They would lecture me really hard if I ever smoked pot.

A young man, whose dad used to grow pot and reportedly told hell-raising stories about it, described himself as having gone in the opposite direction. But he liked the script because its openness would make the teen feel he didn't have to "hide stuff," and that the teen would "feel relieved." Another young man liked the script because it addressed the dangers, health risks, legal risks, and inevitable exposure: "The parent seems very well informed about the teen's situation, which would make the kid feel more secure and understood."

Whereas teens were uniformly positive about Script 4, the script split the general consensus that had prevailed in the parents' responses to the prior scripts. Reformed former pot users found the safety net script too permissive. For example, the mother of the "pot baby," described previously, felt that the script "encourages the kid to experiment. It's important to send a strong no-pot message." This mother felt that she perpetually had to battle her son's peer culture and her ex-husband's permissiveness to keep her son away from marijuana. To her, the issue was black and white because of her fear that her son would become like her former self, and like her ex-husband, an unrepentant daily pot-smoker.

Parents who favored the safety net script were abstainers who had never smoked pot but had indulged in alcohol, or were recreational pot-smoking parents. The former group included a mother of three teenagers, the youngest of whom she was "worried about." She said she uses this script because "it makes them feel I'll be there for them if they make a mistake, and that I'll be disappointed if they go too far." She thinks the narrative instills a dual sense of security and guilt, and also keeps the lines of communication open. A recreational pot-smoking mother said that she emphasized how not to cross the line with regard to pot smoking. She told her teens:

> Don't take it to school, don't carry it around because it's illegal and you'll get into trouble; you can smoke it at home with your friends before you go to a dance, but if you are ever in a situation where you can't get home safely you call me, no questions asked, no lectures.

Another recreational pot-smoking mother said, "We've never pretended that our kids don't smoke pot, but we remind them not to go too far; use your brain and be careful." The illegality bothers her, and the excess, but she feels that experimentation is inevitable and so far she feels that their teenagers are open with them about their experimentation and able to be moderate about it.[5]

IMPLICATIONS

We were surprised at the eagerness with which parents volunteered to participate in the study, and their vested interest in the findings. Many sought from us the perfect script, or as one mother phrased it, the "magic bullet" for how to talk to one's children about one's personal experiences with marijuana. We cannot provide a magic bullet on the basis of three dozen interviews, but the themes that emerged suggest some guidelines for what virtues matter for American parents and teens with regard to the narrative management of this illicit transgression. These virtues—honesty, knowledge, regret, and, for most parents and all of the teens, safe experimentation—will be discussed in this section along with larger implications for the field of family narrative.

The most prominent virtue across all parents and 18-year-olds was the importance of answering the question "Did you ever smoke pot when you were younger?" honestly and straightforwardly. A simple, immediate, and honest "yes" or "no" was highly valued because it was felt to create a *climate of mutual honesty.* Parents who were honest with their children could more often expect their children to be honest with them. Sharing stories about

---

[5]As an interesting side note for the study of family narrative, we noticed that among the currently married informants, the recreational pot smokers more often used the collective voice, using "we" instead of "I" in their discourse, for example, "*We* say be smart about it and don't get in a car. Call *us,* and try to be moderate." Such indications of parental consensus (Steuve & Pleck, 2001) were less prevalent among married informants who had reportedly not smoked pot, or who were reformed ex-drug abusers.

one's illicit past may signify a turning point toward an egalitarian relationship between parent and child, which tends to surface in emerging adulthood (Arnett, 2000). Whereas offering one's adolescent more freedom (e.g., to use the family car or to stay out later) communicates a one-way trust in the child, disclosing one's illicit behavior communicates a mutual trust. The disclosure trusts the child to use the information wisely and to understand the parent from a more mature perspective.

To our surprise, parents who had not smoked pot were not off the hook with regard to the Question because such parents ran the risk of being dismissed by their teens as naïve and out of touch with the child's reality. Parents who had not smoked pot tended to be regarded by their children as ignorant of basic drug facts. The teens in our study, relative to their parents, tended to be more formally educated about the inaccuracy of the claim that marijuana is usually the gateway to hard drugs. However, some teens felt that accurate knowledge of drug facts was not sufficient to render their parents credible sources with regard to the effects of marijuana, or to fully understand the child's experience. These teens felt that parents had to have smoked marijuana themselves in order to understand the "whole story" and to more fully open the lines of communication between parent and child. This view raises the interesting question of whether engaging in the same activity (although not necessarily with one's child) opens lines of communication about the experience. For example, the full story of a parent's sexual experiences is not usually discussed in American families, regardless of the age of the child (Bartle, 1998).

In talking about their past experiences with marijuana, parents tended to place much more emphasis on conveying risks than benefits. Even parents who were current occasional users endorsed the expression of regret in an effort to promote caution and long-term achievement over the pleasures of a short-term high. While honesty about whether one had ever smoked pot was an important theme, honesty about the full range of consequences—bad and good, short-term and long-term—was less valued. Thus, even for parents who appeared to have enjoyed marijuana with few negative consequences, *expressing regret about potentially negative consequences trumped honesty about experienced consequences.*

The final virtue, safe experimentation, was enthusiastically endorsed by all the teens and by most of the parents. This virtue did not focus on the parent's marijuana experience, but instead emphasized the inevitability of the temptation, the potential physiological and legal dangers, and the importance of being cautious and calling the parent for help, if need be. Teenagers were enthusiastic about the realism, freedom and responsibility that were simultaneously conveyed by this script. The dissenting parents were perhaps the most interesting informants in the study. For parents who viewed marijuana as partly responsible for their own extended life problems, the child's well-being did not seem well served by opening the doors to experimentation, doors which they themselves had passed through in their youth and now tried to keep tightly shut. The "safe experimentation" script was viewed as too permissive by such parents, whereas it was viewed as appropriate by parents who felt that marijuana had not compromised the quality of their lives and who felt that their children could also handle marijuana responsibly.

Larger Implications for the Field of Family Narrative

As noted in the introduction to this chapter, studies of parental stories of transgressions have focused primarily on practices that are common across a community rather than practices that are idiosyncratic to particular families or parents (Miller et al., 2001). We, too, found some commonality across parents and teenagers, but this commonality pertained mostly to common values or beliefs, not practices. Because of the delicacy of the topic, we did not attempt to observe how parents actually talked to their teenagers about their past use of marijuana. However, we did expect that parents would offer vivid narratives about how they had talked to their teenagers in the past.

To our surprise, no parents had a ready story to tell us about a *specific episode* in which they had talked to their children about their own experiences with marijuana. Parents had firm opinions about what *not* to say, but did not usually offer specific stories about what they *did* say. We also observed that although most of the teens seemed confident about their knowledge with regard to whether their parents had or had not smoked pot, the source of this knowledge was not necessarily the result of deliberate disclosure on the part of the parent. Some knowledge was reportedly based on serendipitous observation or eavesdropping: overhearing one's mother and aunt laughing about being stoned on a high school camping trip, the picture in an uncle's photo album of one's dad smoking pot, a baggie full of stale weed tucked into the back of dad's sock drawer. Clearly, children derive information about their parents' past from many sources, only some of which are under the direct control of the parent. The impact on children of indirect knowledge about their parents' lives, such as hearsay, is an interesting domain for future study because it encourages a more distributed conception of narrative selves and lives as extending beyond the nuclear family and into the wider community (Bruner, 1990).

Teenagers were aware of their parents' tendency to shield this part of their past, especially when the children were younger. Generally, the older and the more responsible the child, the more likely the informants (both parents and teens) viewed as appropriate parents' disclosure of their illicit past. This sensitivity to the maturity of the child was striking, although parents on the whole were viewed by teens as continuing to be more protective of their illicit transgressions than the teens felt was necessary. The teens viewed their parents as people who make mistakes but are generally well intentioned, a view that parallels the attitudes of the American parents of young children in the Miller et al. (2001) study. The parents in the present study, however, were less uniform than either Miller's parents or our 18-year-olds in viewing their teenagers as human beings who make mistakes. Many seemed to feel that the fruits of their parenting were still on the vine. The more casual attitude of teens toward parental transgressions than vice versa may reflect differences in investment in the parental project (Steinberg, 2001). For example, parents tend to view their children's transgressions as reflecting on their own failure as a parent, whereas teens do not tend to read such deep meaning into it (Collins, 1990; Smetana, 1988). Sometimes in our interviews with teens, we asked them how they would talk to their own kids about their experiences with illicit drugs. This question tended to produce a more cautious story, one that was reminiscent of the cautionary tales more often portrayed by parents. Possibly, projecting oneself into the future may lead a teenager to cast the present into a longer time perspective and to experience the present with more of an eye to the future.

The most dramatic differences among parents centered on their comfort with their own adolescent selves. The recreational pot-smoking mothers still seemed to value the exploratory mentality to which they viewed marijuana as a route. For such mothers, cautious experimentation was a practice which they felt they had successfully incorporated into their lives; their current selves were relatively conversant with their past selves (Bakhtin, 1981; Hermans, 1996). These mothers expressed pride in their children's academic and extracurricular achievements and confidence in their children's moderation with regard to the use of pot, although they were alert to signs that their children were veering off track. Such mothers seemed to exemplify families who have a sustained generational identity. In a longitudinal study of California counterculture families, Weisner and Bernheimer (1998, p. 212) found that regardless of whether counterculture values had been sustained or abandoned, all of the parents felt that their teenage children's "well-being (or lack thereof) . . . resulted partly from countercultural parental values and life choices." A sustained commitment to these values was found to be associated with greater subjective and objective well being for middle-aged parents and their teenagers, including lower levels of teenage drug use.

The recreational pot-smoking mothers contrasted markedly with the mothers who were worried about their teenage children's use of drugs. The latter mothers had a spouse or an ex-spouse who, in their view, did not use moderation as a philosophy. The disparity between the parents with regard to attitudes toward marijuana was cast as a perpetual obstacle in keeping their children on the good path. A former pot-using mother whose husband smokes marijuana daily said she had never discussed her husband's marijuana use with her 17-year-old:

> My son oftentimes will say, "Well, you know, Dad said this, you say that." You can tell there's a little bit of confusion. On the other hand, I don't think it's reasonable for two people to get their stories straight ahead of time either. I think you just have to go with it. Like I say, "Well, you know, that's what dad thinks and dad is different from me."

Further fracturing the coherence of that family system was the troubled trajectory of the mother's life story. This mother seemed to have psychologically divorced her adolescent drug self from her current sober self, but had not developed a hopeful vision of the future for herself or for her children. This kind of unhopeful personal story has been found to be associated with unfortunate family outcomes (McAdams & Bowman, 2001; Pratt, Norris, van de Hoef, & Arnold, 2001; Singer, 1997).

Clearly an important issue to be pursued by family narrative research concerns the impact of parents' personal stories on family climate and children's well-being. Consistent with Miller et al. (2001), most of the parents in the present study believed that the personal stories that they chose to tell to their children influenced their children's development. We have no independent evidence to support the validity of such beliefs, but we noted some variation with regard to the strength of the conviction. Fathers, although underrepresented in the study, tended to be less concerned than mothers about vividly disclosing past episodes of drug use to their children. Hints of a parallel gender difference also emerged in the "hell-raising" stories that fathers more often told children in Miller's studies of American families (Miller et al., 2001). Overall, we sensed that mothers viewed personal narratives as a more powerful socializing agent than did fathers, who tended to view their stories as serving more of an entertainment than a guidance function. The field of family narrative is just beginning to understand the influence of parents' personal stories on children's well-being. How parents determine which stories are appropriate to tell is a fascinating route for future research.

ACKNOWLEDGMENTS

We are grateful to the parents and teenagers who entrusted us with their experiences, to our interviewers, Mimi Cleary and Christina Chidester, and to Joe Christy and Margarita Azmitia for comments on prior drafts. Preparation of this manuscript was supported in part by a training grant from the National Institute of Mental Health (5 T32 M20025-03) to the second author.

REFERENCES

Alessandri, S. M., & Wozniak, R. (1989). Continuity and change in intrafamilial agreement in beliefs concerning the adolescent. A follow-up study. *Child Development, 60,* 335–339.

Arnett, J. J. (2000). Emerging adulthood: A theory of development from the late teens through the twenties. *American Psychologist, 55,* 469–480.

Bakhtin, M. (1981). *The dialogic imagination.* Austin: University of Texas Press.

Bartle, N. (1998). *Venus in blue jeans: Why mothers and daughters need to talk about sex.* Boston: Houghton Mifflin.

Bruner, J. (1990). *Acts of meaning.* Cambridge, MA: Harvard University Press.

Burton, D. Sussman, S., Hansen, W. B., Johnson, C. A., & Flay, B. R. (1989). Image attributions and smoking intentions among seventh grade students. *Journal of Applied Social Psychology, 19,* 656–664.

Cass, D. (2002, September 6). Government survey finds drug use on the rise. *Santa Cruz Sentinel (Associated Press),* p. A-5.

Collins, W. A. (1990). Parent-child relationships in the transition to adolescence: Continuity and change in interaction, affect, and cognition. In R. Montemayor, G. R. Adams, & T. Gullotta (Eds.), *Advances in adolescent development: Vol. 2. The transition from childhood to adolescence* (pp. 85–106). Beverly Hills, CA: Sage.

Collins, W. A. (1997). Relationships and development during adolescence: Interpersonal adaptation to individual change. *Personal Relationships, 4,* 1–14.

Collins, W. A., & Repinski, D. J. (1994). Relationships during adolescence: Continuity an change in interpersonal perspective. In R. Montemayor & G. R. Adams (Eds.), *Advances in adolescent development: Vol. 6. Personal relationships during adolescence* (pp. 7–36). Thousand Oaks, CA: Sage.

Fiese, B., Hooker, K., Kotary, L., Schwagler, J., & Rimmer, M. (1995). Family stories: Gender differences in thematic content. *Journal of Marriage and the Family, 57,* 763–770.

Fung, H. (1999). Becoming a moral child: The socialization of shame among young Chinese children. *Ethos, 27,* 180–209.

Gabany, S. G., & Plummer, P. (1990). The Marijuana Perception Inventory: The effects of substance abuse instruction. *Journal of Drug Education, 20,* 234–245.

Goodnow, J. J. (1992). Parents' ideas, children's ideas: Correspondence and divergence. In I. E. Sigel, A. V. McGillicuddy-DeLisi, & J. J. Goodnow (Eds.), *Parental belief systems: The psychological consequences for children* (2nd ed., pp. 293–317). Hillsdale, NJ: Lawrence Erlbaum Associates.

Grotevant, G. D., & Cooper, C. R. (1985). Patterns of interaction in family relationships and the development of identity exploration in adolescence. *Child Development, 56,* 415–428.

Habermas, T., & Bluck, S. (2000). Getting a life: The emergence of the life story in adolescence. *Psychological Bulletin, 126,* 748–769.

Hermans, H. J. M. (1996). Voicing the self: From information processing to dialogical interchange. *Psychological Bulletin, 119,* 31–50.

Johnston, L. D., O'Malley, P. M., & Bachman, J. G. (1986). *Drug use among American high school students, college students, and other young adults: National trends through 1985.* Rockville, MD: National Institute on Drug Abuse.

Johnston, L. D., O'Malley, P., & Bachman, J. G. (1998). *National Survey Results on Drug Use from Monitoring the Future Study.* Rockville, MD: U.S. Department of Health & Human Services.

Kandel, D. (1975). Stages in adolescent involvement in drug use. *Science, 190,* 912–914.

McAdams, D. P. (1993). *The stories we live by: Personal myths and the making of the self.* New York: William Morrow.

McAdams, D. P., & Bowman, P. J. (2001). Narrating life's turning points: Redemption and contamination. In D. P. McAdams, R. Josselson, & A. Lieblich (Eds.), *Turns in the road: Narrative studies of lives in transition* (pp. 3–34). Washington, DC: American Psychological Association.

McLean, K. C., & Thorne, A. (2003). Late adolescents' self-defining memories about relationships. *Developmental Psychology, 39,* 635–645.

Miller, P. J., Sandel, T. L., Liang, C.-H., & Fung, H. (2001). Narrating transgressions in Longwood: The discourses, meanings, and paradoxes of an American socializing practice. *Ethos, 29,* 159–186.

Miller, P. J., Wiley, A., Fung, H., & Liang, C.-H. (1997). Personal storytelling as a medium of socialization in Chinese and American families. *Child Development, 68,* 557–568.

Ochs, E., & Schieffelin, B. (1984). Language acquisition and socialization: Three developmental stories and their implications. In R. A. Shweder & R. LeVine (Eds.), *Culture theory: Essays on mind, self and emotion* (pp. 276–320). Cambridge: Cambridge University Press.

Pratt, M. W., Norris, J. E., van de Hoef, S., & Arnold, M. L. (2001). Stories of hope: Parental optimism in narratives about adolescent children. *Journal of Personal and Social Relationships, 18,* 603–623.

Shedler, J., & Block, J. (1990). Adolescent drug use and psychological health. *American Psychologist, 45,* 612–630.

Singer, J. A. (1997). *Message in a bottle: Stories of men and addiction.* New York: The Free Press.

Smetana, J. (1988). Concepts of self and social convention: Adolescents' and parents' reasoning about hypothetical and actual family conflicts. In M. Gunnar (Ed.), *Twenty-first Minnesota symposium on child psychology* (pp. 79–122). Hillsdale, NJ: Lawrence Erlbaum Associates.

Steinberg, L. (2001). We know some things: Parent-adolescent relationships in retrospect and prospect. *Journal of Research on Adolescence,11,* 1–19.

Stueve, J. L., & Pleck, J. H. (2001). "Parenting voices": Solo parent identity and co-parent identities in married parents' narratives of meaningful parenting experiences. *Journal of Social & Personal Relationships, 18,* 691–708.

U.S. Department of Health and Human Services. (1998). *Keeping youth drug-free* (DHHS Publication No. 619-046/90675). Washington, DC: U.S. Government Printing Office.

Weisner, T. S., & Bernheimer, L. P. (1998). Children of the 1960s at midlife: Generational identity and the Family Adaptive Project. In R. A. Shweder (Ed.), *Welcome to middle age (And other cultural fictions)* (pp. 211–257). Chicago: The University of Chicago Press.

PART III

Young Adulthood: Intimacy and Relationship Narratives

9

Marital Attachment and Family Functioning: Use of Narrative Methodology

Susan Dickstein
Brown University

This chapter focuses on the extent to which marriage functions as an attachment relationship reflected in working models incorporating organized representations of the self and of social relationships produced in narrative form. Marriage is an intimate adult relationship embedded within a family system that is linked with quality of functioning in numerous other aspects of family life. For example, research has shown that the marriage is related to a host of outcomes including how parents interact with their infants, how young children express and regulate emotion, and how episodes of depression in women are experienced, maintained, and resolved (Barnett & Gotlib, 1988; Hooley & Teasdale, 1989; Jacobson, Dobson, Fruzetti, Schmaling, & Salusky, 1991; Kowalik & Gotlib, 1987). There has been ongoing examination of the processes by which marriage influences (and is influenced by) various family subsystem functions. In this chapter, focus is placed on attachment processes to examine links among family subsystems.

Attachment research has become a hallmark approach from which to conceptualize interpersonal interaction that has meaning across generational boundaries and relationship contexts (van IJzendoorn, 1992; Waters, Vaughn, Posada, & Kondo-Ikemura, 1995). To date, most of this work has examined adult attachment relationships in the realm of adults' conceptualization of their own early childhood relationships with their parents. In particular, adult attachment relationships have been the focus of attention when attempting to elucidate processes that might help explain attachment status in children. In this chapter, we broaden the lens to examine the marital relationship as an adult attachment construct with associated representational properties (Hazan & Shaver, 1990; Owens et al., 1995; Shaver, Hazan, & Bradshaw, 1988). It is anticipated that conceptualization of the marriage as an attachment construct will elucidate important relational processes and associations within the family. In fact, we believe these marital attachment relationships are an important component for full understanding of the complex pattern of inter- and intragenerational representations of self–other relatedness. For example, from an attachment perspective, it may be the case that the marital relationship has an important potential restorative function, which can promote the development of secure infant-parent attachment relationships in the next generation. In this chapter, our goal is to describe the conceptual underpinnings of the marital attachment construct and highlight the utility of examining "marriage stories" from an attachment perspective.

ATTACHMENT THEORY

Bowlby (1982) theorized that children form internal working models of their relationships with others based on early interactions with significant caregivers. When children have experiences with reliable and responsive caregivers, they construct a working model of that relationship as secure and accessible, and a sense of self as adequate and worthy (Bretherton, 1985; Cummings & Cicchetti, 1990). In contrast, the continual experience of caregiver unavailability or inconsistency leads to expectations that the caregiver cannot be relied on as a secure base from which to explore the world, and that the self is unworthy of love. Overall, attachment theory supports the following points: (a) the child's sense of self is formed within a relationship context; (b) each child potentially has multiple significant relationship contexts within which the sense of self can be differentiated and enriched; and (c) working models are a heuristic for understanding the organized representations of self and relationships corresponding to observable attachment patterns that can be classified through use of standard procedures.

Recent methodological developments have facilitated more direct assessment of adults' current working models of their past relationships, termed *adult attachment* (George, Kaplan, & Main, 1985; Main & Goldwyn, 1988). *Secure* attachment is reflected in a balance between the attachment and exploratory motivational systems. In infants, this is demonstrated when the child seeks proximity to, and obtains comfort from, the caregiver during times of distress, following which the child promptly returns to exploration of the object and social worlds. In adults, secure attachment (labeled *autonomous*) is manifest as the ability to describe early relationships with caregivers in a coherent and consistent manner; these adults convey a strong sense of personal identity; and emphasis is placed on the importance and value of early experiences and current relationships.

Insecure attachment, on the other hand, is characterized by disruptions between the attachment and developmentally appropriate motivational systems. In infants, there are two organized patterns of insecure attachment (avoidant and resistant), which differ on the level of activation of attachment behaviors. There is also one pattern with no clear organization (disorganized). *Avoidant* infant-parent attachment is manifest when a child, during a stressful situation (confirmed by high levels of physiological arousal), de-activates attachment behavior by avoiding contact with the parent in an apparent attempt to minimize the anxiety associated with possible maternal rejection. In adults, the analogous pattern is classified as *dismissing* of attachment in which adults limit, deactivate, or devalue the influence of attachment relationships. *Resistant* infant-parent attachment is manifest when a child overactivates attachment behavior by simultaneously demanding and rejecting parental attention, and exhibits excessive dependence on the parent in an attempt to minimize arousal. In adults, the analogous pattern is classified as *preoccupied* with attachment characterized by descriptions of early attachment relationships that are confused or conflicted, often accented by passivity, fear, or anger.

Finally, the *disorganized* infant-parent attachment classification involves the child exhibiting no consistent way to deal with stressful attachment-related situations. In adults, attachment disorganization is characterized by a lack of resolution with respect to loss or trauma in which there is a pervasive emphasis on continued effects of loss or trauma in connection with current attachment experiences, and/or lapses in the monitoring of discourse or reasoning with the respect to the experience. Transcripts that reflect *unresolved* status exhibit specific lapses in monitoring of reasoning (such as psychologically confused statements or attempts to manipulate the mind with respect to the loss) and/or discourse (such as unusual attention to detail when describing the loss or invasion of loss-related themes into other topics).

Patterns of Attachment

Theoretical and empirical work suggests that mothers' working models of their early relationships with their own parents (reflected in adult attachment classifications) greatly influence the interaction patterns they develop with their children. Maternal insecure adult attachment is related to the development of behavior problems in their children (Crowell & Feldman, 1989; 1991), sleep disorders in their toddlers (Benoit, Zeanah, Boucher, &

Minde, 1989), failure to thrive in their infants (Benoit, Zeanah, & Barton, 1989), and dysregulations in mother-infant affect attunement (Haft & Slade, 1989).

Further, parents' working models of relationships developed early in life are related to the attachment relationships they develop with their own children. Prospective studies have found concordance rates ranging from 66% to 75% between maternal adult attachment classifications (secure versus insecure) obtained by Adult Attachment Interview (AAI) during pregnancy, and infant-mother attachment (secure versus insecure) observed in the Ainsworth, Blehar, Waters, and Wall (1978) Strange Situation more than a year later (Benoit, Vidovic, & Roman, 1991; Fonagy, Steele, & Steele, 1991; Ward, Botyanski, Plunkett, & Carlson, 1991). A similar range of concordance rates was found when the AAI was administered concurrently or following the Strange Situation (Eichberg, 1987; Main & Goldwyn, 1994; Zeanah & Emde, 1994).

Although most of the literature to date has focused on mothers, recent work has highlighted the importance of examining fathers' working models of relationships. In a meta-analysis conducted by van IJzendoorn and Bakermans-Kranenburg (1996), results indicated that the distribution of attachment representations in fathers is remarkably similar to that of mothers. Initial work suggests that mothers' and fathers' representations may differentially correspond with child outcomes. For example, while fathers' attachment representations were significantly related to father-infant security, van IJzendoorn and Bakermans-Kranenburg (1996) found that the association was somewhat less strong than it was for mothers. In addition, in a nonclinical sample, Cowan, Cohn, Cowan, and Pearson (1996) found that fathers' representations were more associated with teacher ratings of externalizing behaviors in preschool age children, whereas mothers' representations were more associated with child internalizing behaviors.

In a related vein, recent work has assessed associations between the quality of the marital relationship and each partner's adult attachment working model of childhood. Cohn, Cowan, Cowan, and Pearson (1992) found no relation between adult attachment (of early childhood relationships) classifications and self-reports of marital satisfaction, obtained from both husbands and wives. For husbands, however, adult attachment security was related to more positive (as opposed to conflictual) behavior in the marriage. Further, the authors speculated that a secure partner may, in fact, buffer negative effects of insecure working models established concerning early experience (i.e., adult attachment) vis-à-vis current marital behavior. Such findings support our working hypothesis that the nature of the attachment relationship *between* the partners may be linked both to marital behavior and to intergenerational continuity of relationship patterns.

In sum, attachment patterns can be examined in different developmental periods; there is correspondence within families across generations; these attachments appear to influence the developing sense of self as well as the developing expectations regarding the extent to which others can be relied on as emotional and social supports; and mothers' and fathers' representations potentially yield differential associations with parent-child and marital behavior. While a high degree of within-family correspondence has been reported between adult and infant-parent attachment classifications, the direction of the effects has not been clearly substantiated. The extent to which this association can be accounted for by intervening variables (such as the nature of mothers' current adult relationships) has not been fully explored. Finally, factors that may account for the observed intergenerational (and relational) matches and mismatches (potentially revealing protective or risk factors) have not been fully investigated.

MARITAL ATTACHMENT

Marital attachment is a concept that extends attachment constructs to the marital domain, and is broader in its cognitive-affective scope than appraisal of current marital satisfaction. Assessment of marital attachment is designed to infer the working model of the marriage. Similar to infant and adult attachment, marital attachment involves the extent to which partners operate from a secure base in order to accomplish developmentally appropriate tasks within adult domains such as effective parenting or employment, return to a safe haven during times of stress or distress, and use of the attachment relationship (the marriage, in this case) to regulate affect (e.g., Cohn, Silver, Cowan, Cowan, & Pearson, 1992; Hazan & Shaver, 1990; Shaver et al., 1988).

As with adult attachment, security of marital attachment is hypothesized to have implications for infant-parent attachment. However, unlike adult attachment, which is an assessment of a current model of caregiving relationships elicited via descriptions of past relationships, marital attachment is an assessment of a current model of intimate relationships elicited via descriptions of a *current* relationship within the context in which infant-parent attachment develops. As such, marital attachment is likely to be associated with the immediate nature of current family functioning, and therefore, may play a moderating role in the continuation of attachment security or insecurity across generations. For example, it is hypothesized that secure marital attachment may function to reduce the likelihood of insecure adult attachment leading to insecure infant-parent attachment. In families where both adult partners are secure in their marital attachment relationship (independent of adult attachment status), better family functioning may be evident due to processes such as effective skills in communication, problem solving, and resolution of negative affect (without implication of directional causality). This, in turn, may be associated with increased parental availability and sensitivity to the infant's needs, and thus secure infant-parent attachment. This moderation of the typical pattern of insecure adult attachment status promoting insecure infant-parent attachment leads to the view of marital attachment as a protective factor in the intergenerational transmission of attachment patterns. Thus, demonstrating an association of marital attachment and family functioning would suggest continued interest in the important hypothesis that secure *marital* attachment may help break the cycle in which insecure *adult* attachment leads to insecure *infant-parent* attachment.

This model rests on the assumptions that (a) adults can acess attachment working models differentially based on relationship context, and (b) marriage constitutes an attachment-relationship domain. We hypothesize that there is only slight (if any) association between marital attachment and adult attachment classifications; any associations between the measures are assumed to be due to overlap in method variance, not to construct concordance. We also hypothesize that there is minimal association between marital attachment classification and marital satisfaction given the assumption that marital representation is different from marital appraisal and behavior. And, finally, we hypothesize that there is substantial association between marital attachment classification and family functioning given the assumption that the working model or representation of the marital relationship is intrinsically tied (in a bi-directional manner) to the ways in which the couple transacts the day-to-day routines and rituals of being a family.

MARITAL ATTACHMENT INTERVIEW (MAI)

The Marital Attachment Interview is a direct extension of the Adult Attachment Interview (George, Kaplan, & Main, 1996), with modifications to address differences between construction of past relationships with the prior generation and the current same-generation marital attachment relationship. The MAI maintains similar properties as the AAI, including use of structured questions about attachment issues, questions asked in a set order, probes for specific information without altering the person's phrasing, no use of interpretive or integrative comments, and questions probing for overall evaluations of experience in conjunction with requests for specific examples. The MAI has a total of 16 questions covering orientation to the current marital relationship; description of the current relationship including expectations, changes over time, and separation experiences; experiences with rejection, threat, and support from the partner; past significant and intimate adult relationships including any prior divorces and/or abusive relationship experiences (from which information is obtained to score Unresolved with Respect to Loss or Trauma); information regarding the person's memories of his/her own parents' marital relationship; description of marital relationship influences on the current personality; and a wrap up.

Marital Attachment Interview Scoring

The narratives generated from verbatim transcripts of the Marital Attachment Interview are coded using the Adult Attachment Interview scoring system in slightly modified form to make marital attachment classifications (Main & Goldwyn, 1994). Attachment classifications from narrative assessment are based on two major dimensions, including security-insecurity and activation-deactivation of attachment behavior (Kobak, Cole, Ferenz-Gillies, & Flemming, 1993). The security-insecurity dimension is assessed from narrative properties including narrative characteristics (how the person presents narrative material) and content regarding actual relationship experiences (what the person says about relationships). The manner in which the person presents narrative material is weighted more heavily in the scoring than the specific content.

Narrative Scales. For the MAI, Loving and Rejection scales are scored consistent with their counterparts in the AAI system. The Loving scale assesses the extent to which the person describes experiences in the current significant adult relationship as loving or unloving, and maintains a firm sense that the partners are emotionally supportive and available. The Rejection scale assesses the extent to which the person describes experiences in the relationship as rejecting and/or avoiding of the person's attachment behaviors, as being emotionally distant or aloof, and/or as desiring to be out of the relationship altogether. Given the adult-adult nature of the marital relationship, these scales are considered bi-directionally; thus, a rating is made based on the person's experience of being rejected by the partner and/or the person's experience of rejecting the partner. Similar to AAI scoring, experience scales are ultimately scored based on the rater's judgments about the quality of the relationship in each domain.

The scales rating Narrative Characteristics include Coherence, Idealization, Anger, Derogation, Lack of Specificity (the analogue of AAI Lack of Recall), Metacognitive Process, Passivity of Thought Processes, and Fear of Loss. These scales are consistent with their AAI counterparts, with Coherence being the primary scale upon which classification is based. Three of these scales were modified to better reflect the current nature of the marital relationship. The Anger scale assesses the extent to which the person indicates anger toward or about the partner during the interview, which reflects current involvement in anger experiences. This scale is intended to assess thematic and pervasive anger, or anger that is presented in an overwhelming manner. Thus, a person who discloses currently felt anger with the partner related to a recent fight, but does so in an organized and reflective manner would *not* receive a high score on this scale. The Lack of Specificity scale corresponds to the AAI Lack of Recall scale. The MAI scale is modified to address the current nature of the marital relationship, and thus emphasis is placed on specificity of disclosure (i.e., ability to provide rich and detailed description of experience) rather than memory for distal events. The Fear of Loss scale was modified to address overwhelming anxiety about the possibility of the partner's death or abandonment (rather than a child as in the AAI scoring).

Narrative Classifications. Similar to the AAI, MAI classifications of Secure (Autonomous) or Insecure (Dismissing or Preoccupied) are made. In addition, a classification of Unresolved with Respect to Loss or Trauma may be assigned. The MAI Unresolved Loss classification reflects lack of resolution with respect to the dissolution (due to separation, divorce, or death) of past intimate adult relationships. The MAI Trauma classification reflects lack of resolution with respect to abusive experiences with past or current partners. Also similar to the AAI system, Cannot Classify is assigned when no organized working model pattern can be detected or when clear evidence of two discrepant models is provided within the transcript.

Secure attachment narratives are coherent, detailed, and responsive to the interview queries. They may be associated with modest levels of either activation or deactivation of attachment behavior. Information is presented in a relatively independent and objective manner, demonstrating perspective, insight, and/or understanding, as well as the ability to manage negative affect. Although specific content and valence of relationships may vary, there is thematic indication of valuing attachment relationships and regard for attachment-related experiences as influential in current personality and functioning.

The two main types of insecure attachment (characterized by incoherence, poor access to attachment relevant-material, and shift of focus away from the interview agenda) are differentiated based on either underactivation of the attachment system (i.e., demonstration of dismissing, distancing, or devaluing of the attachment figure) or overactivation of the attachment system (i.e., demonstration of confusion, conflict, and/or heightened distraction with the attachment figure).

Narratives reflecting the underactivation form of insecurity (Dismissing) are characterized by lack of specificity regarding attachment experiences and their influence on current personality and functioning. Marital attachment narratives characterized by underactivation may be manifest by dismissal of the importance of relationships, description of apparently difficult experiences in the relationship (e.g., marital separation) with denial or failure to address the impact to the self, indication of being cut off from the emotional aspects of relationships, lack of specificity regarding details of relationship experiences, and/or global positive yet unsubstantiated (or contradicted) evaluation of the relationship.

Narratives reflecting the overactivation form of insecurity (Preoccupied) are characterized by an inability to abstract from or make sense of attachment relationship experience (i.e., to coherently access meaningful aspects of the relationship in an objective manner); in addition, these narratives involve current thematic anger, passivity or vagueness of thought, and a sense of being overwhelmed by relationships. Marital attachment narratives characterized by overactivation may be manifest by description of being overwhelmed by the demands of relationships, of increased dependency upon relationships, and/or indication of lack of self–other differentiation.

A second classification (in addition to one of the three strategies just described) is also made regarding presence of Unresolved features with Respect to Loss or Trauma. This is manifest by current confusion and a sense of being overwhelmed by a significant traumatic event that, in the case of marital attachment, may include loss of a former or current partner due to death or dissolution of the relationship, or severe trauma (such as abuse by the current or former partner). Similar to the AAI, MAI transcripts that reflect Unresolved status exhibit specific lapses in monitoring of reasoning (such as psychologically confused statements or attempts to manipulate the mind with respect to the loss or trauma) and/or discourse (such as unusual attention to detail when describing the loss or invasion of loss-related themes into other topics).

A "Cannot Classify" rating is provided for those transcripts that do not meet criteria for one of the three major classifications described previously.

This may involve simultaneous use of distinct strategies (pertaining to the state of mind scales) so that no organized pattern is apparent, or may involve evidence of discrepant states of mind in different portions of the interview.

Marital Attachment Narratives

Attachment classifications are primarily judged with respect to the manner in which the narrative is conveyed (i.e., coherence), although the thematic content of marriage stories provides useful and enriched information about the nature and quality of these relationships. We review relevant themes of narratives rated as secure and insecure, and provide examples next. (While we obtained MAI narratives from men and women, all examples are from narratives provided by women for illustrative purposes. The details of the following excerpts have been altered to protect subject confidentiality.)

Valuing of Relationships. One theme that characterizes secure marital attachment narratives is a fluid and balanced description of the relationship emphasizing the value of attachment relationships and respect for attachment related experiences. Although descriptions of the partner or the relationship are not universally positive, stories are told with minimal defensiveness about dissatisfying aspects. For example, in response to the question, "What's your relationship [with your partner] like now?," Mary (who was in the third trimester of pregnancy) responded, "There's been a lot of strain with this baby coming . . . we are both so busy, and I wonder about how we are going to make the adjustment. . . . Umm, the one thing is we continue to talk and that's the best part. You know, it's funny, when we first started dating everyone was like, oh wait 'til you're married, then things will change or wait 'til you have children—and to us we haven't let it change. I mean we continue to work hard at it and I know for me, and I think I can say for him, too, that my relationship with him is the most important thing in my life, and I work at it—that's the number one priority."

This contrasts with themes from insecure marital attachment narratives in which there tends to be dismissal of the importance of the relationship or of relationships in general. On one hand, these narratives may provide minimal detail and little apparent consideration of the importance of the relationship. For example, in response to the question, "What's your relationship [with your partner] like now?," Joan answered, "Um . . . I don't know how to describe it. . . . He had really nice parents. My parents have nothing to say. I mean you pretty much do your own thing." On the other hand, insecure marital attachment may also be characterized by ongoing ambivalence regarding the relationship, with a sense of being overwhelmed, angry, and/or confused by relationship experiences. For example, when Sasha was asked to describe the one thing that stood out about her wedding day she responded, "I just remember wondering would he show up, would he show up. I just felt that something would go wrong. When I got there he was there. . . . We danced a lot. Everyone had a good time. You know, since then it's not all fun like it used to be. It can get confusing. I feel really safe with him. I don't really know if he will be coming home."

Openness to the Topic of Relationship Importance. Marital attachment stories rated as secure include vivid and rich descriptions of early moments of the relationship, and a clear and coherent sense of the development of (and changes within) the relationship over time. For example, stories describing the start of the relationship vary widely, with relatively few depicting a "love at first sight" romance—instead, there are stories that describe a relationship rooted in friendship that blossomed in intimate ways due to each partner's deliberate efforts; or that describe a relationship initiated in the context of swift passion that gave rise to lives intertwined on pragmatic as well as emotional levels. Despite differences in content, there is a rich and integrated perspective of relationship development over time. For example, Jenny indicated, "I have a feeling of comfort and absolute trust and not, you know, worrying like are we gonna make it. I don't worry about saying the wrong thing anymore because I know that I'm going to at some point, I know he's going to at some point, and we'll just get through it. We found out that we can get through the hard times, you know."

Alternatively, this contrasts to narratives in which relationship experiences are reported with minimal perspective about the meaning, development, or impact of those experiences. For example, in response to the probe, "I'd like you to describe your relationship with Bill from the earliest you can recall by telling me a story that stands out for you," Donna indicated, "Nothing really happened. We went on a lot of dates and then we did a lot of things. We could always talk and we always did things together. Let me see. . . . Like with some guys you don't connect. You know you kind of do your own thing. We just always connected. . . . There's no particular time." The topic seems closed for further elaboration or consideration.

Relationship Influences. Stories based in security also often include an open examination of how the marriage is integrated into other current important relationships (such as friendships and family of origin relationships), and/or knowledge that the relationship has meaning with respect to previous interpersonal experiences (either deliberate breaking with prior patterns or conscious carrying forward of desired features). Overall, these stories convey a clear sense of how the individual came to be in the relationship (on both pragmatic and psychological grounds), the extent to which the relationship has meaning to the individual, and the role of the relationship in the individual's unique growth in adult developmental domains. For example, in response to the question, "What is the main thing you've learned from being in a relationship with [your partner]?" Angela replied, "Umm, that I can trust someone. That's what popped into my head, so maybe I should go with that [reflecting a collaborative participation in the interview]. Not that I wasn't a trusting person before but maybe I'm more so now than I've ever been. I think I have learned to depend on someone and not always feel I need to do it by myself. I'm more trusting now that it's us, not just me."

This is in contrast with Annie's response: "I mean I don't know. I guess this is what I've always wanted. I always wanted to be with someone that I, you know, wanted to love and enjoy being with them, and have a few things in common. I think that's pretty much about it. It's not something that, you know, you think about a lot." In Annie's narrative, there was a striking absence of consideration about how previous relationship experiences may have influenced her current marriage choices nor how the current relationship affects her own self-development.

THE FAMILY RELATIONSHIPS STUDY: MAI PILOT STUDY

There is evidence to suggest that the Marital Attachment Interview (MAI) is a useful narrative-based method for collecting information about current intimate adult relationships (Dickstein, Seifer, St. Andre, & Schiller, 2001). These results were obtained from a pilot study examining links between MAI and AAI narratives. The sample for this pilot study included 24 families, recruited primarily from other ongoing studies of early childhood development. All partners were married and/or living together, and had at least one child 14 months of age (39% were firstborn). All subjects were Caucasian, with 8.6% of the sample of Portuguese ethnicity. On average, the subjects were well educated (mean years of schooling for wives and husbands was 15.5 and 15.7, respectively; range = 10–20 years). They were married on average 4.1 years (range = 1–14 years); one husband had been previously widowed, and four participants (two husbands and two wives) had been previously divorced.

Wives and husbands each completed AAI and MAI interviews, on separate occasions and independent of one another. Each partner also independently completed questionnaires regarding family functioning and marital satisfaction. Family functioning was assessed using the Family Assessment Device (FAD; Epstein, Baldwin, & Bishop, 1983). The FAD is a 60-item self-report questionnaire based on the McMaster Model of Family Functioning to assess six domains of family functioning including Roles, Communication, Problem Solving, Behavior Control, Affective Responsiveness, and Affective Involvement, as well as Total Family Functioning (Epstein, Baldwin, & Bishop, 1983; Epstein, Bishop & Levin, 1978). Subjects rated items on a four-point scale, ranging from very healthy (1) to very unhealthy (4), with *lower* scores indicating healthier family functioning. The Total Family Functioning score for each partner was used in the current analyses. For the sample as a whole, mean FAD scores for wives and husbands were 1.63 (0.40) and 1.75 (0.41), respectively.

Marital satisfaction was assessed using the Dyadic Adjustment Scale (DAS; Spanier, 1976). The DAS is a 32-item instrument that has been widely used to assess dyadic satisfaction, cohesion, consensus, and expression of affection within the current partner relationship, and yields an overall Marital Satisfaction score for each partner. For the sample as a whole, mean DAS scores for wives and husbands were 105.44 (17.03) and 106.41 (15.62), respectively.

Clinical psychologists or child psychiatrists conducted all attachment interviews. For both attachment interview protocols, clinicians were trained to be thoroughly familiar with the interview material, format, and general scoring principles in order to adhere to the interview structure while maintaining a conversation-like and empathic style. Interviews were conducted in a comfortable and private setting in the laboratory, with assurances given that no information would be disclosed to the partner. Participants were assigned to different interviewers to conduct their AAI and MAI interviews; in addition, different interviewers were assigned to each partner of a husband-wife pair.

Altogether, we conducted 47 Adult Attachment Interviews (24 wives and 23 husbands) and 44 Marital Attachment Interviews (24 wives and 20 husbands). There were 44 subjects for whom information was available to compare adult attachment and marital attachment classification (24 wives and 20 husbands). Of the 23 possible couples for whom we obtained both husband and wife data, four couples were excluded because one of the partners received a Cannot Classify rating on the AAI. In one of these four couples, one partner also received a Cannot Classify rating on the MAI. Thus, there were 19 couples for whom information was available to compare spouses' classifications on adult attachment and marital attachment ratings.

All interviews were audiotaped for subsequent verbatim transcription, which were then used to make classification judgments. Prior to scoring, all interviews were re-labeled with a code that was independent of subject identifiers so that raters were blind to family identity. All adult attachment and marital attachment interviews were scored by at least one of two raters, both of whom participated in a 2-week adult attachment interview training institute, and both of whom achieved reliability with a senior institute leader on adult attachment scoring (exact agreement > 80%). The two reliable AAI coders achieved reliability with each other on the MAI (81% exact agreement; kappa = .71).

First, we found that the distribution of MAI primary classifications was similar to the standard norms for AAI classifications (van IJzendoorn & Bakermans-Krannenburg, 1996), suggesting that the MAI taps into a working model system that is similar to the AAI, such that the information obtained via the MAI is considered to be attachment-relevant. (See Table 9.1 for these results). Second, 61% of subjects in this study were classified the same with respect to adult and marital attachment working models (marginal distributions indicate 30% concordance based on chance). This suggests that working models regarding early childhood experiences are powerful, yet not fully explanatory, mechanisms with respect to attachment within marital relationships, and provides evidence that multiple working models may be formed within different important relationship domains (Bretherton, 1999).

Briefly, it may be that marital attachment working models are differentiated from adult attachment working models such that evidence is provided for secure marital attachment despite adult attachment insecurity. This would involve maintaining discrepant working models regarding two relationship domains. In these cases where *discordant* working models are maintained, one would infer that construction of current relationships has little effect on the construction of past family relationships. Considering the case where marital

TABLE 9.1
Distribution of AAI and MAI Scores

	Secure n *(%)*	*Dismissing* n *(%)*	*Preoccupied* n *(%)*	*Can't Classify* n *(%)*	*Unresolved* n *(%)*
AAI (*n* = 47)	25 (53)	9 (19)	9 (19)	4 (9)	13 (28)
MAI (*n* = 44)	25 (57)	9 (21)	9 (21)	1 (2)	8 (18)
AAI Base Rates*	(58)	(24)	(18)	(n/a)	(19)

*From van IJzendoorn and Bakermans-Kranenburg (1996).

and adult attachment classifications are *concordant,* (in some cases) it may be that a current secure marital working model has affected the working model regarding past events such that it gets re-worked. Although the events of the past remain the same, a secure marital working model may provide (or reflect) the context within which the past events are reconstructed in a more secure organization.

We also found that marital attachment security was significantly related to family functioning. Further, our data provide at least preliminary suggestion that marital attachment security may be associated (possibly in a protective manner) with couple and family relationship well-being, both for wives and husbands. Of course, our data do not address the directionality of these effects. Perhaps representations affect appraisal, but it is equally reasonable that appraisal (the extent to which each partner feels satisfied with the relationship and/or rates the family unit as well functioning) is one basis for the construction of marital representations. In general, we found that marital attachment, in contrast to adult attachment, is a more proximal indicator of these important family factors. This makes sense in that marital attachment is, in fact, a model of a current relationship that shares the same context with other current aspects of family life.

Implications and Conclusions

Marital Attachment Construct. Areas of recent debate include the extent to which (a) unique working models (as revealed through narrative description) are developed for each significant relationship partner; (b) each of these multiple working models is a dynamic construction, with the possibility that (c) one constructed working model can affect other working models. On the one hand, it is possible that individuals hold distinct types of working models for different relationship partners—this generalizes to having possible lack of correspondence between adult attachment (with family of origin) and marital attachment (with adult partner). On the other, the cognitive-affective processes in play when constructing marital attachment working models may affect the ongoing construction of past relationships, behavior with parents, and behavior with children. We are particularly interested in the extent to which the marital relationship also has an important potential restorative function in adults with insecure attachment histories, which may promote the development of secure infant-parent attachment relationships in the next generation. More work is necessary to determine the extent to which marital attachment may be a protective mechanism by which adult attachment insecurity is shielded from the next generation.

Further, we need to better clarify the properties of marital attachment. For example, it would be important to determine whether marital attachment is a relatively stable phenomenon (like adult attachment security), and the types of circumstances that may be associated with changes in attachment classification. A related question is whether marital attachment security remains stable during the transition to parenthood, which is known to be a vulnerable time marked by decreases in marital satisfaction and stresses to the family system. Further, in the context of secure (or insecure) marital attachment, one might evaluate whether negative effects of the transition to parenthood on marital satisfaction and family functioning are buffered (or exaggerated).

Some of these issues are directly addressed in a study that was conducted subsequent to this pilot study (data for which are currently being prepared for publication). In the Family Relationships Study we assessed 120 couples during the third trimester of pregnancy, conducting AAI and MAI interviews with each partner (as part of a larger study protocol). We followed up with families when the target child was 4 months of age to conduct an interview to assess quality of family functioning (using the McMaster Structured Interview of Family Functioning) and a Birth Narrative Interview (coded with the Family Narrative Consortium coding system; Fiese et al., 1999) to examine the couple's co-constructed story about their experiences during the transition to parenthood, and their perceptions about how the child has been integrated into the family. In addition, when the child was 12 months of age, we repeated the MAI interview with mothers to assess longitudinal properties of the interview across the transition to parenthood. These data should yield informative insights about narrative construction across family sub-systems and over time.

Use of Narrative Methodology for Understanding Marital Relationships. An important factor to consider when utilizing narrative methodology to understand relationship processes is the properties of the storytelling situation. That is, in our research, similar to most research on adult attachment, individuals produce marital attachment narratives without their partners being present. The classification of attachment (in)security is based on the individual's narrative qualities with respect to the relationship. It would be interesting to determine if similar attachment-relevant properties could be coded when narratives are produced by a couple. We may gain important information about marital attachment process by examining individual narrative-based perspectives compared to those put forth by a couple as they produce the narrative conjointly. In this way, we may be able to better elucidate the mechanisms by which individual's working models of attachment are linked with relationship experiences and interactions. That is, we may be able to more closely and directly examine the impact of discordant individual models on relationship functioning.

Other well-established narrative-based scoring methodologies, such as the Family Narrative Consortium system (Fiese et al., 1999), may be applied to jointly (or individually) constructed marital attachment narratives to not only yield information about the coherence and organization of the content, but to shed light on narrative interaction and relationship beliefs. In a related vein, marital narratives have been examined outside the attachment perspective. For example, Gottman and colleagues (e.g., Buehlman, Gottman, & Katz, 1992) use an oral history interview technique to elicit the couple's co-constructed narrative about the course of their relationship over time to broadly assess affective and intimacy reports of the relationship (coding both content and process variables). They found that one dimension distilled from these interviews predicted the couple's divorce and separation. These results are explained within the framework of physiological reactivity, and help to elucidate the importance of affective processing mechanisms within marital relationships for the well-being of individual partners as well as the health and stability of the marriage.

Alternatively, Veroff and colleagues (e.g., Veroff, Sutherland, Chadiha, & Ortega, 1993) apply symbolic interactionist theory using a reality construction perspective. They evaluate themes derived from marital narratives with respect to how couples arrive at consensual meanings about their relationship to predict marital satisfaction and individual well-being. Their results suggest that quality of narrative construction in fact corresponds with quality of relationship experiences. In addition, they found that couples who are able to describe and integrate relationship experiences over time (or to "reconstruct" these experiences into a current relationship awareness) report better quality relationships. This theoretical perspective seems to compliment attachment theory as related to marriage; this constuctivist approach places emphasis on the "couple-ness" aspects of the narrative, whereas the attachment approach focuses on the individual's construction of the relationship. Further empirical examination of narrative from these distinct theoretical approaches would likely yield exciting and important information for the field.

Clinical Implications. There may be an important place for marital attachment narrative methodology in preventive-intervention contexts. For example, the marital attachment narrative may be an ideal evaluation tool used at the start of marital treatment to assess each partner's expectations of and history with adult intimate relationships; affective and cognitive constructions of this and other important relationships; and unique perspective on the role or meaning of this particular relationship for their own adult development. Couples may be encouraged to develop a "relationship working model" that overtly incorporates or addresses the unique aspects of each partner's individual model of the relationship. Thus, joint re-construction of relationship models to yield more integrated understanding of relationship functioning may be a goal of treatment.

Taken together, the MAI provides evidence that the assessment of relationship representations by use of narrative methodology can be generalized to different relationship domains. It provides another window by which to explore intergenerational processes related to how individuals form relationships with others. Further, it builds on the tradition of other narrative methodologies that examine whole family outcomes, not only parent-child relationship qualities (e.g., Fiese et al., 1999). In sum, the MAI expands the utility of narrative strategies to examine a broader range of family issues beyond the parent-child dyad that currently comprises the vast majority of narrative-based attachment research.

REFERENCES

Ainsworth, M. D. S., Blehar, M. C., Waters, E., & Wall, S. (1978). *Patterns of attachment: A psychological study of the strange situation.* Hillsdale, NJ: Lawrence Erlbaum Associates.

Barnett, P. A., & Gotlib, I. H. (1988). Psychosocial functioning and depression: Distinguishing among antecedents, concomitants, and consequences. *Psychological Bulletin, 104,* 97–126.

Benoit, D., Vidovic, D., & Roman, J. (1991, April). *Transmission of attachment across three generations.* Paper presented at the meeting of the Society for Research in Child Development, Seattle, WA.

Benoit, D., Zeanah, C., & Barton, M. (1989). Maternal attachment disturbances in failure to thrive. *Infant Mental Health Journal, 10,* 185–202.

Benoit, D., Zeanah, C. H., Boucher, C., & Minde, K. (1989). Sleep disorders in early childhood: Association with insecure maternal attachment. *Journal of the American Academy of Child and Adolescent Psychiatry, 31*(1), 86–93.

Bowlby, J. (1982). *Attachment and loss (Vol. 1). Attachment.* New York: Basic. (Original work published 1969)

Bretherton, I. (1985). Attachment theory: Retrospect and prospect. In I. Bretherton & E. Waters (Eds.), *Growing points of attachment theory and research* (Monographs of the Society for Research in Child Developent, 50 [Serial No. 209]), 3–35.

Bretherton, I. (1999). Updating the "internal working model" construct: Some reflections. *Attachment and Human Development, 1*(3), 343–357.

Buehlman, K. T., Gottman, J. M., & Katz, L. F. (1992). How a couple views their past predicts their future: Predicting divorce form an oral history interview. *Journal of Family Psychology, 5,* 295–318.

Cohn, D. A., Cowan, P. A., Cowan, C. P., & Pearson, J. L. (1992). Mothers' and fathers' working models of childhood attachment relationships, parenting styles, and child behavior. *Development and Psychopathology, 4,* 417–431.

Cohn, D. A., Silver, D. H., Cowan, C. P., Cowan, P. A., & Pearson, J. (1992). Working models of childhood attachment and couple relationships. *Journal of Family Issues, 13,* 432–449.

Cowan, P. A., Cohn, D. A., Cowan, C. P., & Pearson, J. L. (1996). Parents' attachment histories and children's externalizing and internalizing behaviors: Exploring family systems models of linkage. *Journal of Consulting and Clinical Psychology, 64,* 53–63.

Crowell, J. A., & Feldman, S. (1989). Assessment of mothers' working models of relationships: Some clinical implications. *Infant Mental Health Journal, 10,* 173–184.

Crowell, J. A., & Feldman, S. (1991). Mothers' working models of attachment relationships and mother and child behavior during separation and reunion. *Developmental Psychology, 27,* 597–605.

Cummings, E. M., & Cicchetti, D. (1990). Toward a transactional model of relations between attachment and depression. In M. T. Greenberg, D. Cicchetti, & E. M. Cummings (Eds.), *Attachment in the preschool years: Theory, research and intervention* (pp. 339–372). Chicago: University of Chicago Press.

Dickstein, S., Seifer, R., St. Andre, M., & Schiller, M. (2001). Marital Attachment Inverview: Adult Attachment Assessment of Marriage. *Journal of Personal and Social Relationships, 18*(5), 651–672.

Eichberg, C. G. (1987, April). *Quality of infant-parent attachment: Related to mother's representation of her own relationship history.* Paper presented at the biennial meeting of the Society for Research in Child Development, Baltimore, MD.

Epstein, N. B., Baldwin, L. M., & Bishop, D. S. (1983). The McMaster family assessment device. *Journal of Marital and Family Therapy, 9,* 171–180.

Epstein, N. B., Bishop, D. S., & Levin, S. (1978). The McMaster Model of Family Functioning. *Journal of Marriage and Family Counseling, 4,* 19–31.

Fiese, B. H., Sameroff, A. J., Grotevant, H. D., Wamboldt, F. S., Dickstein, S., & Fravel, D. (1999). The stories that families tell: Narrative coherence, narrative interaction, and relationship beliefs. *Monographs of the Society for Research in Child Development, 64*(2, Serial No. 257).

Fonagy, P., Steele, H., & Steele, M. (1991). Maternal repersentations of attachment during pregnancy predict the organization of infant-mother attachment at one year of age. *Child Development, 62,* 891–905.

George, C., Kaplan, N., & Main, M. (1985). *Adult attachment interview.* Unpublished manuscript, University of California at Berkeley.

George, C., Kaplan, N., & Main, M. (1996). *Adult attachment interview.* Unpublished manuscript (3rd ed.), University of California at Berkeley.

Haft, W. L., & Slade, A. (1989). Affect attunement and maternal attachment: A pilot study. *Infant Mental Health Journal, 10,* 157–172.

Hazan, C., & Shaver, P. R. (1990). Love and work: An attachment-theoretical perspective. *Journal of Personality and Social Psychology, 59,* 270–280.

Hooley, J. M., & Teasdale, J. D. (1989). Predictors of relapse in unipolar depressives: Expressed emotion, marital distress, and perceived criticism. *Journal of Abnormal Psychology, 98,* 229–235.

Jacobson, N. S., Dobson, K., Fruzetti, A. E., Schmaling, K. B., & Salusky, S. (1991). Marital therapy as a treatment for depression. *Journal of Consulting and Clinical Psychology, 59,* 547–557.

Kobak, R. R., Cole, H. E., Ferenz-Gillies, R., & Flemming, W. S. (1993). Attachment and emotion regulation during mother-teen problem solving: A control theory analysis. *Child Development, 64,* 231–245.

Kowalik, D. L., & Gotlib, I. H. (1987). Depression and marital interaction: Concordance between intent and perception of communication. *Journal of Abnormal Psychology, 96,* 127–134.

Main, M., & Goldwyn, R. (1988). *Adult attachment classification system* (version 3). Unpublished manuscript, University of California at Berkeley.

Main, M., & Goldwyn, R. (1994). *An adult classification and rating system.* Unpublished manuscript, University of California, Berkeley. (Updated 1996)

Miller, I. W., Epstein, N. B., Bishop, D. S., & Keitner, G. I. (1985). The McMaster family assessment device: Reliability and validity. *Journal of Marital and Family Therapy, 11*(4), 345–356.

Owens, G., Crowell, J. A., Pan, H., Treboux, D., O'Connor, E., & Waters, E. (1995). The prototype hypothesis and the origins of attachment working models: Adult relationships with parents and romantic partners. In E. Waters, B. E. Vaughn, G. Posada, & K. Kondo-Ikemura (Eds.), Caregiving, cultural, and cognitive perspectives on secure-base behavior and working models: New growing points of attachment theory and research. *Monographs of the Society for Research in Child Development, 60* (2–3, Serial No. 244).

Shaver, P., Hazan, C., & Bradshaw, D. (1988). Love as attachment: The integration of three behavioral systems. In R. J. Stenberg, M. L. Barnes (Eds.), *The psychology of love.* New Haven, CT: Yale University Press.

Spanier, G. (1976). Measuring dyadic adjustment: New scales for assessing the quality of marriage and similar dyads. *Journal of Marriage and the Family, 38,* 15–28.

van IJzendoorn, M. H. (1992). Intergenerational transmission of parenting: A review of studies in nonclinical populations. *Developmental Review, 12,* 76–99.

van IJzendoorn, M. H., & Bakermans-Kranenburg, M. J. (1996). Adult Attachment Interview classifications in mothers, fathers, adolescents, and clinical groups: A meta-analytic search for normative data. *Journal of Consulting and Clinical Psychology, 64*(1), 8–21.

Veroff, J., Sutherland, L., Chadiha, L. A., & Ortega, R. M. (1993). Predicting marital quality with narrative assessments of marital experience. *Journal of Marriage and the Family, 55,* 326–337.

Ward, M. J., Botyanski, N. C., Plunkett, S. W., & Carlson, E. A. (1991, April). *The concurrent and predictive validity of the AAI for adolescent mothers.* Paper presented at the biennial meeting of the Society for Research in Child Development, Seattle, WA.

Waters, E., Vaughn, B. E., Posada, G., & Kondo-Ikemura, K. (1995). Caregiving, cultural, and cognitive perspectives on secure-base behavior and working models: New growing points of attachment theory and research. *Monographs of the Society for Research in Child Development, 60* (2–3, Serial No. 244).

Zeanah, C. H., & Emde, R. N. (1994). Attachment disorders in infancy and childhood. In M. Rutter, L. Hersov, & E. Taylor (Eds.), *Child and adolescent psychiatry: Modern approaches* (pp. 490–504). Oxford: Blackwell.

PART IV

Midlife: Parenting and Narrative Socialization Processes in the Family

10

Generativity and the Narrative Ecology of Family Life

Dan P. McAdams
Northwestern University

Even the smallest family has many stories to tell. Two partners have a story about how they met, how they came together in love, where their relationship is headed for the future. They each have stories about their own families of origin and how those families connect to and conflict with the nuclear family they have established together. Their parents and siblings have their stories about the relationship, too, about how, for instance, this is a match that was definitely *not* made in heaven, about how this couple defied the odds to create something spectacular, or settled into a predictable pattern of domestic tedium. Add a child to this nuclear unit, and the narrative possibilities grow even more, for now there is the story of that birth and development, of what it means for the future as well as the past. And from the past come stories passed down from one generation to the next, stories these two partners will tell their child when she is old enough to appreciate them, stories that their child may cherish as narrative keepsakes from the past or reject as boring, irrelevant, or contrary to her own narrative sense of who she wants to be. She will create her own stories, and borrow many others. Her siblings will do the same, and their children; and on it goes.

Every family develops within a complex and dynamic ecology of narrative. Stories are created, revised, retold, and forgotten. Different storytellers occupy different narrative niches. Grandfather rarely tells a story, but when he does you know it will have a moral lesson. Aunt Vicky dishes the gossip, but never in the presence of the men and only during peaceful and pleasant times. Certain people are good listeners, and they get to hear many different tales. Others specialize as audiences for particular genres and performances. For example, Jeff loves to hear his father's war stories, but little else really interests him. The family operates according to implicit rules of storytelling, regarding what should be said, when, where, how—except, of course, when the rules are broken, which is not infrequent. In this uneven and shifting ecology, stories may function in different ways for different tellers and listeners. In the opening chapter of this volume, Pratt and Fiese identify three especially important functions of family storytelling. They argue that stories told in and about families may provide (a) opportunities to *act* through which family members learn to become competent narrators, (b) moral *messages* and lessons aimed to instill values and promote socialization in the family, and (c) narrative material for the formulation of personal and family *identity*.

As parents foster storytelling in their children, impart moral messages through stories, and use narrative to promote identity development for the next generation, they express the universal psychosocial urge that Erikson (1950) named *generativity*. Generativity is an adult's concern for and commitment to promoting the well-being of future generations through parenting, teaching, mentoring, and engaging in a wide range of endeavors aimed at leaving a positive legacy for the future (McAdams & de St. Aubin, 1992). The past decade has witnessed an upsurge of empirical research on the concept of generativity (see McAdams, 2001a; McAdams & de St. Aubin, 1998, for reviews). Storytelling is one important aspect of generativity, especially in families (Kotre, 1999, 2004; Pratt, Norris, Arnold, & Filyer, 1999). In their efforts to provide guidance and care for the next generation, parents read nursery rhymes and fairy tales to their children, tell their children cautionary tales from their own lives, help their children tell their own stories about personal experience, pass on valued family stories from the past, and engage in a wide range of other narrative practices that serve, among other things, as manifestations of generativity.

My aim in this chapter is to explore the narrative ecology of family life from the standpoint of current research and theorizing on generativity. I first consider the role of narrative in the human life course and then move to the topics of generative lives and generativity in the family. In the last part of the chapter, I introduce new data on family stories told by a sample of midlife adults, half of whom were chosen for interviews based on their extremely high scores on measures of generativity and half of whom because they scored very low on generativity. My conceptual integration and analysis of the new data on family stories and generativity will identify a particular genre of family stories that appears to contain considerable generative power. These especially generative family stories are often structured as tales of *suffering* and *growth* against a backdrop of human *kindness*. Although generativity can be expressed in many different narrative forms, family stories that emplot episodes or periods of profound human suffering which ultimately result in growth and/or redemption appear to carry strong messages of generativity that are passed down from one generation to the next.

NARRATIVE AND THE LIFE COURSE

A story is an account of how human or human-like agents act upon their desires and beliefs over time (Bruner, 1990). As such, a story typically contains a setting within which action makes sense, an actor whose intentions are translated into goal-directed behavior, and an ending through which the emotional tension created by the story's events is resolved or dismissed. In order to be a storyteller, therefore, an organism must first have an understanding of human intention organized in time (McAdams, 2001b). Research suggests that by the age of 12–16 months, human children have typically attained a tacit understanding of human intentionality. For example, Tomasello (2000) reports that 16-month-old infants will imitate complex behavioral sequences exhibited by other human beings only when those activities appear intentional. With the emergence of what Dennett (1987) calls the *intentional stance,* children in the second year of life can experience the world from the subjective standpoint of an intentional causal agent. In other words, the young child develops a sense of the self as an active, intentional, agentic "I"—a subjective source from which desires flow and action springs (Kagan, 1994). By the age of 2, I implicitly know that "I" exist as an intentional being, that I have *my* own thoughts and feelings and that I can act upon them, that what happens to *me* is *my* experience. According to Howe and Courage (1997), 2-year old children are able to collect and personalize episodic memories as "things that *I* did," building up an autobiographical memory store of little stories about what has transpired in "my life."

Children's understanding of intentionality and narrative expands further in the preschool years as they consolidate a *theory of mind* (Wellman, 1993). Theory of mind refers to the ability of normal children to attribute mental states (such as desires, beliefs, and intentions) to themselves and to other people as a way of making sense of and predicting behavior. In the third and fourth years of life, children come to understand that people (like themselves) formulate desires and beliefs in their minds and then translate those mentalistic phenomena into motivated action. Interpreting the actions of others (and oneself) in terms of their predisposing desires and beliefs is a form of *mind reading,* according to Baron-Cohen (1995), a competency that is essential for effective social interaction. Such a competency is also essential for storytelling and story comprehension, for it is virtually impossible to narrate human experience in a meaningful way without attributing desires, beliefs, and intentions to human actors, and linking their behaviors to these mental states. As children consolidate theory of mind, they develop a basic understanding of what a story must have in order to be a story. Thus, 5-year-olds typically know that stories are set in a particular time and place and involve characters that act on their desires and beliefs over time, that characters react to each other to build a plot in the narrative, that these motivated actions and interactions create suspense or curiosity in the listener, and that the actions and the attendant suspense should be resolved by a satisfying story ending. If a story does not conform to these narrative conventions, children may find it confusing or difficult to remember, or they may recall it later with a more conventional (storylike) structure than it originally had (Mandler, 1984).

Storytelling and narrative understanding develop in a social context. Parents typically encourage children to put their experiences into narrative form as soon as children are verbally able to do so (Fivush & Kuebli, 1997). Early on, parents may take the lead in stimulating the child's recollection and telling of the past by reminding the child of recent events, such as this morning's breakfast or yesterday's visit to the doctor. Taking advantage of this initial conversational scaffolding provided by adults, the young child soon begins to take more initiative in sharing personal stories. In conversations with adults about personal memories, young children become acquainted with the narrative structures through which events are typically discussed by people in their world. Cultural differences may loom large in family storytelling with young children (Wang, this volume). For example, Chinese parents appear to be more likely to utilize early storytelling as opportunities for teaching lessons to the child, whereas North American families are likely to emphasize instead the child's creativity and autonomy in the stories (Miller, Wiley, Fung, & Liang, 1997). Furthermore, cultural factors may prioritize different roles in narrative experience. Fung, Miller, and Lin (this volume) suggest that relative to North American families, Taiwanese parents tend to see the child's role as that of the active and reflective listener, rather than the teller of the tale. Rooted in the Confucian value of filial piety, one must first be a good listener of stories told by others, especially by other authority figures, before one is accorded the status of storyteller.

Although children are able to narrate their own experience in ways that conform to culturally established scripts, it is not until adolescence, some have argued, that individuals begin to see their own lives as large, evolving stories (Habermas & Bluck, 2000; McAdams, 1985). As children move through the elementary-school years, they gather knowledge about what typically happens in people's lives across the full life course. In middle-class

American society, for example, they learn that people go to school through their teenage years, that they are likely to leave home in late adolescence for further schooling or work, that they get married and usually have children sometime after that, that people have jobs or careers that take them well into middle age, that retirement occurs after that, and so on. This kind of *biographical coherence,* strongly shaped by cultural norms (Denzin, 1989), must be in place in a child's mind before he or she can begin to understand his or her own life as an integrated story, with beginning, middle, and (anticipated) ending (Habermas & Bluck, 2000). Furthermore, the individual must be able to explain current events in life in terms of previous events, what Habermas and Bluck call *causal coherence.* Thus, a 16-year-old girl may explain her reluctance to respond to boys' romantic overtures in terms of a failed romance in junior high school. She is able to link in narrative two disparate events or chapters in her life story in such a way as to suggest that the previous event explains or provides the origin for the later event. Beyond that, she may be able to extract a general theme or lesson from her narration, a propensity that Habermas and Bluck call *thematic coherence.* First-person autobiographical accounts reveal greater levels of causal and thematic coherence as individuals move through adolescence and into young adulthood.

The cognitive emergence of causal and thematic coherence in adolescence dovetails with social and emotional changes occurring at this time to usher in an appreciation for and concern with finding or making a story out of one's life. And these developments dovetail with the emergence of *ego identity* as a central developmental task for young people in their teens and 20s living in modern societies (Arnett, 2000; Erikson, 1959). In my own theoretical and empirical work, I have argued that the identity challenge of modern life is a narrative challenge (McAdams, 1985, 1993, 2001b). The central task in identity, beginning in late adolescence and young adulthood, is to construct a life story for oneself that makes sense of who one was, is, and will be within the social, economic, and ideological world in which a person lives. A life story is an internalized and evolving narrative of the self that reconstructs the past and anticipates the future in such a way as to provide one's life with some degree of unity and purpose. Life stories are based on biographical facts, but they go considerably beyond the facts as people selectively appropriate aspects of their experience and imaginatively construe both past and future to construct stories that make sense to them and to their audiences, that vivify and integrate life and make it more-or-less meaningful. Life stories are psychosocial constructions, co-authored by the person himself or herself and the cultural context within which that person's life is embedded and given meaning. As such, individual life stories reflect cultural values and norms, including assumptions about gender, race, and class (Rosenwald & Ochberg, 1992; Stewart, 1994). Life stories are intelligible within a particular cultural frame, and yet they also differentiate one person from the next. Individual differences in people's internalized and evolving self-narratives constitute differences in personality between people that are as important as, though very different from, differences in dispositional personality traits (McAdams, 1996).

Identity stories continue to develop well into and through the midlife years. Some research suggests that the move from early to middle adulthood may be occasioned by an increase in life-narrative themes concerned with generativity (McAdams, 2001a; McAdams, de St. Aubin, & Logan, 1993). Many life stories constructed by middle-aged adults contain aspects of what McAdams (1985) called a generativity script—that is, an outline or plan regarding how the individual hopes to leave a positive legacy for the next generation. In an existential sense, a generativity script can provide a life story with a satisfying "ending," by suggesting that even though the protagonist of the story will someday die, he or she will leave behind something worthy (see also Becker, 1973; Kotre, 1984). Generativity scripts, therefore, provide life narratives with anticipated endings that in themselves are suggestive of new beginnings and of the continuity of life from one generation to the next. It is this sense of "giving birth to" (generating life) and working to assure continuity from one generation to the next that is at the heart of the human experience of generativity.

GENERATIVITY IN ADULTHOOD

Both within and outside of the family, modern adults find many opportunities to express generativity. Kotre (1984) identified four forms of generative expressions: biological (conceiving children, giving birth), parental (caring for offspring, providing guidance and discipline), technical (teaching skills, modeling behaviors), and cultural (passing on meaning systems, creating new knowledge for the next generation) generativity. The various forms of generativity are often expressed within particular social roles and domains, in family or work roles, for example, in political and civic domains, even in leisure-time pursuits (MacDermid, Franz, & de Reus, 1998). Within and across these different role domains, furthermore, generativity can manifest itself in activities aimed at *generating* or producing new things and people, in *caring for* people and maintaining those most valued aspects of society, and in eventually *offering up* or letting go of those people and things that have been generated and cared for (McAdams & de St. Aubin, 1992). The task of letting go, of granting autonomy to one's biological, parental, technical, or societal progeny, is one of the great challenges of generativity, as many parents know.

Erikson contended that *generativity versus stagnation* is the psychosocial centerpiece of the seventh stage in his grand developmental scheme, the stage associated with midlife. Research provides some qualified support for Erikson's developmental argument. For example, cross-sectional studies, including a nationwide survey of over 3,000 adult U.S. citizens, suggest that generativity concerns and behaviors may peak in the midlife years (e.g., Keyes & Ryff, 1998; McAdams et al., 1993; Peterson & Stewart, 1990; Rossi, 2001). Longitudinal data, however, provide more of a mixed picture, with at least one study showing no relation between age and generativity in the adult years (Whitbourne, Zuschlag, Elliot, & Waterman, 1992) and another showing a smooth stage sequence in accord with Erikson's theory (Vaillant & Milofsky, 1980). Furthermore, the developmental course of generativity is strongly and sometimes unpredictably shaped by social and cultural forces (Cohler, Hostetler, & Boxer, 1998). Different aspects of generativity may ebb and flow at different times over the life course. For example, Stewart and Vandewater (1998) have shown that the *motivation* to be generative may be very high in young adulthood, but that people may not typically be able to fully actualize their generative desires until they reach the midlife years. The conclusion to be drawn, then, from the research on the relation between age and generativity is that generativity may indeed be an especially salient psychosocial issue in midlife, but that generative concerns and issues can arise at virtually any point in the adult life course (McAdams, 2001a).

Adults differ from each other with respect to the strength and scope of their generativity. In recent years, researchers have developed self-report, behavioral, Q-sort, interview-based, and projective measures of individual differences in adult generativity (e.g., Bradley, 1997; McAdams & de St. Aubin, 1992; Peterson & Klohnen, 1995; Stewart, Franz, & Layton, 1988). High scores on generativity measures are positively associated with a wide range of prosocial behaviors and societal engagements. For example, research has shown that generativity is positively associated with prosocial personality characteristics (Peterson & Klohnen, 1995), strong social support networks (Hart, McAdams, Hirsch, & Bauer, 2001), interest in political issues and involvement in the political process (Cole & Stewart, 1996; Hart et al., 2001; Peterson & Duncan, 1999; Peterson, Smirles, & Wentworth, 1997), church attendance and involvement in religious/spiritual activities (Dillon & Wink, 2004; Hart et al., 2001; Rossi, 2001), and community voluntarism (Rossi, 2001). Self-report generativity is also positively associated with ratings of subjective mental health and life satisfaction (Ackerman, Zuroff, & Moscowitz,

2000; de St. Aubin & McAdams, 1995; Grossbaum & Bates, 2002; Keyes & Ryff, 1998; Snarey, 1993; Vandewater, Ostrove, & Stewart, 1997). With respect to demographic considerations, women occasionally score higher than men on generativity, though the difference is not always statistically significant, and more highly educated individuals tend to score slightly higher than those with low levels of education (Kim & Youn, 2002; McAdams & de St. Aubin, 1992; Rossi, 2001).

Linking generativity and life narrative (identity), McAdams and his colleagues have compared the life stories of highly generative and less generative midlife adults in two intensive, interview-based studies (McAdams, Diamond, de St. Aubin, & Mansfield, 1997; McAdams, Reynolds, Lewis, Patten, & Bowman, 2001). They have identified a set of themes that appear significantly more often in the life stories of highly generative adults compared to their less generative peers. Among these themes is an early sense of being special or advantaged compared to others, a sensitivity to the suffering of other people, ideological continuity and certitude across the life course, and the transformation of bad scenes into good outcomes. The last theme is called a *redemption sequence* in life narrative, wherein a bad scene is redeemed, salvaged, or made better by that which follows. Generativity is strongly associated with employing the rhetoric of redemption, reform, and recovery in the identity stories people construct to make sense of their lives (Maruna, 2001; McAdams & Bowman, 2001). It is interesting to note that the very concept of generativity itself entails an implicit message of human redemption. The hard work that the highly generative adult displays in his or her efforts to promote the well-being of future generations may entail a good deal of pain, suffering, and sacrifice. Scenes of sacrifice and hard work, therefore, may lead to scenes of blessing and reward. Indeed, generativity is often about progress, improvement, transforming the bad into good. In life stories, in folk tales, in modern fiction and cinema, the discourse of generativity is full of stories about people suffering and making sacrifices in order to make a better world for generations to come (de St. Aubin, McAdams, & Kim, 2004).

GENERATIVITY IN THE FAMILY

The prototype of generativity is probably the bearing and raising of children. One's own biological child is literally an extension of the self, biologically generated in one's own image, flesh of one's flesh, nurtured, cared for, mentored, educated, disciplined, and eventually granted some degree of autonomy to carry forward life for generations to come. It is in the bearing and raising of children that many adults confront their biggest challenges, fulfillments, and frustrations in generativity. Parenting, therefore, can be seen as a primary instantiation of generativity itself, and the family, generativity's most sacred domain.

Yet many observers of contemporary family life, especially family life in America, contend that something has gone terribly awry in the realm of generativity. Myers (2000) points to a wide range of social indices suggesting that while Americans' material well-being has increased markedly since 1960, the well-being of families and children has steadily declined. In the United States since 1960, Myers observes, the divorce rate has roughly doubled, teen suicide rates have tripled, recorded violent crime has quadrupled, the percent of babies born to unmarried parents has sextupled, and clinical depression has soared to ten times the pre–World-War-II level. Add to this picture increases in childhood poverty and child abuse, and the idealized story of a nurturing American family where generative adults provide care and wisdom for their cherished offspring may prove to be a badly distorted myth. In keeping with Myers' view, Twenge (2000) has documented an alarming increase in children's anxiety scores since the 1950s. Casting an even broader net that encompasses both family and civic life, Putnam (2000) assembles an awesome array of statistical findings to show that social capital of all kinds—from quality family time to charitable giving—has dropped precipitously since the late 1950s. The title of Putnam's (2000) book—*Bowling Alone*—leaves us with a starkly nongenerative image of American life.

These kinds of societal critiques, however, have not gone unchallenged. In her book, *Caring and Doing for Others,* Rossi (2001) reports data from a nationwide survey of Americans' family and civic life to suggest that while many of the problems that Putnam and Myers observe cannot be denied, there is ample sociological evidence to argue for impressive strength in the American family and the continued power and prevalence of prosocial and generative activities among Americans, both in the family and in wider societal contexts. Along with Putney and Bengston (2001), Rossi shows that despite the problems facing contemporary American families, intergenerational attachments remain very strong. Compared to the 1950s, American families are structured in a wide assortment of nontraditional ways today. Yet adults care and provide for children in ways that often defy the negative expectations that many social critics put forth. Grandparents, baby sitters, child-care workers, fictive kin, same-sex partners, and a host of other nontraditional caregivers supplement parenting done by mothers and fathers in the many different kinds of family structures that prevail on the American scene today (e.g., Hill, 1997).

While Myers and Putnam review a large corpus of sociological data, Rossi (2001) provides data of her own from her nationwide study showing that generativity is a powerful force in caring and doing for others within the family. Individual differences in adult's self-reported concern about generativity were strongly predictive of the extent to which both men and women involved themselves in family care. Generativity was positively associated with providing both monetary and social/emotional support for family members. Among midlife adults, support may be provided for those of both the younger generation (children) and the older (grandparents). In a longitudinal study of midlife women, Peterson (2002) shows that women who attained a generative stance in life by the age of 43 reported greater investment 10 years later in intergenerational roles, such as daughter and mother. Highly generative women in Peterson's study reported less subjective burden in caring for elderly parents and more knowledge about community elder care programs. Peterson and Klohnen (1995) found that highly generative women who were also mothers invested considerably more energy and commitment in parenting and showed an "expanded radius of care" (p. 20) compared with less generative mothers.

Generative parents actively promote their children's education. In a large-scale study of parents whose children were enrolled in a major metropolitan school system in the United States, Nakagawa (1991) found that mothers and fathers with high scores on a self-report measure of generativity tended to be more involved in their children's schooling than parents scoring lower. Parents scoring high on generativity tended to help their children with their homework more, showed higher levels of attendance at school functions, and evidenced greater knowledge about what their children were learning and doing in school, compared to parents scoring lower in generativity. In another study of African-American and Euro-American parents, researchers found that high levels of generativity were associated with valuing trust and communication with one's children and viewing parenting as an opportunity to pass on values and wisdom to the next generation (Hart et al., 2001). Although Black and White parents showed some differences in their descriptions of their own approaches to parenting, generativity predicted the same parenting qualities for both groups.

Two recent studies suggest that generativity may be associated with an *authoritative* parenting style. Peterson and colleagues (1997) found that middle-aged parents of college students expressed more authoritative attitudes about parenting if they were high in generativity. Pratt, Danso, Arnold, Norris, and Filyer (2001) found that generativity among mothers of teenaged children predicted authoritative styles, but generativity among fathers was unrelated to parenting style. Authoritative parenting combines an emphasis on high standards and discipline with a warm, child-centered, and caring approach to raising children. Authoritative parents provide their children with a good deal of structure and guidance, but they also give their children a strong voice in making family decisions. In studies done primarily in the United States, authoritative patterns of parenting have been consistently associated with higher levels of moral development and greater levels of self-esteem (Maccoby & Martin, 1983). In Peterson et al. (1997), authoritative parenting predicted attitudinal similarity between parents and college-age children, and it was negatively associated with parent/child conflict.

The role of generativity in family life can sometimes manifest itself in surprising ways. For example, Kay (1998) conducted intensive interviews of male Holocaust survivors to examine the ways in which they expressed generativity in their families. He found that these survivors, now in their 70s and older, scored significantly higher on self-report measures of generativity compared to a demographically matched sample of men. However, the survivors viewed their generative contributions almost exclusively in terms of biological reproduction and providing financial assistance for their children. They were reluctant, by contrast, to form close emotional bonds with their families, and they rarely felt comfortable sharing stories of their lives or passing down family culture and belief systems to the next generation. Kay suggests that these men's histories were so painful and devastating that they could not or would not revisit their past in the presence of their family members. In a related vein, Kotre and Kotre (1998) provide case examples of generativity expressed in the *refusal to pass on* traditions or behaviors from the past. Kotre and Kotre argue that in some instances generativity is best expressed by taking the role of an *intergenerational buffer* within the family. For example, in a family with a history of abuse or addiction, a parent can decide that "the suffering ends here." By actively blocking the transmission of destructive practices or beliefs from one generation to the next, a person can create a more generative family environment and provide new hope for future growth and the generation of more beneficent meaning systems in the family.

FAMILY STORIES AND GENERATIVITY

In the famous first sentence of *Anna Karenina,* Leo Tolstoy (1995, p. 1) wrote: "All happy families resemble one another, but each unhappy family is unhappy in its own way." Tolstoy's assertion poses significant problems for the concept of family stories, as the literary critic Morson (1995) astutely points out. For Tolstoy, unhappy families deviate from the expected domestic script of the 19th-century Russian elite. Anna leaves her husband to follow a passionate but destructive affair with Vronsky, resulting in overwhelming public shame and her eventual suicide. Hers is a beautifully tragic story to tell, a story about how a woman's passion and narcissism leave her ostracized from high society and eventually ruin her family. Writes Morson, "romantic destiny, the sense that one has been chosen for a special and tragic story, feeds [Anna's] narcissism" (p. 836). By contrast, Levin and Kitty represent the happy family, whose members find their happiness in the mundane and unstoried details of everyday life. In a deeply generative scene on the book's last page, Levin concludes that he now understands the meaning of his life, minutes after gazing upon the face of his newborn son. For Tolstoy, happy family life

> is lived in the small and ordinary details. It is prosaic and undramatic and is lived best when there is no story to tell. The reason that all happy families resemble each other whereas each unhappy family is unhappy in its own way is that unhappy families, like unhappy lives, are dramatic; they have a story and each story is different. But happy families and happy lives, filled with undramatic incidents, do not make a good story; and it is in this sense that they all resemble each other. (Morson, 1995, p. 835)

Morson's reading of Tolstoy fits nicely with a sentiment expressed by Bruner (1990), who argues that good stories involve some kind of "deviation from a canonical cultural pattern" (p. 50). In other words, stories are told when events occur that are unexpected and discrepant from the mundane and predictable patterns of everyday social life. I could conceivably give you an account of the breakfast I ate yesterday morning, how I even managed to read the newspaper as I ate my cereal, but you would not want to hear it and I would not want to tell it because nothing especially interesting or unusual happened yesterday morning. In a sense, there is no story to tell. Bruner suggests that life becomes tellable only when it deviates from the mundane and predictable. Often such a move involves risk, danger, or suffering. Serious threats, dangerous circumstances, and human suffering are the stuff of good stories; they motivate a teller to tell and a listener to listen, they build suspense and curiosity, they promise a resolution in the end.

With all due respect to Tolstoy, however, research on family stories seems to assume that even happy families have their own, unique, and maybe even dramatic stories to tell. Indeed, Tolstoy himself devotes considerable space in his novel to telling the happy story of Levin and Kitty, even if it is rather less exciting that Anna's and Vronsky's tragic fate. Deviations from the canonical cultural patterns could conceivably be positive as well as negative. When it comes to family stories, perhaps unexpected uplifts and high points might compete with danger for narrative credibility. Light-hearted tales of funny or frivolous times may make good material for the stories families tell. These tellings may be embedded in family rituals such as dinnertime, reunions, favorite pastimes, religious gatherings, and the like (Riess, 1989). It seems likely, furthermore, that the canonical nature of some family practices might enhance the meaningfulness of certain kinds of stories—stories aimed to comfort and reassure, for example, or those told again and again to affirm some aspect of family identity. As Pratt and Fiese (this volume) point out, families are often their own audiences for their own stories, setting expectations for what kinds of stories should be told, when, and by whom. Each family's narrative ecology, therefore, may affirm its own literary tradition, be it one filled with happy stories or one tending toward the tragic or ironic.

The term *family stories* would seem to cover two somewhat different kinds of phenomena. First, there are those stories that are told *by* family members in the presence of other family members. These kinds of family stories, which may or may not themselves be about family events, may offer opportunities for individuals in the family to connect across generations and create a sense of family history and identity (Martin, Hagestad, & Diedrick, 1988). Family story tellings may be interpreted from the standpoints of *practice* (How was the story told? What was the performance like?) and *representation* (What was the story about? What does the story reveal about family beliefs?) (Fiese et al., 1999). Researchers have analyzed such performances for variables like narrative coherence, interaction patterns, and relationship beliefs (Fiese et al., 1999). They have also examined the main themes that these stories may contain. For example, researchers have examined the content of stories that parents tell about their own childhood to their young children (Fiese, Hooker, Kotary, Schwagler, & Rimmer, 1995). The research shows that when telling stories to their infants parents tend to emphasize affiliative themes, whereas their stories for preschool children tend to emphasize achievement. In addition, mothers tend to tell stories with more affiliative themes overall, while fathers tell stories with more achievement themes (Fiese et al., 1995).

Second, there are stories that are told *about* family. The audiences for these stories may or may not be other family members. According to Mackey, Arnold, and Pratt (2001), stories about their families dominate mid-adolescents' descriptions of key turning points in their lives. Oppenheim, Wamboldt, Gavin, Renouf, and Emde (1996) showed that when couples' stories about their children's births were especially coherent and emotionally expressive, the couples also showed greater levels of marital satisfaction. For both men and women in later life, stories about family provide threads of continuity for their individual life stories (Pratt & Fiese, this volume). As Pratt and Norris (1999) have noted, the life stories of older adults are often given coherence by their sense of having learned important lessons from a more mature family member or other adult figure from their earlier lives. Yet stories told about families do not always play a beneficent role in individual identity. In the cases clinicians know best, family stories may be seen as the reasons for significant problems in one's life (White & Epston, 1990). Family stories may stifle identity as much as they enhance it (Pratt & Fiese, this volume).

What kinds of family stories do highly generative people tell? Pratt et al. (1999) asked adults to identify critical moral incidents in their own lives and to tell those incidents as if they were telling them to an adolescent. The respondents also completed a self-report measure of generativity. Adults who scored high on the generativity measure told personal stories for adolescents that tended to emphasize the development of their own values and important lessons they had learned from their past, to a greater extent than did adults scoring low in generativity. In addition, the narratives told by the highly generative adults tended to be rated by the readers of the accounts as more engaging and well-formed, compared to the stories told by less generative adults. Kotre (2004) has argued that any generative community must include storytellers who are invested in passing down words of wisdom from one generation to the next. The data in Pratt et al. (1999) suggest that highly generative adults may see family storytelling in this way. In telling personal stories to an adolescent audience, highly generative adults tell coherent and engaging stories about how they developed their own values and what lessons can be taken from the experiences that they had growing up.

Between the years 1996 and 1998, my students and I interviewed 74 men and women for a study of generativity and life stories among African-American and Euro-American adults (see Hart et al., 2001; McAdams & Bowman, 2001; McAdams et al., 2001, for details). The 74 were chosen from a sample of over 260 adults between the ages of 35 and 65 years, approximately half African-American and half Euro-American, who completed a series of questionnaires and surveys, including self-report measures of generativity. The 74 who were interviewed were chosen because they each scored extremely high or extremely low on the generativity measures. The major aim of the study was to compare and contrast the narrative identities of highly generative and relatively nongenerative African-American and Euro-American men and women. Each life story interview required between 2 and 3 hours of time to complete. Toward the end of the interview protocol, each respondent was given this request:

> Growing up, many of us hear stories in our families or from our friends that stick with us, stories that we remember. Family stories include things parents tell their children about "the old days," their family heritage, family legends, and so on. Part of what makes life fun, even in adulthood, involves friends' and families' telling stories about themselves and about others. Try to identify one story like this that you remember, one that has stayed with you. Tell me a little bit about the story, why you like it or why you remember it, and what impact, if any, you think it has had on your life.

From the 74 interviews conducted, 68 participants (37 participants high in generativity and 31 low in generativity) provided viable responses to this request. In virtually every instance, the participant told a story that came from his or her family. (Only two participants told stories that originated with a friend.) In a majority of the instances (46 out of 68, or 67%), the participant identified the teller of the story as a particular family member (most often grandmothers), whereas in most of the rest of the cases (with the exception of the two "friend stories") they said that the story was something that they had heard in their family or that derived in some way from family lore.

How did the family stories of highly generative and less generative adults differ from each other? In many ways, the stories of the two groups did not differ. For example, the highly generative adults were no more or less likely to identify a particular family member as the teller of the tale. The stories of the two groups were comparable in length and narrative coherence. Somewhat surprisingly perhaps, the two groups were equally likely to tell a family story that exemplified a valued character trait or important life lesson. Among the traits and values celebrated by both highly generative and less generative adults in family stories were courage, self-sufficiency, hard work, and faith. For both groups, the stories frequently contained humor and irony.

Nonetheless, the two groups of responses did differ in a few dramatic ways. First, the less generative adults were more likely to say that they had a difficult time coming up with a good example of a family story that was worth relating. The two "friends" stories came from the less-generative sample; five of less-generative participants said that their families told very few stories ("We just didn't do that"), that their families had many secrets, or that they didn't think that family stories were very useful ("You shouldn't dwell on the past"), even though they eventually did relate a family story to the interviewer; and one less-generative participant described how her mother used to humiliate her by telling other family members stories about her [the participant's] stupidity and awkwardness. Among the highly generative adults, there were no examples like these. The examples themselves suggest that some less-generative adults recall and perceive less interaction among family members and less investment in sharing the kinds of stories that build family solidarity and warmth. Their memories of family life are bereft of incidents in which people enjoyed the simple act of telling and listening to each other's life tales.

A second set of differences pertains to the content of the family stories told. To get a sense of the overall difference, contrast the following two accounts, the first of which is told by a highly generative 61-year-old woman and the second by a 46-year-old man whose questionnaire responses put him in the low-generativity group:

> *High generative:* My grandmother, she told me about her escape from Russia, and that was just probably the most phenomenal story of adventure and bravery. I don't know how she could do it; I couldn't. My grandfather had come to America a year and a half or two years before and worked and sent her a ticket back. . . . She had the baby, or maybe two of them by then. But they had to go in an ox cart under the hay because they had no papers all across Europe and be handed from people to people over the borders. They got to some port in Germany where she did get on this big boat in steerage in the bottom with the baby. And she arrived in the United States, New York, Ellis Island, and all she had was a train ticket to South Bend, Indiana. . . . She was about 22 or 23, no money, no food. And she said, "People were so nice to me. When they'd see the baby crying, they'd give him a piece of bread." [The story goes on to detail her reunion with her husband and the happiness they experienced as a family.]

> *Low generative:* My dad telling the sea story. My dad would tell stories about trips, actually a more extended kind of adventure he had in the 1930s with my uncle. They got jobs on a banana boat. I think it was based in Cuba at that point. Cuba was open then, of course. So they did that for a while and then they took a trip through Central America and ended up working their way back, and spent some time in New Orleans, and then back to Chicago. . . . lots of aspects of what went on at sea. Then going through a hurricane in the Caribbean, and then in jungles. . . . It had a big effect on me. As I mentioned before, that became a model for my early years of what it meant to be a man. . . .

The two stories share surface similarities. They are both stories about adventure and survival. They both involve travel. In both cases, the participant remarks that the story had some kind of effect on her or him: The highly generative woman finds her grandmother's story inspiring, but she feels she could never live up to the protagonist's role; the less-generative man sees the protagonist of his family story, his father, as a role model for masculinity. Both stories involve significant dangers: oppressive governments and hurricanes. A major difference between the two stories concerns gender. The former is a woman's story about a female protagonist and domestic heroism; the latter is a man's story about his father's and uncle's exploits. But the highly generative woman's story contains three themes that are prevalent in many of the family stories told by the highly generative adults, both men and women, Black and White (and relatively scarce in the stories of less generative men and women). These are the themes of *suffering, growth,* and human *kindness.*

In the current sample, highly generative adults were almost three times more likely to describe a protagonist's suffering and deprivation than were less-generative adults. A total of 27 out of the 37 family stories from highly generative adults (73%) contained the suffering theme, whereas only 8 of the 31 family stories from less generative adults described a protagonist's suffering (26%). Stories described poverty, discrimination, disability, poor health, and a host of other deprivations. In the preceding story, we see that suffering eventually pays off. The protagonist is reunited with her husband, and they proceed to raise a family. By a 5-to-1 margin (32% versus 6%), highly generative adults, compared to less generative adults, told family stories in which the protagonist's suffering led directly to the expansion or growth of the self, one's family, one's career, or some other aspect of the protagonist's world. The move from suffering to growth is similar to the redemption sequences that McAdams et al. (1997) have identified as characteristic of the overall life stories told by highly generative adults. Finally, generative adults in the current sample were eight times more likely than their less generative counterparts (24% versus 3%) to tell family stories in which people provide help and care for others or exhibit extraordinary acts of kindness. In the first of the preceding stories, strangers give food to a hungry baby. In other family stories told by highly generative adults, neighbors help each other out in tough economic times, a woman tends to her sick sister, Whites help runaway Black slaves, an aunt is especially nice to her nieces and nephews when they are forced to leave their mother, and so on. Human kindness is often instrumental in the transformation of suffering into growth.

The results of my exploratory study of 68 family stories and their relation to generativity are merely suggestive and in need of a more rigorous replication. Researchers need to conduct more formal tests of the hypothesis that family stories of suffering, growth, and kindness are especially characteristic of highly generative adults. But the results are consistent with past research showing high levels of redemptive imagery in the life narratives of highly generative adults (e.g., Colby & Damon, 1992; McAdams et al., 1997). The intimate link between suffering and growth, furthermore, is arguably the experiential core of the most basic expression of human generativity—giving birth. Even in our modern technological age, labor and delivery are painful experiences for most pregnant women. But the suffering is necessary if new life is to emerge and, eventually, grow. A successful birth and subsequent growth, furthermore, rely on the kindness of a human community, a family or group who provide support, assistance, and sustenance for the helpless infant and the suffering mother. The family stories told by highly generative adults were rarely about birth or child development per se. But they frequently employed imagery, metaphors, and plot lines that suggest the same kind of generative human experience. In autobiographical memory, highly generative adults may be especially sensitive or dispositionally "primed" to recall family narratives of this sort (Conway & Pleydell-Pearce, 2000). Or it may be the case that families who tell stories like these are more likely to produce children who grow up to be highly generative adults.

CONCLUSION

Every family has its own unique narrative ecology. Stories told in and about families function in a wide variety of ways. They provide entertainment; they offer opportunities for self-expression; they promote belief systems and exemplify character traits that members of the family value; they help to shape individual and family identity. Family stories are sometimes employed in the service of generativity. Stories are passed down from one generation to the next, linking different family members together within a socio-literary tradition. Adults construct stories and tell stories to promote the well-being of future generations. This storytelling becomes part of the warm and supportive family life that highly generative adults seek to cultivate. Research has shown that highly generative adults foster trust and commitment in family relations, blend warmth and discipline in their parenting practices, are deeply invested in their children's education, and seek to pass on values and wisdom to their children. Family storytelling provides valuable opportunities through which highly generative adults are able to exert a positive and long-lasting influence on children and on the family system as a whole.

Highly generative adults may favor certain kinds of family stories over others. They may find especially compelling those family narratives in which the protagonist suffers through difficult times, but the suffering pays off in growth, expansion, and the realization of a full family life. Family stories may be filled with unsavory characters, mean-spirited and irresponsible uncles, wayward aunts, fools, miscreants, and buffoons. But some of the characters, some of the time, show remarkable acts of kindness. If they did not, suffering could not possibly lead to growth. Family life should be fun and playful; families should provide us all with a safe haven from the relentless challenges and confusion of modern life. But from the standpoint of generativity, family life is also serious business, for it is in the family that the greatest suffering and the most stupendous growth and fulfillment in life will likely be experienced. Highly generative adults seem to have a tacit understanding and appreciation of this fact of family life. You can tell that from their stories.

ACKNOWLEDGMENT

The preparation of this chapter was aided greatly by a grant from the Foley Family Foundation to establish the Foley Center for the Study of Lives at Northwestern University. The study of life stories and generativity described in the last part of the paper was funded by a grant to the author from the Spencer Foundation. The author would like to thank Reginald Blount, Phil Bowman, Jennifer Goldberg, Holly Hart, Amy Himsel, Renee Janz-Diamond, Amy Kegley, Erin Kennedy, Kenya Key, Martha Lewis, Jane Maring, Nathania Montes, David McConville, Derek McNeil, Lakshi Ramanathan, Elizabeth Reyes, and Janet Shlaes for their assistance in various aspects of that study.

REFERENCES

Ackerman, S., Zuroff, D., & Moscowitz, D. S. (2000). Generativity in midlife and young adults: Links to agency, communion, and well-being. *International Journal of Aging and Human Development, 50,* 17–41.

Arnett, J. J. (2000). Emerging adulthood: A theory of development from the late teens through the twenties. *American Psychologist, 55,* 469–480.

Baron-Cohen, S. (1995). *Mindblindness: An essay on autism and theory of mind.* Cambridge, MA: MIT Press.

Becker, E. (1973). *The denial of death.* New York: The Free Press.

Bradley, C. (1997). Generativity-stagnation: Development of a status model. *Developmental Review, 17,* 262–290.

Bruner, J. S. (1990). *Acts of meaning.* Cambridge, MA: Harvard University Press.

Cohler, B. J., Hostetler, A. J., & Boxer, A. (1998). Generativity, social context, and lived experience: Narratives of gay men in middle adulthood. In D. P. McAdams & E. de St. Aubin (Eds.), *Generativity and adult development* (pp. 265–309). Washington, DC: APA Press.

Colby, A., & Damon, W. (1992). *Some do care: Contemporary lives of moral commitment.* New York: The Free Press.

Cole, E. R., & Stewart, A. J. (1996). Meanings of political participation among Black and White women: Political identity and social responsibility. *Journal of Personality and Social Psychology, 71,* 130–140.

Conway, M. A., & Pleydell-Pearce, C. W. (2000). The construction of autobiographical memories in the self-memory system. *Psychological Review, 107,* 261–288.

de St. Aubin, E., & McAdams, D. P. (1995). The relations of generative concern and generative action to personality traits, satisfaction/happiness with life, and ego development. *Journal of Adult Development, 2,* 99–112.

de St. Aubin, E., McAdams, D. P., & Kim, T. C. (Eds.). (2004). *The generative society.* Washington, DC: APA Press.

Dennett, D. (1987). *The intentional stance.* Cambridge, MA: MIT Press.

Denzin, N. (1989). *Interpretive biography.* Newbury Park, CA: Sage.

Dillon, M., & Wink, P. (2004). Religion, cultural change, and generativity in American society. In E. de St. Aubin, D. P. McAdams, & T. C. Kim (Eds.), *The generative society* (pp. 153–174). Washington, DC: APA Press.

Erikson, E. H. (1950). *Childhood and society.* New York: Norton.

Erikson, E. H. (1959). Identity and the life cycle: Selected papers. *Psychological Issues, 1*(1), 5–165.

Fiese, B. H., Hooker, K. A., Kotary, L., Schwagler, J., & Rimmer, M. (1995). Family stories in the early stages of parenthood. *Journal of Marriage and the Family, 57,* 763–770.

Fiese, B. H., Sameroff, A., Grotevant, H., Wamboldt, F., Dickstein, S., & Fravel, D. (1999). The stories that families tell: Narrative coherence, narrative interaction, and relationship beliefs. *Monographs of the Society for Research in Child Development, 64* (Serial No. 257).

Fivush, R., & Kuebli, J. (1997). Making everyday events emotional: The construal of emotion in parent-child conversations about the past. In N. L. Stein, P. A. Ornstein, B. Tversky, & C. Brainerd (Eds.), *Memory for everyday and emotional events* (pp. 239–266). Mahwah, NJ: Lawrence Erlbaum Associates.

Grossbaum, M. G., & Bates, G. W. (2002). Correlates of psychological well-being at midlife: The role of generativity, agency and communion, and narrative themes. *International Journal of Behavioral Development, 26,* 120–127.

Habermas, T., & Bluck, S. (2000). Getting a life: The emergence of the life story in adolescence. *Psychological Bulletin, 126,* 748–769.

Hart, H. M., McAdams, D. P., Hirsch, B. J., & Bauer, J. J. (2001). Generativity and social involvement among African-Americans and White adults. *Journal of Research in Personality, 35,* 208–230.

Hill, R. B. (1997). *The strengths of African American families: Twenty-five years later.* Washington, DC: R & B Publishers.

Howe, M. L., & Courage, M. L. (1997). The emergence and early development of autobiographical memory. *Psychological Review, 104,* 499–523.

Kagan, J. (1994). *Galen's prophecy.* New York: Basic Books.

Kay, A. (1998). Generativity in the shadow of genocide: The Holocaust experience and generativity. In D. P. McAdams & E. de St. Aubin (Eds.), *Generativity and adult development* (pp. 335–359). Washington, DC: APA Press.

Keyes, C. L. M., & Ryff, C. D. (1998). Generativity in adult lives: Social structural contours and quality of life consequences. In D. P. McAdams & E. de St. Aubin (Eds.), *Generativity and adult development* (pp. 227–263). Washington, DC: APA Press.

Kim, G., & Youn, G. (2002). Generativity differences between employed and non-employed women in Korea: A role of education level. *Psychological Reports, 91,* 1205–1212.

Kotre, J. (1984). *Outliving the self: Generativity and the interpretation of lives.* Baltimore, MD: Johns Hopkins University Press.

Kotre, J. (1999). *Making it count: How to generate a legacy that gives meaning to your life.* New York: The Free Press.

Kotre, J. (2004). Generativity and culture: What meaning can do. In E. de St. Aubin, D. P. McAdams, & T. C. Kim (Eds.), *The generative society* (pp. 35–49). Washington, DC: APA Press.

Kotre, J., & Kotre, K. B. (1998). Intergenerational buffers: The damage stops here. In D. P. McAdams & E. de St. Aubin (Eds.), *Generativity and adult development* (pp. 367–389). Washington, DC: APA Press.

Maccoby, E. E., & Martin, J. A. (1983). Socialization in the context of the family: Parent-child interaction. In P. Mussen (Ed.), *Handbook of child psychology* (4th ed., Vol. 4, pp. 1–102). New York: John Wiley & Sons.

MacDermid, S. M., Franz, C. E., & De Reus, L. A. (1998). Generativity: At the crossroads of social roles and personality. In D. P. McAdams & E. de St. Aubin (Eds.), *Generativity and adult development* (pp. 181–226). Washington, DC: APA Press.

Mackey, K., Arnold, M. L, & Pratt, M. W. (2001). Adolescents' stories of decision-making in more or less authoritative families: Representing the voices of parents in narrative. *Journal of Adolescent Research, 16,* 243–268.

Mandler, J. M. (1984). *Stories, scripts, and scenes: Aspects of schema theory.* Hillsdale, NJ: Lawrence Erlbaum Associates.

Martin, P., Hagestad, G. O., & Diedrick, P. (1988). Family stories: Events (temporarily) remembered. *Journal of Marriage and the Family, 50,* 533–541.

Maruna, S. (2001). *Making good: How ex-convicts reform and rebuild their lives.* Washington, DC: APA Press.

McAdams, D. P. (1985). *Power, intimacy, and the life story: Personological inquiries into identity.* New York: Guilford Press.

McAdams, D. P. (1993). *The stories we live by: Personal myths and the making of the self.* New York: William Morrow.

McAdams, D. P. (1996). Personality, modernity, and the storied self: A contemporary framework for studying persons. *Psychological Inquiry, 7,* 295–321.

McAdams, D. P. (2001a). Generativity in midlife. In M. Lachman (Ed.), *Handbook of midlife development* (pp. 395–443). New York: Wiley.

McAdams, D. P. (2001b). The psychology of life stories. *Review of General Psychology, 5,* 100–122.

McAdams, D. P., & Bowman, P. J. (2001). Narrating life's turning points: Redemption and contamination. In D. P. McAdams, R. Josselson, & A. Lieblich (Eds.), *Turns in the road: Narrative studies of lives in transition* (pp. 3–34). Washington, DC: APA Press.

McAdams, D. P., & de St. Aubin, E. (1992). A theory of generativity and its assessment through self-report, behavioral acts, and narrative themes in autobiography. *Journal of Personality and Social Psychology, 62,* 1003–1015.

McAdams, D. P., & de St. Aubin, E. (Eds.). (1998). *Generativity and adult development: How and why we care for the next generation.* Washington, DC: APA Press.

McAdams, D. P., de St. Aubin, E., & Logan, R. (1993). Generativity among young, midlife, and older adults. *Psychology and Aging, 8,* 221–230.

McAdams, D. P., Diamond, A., de St. Aubin, E., & Mansfield, E. (1997). Stories of commitment: The psychosocial construction of generative lives. *Journal of Personality and Social Psychology, 72,* 678–694.

McAdams, D. P., Reynolds, J., Lewis, M. L., Patten, A., & Bowman, P. T. (2001). When bad things turn good and good things turn bad: Sequences of redemption and contamination in life narrative, and their relation to psychosocial adaptation in midlife adults and in students. *Personality and Social Psychology Bulletin, 27,* 472–483.

Miller, P., Wiley, A., Fung, H., & Liang, C. H. (1997). Personal story-telling as a medium of socialization in Chinese and American families. *Child Development, 68,* 557–568.

Morson, G. S. (1995). Anna Karenina's omens. In G. Gibian (Ed.), *Anna Karenina: A Norton critical edition* (2nd ed., pp. 831–843). New York: W. W. Norton.

Myers, D. G. (2000). *The American paradox: Spiritual hunger in an age of plenty.* New Haven, CT: Yale University Press.

Nakagawa, K. (1991). *Explorations into the correlates of public school reform and parental involvement.* Unpublished doctoral dissertation, Northwestern University.

Oppenheim, D., Wamboldt, F., Gavin, L., Renouf, A., & Emde, R. (1996). Couples' co-construction of the story of their child's birth: Associations with marital adaptation. *Journal of Narrative and Life History, 6,* 1–21.

Peterson, B. E. (2002). Longitudinal analysis of midlife generativity, intergenerational roles, and caregiving. *Psychology and Aging, 17,* 161–168.

Peterson, B. E., & Duncan, L. E. (1999). Generative concern, political commitment, and charitable actions. *Journal of Adult Development, 6,* 105–118.

Peterson, B. E., & Klohnen, E. C. (1995). Realization of generativity in two samples of women at midlife. *Psychology and Aging, 10,* 20–29.

Peterson, B. E., Smirles, K. A., & Wentworth, P. A. (1997). Generativity and authoritarianism: Implications for personality, political involvement, and parenting. *Journal of Personality and Social Psychology, 72,* 1202–1216.

Peterson, B. E., & Stewart, A. J. (1990). Using personal and fictional documents to assess psychosocial development: A case study of Vera Brittain's generativity. *Psychology and Aging, 5,* 400–411.

Pratt, M. W., Danso, H. A., Arnold, M. L., Norris, J. E., & Filyer, R. (2001). Adult generativity and the socialization of adolescents: Relations to mothers' and fathers' parenting beliefs, styles, and practices. *Journal of Personality, 69,* 89–120.

Pratt, M. W., & Norris, J. E. (1999). Moral development in maturity: Lifespan perspectives on the process of successful aging. In T. Hess & F. Blanchard-Fields (Eds.), *Social cognition and aging* (pp. 291–317). New York: Academic Press.

Pratt, M. W., Norris, J. E., Arnold, M. L., & Filyer, R. (1999). Generativity and moral development as predictors of value-socialization narratives for young persons across the adult life span: From lessons learned to stories shared. *Psychology and Aging, 14,* 414–426.

Putnam, R. D. (2000). *Bowling alone: The collapse and revival of American community.* New York: Simon & Schuster.

Putney, N., & Bengston, V. (2001). Families, intergenerational relationships, and kinkeeping in midlife. In M. Lachman (Ed.), *Handbook of midlife development* (pp. 528–570). New York: Wiley.

Riess, D. (1989). The practicing and representing family. In A. J. Sameroff & R. Emde (Eds.), *Relationship disturbances in early childhood* (pp. 191–220). New York: Basic Books.

Rosenwald, G. C., & Ochberg, R. L. (Eds.). (1992). *Storied lives.* New Haven, CT: Yale University Press.

Rossi, A. (Ed.). (2001). *Caring and doing for others: Social responsibility in the domains of family, work, and community.* Chicago: University of Chicago Press.

Snarey, J. (1993). *How fathers care for the next generation: A four-decade study.* Cambridge, MA: Harvard University Press.

Stewart, A. J. (1994). Toward a feminist strategy for studying women's lives. In C. Franz & A. J. Stewart (Eds.), *Women creating lives* (pp. 11–35). Boulder, CO: Westview Press.

Stewart, A. J., Franz, E., & Layton, L. (1988). The changing self: Using personal documents to study lives. *Journal of Personality, 56,* 41–74.

Stewart, A. J., & Vandewater, E. A. (1998). The course of generativity. In D. P. McAdams & E. de St. Aubin (Eds.), *Generativity and adult development* (pp. 75–100). Washington, DC: APA Press.

Tolstoy, L. (1995). *Anna Karenina.* New York: W. W. Norton. (Original work published 1877)

Tomasello, M. (2000). Culture and cognitive development. *Current Directions in Psychological Science, 9,* 37–40.

Twenge, J. (2000). The age of anxiety? Birth cohort change in anxiety and neuroticism, 1952–1993. *Journal of Personality and Social Psychology, 79,* 1007–1021.

Vaillant, G. E., & Milofsky, E. (1980). The natural history of male psychological health: IX. Empirical evidence for Erikson's model of the life cycle. *American Journal of Psychiatry, 137,* 1348–1359.

Vandewater, E. A., Ostrove, J. M., & Stewart, A. J. (1997). Predicting women's well-being in midlife: The importance of personality development and social role involvements. *Journal of Personality and Social Psychology, 72,* 1147–1160.

Wellman, H. M. (1993). Early understanding of mind: The normal case. In S. Baron-Cohen, H. Tager-Flusberg, & D. Cohen (Eds.), *Understanding other minds: Perspectives from autism* (pp. 10–39). New York: Oxford University Press.

Whitbourne, S. K., Zuschlag, M. K., Elliot, L. B., & Waterman, A. S. (1992). Psychosocial development in adulthood: A 22-year sequential study. *Journal of Personality and Social Psychology, 63,* 260–271.

White, M., & Epston, D. (1990). *Narrative means to therapeutic ends.* New York: Norton.

11

Pin-Curling Grandpa's Hair in the Comfy Chair: Parents' Stories of Growing Up and Potential Links to Socialization in the Preschool Years

Barbara H. Fiese
Nicole L. Bickham
Syracuse University

"Tell me a story about when you were little . . ." This is a request heard often by parents of young children. When asked if they ever talked about their growing up experiences with their children, nine out of ten parents reported that they had done so on several occasions. Six out of ten parents of preschoolers reported that they did so on at least a weekly basis (Fiese, Hooker, Kotary, Schwagler, & Rimmer, 1995). But what do they talk about? In this chapter we place family stories in the ecological context of child rearing. We propose that parents use stories of their growing up experiences as opportunities for socialization and that these stories convey messages about being close to others, doing good work, and striving for independence. Woven into the fabric of everyday life, these stories can serve as guideposts for behavior, providing children with rich images of their parents' experiences as well as more subtle nuances of what it means to be a member of a family.

To illuminate this process, we describe a study of 120 parents who were asked to tell a story to their 4-year-old child about when they were growing up. In examining socialization via family stories, we highlight variations in story themes of both storyteller and listener. We propose that there is a developmental press in the thematic content of family stories. Second, as a process, telling stories about growing up provides generational links. Many of the stories include a description of family kinship ties and provide vibrant images of family members who are important to understanding family history but are removed from the child's everyday experiences. Family stories provide a unique opportunity to examine both stability and change within the context of the family system. Stories may serve to both preserve family identity across generations, insuring continuity, as well as help members navigate developmental passages, reflecting the changing nature of family life. We also take this opportunity to demonstrate how the study of family stories lends itself well to the systematic integration of qualitative and quantitative research methods.

Family stories are complex, due in part to the simultaneous existence of two distinct layers to stories—the *act* of storytelling and the *content* of the story itself. The act of telling family stories provides an opportunity to connect generations as well as introduce new members to the family. Several researchers have noted that during the early stages of relationship formation, couples disclose accounts of unique as well as common personal experiences as they face the task of creating a shared identity (Veroff, Sutherland, Chadiah, & Ortega, 1993; Wamboldt, 1999). In many cases, the parent generation may use introductory gatherings as opportunities to bring the potential son- or daughter-in-law into the fold of the family through stories told about their future husband or wife. Much to the chagrin of the soon-to-be bride or groom, these stories may include recountings of previous boyfriends or girlfriends, times of success and failure, or just plain silly acts displayed as a youngster. Though on the surface these stories may appear to function purely as entertainment, they allow the novice family member to become acquainted not only with their soon-to-be-betrothed but also members of the family still to be introduced (e.g., distant uncles, grandparents, old boyfriends/girlfriends).

Family stories can be used to teach lessons as well as to initiate members into the family. Miller and colleagues describe how parents of preschool-age children remark on children's transgressions and use these opportunities to reinforce cultural norms of acceptable behavior (Miller, Wiley, Fung, & Liang, 1997). Thorne, McClean, and Dasbach (this volume) suggest that stories of parental transgressions provide opportunities for value learning in adolescence as well. Pratt and colleagues have demonstrated that there are explicit moral tones in the stories conveyed by grandparents to their grandchildren (Pratt, Norris, Arnold, & Filyer, 1999). Examples drawn from studies of early couple formation and lessons shared between grandparent and grandchild highlight how family stories may serve as roadmaps of what to expect in relationships and how to handle common challenges such as disappointments and moral dilemmas. Thus, stories can be used to engage members as well as to instruct them in family lore.

THEMATIC CONTENT OF FAMILY STORIES

There are a variety of ways to analyze family stories, as evidenced in this volume. One approach is to consider the relative coherence of the narrative. Coherence may be an important marker of emotional resolution of a personal event as well as reflective of how well the individual has been able to integrate different aspects of an experience into a synthesized whole (Fiese & Sameroff, 1999). This process of integration and synthesis has been shown to be important in studies of attachment (Main & Goldwyn, 1984), identity formation (Grotevant, 1993), and relationship satisfaction (Dickstein, St. Andre, Sameroff, Seifer, & Schiller, 1999). The coherence of a narrative is proposed to reflect the meaning-making process inherent in telling a story of personal relevance.

The thematic content of stories, on the other hand, may be more closely linked to socialization. By focusing on the thematic content of stories it is possible to identify enduring themes that are associated with creating an integrated identity as well as themes that shift with developmental changes. McAdams (this volume) describes different storied themes that evolve across the lifespan. The thematic content of stories has been proposed to reflect intentions and motives (McAdams, 1993). Henry Murray (1938) catalogued these themes based on stories told about cards depicting ambiguous visual stimuli. Although originally identifying a multitude of motivational themes, they have been distilled into two overarching constructs: agency and communion (Bakan, 1966). Typically described in the context of what motivates adults to behave in the ways that they do, these themes revolve around strivings to be independent and autonomous and strivings to form close relationships. McAdams (this volume) has extended these core themes to include strivings for generativity and investment in future generations. The bulk of the narrative work that has been done on thematic content has focused on adolescents and adults, with a particular focus on identity. Certainly, this makes sense when considering how stories may be part and parcel of who we are and how we come to be (McAdams, 1993). Implicit in a thematic emphasis is the notion that through the telling of stories and integration of experiences there are unifying themes that characterize personal identity. It would be an egregious error to consider this as a solitary activity and one that is only born when reaching adolescence. The stories we come to create are built not only on our own personal experiences but also through an integration of the stories that we have heard over many years.

There is a small literature on the thematic content of family stories. Martin and colleagues (Martin, Hagestad, & Diedrick, 1988) set out to identify generational links in family stories by asking parents and grandparents of college students to recall stories told about relatives, even those they had not met. The majority of the stories were of a personal nature falling into the broad categories of personality descriptions, work, family, death and dying, and general family activities. Interestingly, stories told about unique personalities (such as "Crazy Freddie" who owned hundreds of cuckoo clocks) tended to portray males as the protagonist. Work-related stories also typically portrayed heroes rather than heroines. Females, on the other hand, were most often the center of the story when the event focused on family life, such as relying on a grandparent in times of need. A similar pattern was noted by Nussbaum and Bettini (1994) in another study of college students and stories told by their grandparents. Grandfathers tended to tell stories that emphasized the value of life and survival. In contrast, grandmothers were more likely to tell stories about relationships and how the family developed, with particular attention to the value of family history and preservation.

Stories can serve as historical accounts of who is in the family, who left the family, and how the family was preserved across generations. These accounts tend to fall along gendered lines with the primary player in work and survival stories being male and leading ladies starring in relationship and family history stories. The study of grandparent-grandchild storytelling emphasizes the epochal potential of family stories. In contrast, the stories between parent and child may be less grand and dramatic, with more attention to the details of everyday life.

Fivush and colleagues (Fivush & Fromhoff, 1988; Reese, Haden, & Fivish, 1993) have eloquently demonstrated that there are important differences in how parents and children engage in reminiscing about the past. Some parents tend to elaborate and encourage their children to participate in the act of storytelling with obvious turn taking that results in a more complete story. Other parents tend to just "give the facts" and are less likely to include their children in the act of storytelling. These stylistic differences are predictive of the child's own narrative style during the preschool years (Peterson & McCabe, 1994). Interestingly, gender differences have also been noted in parent-child stories, whereby daughters are more likely to be elaborative partners than sons and more likely to develop elaborative and detailed narratives of their past compared to sons.

How might we go about integrating these findings? A simplistic approach would be to call upon global theories of gendered talk and catalogue these findings as additional evidence that men and women differ in what they say and what they believe they have said (Gilligan, 1982). However, this solution is inadequate because it ignores the transactional value of storytelling and the broader context in which family stories are relayed. As we set out on this analysis of family stories, we were sensitive to the fact that mothers and fathers may differ in how they approach the task of telling stories. We were interested in identifying a catalogue of themes that would summarize the stories that families told about their growing up experiences. If family stories are used as one medium of conveying lessons then we expect those messages to be compatible with the developmental task of the child receiving the story as well as the cultural context of the storyteller. Because we were venturing into relatively uncharted territory, we opted to take a qualitative approach in detecting thematic content rather than relying on a priori categories. We recognize that the themes we identified may be subject to our personal biases. However, as an initial foray we felt that this approach would allow for a more extensive examination of potential and emerging themes.

In addition to identifying themes, we were also interested in whether the content of the stories would differ by gender of parent and/or child. Thus, we used the themes identified in our qualitative analysis as categories that could be subjected to more quantitative comparisons across groups.

SAMPLE OF STORY-TELLERS AND LISTENERS

The stories we describe were drawn from 120 families with 4-year-old children (56 boys and 64 girls). The families were recruited through area nursery schools as part of a larger study on family traditions and intergenerational family process. Twenty-five of the children were the only child in the family, 38 were first-born with younger siblings, 39 were the youngest with older siblings, and 18 had both younger and older siblings. The sample was primarily Caucasian (91%) with the remainder Black (4%), Latino (2%), and Asian (2%). The families were primarily middle and upper middle class with an average Hollingshead (1975) 4-factor score of 56 distributed across four classes (I [upper middle] 61%, II 34%, III 4%, IV [unemployed] 1%). The average age of the mothers was 34 years, and the average age of the fathers was 36 years.

STORY-TELLING TASK

Each parent was presented with a 3 × 5" index card detailing the following instructions: "Tell your child a story about when you were growing up . . . when you were a little girl (boy)." Although the other parent was present when the story was being told, each parent was asked to tell the story directly to the target child. We realize that the procedure itself may have been somewhat artificial and may not reflect the spontaneous stories told in everyday life. However, we did find that in some cases these were stories that had been told before. In several instances, the parent would preface the story with, "Should I tell the one about . . . ?" indicating that it was a story the child had already heard. Children would also indicate recognition of the story by filling in details or egging the parents on. Certainly, not every story was one that had been told before. However, there appears to be some evidence that telling stories about growing up experiences is not an entirely novel behavior (Fiese et al., 1995; Miller & Moore, 1989). In our own study the following example serves to illustrate:

Mother: Did I ever tell you the time we went on vacation? And we were playing. And did I tell you this before?
Child: Yeah, you ran down the hill and you fell.
Mother: I did, and I had that glass bottle.
Child: And it had a sharp edge.

It is evident in this case that not only had the child heard the story before, he could fill in details that were important in following the storyline.

QUALITATIVE STRATEGY

In a previous report, we limited our analysis to identifying the strength of achievement and affiliation themes, based on theoretical considerations (Fiese & Skillman, 2000). We felt, however, that these two themes did not capture the richness of the stories and that parents were imparting messages that went beyond drawing close and striving for success. Therefore, in the current analysis we relied on a qualitative method referred to as the *constant comparative method* for identifying content themes (Taylor & Bogdan, 1998). Based on grounded theory (Glaser & Strauss, 1967), this strategy allows the researcher to identify themes that are then compared across the data (in this case, the stories) and revised as new themes emerge or need to be refined given conflicting evidence in the data.

For the first pass on the stories, each story was read by the first author, who made notes on emerging themes. A preliminary set of categories was identified that included themes of affiliation, achievement, independence, getting into trouble, and kinship ties. The second author independently reviewed 60 of the stories and their thematic assignments. The two authors agreed on the

TABLE 11.1
Themes Identified in Family Stories

Theme	*Working Definition*
Relationships/Affiliation	
Family	Story includes being close with or engaging in activities with family members. Often includes activities noted by "spending time together."
Non-family	Being close or spending time with nonfamily members, includes pets. May include several activities or just spending time together.
Family Life	
Roles	Roles are assigned through work or place in family (e.g., parent as authority figure or youngest sibling).
Routines	Something that occurs on a regular basis. Often preceded by phrases such as "always," "we used to," "every ____ we would."
Work	
How Things Work	Narrator explains how something works or how something is done (e.g., method of fishing, how to make a pie).
Achievement	Story focuses on an accomplishment or the importance of an achievement (e.g., working hard at something), regardless of the outcome.
Independence	
Autonomy	Child acts independently or seeks independence. May be implied (spending solitary time) or explicit (defying authority figures) or going beyond what would be expected of a child of a particular age (e.g., riding bus home alone when 5 years old).
Risk Taking	Doing something on one's own or engaging in joint activity that leads to or could lead to child being harmed.
Getting Into Trouble	Doing something that resulted in the child being punished or reprimanded.

presence or absence of the themes on average 90% of the time. Definitions of the themes were revised, and in some cases a larger category was refined to reflect two or more separate themes. The resulting categories and their definitions are presented in Table 11.1.

THEMATIC LANDSCAPE

We reviewed 220 stories; 109 were told by mothers and 111 by fathers. The number of themes evident in each story were relatively evenly distributed across the sample, with 25% of the stories including one theme, 25% two

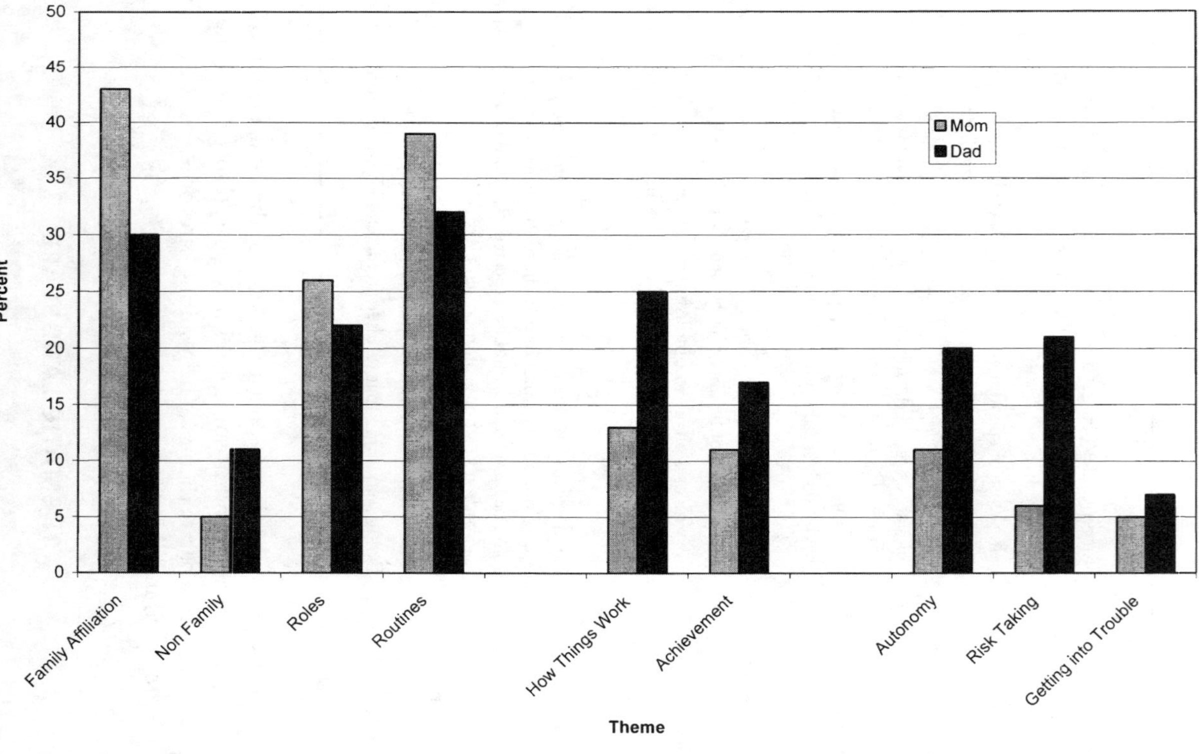

FIG. 11.1. Percent of stories containing theme.

themes, 25% three themes, and 25% containing four or more themes. Figure 11.1 depicts the percentage of stories containing the themes that we identified.

STORY ORIENTATION: PEOPLE AND PLACES

In addition to content themes, we first address the issue of how the parents approached the task and structured the story to engage the child. Researchers who study parent-child reminiscing point out that there are distinct styles of engaging children in narrative tasks (e.g., Fivush, Bohanek, Robertson, & Duke, this volume; Peterson & McCabe, this volume). Thus we expected individual differences in how parents approached the storytelling task. Approximately half of the parents took the child's perspective into account when recounting their childhood experiences. Mothers and fathers were just as likely to incorporate the child's perspective, whether told to sons or daughters. There were multiple ways that parents would incorporate the child's perspective into the story. The over-arching strategy was to use leading phrases such as, "remember when you . . ." There were several variations that we found interesting in this regard. Close to one third of the stories included reference to geographical locations to orient the child to the story. The locations ranged from recognizable landmarks (e.g., Niagara Falls) to sites of family significance (e.g., a summer house). Parents also used kinship ties as a means to engage children in the story, highlighting how members of the family were related to each other. The following excerpt includes several of these orientation features.

Father: Remember when we went walking with Grandpa?
Child: Yeah.
Father: Well, when I was a little boy, I used to go walking with my grandpa all the time and in fact we used to go on walking trips. I used to go walking with my Dad, who's your grandpa, and uhm . . . remember when we went down to the pond?
Child: Yeah.
Father: Do you remember that? The pond behind Grandma and Grandpa's house?
Child: Yeah.
Father: Well when I was a little boy, every Thanksgiving—and that's what we had last week, remember? We had Thanksgiving. We had a big dinner at Grandma and Grandpa's house. Every Thanksgiving when it was cold enough we would go skating on the pond and we would play hockey. Remember? Playing hockey?

In this excerpt, the father engages the child through recalling people and places that were familiar to the child even though the story itself was about a nonshared experience.

Relationships, Roles, and Routines

The most predominant theme was affiliation. Close to half (43%) of the stories included some aspect of shared activities or being close to family or nonfamily members. Stories with affiliative themes ranged from a focus on shared activities (e.g., sharing a tent with brothers and sisters) to explicit statements about feeling good when with family members. When we examined the likelihood that the affiliation stories would be told by mothers or fathers we found some interesting results. Mothers were more likely, overall, to tell a story that included an affiliation theme with family members, χ^2 (218) = 3.70, $p < .05$. Many of the stories told by mothers described feeling close to family members. In the following story, the mother's fondness for her grandfather is revealed:

> This is true. This really happened. When I was a little girl and I lived with my grandfather and grandmother. Grandpa had a big comfy chair as comfy as that chair over there and he used to snuggle down in that chair and I would walk around in front of my grandfather and look at him and he would know that I wanted to crawl up in his lap and you know how that feels? So I would crawl up in his lap and he would hold me in his lap and he would tell me stories. And you know what one of my favorite things to do was to comb Grandpa's hair. One day I decided to comb Grandpa's hair and I took my little hair brush and comb and I stood up behind Grandpa and his comfy chair and I started to comb his hair and he said, "Oh that feels so nice," and I combed his hair and he didn't know it but I had some little ponytail holders and some pins and I started making pin curls in grandpa's hair and I put little curls all on the top of his head and he fell asleep. And when he woke up he had the prettiest curls you ever saw all over his head and he didn't even mind. Wasn't that nice?

It was relatively common for mothers, and to a lesser extent fathers, to incorporate themes of being close with others even in the face of childhood antics. This view of family relationships is somewhat different from those portrayed in attachment stories where the primary focus is on felt security. Although not incompatible with secure attachment relationships, the more mundane descriptions of daily exchanges underscore that family relationships are characterized by repetitive, sometimes fleeting, interactions involving warmth, cohesion, and trust. From the perspective of general systems theory, these are often considered key ingredients of a healthy family (Parke & Buriel, 1998). Another aspect of family organization that was often included in stories marked by closeness was the mention of family roles and routines. Taken together, these three themes appear to form a constellation that reflects trust in relationships as well as how family life is organized around roles and routines. An example serves to illustrate:

> At night, sometimes, Grandpa Franklin would come into me and Justine's, you know Aunt Justine, well he'd come into our bedroom and sing us some songs. And me and Justine shared a room, he'd go into our room, and we would have one bed, just like you and Sam share a room; we would each be laying in our bed and he would sing us some silly songs. And we'd say "Please daddy, please sing 'There was an old lady who swallowed a fly.'" And that was our favorite, and do you know why we liked that song? You know that song . . . "there was an old lady who swallowed a fly, I don't know why she swallowed a fly . . ." Well Grandpa would tickle every time he got to that part, "it tickled inside her." Has Grandpa ever done that to you when he sung that song to you? Well we'd be in our beds and Grandpa would come in and me and Justine would be in our beds and he'd reach his hands and go "and wiggled and jiggled and tickled inside her." And he'd tickle us when he used to sing those songs. And then he'd give us a big kiss and hug goodnight. And that was a nice way to end the day.

We examined whether stories told to daughters were different from those told to sons. We created a summary score totaling the presence or absence of the themes of affiliation, roles, and routines (see Table 11.2). We found a trend ($F(3, 216) = 2.26$, $p < .08$) for stories told by mothers to daughters to be strongest on these dimensions. Women have been referred to as the "kin-keepers" of the family, being responsible for organizing family gatherings (Leach & Braithwaite, 1996), maintaining contact across generations (Rosenthal & Marshall, 1988), and ensuring that family traditions are preserved (Meske, Sanders, Meredith, & Abbott, 1994). Evident in these stories are roles and routines that demark everyday family relationships.

Work and Success

A second grouping of stories we identified can be summarized along the lines of work and strivings for success. We examined gender differences in the likelihood of such themes being expressed in the stories. We totaled the absence or presence of achievement and how things work themes to create a summary of work themes. We found that overall there was a gender difference in the likelihood of such themes being included ($F(3, 216) = 3.16$, $p < .02$). Overall, fathers were significantly more likely to tell stories of work and stories told

Table 11.2
Presence of Story Themes by Parent-Child Dyad

	Mother		*Father*	
	Daughter	*Son*	*Daughter*	*Son*
Percent of Stories[a]				
Relationships				
Affiliation	46	39	32	28
Non-Family	02	08	08	13
Family Life				
Roles	38	11	24	18
Routines	41	38	31	32
Roles & Routines Combined	64	46	49	41
Work				
How Things Work	08	17	24	26
Achievement	05	17	18	15
Work & Achievement Combined	12	28	33	36
Independence				
Autonomy	10	12	22	17
Risk Taking	07	06	20	21
Getting Into Trouble	03	05	05	09
Trouble & Autonomy Combined	16	18	34	38

[a]Percent of all stories told within dyads: mother/daughter; mother/son; father/daughter; father/son.

by mothers to daughters were the least likely to include work themes. A story told by a father to his son serves to illustrate the work stories:

> **Father:** When I was a little boy, we had a house that was on a corner, we had 180 feet of sidewalk to shovel. And you know what? I had to do one side. Every time it snowed I had to get up early and go out and shovel one side. And I shoveled the sidewalk that was on Maple Street. Everybody else had to shovel the side that was on Oak Avenue. Now, I had to shovel 60 feet, and nobody else had to shovel so much. You know why I had to shovel 60 feet, and nobody else shoveled so much? 'cause I would get up early and there was a lot of people who used to walk down Maple Street where I shoveled and I had to get it done early, 'cause otherwise it would all get packed down, and it would be hard and slippery and you couldn't shovel it and it was really tough, but if I got early on it and I got it all done it was really easy, and I got the whole thing shoveled and it would be done in no time at all. So, I got all my shoveling done for the whole day before I went to school. But nobody helped me. I had to

do it all by myself. Sometimes it was really deep, and it was a heavy shovel and it was a steel shovel. When I used the steel shovel. Do you know why I used the steel shovel? 'Cause it didn't bend like the aluminum shovel did. Even though it was heavier it was better, because the sidewalk wasn't very smooth and so you had to scrape it to get the snow off 'cause even when I got up early there were some people who had gotten up earlier than I had and had already started to pack down the snow.

Son: Who packed down the snow?

Father: They walked on it. STOMP . . . STOMP . . . STOMP. And they would pack it down so that it would be really hard to shovel and that's why I'd try to get up early and get it done.

In this account, the father describes not only his hard work but also the tools (a steel shovel) that are necessary to complete the task. Indeed, one quarter of the fathers' stories included reference to tools or lengthy descriptions of how things work.

Being Independent: Getting Into Trouble

A third broad category we identified were stories that had to do with being independent and striving for autonomy. In many cases, the striving for independence included risk taking which ultimately got the child in trouble. We totaled the presence or absence of autonomy, risk taking, and getting into trouble to create an independence score. We found that fathers, overall, were more likely to tell stories that included being independent, risk taking, and getting into trouble ($F(3, 216) = 3.06, p < .03$). Fathers were twice as likely to tell stories about independence and over three times as likely to tell stories that involved some type of risk taking. The following story serves to illustrate:

> When I was a little boy a long time ago, I used to be very hazardous. When I used to get together with my brothers, daddy's daddy he would always tell us don't cause any trouble. Ok, but I always used to get into trouble. I remember one summer I got in so much trouble that I wasn't allowed to go outside and play. I ended up going through a window. I got hit by a car. I got my teeth knocked out. This is all in one summer. My daddy wasn't very happy with me. I told him, don't worry about it, I'm OK. He says, well when you get older and you become a daddy and you'll know why I worry. I never understood that too much until you guys came along. But I didn't care then. So I just went out and got hit by another car. So that's why, what do I say when you are out riding your bike? What do I say? Watch both ways right? That's my story and I'm still alive.

Although we found few stories that contained an explicit moral, fathers' stories about getting into trouble and risk taking oftentimes reflected the implicit message, "Do as I say not as I did!"

TREES OF FAMILY STORIES

The stories that parents have to tell about their growing up experiences can be thought of as reflecting the different branches of family life as well as imparting messages consistent with socialization in the context of American middle-class Caucasian families. We suspect that other themes may be evident under different contexts of child raising. Indeed, Miller points out that mothers in Chinese cultures are more likely to emphasize personal transgressions in recounting past events of their children, and mothers in America are more likely to focus on their child's independence and personality characteristics (Miller et al., 1997). Other researchers have noted differences in conversational content, with Western cultures more likely to talk about individual accomplishments and Asian cultures to focus on shared family experiences (Martini, 1996). As Wang (this volume) points out, cultures may differ in regard to emphasis on learning from past experiences. Within a cultural context where ancestors are revered and family history is considered an essential ingredient in development, personal stories of growing up may take on characteristics beyond those found in our primarily upper middle-class American sample. Certainly, more research is warranted to include storytelling across cultures to focus on similarities as well as differences. Our discussion, thus, is limited to the overarching themes found in this sample of stories collected from two-parent families in middle-class America.

The ways in which the parents approached the task of storytelling is consistent with the work reported by researchers who have studied parent-child reminiscence (e.g., Fivush et al., this volume; Peterson & McCabe, this volume). Consistent with other reports, we found that there were individual differences in how parents engaged in the narrative task such that some parents were more elaborative and used cues of orientation (geography, kinship ties, common experiences) to elaborate on story themes. It is interesting to note that these individual differences have been previously noted when the task is aimed at encouraging the child to recount an experience. In the case of growing up stories the task is aimed at the parent telling the story to the child. As Fung and Miller (this volume) point out, the narrative environment is regulated by the role of listener as well as the teller.

We grouped our findings across three thematic categories: family relationships, work, and independence. We find it interesting that these summarizations are consistent with Erikson's first four ages of man that span the developmental period from birth to the early school years. The age of trust is characterized by close relationships and feelings of "inner goodness." Upon review of Erikson's account of this pivotal initial stage it is interesting to note that he describes building trust in relationships through everyday parent care and responsiveness that is embedded in larger cultural institutions aimed at providing a sense of belonging and connectedness to the "ritual practice of many" (p. 250). Family relationship stories were often framed in the context of everyday routines and special family rituals. Bedtime stories, baking cookies with Grandma, and the summer camping trip provided opportunities to comment on not only the organization of family life but also on how routine events provide a stage for close and meaningful relationships.

Previous research has focused on narratives of close relationships as they pertain to attachment security (Oppenheim, this volume). The study of family stories, as distinct from story-stem techniques, is not inconsistent with findings relating attachment security and narrative practices in that positive accounts of relationships may be expressed both through narrative and through practice. The study of family stories is distinct, however, by inclusion of multiple aspects of family life. Individuals may represent the trustworthiness of relationships in their cognitive working models (Main & Goldwyn, 1984), but when cast as a narrative about family members and group interaction, the setting and organizational features of the family become foreground. We did not examine the content of these growing up stories in relation to how parents and children interact with each other. However, there is evidence to suggest that narrative accounts of family events are related to how families interact with each other as a group (Dickstein et al., 1999; Fiese & Marjinsky, 1999). In this regard, family stories reflect not only whether relationships are sources of reward but also clues as to how such relationships are played out in everyday life.

Our findings that mothers were more likely to include themes of closeness in the context of family routines is consistent with previous reports on women and their roles as kinkeepers in the family. Previous research has focused on how women are more likely to carry out family routines and shoulder the responsibility of keeping the family heritage. It may be that family stories are one way that young girls begin to be indoctrinated into the family system of kinkeepers. Broad characterizations of gender differences have focused on the contrast between relationships and work. Our findings are consistent with these depictions but also expand the emphasis. It is not just that mothers were more likely to talk about relationships than fathers and that daughters were more likely to hear these stories, but also that relationships are framed in the context of everyday routines and special rituals that may provide a sense of belonging related to individual identity (Fiese, 1992).

Erikson's second and third ages focus on autonomy and initiative. He describes the emotional life of the preschooler as resolving tensions between acting on one's own and feelings of guilt and doubt. In the stories told by parents, particularly fathers, there was an emphasis on acting on one's own with a tension of getting into trouble. We suspect that these stories may have been told as warnings to children. There is reason to expect that boys are more likely overall to take physical risks and it is likely that, if caught, there would be repercussions of some sort. In the stories of risk taking and autonomy fathers appeared to be relaying themes of caution, recognizing that their offspring may be engaging in very similar adventures. Fathers, overall, highlighted the potential for danger in their family stories and interestingly boys as well as girls were as likely to hear such stories.

Erikson's fourth age focuses on industry. In this age he describes the child's interest and ability to handle tools and technology. We found it interesting that in the stories told about work and striving for success there was often mention of tools and explanations of how things work. Fathers were twice as likely as mothers to include accounts of how things work.

Linking story content with Erikson's ages of man, even on a post-hoc basis, highlights the potential enduring nature of these themes and their potential to be part of the socialization process in early childhood. There is another aspect of these stories that may also reflect not only the ways in which there are common challenges across the life span but how family organization fosters personal meaning in everyday life. We found it very interesting that the second most prevalent theme, after family affiliation, was the depiction of routines. As is the case with stories, family routines may be multilayered and reflect not only acts but also a meaning-making process within the family. Fiese and colleagues have made the distinction between routines of daily living and rituals in family life (Fiese et al., 2002). Whereas routines may be relatively perfunctory and rarely thought about once they are completed, rituals possess a symbolic component that emotionally connects family members. In our study, we illustrated the routine theme by reference to a regular bedtime activity. This story may relay to the child not only the predictability of daily routines but also that these activities provide an opportunity to reaffirm close family relationships. Heard over and over again, stories of routines may accentuate feelings of belongingness and offer signposts to the child, signifying "This is what it means to be a member of our family."

APPLICATIONS AND FUTURE DIRECTIONS

Educators and clinicians alike may benefit from the use of family stories. Previous authors have reported employing college students to collect family stories via their grandparents. Early childhood educators may follow suit by enlisting the aid of teachers and parents in sharing childhood stories. These stories may serve to illustrate common developmental phenomena as well as unique cultural variations. For clinicians, there is a long-standing heritage in the use of storytelling to promote change. What may be unique, from our perspective, is the possibility to include dyadic storytelling between parent and child as part of a therapeutic process.

We consider this an initial effort to examine how family stories may be part of socialization in early childhood. If these stories do reflect important developmental phenomena it will be important to compare themes across different ages. It may be that themes of personal identity may not be cemented until early adulthood. Longitudinal data would allow for a closer examination of whether there are stable themes within a family or whether the themes change based on age of children. A glaring omission in this work has been an inclusion of the child's perspective on these stories. To date, we do not have a clear picture of what the child is gaining (if anything) by hearing these stories. Furthermore, does it matter whether children hear the same story over and over again, or is frequency of storytelling overshadowed by the themes inherent in the stories? We would like to see the context of family stories expanded to include direct links between story themes and child behavior.

ACKNOWLEDGMENT

Preparation of this manuscript was supported, in part, by a grant to the first author from the National Institutes of Health (MH51771).

REFERENCES

Bakan, D. (1966). *The duality of human experience: Isolation and communion in Western man.* Boston: Beacon Press.

Dickstein, S., St. Andre, M., Sameroff, A. J., Seifer, R., & Schiller, M. (1999). Maternal depression, family functioning, and child outcomes: A narrative assessment. In B. H. Fiese,

A. J. Sameroff, H. D. Grotevant, F. S. Wamboldt, S. Dickstein, & D. L. Fravel (Eds.), *The stories that families tell: Narrative coherence, narrative interaction, and relationship beliefs. Monographs of the Society for Research in Child Development, 64*(2), Serial No. 257 (pp. 84–104). Malden, MA: Blackwell.

Fiese, B. H. (1992). Dimensions of family rituals across two generations: Relation to adolescent identity. *Family Process, 31,* 151–162.

Fiese, B. H., Hooker, K. A., Kotary, L., Schwagler, J., & Rimmer, M. (1995). Family stories in the early stages of parenthood. *Journal of Marriage and the Family, 57,* 763–770.

Fiese, B. H., & Marjinsky, K. A. T. (1999). Dinnertime stories: Connecting relationship beliefs and child behavior. In B. H. Fiese, A. J. Sameroff, H. D. Grotevant, F. S. Wamboldt, S. Dickstein, & D. Fravel (Eds.), *The stories that families tell: Narrative coherence, narrative interaciton, and relationship beliefs. Monographs of the Society for Research in Child Development, 64*(2), Serial No. 257 (pp. 52–68). Malden, MA: Blackwell.

Hollingshead, A. B. (1975). *A four-factor classification of social status.* Unpublished manual. New Haven, CT: Yale University.

Fiese, B. H., & Sameroff, A. J. (1999). The family narrative consortium: A multidimensional approach to narratives. In B. H. Fiese, A. J. Sameroff, H. D. Grotevant, F. S. Wamboldt, S. Dickstein, & D. L. Fravel (Eds.), *The stories that families tell: Narrative coherence, narrative interaction, and relationship beliefs. Monographs of the Society for Research in Child Development, 64*(2), Serial No. 257 (pp. 1–36). Malden, MA: Blackwell.

Fiese, B. H., & Skillman, G. (2000). Gender differences in family stories: Moderating influence of parent gender role and child gender. *Sex Roles, 43,* 267–283.

Fiese, B. H., Tomcho, T., Douglas, M., Josephs, K., Poltrock, S., & Baker, T. (2002). Fifty years of research on naturally occuring rituals: Cause for celebration? *Journal of Family Psychology, 16,* 381–390.

Fivush, R., & Fromhoff, F. A. (1988). Style and structure in mother-child conversations about the past. *Discourse Processes, 11,* 337–355.

Gilligan, C. (1982). *In a different voice: Psychological theory and women's development.* Cambrdige, MA: Harvard University Press.

Glaser, B. G., & Strauss, A. (1967). *The discovery of grounded theory: Strategies for qualitative research.* Chicago: Aldine.

Grotevant, H. D. (1993). The integrative nature of identity: Bringing soloists to sing in the choir. In J. Kroger (Ed.), *Discussions in ego identity* (pp. 121–146). Hillsdale, NJ: Lawrence Erlbaum Associates.

Leach, M. S., & Braithwaite, D. O. (1996). A binding tie: Supportive communication of family kinkeepers. *Journal of Applied Communication Research, 24,* 200–216.

Main, M., & Goldwyn, R. (1984). Predicting rejection of their infant from mother's representation of her own experience: Implications for the abused and abusing intergenerational cycle. *Child Abuse and Neglect, 8,* 203–217.

Martin, P., Hagestad, G. O., & Diedrick, P. (1988). Family stories: Events (temporarily) remembered. *Journal of Marriage and the Family, 50,* 533–541.

Martini, M. (1996). "What's new?" at the dinner table: Family dynamics during mealtimes in two cultural groups in Hawaii. *Early Development and Parenting, 5,* 23–34.

McAdams, D. P. (1993). *The stories we live by: Personal myths and the making of the self.* New York: William Morrow & Co., Inc.

Meske, C., Sanders, G. F., Meredith, W. H., & Abbott, D. A. (1994). Perceptions of rituals and traditions among elderly persons. *Activities, Adaptation, & Aging, 18,* 13–26.

Miller, P. J., & Moore, B. B. (1989). Narrative conjunctions of caregiver and child: A comparative perspective on socialization through stories. *Ethos, 17,* 43–64.

Miller, P. J., Wiley, A. R., Fung, H., & Liang, C. (1997). Personal storytelling as a medium of socialization in Chinese and American families. *Child Development, 68,* 557–568.

Murray, H. (1938). *Explorations in personality.* New York: Oxford University Press.

Nussbaum, J. F., & Bettini, L. M. (1994). Shared stories of the grandparent–grandchild relationship. *International Journal of Aging and Human Development, 39,* 67–80.

Parke, R. D., & Buriel, R. (1998). Socialization in the family: Ethnic and ecological perspectives. In W. Damon (Ed.), *Handbook of child psychology* (Vol. 3, pp. 463–552). New York: Wiley.

Peterson, C., & McCabe, A. (1994). A social interactionist account of developing decontextualized narrative skill. *Developmental Psychology, 30,* 937–948.

Pratt, M. W., Norris, J., Arnold, M. L., & Filyer, R. (1999). Generativity and moral development as predictors of value socialization narratives for young persons across the adult lifespan: From lessons learned to stories shared. *Psychology and Aging, 14,* 414–426.

Reese, E., Haden, C. A., & Fivush, R. (1993). Mother-child conversation about the past: Relationships of style and memory over time. *Cognitive Development, 8,* 403–430.

Rosenthal, C. J., & Marshall, V. W. (1988). Generational transmission of family ritual. *American Behavioral Scientist, 31,* 669–684.

Taylor, S. J., & Bogdan, R. (1998). *Introduction to qualitative research methods* (3rd ed.). New York: John Wiley & Sons, Inc.

Veroff, J., Sutherland, L., Chadiah, L. A., & Ortega, R. M. (1993). Predicting marital quality with narrative assessments of marital experience. *Journal of Marriage and the Family, 55,* 326–337.

Wamboldt, F. S. (1999). Co-constructing a marriage: Analyses of young couples' relationship narratives. In B. H. Fiese, A. J. Sameroff, H. D. Grotevant, F. S. Wamboldt, S. Dickstein, & D. L. Fravel (Eds.), *The stories that families tell: Narrative coherence, narrative interaction, and relationship beliefs. Monograph of the Society for Research in Child Development, 64*(2), Serial No. 257 (pp. 37–51). Malden, MA: Blackwell.

12

The Cultural Context of Parent-Child Reminiscing: A Functional Analysis

Qi Wang
Cornell University

The social-interactionist approaches to cognitive development highlight the developmental significance of face-to-face interactions between the child and more competent members of the society (Cole, 1996; Gauvain, 2001; Rogoff, 1990; Vygotsky, 1978; Wertsch, 1991). Vygotsky (1978) contended that development takes place when children internalize culturally valued skills, knowledge, and concepts into their own mental framework, a process that initiates *between* the child and the partner (e.g., parents, teachers, older siblings) and leads to higher mental functions *in* the child. Rogoff (1990) further asserted that adult-guided participation serves as a forum of "apprenticeships in thinking" that "provide the beginner with access to both overt aspects of the skill and the more hidden inner processes of thought" (p. 40). Thus, by actively engaging in everyday joint activities, children gradually incorporate the meaning and utility of their culture's material and symbolic tools into their own repertoire of thinking, and further develop culture-specific qualities and competencies (Gauvain, 2001; Goodnow, 2000; Valsiner, 2000).

Building upon this conceptualization of cognitive growth as an active construction embedded in a social weave of shared activities, many memory researchers underscore parent-child conversations about the shared past and the long-term consequences of such conversations for children's autobiographical memory (Fivush, 1994; Hudson, 1990; Nelson, 1993; Pillemer & White, 1989). Studies of reminiscing activities in European and Euro-American families have uncovered important factors, such as the amount and style of parent-child memory talk, in shaping children's subsequent remembering (Harley & Reese, 1999; Leichtman, Pillemer, Wang, Koreishi, & Han, 2000; Peterson & McCabe, 1994; Reese, Haden, & Fivush, 1993; Tessler & Nelson, 1994). Parents who converse in a more elaborate, detailed manner tend to have children who remember more information over time. Some researchers further maintain that parent-child reminiscing serves important functions beyond facilitating memory development: It is a primary channel through which children learn how to formulate stories about themselves and further develop an enduring self-concept; it is also a crucial means by which children come to understand the social significance of memory sharing (Fivush, 1994; Nelson, 1993).

Does parent-child reminiscing serve the same functions in other cultures? Psychological and anthropological studies indicate that people in different cultures show varied orientations toward autonomy versus relatedness in their cognition, emotion, and social behavior, orientations that are crystallized in their cultural heritages, particularly related to the conception of selfhood (Geertz, 1973; Markus & Kitayama, 1991; Triandis, 1989; Wang & Brockmeier, 2002). The prevailing social orientation and view of the self in a particular culture may play a paramount role in determining the purposes for which parents converse with their children about personal experiences from the past. Empirical data have revealed marked cultural differences in the structural organization and thematic content of parent-child reminiscing (Miller, Fung, & Mintz, 1996; Miller, Wiley, Fung, & Liang, 1997; Mullen & Yi, 1995; Wang, Leichtman, & Davies, 2000; Wang, 2001a). Such differences may be mapped onto the *functional variation* in everyday uses of memory across cultures.

The current emphasis on the functional aspect of sharing memory narratives reflects a general interest among philosophers and psychologists in the functions of autobiographical memory. Studies have examined memory functions from different perspectives in areas of developmental, cognitive, social, personality, and clinical research and have identified a variety of uses ranging from self definition, relationship maintenance, and behavior guidance (e.g., Baddeley, 1988; Neisser, 1988; Pillemer, 1998). This chapter analyzes the cultural context of parent-child reminiscing from a functional perspective, using the three major functions of autobiographical memory—self, social, and directive—as a framework. I first briefly review theories of memory functions that researchers have proposed based primarily on data of Western populations. Then I discuss the various ways that culture may shape each memory function and how that may result in different contents and styles of family memory sharing. The discussion focuses on Euro-American and Chinese families, analyzing conversational excerpts collected in our past studies of parent-child reminiscing in the two cultures.[1] Build-

[1]These conversations were collected in the cited empirical studies. They were not presented in previously published papers except otherwise noted.

ing upon the empirical data, I demonstrate that the same memory functions appear in nuanced versions across cultures and are manifested in everyday personal storytelling, which creates different cultural contexts of parent-child reminiscing.

A FUNCTIONAL APPROACH TO MEMORY AND MEMORY SHARING

The uses of memory give reasons for memory to persist. Many contemporary researchers have emphasized the functions of autobiographical memory in shaping the processes and consequences of remembering (Bluck & Alea, 2002; Bruce, 1989; Conway & Pleydell-Pearce, 2000; Hyman & Faries, 1992; Pillemer, 1998; Ross, 1989; Singer & Salovey, 1993). According to the functional view, both encoding and retrieval of personal information strongly depend on the structures of mental schemata containing an individual's implicit self-theories, attitudes, and beliefs. Memories that are not consistent with or functional to current goals are eventually either reconstructed or forgotten. Some researchers further underscore the importance of identifying the primary functions of autobiographical memory, claiming that the major purposes memory serves may directly affect the organization of and access to the memory system (Baddeley, 1988; Hyman & Faries, 1992; Neisser, 1988; Robinson & Swanson, 1990).

Taking an adaptive evolutionary perspective, Nelson (1993, 1996) makes an explicit distinction between the function of autobiographical memory and other, earlier established (in development and evolution) memory systems. She contends that, through the medium of language, shared memory narrative gives rise to an autobiographical memory system, which, once established, serves as an important device for social solidarity and a necessary ingredient in the human concept of the self. Pillemer (1998, 2001) further elaborates on the various functions of remembering and recounting personal event memories. In his theorization, *adaptive functions* entail the real-world usefulness of memory in everyday life. Remembering and recounting past events, particularly those that are highly intense (e.g., trauma), serve *emotional or therapeutic functions.* By learning from the past about what is to be avoided in the future, one benefits from the *directive functions* of memory. And finally, narrative reconstruction of the past gives rise to the believability and emotionality of a memory and makes possible its essential *communicative functions.* Similarly, Robinson and Swanson (1990) suggest that autobiographical memory serves at least four functions: interpretation of others' actions, relationship maintenance, mood regulation, and self-definition.

Studies with psychometric instruments of reminiscence functions have also revealed similar uses that memories assume (Merriam, 1993; Romaniuk & Romaniuk, 1981; Watt & Wong, 1991; Webster, 1993). For example, Webster (1993, 1997) developed a 43-item Reminiscence Functions Scale (RFS) in which participants indicate on a 6-point scale how often they reminisce with a particular function in mind. Webster administered the RFS to 710 adults ranging in age from 17 to 91 and identified eight functions:

1. Boredom reduction (reminiscence as a way to pass the time).
2. Death preparation (using the past to reach a sense of closure and calmness).
3. Identity (using the past to discover, clarify, and crystallize one's sense of self).
4. Problem solving (remembering past problem-solving strategies for the present purpose).
5. Conversation (reminiscence as a means of connecting with others in an informal way).
6. Intimacy maintenance (using the past to resurrect thoughts and feelings about an important other).
7. Bitterness revival (remembering past events to justify negative thoughts and emotions towards others).
8. Teach/inform (using reminiscence to relay to others instructional information).

Most of the memory functions postulated in autobiographical memory and reminiscence literature can be mapped onto three broad purposes of memory—self (for self definition and regulation), social (for relationship creation and maintenance), and directive (for the guidance of behavior and problem solving) (for reviews, see Bluck & Alea, 2002; Webster & Cappeliez, 1993). These memory functions have been identified among individuals of different ages, genders, and ethnic backgrounds (Pillemer, 1998, 2001; Webster, 2002). However, although these functions may be universal, the specific ways they manifest may differ markedly in different cultures (Nelson, 1993; Wang, 2003a; Wang & Brockmeier, 2002). By examining data on parent-child reminiscing in Euro-American and Chinese families, I show that cultural variations exist in the three primary functions of autobiographical memory. I here analyze each of the functions in turn, situating them in a cultural context of family memory sharing.

THE SELF FUNCTION: MEMORY AND CULTURAL CONSTRUCT OF THE SELF

Given that the central feature of autobiographical memory is self-relevance, the prevailing view of the self in a particular culture may play a predominant role in defining memory functions. The societal emphasis on individuality and autonomy in Euro-American culture facilitates the development of an "independent" self. It is conceived of as a well-bounded entity comprising an individual's private beliefs, attributes, and personality traits that are impervious to other people, social groups, or interpersonal contexts. In contrast, in many East-Asian societies, like China, great emphasis is placed on group solidarity and interpersonal relatedness. Such a cultural ideology gives rise to an "interdependent" self that is viewed as part of ongoing relationships, as unbounded, and as containing significant social roles, duties, and responsibilities (Geertz, 1973; Markus & Kitayama, 1991; Triandis, 1989). Notably, these two modes of self-conception are not polarized categories. Many researchers concur that the differences may well be a matter of degree, such that the self in any given culture is bound to comprise both autonomy and relatedness, with only the relative salience and prominence of each component differing markedly across cultures (e.g., Barth, 1997; Harter, 1998; Hollos & Leis, 2001; Spiro, 1993; Raeff, 1997; Wang & Li, 2003).

The culturally promoted self-conception may affect the self-function of autobiographical memory in two major ways (Wang, 2003a). First, a focus on autonomy versus relatedness in the self influences the content and structure of memories, which, in turn, reflect, express, and reinforce such a focus. For independent selves, personal event memories with specific details and elaboration, especially those of one-moment-in-time events unique to an individual and with the individual cast as the central character (e.g., "the time I won the spelling bee competition"), are an important way to differentiate the self from others, thereby reaffirming the self as an autonomous entity. In contrast, there may be less need for elaborate, detailed, self-focused autobiographical memories among interdependent selves whose paramount concern is collectivity and interconnectedness. Memories in this case often concern script events and preserve a salient social orientation (e.g., "family dinners"), which help to engage individuals in ongoing relationships and social activities, thereby reinforcing the self as a relational entity (Mullen, 1994; Wang, 2001b, 2004; Wang & Leichtman, 2000). Thus, by taking different forms and contents, autobiographical memories appear to sustain different modes of selfhood in different cultures.

Second, cultural conceptions of selfhood may determine the perceived importance of autobiographical memory in constituting one's self and identity. It is a predominant view in Western philosophy and psychology that the self is developed, expressed, and reconstructed from one's accumulated life history (Bruner, 1990; Hume, 1739/1882; McAdams, 1993; Nelson, 1996; Pillemer, 1998). As Polkinghorne (1988, p. 152) claims, "the self is that temporal order of human existence whose story begins with birth, has as its middle the episodes of a lifespan, and ends with death." Through recollecting and identifying with the past, even the most traumatically painful experiences, one's existence is given meaning, purpose, and value (Antze, 1996; Herman, 1992; Lowenthal, 1985). In many East-Asian cultures, on the other hand, the self is defined less by one's unique autobiographical history but more by an individual's place within his or her system of relationships (Markus & Kitayama, 1991; Triandis, 1989; Wang, 2001b). Social status and roles, be it as a member of a family, a profession, a group, or a nation, are regarded as crucial elements constituting one's self and identity. Thus, autobiographical memories seem more important to independent than to interdependent selves in this respect. Indeed, Wang and Conway (in press) found in their recent study that Euro-American middle-aged adults ($M = 3.57$) rated (on 5-point scales) their memories as more personally important than did Chinese ($M = 2.94$), regardless of the life period when the events occurred.

These differences in the self-function of memory are directly reflected in the content and style of parent-child reminiscing in respectively cultures. Comparative data have revealed that Euro-American parents often employ what Fivush and colleagues (e.g., Fivush, 1994; Reese et al., 1993) termed a *high-elaborative* conversational style. They often initiate lengthy memory conversations with their children, scaffold the child's participation by providing embellished information about the past event, and invite the child to co-construct a shared story. In addition, memory conversations between Euro-American parents and children often focus on the child's roles, predilections, and feelings, with the child cast as the central character of the story (Mullen & Yi, 1995; Wang, 2001a; Wang et al., 2000). Joint reminiscing, in this context, serves as a forum of self-expressive behavior for the child. These characteristics are illustrated in the following excerpt from a memory conversation between a Euro-American mother and her 3-year-old daughter (Wang et al., 2000):

Mother (M): Do you remember when we're at Nana's on vacation, and we went down to the dock at Grandmommy's? You went swimming?
Child (C): Um-hum.
M: What did you do that was really neat?

C: Jump off the dock.
M: Yeah. That was the first time you've ever done that.
C: That was like a diving board.
M: You're right, it was. And where did Mommy have to stand?
C: In the sandy spot.
M: In the sandy spot, right. Mommy said, "Wait, wait, wait! Don't jump 'til I get into my sandy spot!"
C: Why?
M: 'Cause you remember how I told all the leaves pile up on the bottom of the lake? And it makes it a little mushy. And so, you jumped off the dock and then what did you do?
C: Swim.
M: To . . .
C: Nana.
M: Yeah. All by yourself with what on your back?
C: Bubbles.
M: Yeah.

Contrasting to the child-centered, high-elaborative conversational style of Euro-American parents, parents in Chinese culture tend to use a hierarchically organized, low-elaborative conversational style (Wang, 2001a; Wang et al., 2000). They often play a leading role during a memory conversation, posing pointed questions in an attempt to elicit single correct answers or yes/no responses from children, with the conversation similar to a memory test. In addition, the conversation often focuses on group activities and emphasizes the importance of concerted actions. The following conversational excerpt between a Chinese mother and her 3-year-old daughter illustrates these characteristics:

Mother (M): That day, mom took you to take a big bus and go skiing in the park. What did you play at the place of skiing? What did you play?
Child (C): Played . . . played the . . .
M: Sat on the ice ship, right?
C: Yes. Then. . . .
M: We two rowed together, right?
C: Then . . . then . . .
M: Then we rowed and rowed, rowed round a couple of times, right?
C: Um.
M: We rowed around a couple of times. Then you said, "Stop rowing. Let's go. Go home." Right?
C: Um.
M: Then we took a bus to go home, right?
C: Um.

Note that this Chinese mother-child pair indeed referred to fewer people (i.e., mother and child) in their memory conversation than did the American mother-child pair described earlier (i.e., mother, child, and Nana). However, the American conversation focused more on what the child did (accomplished) in the past event, whereas the Chinese conversation focused more on the activities of the "we" group. Both events were situated in a social context, with the American child portrayed as a courageous little heroine and the Chinese child an integral part of a coordinated social unit.

These two revealing cases suggest that the self-function of autobiographical memory manifests in varied forms during parent-child reminiscing, which, in turn, sustains the development of a particular mode of self-construct corresponding with the prevailing ideas of selfhood in a given culture. Conversations that depict the child as a protagonist in coherent, elaborate, detailed stories of the past highlight the importance of a unique autobiographical history in constructing an autonomous, independent self. In contrast, conversations that aim at getting correct information from the child and de-center the focus of the past event on a collective group downplay the use of memory to construct one's unique personal history. Instead, they situate the child in a nexus of social roles, facilitating the development of a relational, interdependent self.

THE SOCIAL FUNCTION: WAYS OF INTERPERSONAL CONNECTION

In relation to the social function, the extent to which memory and memory-sharing serve to strengthen interpersonal ties may vary, depending on how social boundaries are defined and sustained in a given culture. In Euro-American culture, which promotes an independent self, individuals generally perceive themselves as separate relative to others, including significant others such as family members. To establish emotional intimacy or to maintain social relations often requires not only desire but also effort from all parties involved. Sharing personal memories with others creates an optimal context where such bonding can take place and take shape. It often elicits strong empathic and emotional responses that serve to deepen the intimacy between the conversational partners. Memory sharing in the family often occurs naturally at any place and any time—dinner table, bathtub, pretend play, and bedtime, during which parents and children co-construct a context of shared experiences and further, shared thoughts and feelings. It is therefore an effective and relatively effortless way to strengthen emotional bonding between parents and children and is viewed as a valuable childrearing practice (Fivush, 1994; Nelson, 1993; Pillemer, 1998).

In comparison, individuals in East-Asian cultures, which promote an interdependent self, often view the lines between themselves and others as fluidly defined, with people in the social environment being considered as a consistent feature of the self. As a result, social relations in these cultures tend to be less voluntary and effortful. They are largely defined and governed by strict roles and group identities and often effectively achieved through existing social orders such as kinship and relational hierarchy (Hsu, 1953). Intentional recounting of one's past with others for the purpose of making social connections may be unnecessary or even improper in this context. Accordingly, for Asian parents, it is more important during a memory conversation to situate the child in a nexus of relational hierarchy and define the child's right position in his or her social world (e.g., "you're bigger than her, so you should yield to her"). In this way, the relationship between the child and a significant other is highlighted and reinforced, and the child's future behavior in observance of the nature of this relationship is ensured.

Consistent with this view, empirical data have shown that compared with Asian parents, Euro-American parents are often more eager to engage their children in conversations of the past and focus more on the child's feeling states during the conversation. Mullen and Yi (1995) observed American and Korean mother-child conversations during an entire day. They found that American mothers talked with their 3-year-olds about past events three times as often as Korean mothers did. In a recent study, Wang (2001a) asked American and Chinese mothers to discuss with their children at home four past events during which the child experienced happiness, sadness, fear, or anger. American mother-child pairs used an "emotion-explaining" style in which both conversational partners provided rich elaborations and explanations for the antecedents of emotions. The focus on the child's emotions and the mother's corresponding sympathetic responses would help to reinforce the intimacy of a conversational exchange.

Chinese mother-child pairs, in contrast, employed an "emotion-criticizing" style where emotion was instrumental for installing proper behavior in the child rather than being a means of social bonding. During the conversations, Chinese mothers initiated little discussion with their children about the antecedents of emotions and often gave moral judgments about children's emotional experience or behavior. This use of emotional memory sharing is vividly illustrated in the following dialogue: After a Chinese mother discussed with her 3-year-old daughter about a past misdeed of the child, the mother asked, "Did you feel sad that you made a mistake?" and the child answered,

"Very sad." The mother seemed satisfied, "Xuexue is a good child. You understand that you made a mistake" (Wang, 2001a, p. 712).

Interestingly, Wang (2001a) found that when a conversation involved a social conflict between the child and a significant other, Chinese mothers (32%) were more likely than American mothers (5%) to provide a resolution that helped to restore the damaged relationship. The following two conversational excerpts illustrate such a difference. The first one is between an American mother and her 3-year-old daughter about an angry incident involving the child's older brother:

Mother (M): Remember last night when you got very upset with Noah?
Child (C): Yeah.
M: What happened?
C: I don't know.
M: He took your Pokemon ball . . .
C: Yeah!
M: Out of the toy drawer. Why did you get so upset?
C: Because . . . he took my Pokemon ball!
M: Did he think it was his?
C: Yeah!
M: And you thought it was yours?
C: It was mine.
M: Yeah. Are you sure?
C: Yeah.
M: Did he give it back to you?
C: No!
M: No. I'm sorry that happened. It made you very upset.
C: Yeah.
M: Does that happen to you a lot?
C: Yeah.
M: Does Noah take your things? It must be hard being the youngest one in the family. Is it hard? Or do you like it?
C: It's hard.

Here the mother, while sympathetic and responsive to the child's feelings, did not intend to resolve the conflict between the child and her older brother. Although such a social exchange may help to strengthen the relationship between the conversational partners involved, it seems not to facilitate any reconciliation with the third party.

The second conversation about an angry episode was between a Chinese mother and her 3-year-old daughter:

Mother (M):	Did we go mountain-climbing?
Child (C):	We did.
M:	Who carried you up to the hill?
C:	I don't know.
M:	Who carried you the longest? Think hard.
C:	Papa.
M:	What did we do after coming down the hill?
C:	I don't know.
M:	Why do you always say "I don't know?" Think hard. Did we go boat-rowing with Huzi brother?
C:	Yes.
M:	What did you want to do taking off your shoes?
C:	To step into the water. Papa didn't let me.
M:	You were mad and cried, right?
C:	Yes.
M:	Papa was afraid you might catch a cold. He let you later, right?
C:	Right.

Here the Chinese conversation was focused on reestablishing the relationship between the child and her "perpetrator" father who caused her a negative emotion. The mother first reminded the child how good her father was to her (i.e., carrying her up to the hill) and then explained the good intention of her father for not granting her wish (i.e., caring for her health). She further emphasized what the father did eventually (i.e., allowing the child to step into the water) and acquired consensus from the child. Little attention was paid to the relationship between the actual conversational partners.

Thus, memory sharing in Euro-American and Chinese families serves the social function in seemingly different ways. American parents frequently initiate joint reminiscing, using it as an effective means to develop and reinforce emotional bonding with their children. The context of memory sharing is often *exclusive,* focusing on the ongoing relationship between the conversational partners. Although the conversations often contain references to other people and sometimes address interpersonal conflict between the child and a third party, their central theme is the emotional exchange between the two conversational partners who show concerns, articulate feelings, express sympathies, and develop intimacy.

In contrast, Chinese parents are less concerned with sharing experiences, thoughts, and feelings with their children for the purpose of relationship maintenance or extension. Their commentary on children's feeling states often intends to "teach the child a lesson," rather than to help the child articulate and understand the emotion. Such conversations help to define the child's right place in a nexus of relationships and, thereby, reinforce existing social orders. The context of parent-child reminiscing tends to be *inclusive,* paying great attention to the roles of significant others who are not present during the conversation. When a conversation invokes a social conflict between the child and a third party, Chinese parents often provide resolutions to restore the relationship. Instead of making emotional connections between the conversational partners, memory sharing in this case is used for reconciliation of the child with a significant other and, thus, for the good of the larger collective.

THE DIRECTIVE FUNCTION: LESSONS FROM THE PAST

Finally, pertaining to the directive function, cultures may differ in how much they value the moral, social, and intellectual importance attached to past events. In Chinese culture there is traditionally a great emphasis on history and respect for the past, where "learning implies full knowledge of the precedents of a past age" (Nakamura, 1964, p. 205). Individuals are encouraged to learn from experiences of the past lived by themselves, others, and their ancestors. The long-lasting influence of the Confucian fundamental concept of *ren* (仁), the supreme virtue of benevolence, moral vitality, and a sensitive concern for others, further gives the past its ultimate moral purpose. An individual is not born with but must learn to become *ren,* which is regarded as the highest purpose of life and possible for anyone who seeks it in the Confucian belief system. The *ren* pursuit requires self-reflection (zi-xing, 自省), an essential practice that urges individuals to examine their past mistakes on a daily basis for the purpose of perfecting the self. Applying to childrearing, Chinese parents and other socialization agents often unwittingly or deliberately draw upon past events to convey moral messages to children, such as obedience to authority, proper conduct, and a sense of belonging (Fang & Chen, 2001; Hsu, 1953; Miller et al., 1997; Wang et al., 2000). Note that recollections under these circumstances often focus on negative experiences of the individual or the child so that a lesson can be learned or taught.

Research has shown that didactic talk, where parents bring about the child's past transgressions and explicitly instruct the child to observe the rules and to behave properly in the future, is predominant in memory conversations of Asian parents and children. It is commonly observed in both semi-structured parent-child reminiscing (Wang et al., 2000; Wang, 2001a) and naturally occurring family conversations (Miller et al., 1996, 1997; Mullen & Yi, 1995). The following excerpt from a dinner-table conversation of a Chinese family demonstrates the characteristics of such a directive function of memory sharing.[2] The dinner conversation started with a discussion about a transgression of the 4-year-old son, Bao Bao:

Mother (M): Bao Bao, did you tell papa what you did wrong today?
Father (F): He made mistake again?
M: Did you tell Papa? Huh?
Child (C): (makes noise, sounds like yes)
M: Huh?
C: Already told Papa.
M: You already told Mama, right?
C: Right.
M: Did you tell Papa? Papa doesn't know.
C: No.
M: What happened to you at Aunty Lee's house?
C: Bao Bao didn't want to go in.
M: Hmm . . . you were at the door and didn't want to go in. And then what?
C: Didn't play with Edward.
M: Hmm . . . you didn't want to play with Edward. Hmm . . . anything else?
C: At the staircase, didn't say "bye-bye."
M: Hmm . . .
C: Didn't close the door properly.
M: Hmm . . . Did you hear, Papa?
F: I heard. Bao Bao told Papa already.
M: Already told Papa?
F: Papa already knew. Next time (Bao Bao) will behave better, right?
M: Next time don't make mistakes, okay?

As illustrated, even though Bao Bao initially seemed reluctant to talk about what he did wrong that day, his mother insisted that he recount to his father his every "inappropriate" behavior during a visit to a friend's house. Under his mother's prompts, Bao Bao did a wonderful job in his "confession." This family conversation served a directive function where, by making the child reflect on his own past transgressions, the parents intended to install proper

[2]The family participated in an ongoing longitudinal study that examines effects of early parent-child interaction on the development of memory, self, and emotion across preschool years. Mothers recorded their family dinner-table conversations monthly over a 6-month period.

behavioral conduct in the child. The past event was portrayed with a moral significance that goes beyond the present reminiscing context and projects its influence into the future.

Nothing comparable was observed in memory conversations between Euro-American parents and their children. Contrasting to Asian parents, American parents rarely discuss children's past transgressions for the purpose of correction, nor do they explicitly evaluate or criticize children's rule-violating behavior at the possible risk of damaging children's self-esteem. Miller and colleagues (1996, 1997) observed that American parents, in the rare instances when they acknowledged the child's past transgressions, tended to downplay the child's wrongdoing and to tell the story in a humorous, nonserious manner. For example, an American mother narrated a story about her 2-year-old daughter who wrote on the wall with a key and then tried to evade responsibility for her misdeed by falsely blaming her sister. After telling the story in front of the child, the older sister, and a visitor, the mother commented, "But it's so funny. You look at her and she's like, 'I didn't use pencil'" (Miller et al., 1996, p. 260). Obviously, the rule violation was not the main point of this conversation. Instead of encouraging children to learn from their past mistakes, American parents often use the past to make children feel good about themselves, in other words, to protect or enhance children's self-esteem.

In general, individuals in Euro-American culture may not appreciate the directive function of memories to the same extent as they do for the self and social functions. Using two different methods to solicit autobiographical memories, Hyman and Faries (1992) asked their U.S. participants to describe previous times when they had consulted their memories of past events. They found that self-definitional and social functions were very common uses of autobiographical memories. People often told a personal story to others for the purpose of describing themselves and solidifying relationships. In comparison, the directive function of memory was rarely evident in either of their two data sets. The researchers argued that, although this finding might be related to their methodology, which did not provide a problem-oriented context, it could also reflect that autobiographical memories were not particularly important for guiding behavior on a daily basis. Consistent with this view, Wang and Conway (in press) found that, when recalling life events, American middle-aged adults (9%) were less likely than their Chinese counterparts (48%) to reflect upon mores or worldviews that derived from or extended beyond the actual memories (e.g., "Since then, I have realized that there are more nice people than bad ones in this world," and "I learned that perfection takes practice"). As mentioned earlier, "learning-from-the-past" modes of conversation are rarely observed between Euro-

American parents and their children (Miller et al., 1996, 1997; Mullen & Yi, 1995; Wang et al., 2000).

The lack of emphasis on the directive function of memory may be historically patterned in the West such that the use of past experiences for value and moral teaching is more readily observed in older than in younger generations (Michael Pratt, personal communication). In a fast-changing society like the U.S., the past and the present become so dissimilar sometimes that past experiences may no longer be valuable or informative to current situations. Nevertheless, the directive function of memory is not completely absent from modern life. Although not particularly focusing on the moral value of the past, as the Chinese often do, Euro-American individuals do use their memories for current problem-solving and behavior guidance. This is reflected in the following dialogue (Wang et al., 2000), where an American mother initiated a memory conversation with her 3-year-old son that seemed to serve a directive function in guiding the child's current behavior.

Mother (M): Why is this toy special? Why did we get this toy? Where did we go to get this?
Child (C): At the toy store.
M: We got it at the toy store. Why did I get this for you?
C: Because I'm trying to use a potty!
M: Because you're gonna use the potty?
C: Yeah.
M: Yeah. And do you remember when we went to the toy store together? What did we see there? What kinds of things did you like that was at the toy store?
C: Power Ranger guy.
M: Power Ranger guy. . . . Oh. And tell me about . . . What was my deal with you? Why did we decide to get this?
C: Because gonna use a potty!
M: You're gonna to use the potty and what do you get to . . . What does that mean? Do you wear diapers?
C: No.
M: What are you . . .
C: Big boy pants.

During this memory conversation, the mother repeatedly prompted her child to recount the reason for buying a special toy, that is, a reward for toilet training. No explicit moral teaching was conveyed. However, implicit messages were delivered to remind the child of the decision (deal!) and thus to reinforce the child's current behavior (i.e., wearing "big boy pants") resulting from the decision. Conversations like this one serve practical functions in utilizing the past to understand present situations, direct current activities, and solve here-and-now problems.

Taken together, Chinese individuals often use past experiences for moral and intellectual consultations, a practice necessary for the *ren* pursuit emphasized in Confucian ethics. Correspondingly, family reminiscing often appears in a didactic mode where the child's past transgressions are frequently scrutinized and evaluated under the expectation that "history" will not repeat itself. Such a directive function of memory and memory sharing is less common in Euro-American culture, especially among younger generations. Euro-American parents are cautious of making explicit judgment on children's rule-violating behavior for the protection of their self-esteem. On the other hand, in contexts where Euro-American individuals use their memories for behavior guidance, the directive function of autobiographical memory tends to take a different form. In this case, past experiences are instrumental for individuals' current problem solving—a pragmatic goal (Hyman & Faries, 1992; Pillemer, 1998; Singer & Salovey, 1993), as opposed to one's moral or intellectual self-perfection—a metaphysical goal. The focus of the reminiscing is now on the affirmation of the present, rather than the negation of the past. Recollections, therefore, often concern both positive and negative experiences to inform current decisions and activities (Pillemer, 2001).

MEMORY, CULTURE, AND PARENT-CHILD REMINISCING

Analysis of parent-child sharing of memory narratives in Euro-American and Chinese families indicates that family conversations about the past show manifest variation in functions between the two cultures. The three primary functions of autobiographical memory—i.e., self, social, and directive—appear in varied forms and focuses during American and Chinese parent-child reminiscing. Consistent with the cultural emphasis on individuality and autonomy in defining the self and in carrying out everyday social activities, American parents use the joint conversational remembering as a means to encourage the child to express himself or herself (self), to elicit interest and show concern to strengthen the parent-child relationship (social), and to facilitate here-and-now, practical problem solving and guidance (directive). In contrast, in accordance with the Chinese value of interrelatedness and collectivity, Chinese parents use memory sharing as an instrument to assimilate the child into the larger collective (self), to solve interpersonal conflicts and promote social harmony (social), and to perfect a moral and intellectual being as idealized by traditional Chinese teachings (directive).

The functional differences in parent-child reminiscing between Euro-American and Chinese families reflect different socialization goals in the two cultures, and appear to directly affect the ways that children come to use their memories. In studies (Han, Leichtman, & Wang, 1998; Wang, in press; Wang & Leichtman, 2000) where preschool children were asked to independently recount their personal experiences, such as how they spent their last birthday or a recent time when they felt a particular emotion (e.g., anger), Chinese children focused more on skeletal routine events, talked more frequently about social interactions and group activities, and made more references to social rules and behavioral standards than did their American peers. In contrast, American children provided elaborate accounts of personal experiences that often focused on detailed, one-moment-in-time events and contained rich spontaneous references to personal predilections and opinions. Such structural and content differences in children's autobiographical memories mirror those between adults in Euro-American and Asian cultures (Mullen, 1994; Wang, 2001b; Wang & Conway, in press).

Thus, early parent-child reminiscing serves as an ideal social context in which parents transmit to their children culture-specific functions of memory and memory sharing and encourage the development of culturally adaptive qualities. The child-centered, highly elaborate conversational style of American parent-child pairs is well-suited to the goal of facilitating the development of children's autonomy and individuality, whereas the didactic, group-oriented conversational style of Chinese parent-child pairs conveys to children social rules and standards to build an affiliation with the larger society and prepares children for the life-long *ren* (仁) pursuit. Consequently, before the onset of formal schooling, children have already internalized culturally appropriate ways of reminiscing, using memory narrative as an effective medium to construe and express their belief systems acquired in a myriad of daily exchanges with their parents and significant others. This enculturational process is consonant with the social-interactionist view of cognitive development that emphasizes the social contexts of acting, experiencing, collaborating, and remembering (e.g., Fivush, 1994; Nelson, 1996; Rogoff, 1990; Vygotsky, 1978). Through joint parent-child reminiscing, family narratives not only serve as a model for children to construct their self-narratives, but eventually become an integral part of their self-narratives.

Notably, the self, social, and directive functions of autobiographical memory denote particular ways of parent-child reminiscing that may be interconnected within each cultural context. For example, focusing on children's development of autonomy and self-assertiveness (self) may be linked to the fact that American parents tend to avoid criticizing children's past wrongdoings (directive) during memory conversations, whereas focusing on equipping the child with appropriate social roles and duties (self, social) may lead Chinese parents to pay little attention to the personally unique aspects of past events (self) and to emphasize moral rectitude and behavioral standards to their children (directive). Therefore, the three primary functions of memory and memory sharing should not be viewed as isolated entities, but instead interrelated dimensions of everyday memory uses as defined by the sociocultural context where the reminiscing takes place.

Cultural variation in memory functions entailed in the context of parent-child reminiscing may be only one of degree, such that a particular version of a memory function is more valued and therefore, more frequently implemented in the practice of conversational remembering in one culture than in the other. It would be unwarranted to claim that a particular memory use is completely absent in a culture. For example, individuals in Euro-American culture also use memories as moral guidance (Lambek, 1996; Pillemer, 1998), although this use may appear to a lesser extent and in a more subtle manner compared with that in Chinese culture. Obviously, much more empirical research is required to examine how people use memory and memory sharing in service of particular goals across various situations, taking into consideration the influence of the larger cultural milieu. Such research will focus on the dynamic exchange between conversational partners such as family members, identifying important characteristics of reminiscing activities within specific social contexts, and further explicating the nature of cultural similarities and differences in memory use.

Of particular importance, sharing memory narrative as a crucial means of coping with traumatic experiences has drawn wide attention in both empirical and clinical research in European and American cultures (e.g., Antze, 1996; Fivush, in press; Herman, 1992; Young, 1996). It is less clear how the therapeutic function of "telling" manifests in cultures that tend to de-emphasize memory sharing. Studies with Western families have revealed that family narrative interaction plays an important role in helping children regulate and understand their emotions (Bretherton, Fritz, Zahn-Waxler, & Ridgeway, 1986; Fivush, 1993; Sher-Censor & Oppenheim, this volume). In contrast, emotion discourse is less frequent in East-Asian families, where verbalization about feeling states is often treated as superfluous and even improper (Bond, 1991; Ho, 1986; Hsu, 1953; Wang, 2001a). The different attitudes toward and styles of family discourse about emotions appear to have long-term consequences on children's emotional understanding (Wang,

2003b). We are currently conducting studies to further explore cultural variations in trauma-coping strategies during the act and process of telling family stories.

Culture evokes functional variations in family reminiscing for the socialization of the young. The revealing cases of memory conversations in Euro-American and Chinese families suggest that the functions of sharing memory narrative are not an intrinsic given, but a social creation, and hence subject to variation across cultures. The functions of remembering and recounting personal experiences and the ways the functions are achieved are derived from and shaped by a culture's philosophical and religious traditions, its structural organization of the society and the family, and its prevailing ideas about the self. The functional variations in family storytelling, in turn, have direct impact on the developing child as well as on the dynamic system of the family. Different cultural beliefs about memory usages are manifested in the processes and outcomes of everyday mnemonic activities, affecting how personal experiences are remembered and shared, and constituting a cultural context of parent-child reminiscing.

ACKNOWLEDGMENT

I thank Jeff Webster and Faith Markle for their thoughtful comments on an earlier version of this manuscript.

REFERENCES

Antze, P. (1996). Telling stories, making selves: Memory and identity in multiple personality disorder. In P. Antze & M. Lambek (Eds.), *Tense past: Cultural essays in trauma and memory* (pp. 3–24). New York: Routledge.

Baddeley, A. (1988). But what the hell is it for? In M. M. Gruneberg, P. E. Morris, & R. N. Sykes (Eds.), *Practical aspects of memory: Current research and issues* (Vol. 2, pp. 1–18). New York: John Wiley & Sons.

Barth, F. (1997). How is the self conceptualized? Variations among cultures. In U. Neisser & D. A. Jopling, *The conceptual self in context* (pp. 75–91). New York: Cambridge University Press.

Bluck, S., & Alea, N. (2002). Exploring the functions of autobiographical memory: Who do I remember the autumn? In J. D. Webster & B. K. Haight (Eds.), *Reminiscence work: From theory to application* (pp. 61–75). New York: Springer.

Bond, M. H. (1991). *Beyond the Chinese face.* Hong Kong: Oxford University Press.

Bretherton, I., Fritz, J., Zahn-Waxler, C., & Ridgeway, D. (1986). Learning to talk about emotions: A functionalist perspective. *Child Development, 57,* 529–548.

Bruce, D. (1989). Functional explanations of memory. In L. W. Poon, D. C. Rubin, & B. A. Wilson (Eds.), *Everyday cognition in adulthood and late life* (pp. 44–58). New York: Cambridge University Press.

Bruner, J. (1990). *Acts of meaning.* Cambridge, MA: Harvard University Press.

Cole, M. (1996). *Cultural psychology.* Cambridge, MA: Harvard University Press.

Conway, M., & Pleydell-Pearce, C. W. (2000). The construction of autobiographical memories in the self-memory system. *Psychological Review, 107*(2), 261–288.

Fang, H., & Chen, E. C. (2001). Across time and beyond skin: Self and transgression in the everyday socialization of shame among Taiwanese preschool children. *Social Development, 10,* 420–437.

Fivush, R. (1993). Emotional content of parent-child conversations about the past. In C. A. Nelson (Ed.), Memory and affect in development. *Minnesota Symposia on Child Psychology, 26,* 39–77. Hillsdale, NJ: Lawrence Erlbaum Associates.

Fivush, R. (1994). Constructing narrative, emotions, and self in parent-child conversations about the past. In U. Neisser & R. Fivush (Eds), *The remembering self: construction and accuracy in the self-narrative* (pp. 136–157). New York: Cambridge University Press.

Fivush, R. (in press). A feminist model of autobiographical memory. in J. Lucariello, J. A. Hudson, R. Fivush, & P. J. Bauer (Eds.), *The mediated mind: Essays in honor of Katherine Nelson.* Hillsdale, NJ: Lawrence Erlbaum Associates.

Geertz, C. (1973). *The interpretation of cultures.* New York: Basic Books.

Gauvain, M. (2001). Cultural tools, social interaction and the development of thinking. *Human Development, 44,* 126–143.

Goodnow, J. J. (2000). Combing analyses of culture and cognition: Essay review of mind, culture, and activity. *Human Development, 43,* 115–125.

Han, J. J., Leichtman, M. D., & Wang, Q. (1998). Autobiographical memory in Korean, Chinese, and American children. *Developmental Psychology, 34*(4), 701–713.

Harley, K. & Reese, E. (1999). Origins of autobiographical memory. *Developmental Psychology, 35*(5), 1338–1348.

Harter, S. (1998). The development of self-representations. In W. Damon (Ed.), *Handbook of child psychology,* (5th ed., pp. 553–617). New York: Wiley.

Herman, J. (1992). *Trauma and recovery: The aftermath of violence—From domestic abuse to political terror.* New York: Basic Books.

Hollos, M., & Leis, P. E. (2001). Remodeling concepts of the self: An Ijo example. *Ethos, 29*(3), 371–387.

Ho, D. Y. F. (1986). Chinese patterns of socialization: A critical review. In M. H. Bond (Ed.), *The psychology of the Chinese people* (pp. 1–37). Hong Kong: Oxford University Press.

Hsu, F. L. K. (1953). *Americans and Chinese: Purpose and fulfillment in great civilizations.* New York: The Natural History Press.

Hudson, J. A. (1990). The emergence of autobiographical memory in mother-child conversation. In R. Fivush & J. A. Hudson (Eds.), *Knowing and remembering in young children* (pp. 166–196). New York: Cambridge University Press.

Hume, D. (1882). *A treatise of human nature* (Vol. 1). London: Longmans Green. (Original work published 1739)

Hyman, I. E., & Faries, J. M. (1992). The functions of autobiographical memory. In M. A. Conway, D. C. Rubin, H. Spinnler, & W. A. Wagenaar (Eds.), *Theoretical perspectives on autobiographical memory* (pp. 207–221). Dordrecht, The Netherlands: Kluwer Academic Publishers.

Lambek, M. (1996). The past imperfect: Remembering as moral practice. In P. Antze & M. Lambek (Eds.), *Tense past: Cultural essays in trauma and memory* (pp. 235–254). New York: Routledge.

Leichtman, M. D., Pillemer, D. B., Wang, Q., Koreishi, A., & Han, J. J. (2000). When Baby Maisy came to school: Mothers' interview styles and preschoolers' event memories. *Cognitive Development, 15,* 1–16.

Lowenthal, D. (1985). *The past is a foreign country.* New York: Cambridge University Press.

Markus, H. R., & Kitayama, S. (1991). Culture and the self: Implications for cognition, emotion, and motivation. *Psychological Review, 98*(2), 224–253.

McAdams, D. P. (1993). *The stories we live by: Personal myths and the making of the self.* New York: Morrow.

Merriam, S. B. (1993). The uses of reminiscence in older adulthood. *Educational Gerontology, 19,* 441–450.

Miller, P. J., Fung, H., & Mintz, J. (1996). Self-construction through narrative practices: A Chinese and American comparison of early socialization. *Ethos, 24*(2), 237–280.

Miller, P. J., Wiley, A. R., Fung, H., & Liang, C. H. (1997). Personal storytelling as a medium of socialization in Chinese and American families. *Child Development, 68*(3), 557–568.

Mullen, M. K. (1994). Earliest recollections of childhood: A demographic analysis. *Cognition, 52*(1), 55–79.

Mullen, M. K., & Yi, S. (1995). The cultural context of talk about the past: Implications for the development of autobiographical memory. *Cognitive Development, 10,* 407–419.

Nakamura, H. (1964). *Ways of thinking of Eastern peoples: India-China-Tibet-Japan.* Honolulu: East-West Center Press.

Neisser, U. (1988). Time present and time past. In M. M. Gruneberg, P. E. Morris, & R. N. Sykes (Eds.), *Practical aspects of memory: Current research and issues* (Vol. 2, pp. 545–560). New York: John Wiley & Sons.

Nelson, K. (1993). Explaining the emergence of autobiographical memory in early childhood. In A. F. Collins, S. E. Gathercole, M. A. Conway, & P. E. Morris (Eds.), *Theories of memory* (pp. 355–385). Hillsdale, NJ: Lawrence Erlbaum Associates.

Nelson, K. (1996). *Language in cognitive development: The emergence of the mediated mind.* New York: Cambridge University Press.

Peterson, C., & McCabe, A. (1994). A social interactionist account of developing decontextualized narrative skill. *Developmental Psychology, 30,* 937–948.

Pillemer, D. B. (1998). *Momentous events, vivid memories.* Cambridge, MA: Harvard University Press.

Pillemer, D. B. (2001). Momentous events and the life story. *Review of General Psychology, 5*(2), 123–134.

Pillemer, D. B., & White, S. H. (1989). Childhood events recalled by children and adults. In H.W. Reese (Ed.), *Advances in child development and behavior* (Vol. 21, pp. 297–340). New York: Academic Press.

Polkinghorne, D. E. (1988). *Narrative knowing and the human sciences.* Albany, NY: State University of New York Press.

Raeff, C. (1997). Individuals in relationships: Cultural values, children's social interactions, and the development of an American individualistic self. *Developmental Review, 17,* 205–238.

Reese, E., Haden, C. A., & Fivush, R. (1993). Mother-child conversations about the past: Relationships of style and memory over time. *Cognitive Development, 8,* 403–430.

Robinson, J. A., & Swanson, K. L. (1990). Autobiographical memory: The next phase. *Applied Cognitive Psychology, 4,* 321–335.

Rogoff, B. (1990). *Apprenticeship in thinking: Cognitive development in social context.* New York: Oxford.

Romaniuk, M., & Romaniuk, J. G. (1981). Looking back: An analysis of reminiscence functions and triggers. *Experimental Aging Research, 7,* 477–489.

Ross, M. (1989). Relation of implicit theories to the construction of personal histories. *Psychological Review, 96,* 341–357.

Singer, J. A., & Salovey, P. (1993). *The remembered self: Emotion and memory in personality.* New York: The Free Press.

Spiro, M. E. (1993). Is the Western conception of the self "peculiar" within the context of the world cultures? *Ethos, 21*(2), 107–153.

Tessler, M., & Nelson, K. (1994). Making memories: The influence of joint encoding on later recall by young children. *Consciousness and Cognition, 3,* 307–326.

Triandis, H. C. (1989). The self and social behavior in differing cultural contexts. *Psychological Review, 96*(3), 506–520.

Valsiner, J. (2000). *Culture and human development.* London: Sage Publications.

Vygotsky, L. (1978). *Mind in society.* Cambridge, MA: Harvard University Press.

Wang, Q. (2001a). "Did you have fun?": American and Chinese mother-child conversations about shared emotional experiences. *Cognitive Development, 16,* 693–715.

Wang, Q. (2001b). Cultural effects on adults' earliest childhood recollection and self-description: Implications for the relation between memory and the self. *Journal of Personality and Social Psychology, 81,* 220–233.

Wang, Q. (2003a). Infantile amnesia reconsidered: A cross-cultural analysis. *Memory, 11*(1), 65–80.

Wang, Q. (2003b). Emotion situation knowledge in American and Chinese preschool children and adults. *Cognition & Emotion, 17*(5), 725–746.

Wang, Q. (2004). The emergence of cultural self-construct: Autobiographical memory and self-description in American and Chinese children. *Developmental Psychology, 40*(1).

Wang, Q., & Brockmeier, J. (2002). Autobiographical remembering as cultural practice: Understanding the interplay between memory, self and culture. *Culture & Psychology, 8,* 45–64.

Wang, Q., & Conway, M. A. (in press). The stories we keep: Autobiographical memory in American and Chinese middle-aged adults. *Journal of Personality.*

Wang, Q., & Leichtman, M. D. (2000). Same beginnings, different stories: A comparison of American and Chinese children's narratives. *Child Development, 71*(5), 1329–1346.

Wang, Q., Leichtman, M. D., & Davies, K. (2000). Sharing memories and telling stories: American and Chinese mothers and their 3-year-olds. *Memory, 8*(3), 159–177.

Wang, Q., & Li, J. (2003). Chinese children's self-concepts in the domains of learning and social relations. *Psychology in the Schools, 40*(1), 85–101.

Watt, L., & Wong, P. T. P. (1991). A taxonomy of reminiscence and therapeutic implications. *Journal of Mental Health Counseling, 12,* 270–278.

Webster, J. D. (1993). Construction and validation of the Reminiscence Functions Scale. *Journal of Gerontology: Psychological Sciences, 48,* 256–262.

Webster, J. D. (1997). The Reminiscence Functions Scale: A replication. *International Journal of Aging and Human Development, 44,* 137–148.

Webster, J. D. (2002). Reminiscence functions in adulthood: Age, race, and family dynamics correlates. In J. D. Webster & B. K. Haight (Eds.), *Critical advances in reminiscence work: From theory to application* (pp. 140–152). New York: Springer.

Webster, J. D., & Cappeliez, P. (1993). Reminiscence and autobiographical memory: Complementary contexts for cognitive aging research. *Developmental Review, 13,* 54–91.

Wertsch, J. V. (1991). *Voices of the mind: A sociocultural approach to mediated action.* Cambridge: Harvard University Press.

Young, D. J. (1996). Remembering trouble: Three lives, three stories. In P. Antze & M. Lambek (Eds.), *Tense past: Cultural essays in trauma and memory* (pp. 25–44). New York: Routledge.

13

Listening Is Active: Lessons From the Narrative Practices of Taiwanese Families

Heidi Fung
Academia Sinica, Taipei, Taiwan

Peggy J. Miller
Lu-Chun Lin
University of Illinois, Urbana-Champaign

> *When your parents call for you, respond without delay; when your parents issue an order, carry it out at the best of your ability; when your parents give you instructions, listen with respect; when your parents rebuke you, take it with an easy grace. . . . Whenever you speak, earnest comes first; deception and presumption: two evils to avoid; as for words, consider less better than a lot; the more you speak, the more mistakes you are likely to make; you speak less, good results are warranted . . .*
>
> —Y. X. Li, Qing Dynasty, *The Rules of the Disciples*

We have been studying everyday socialization in Taiwanese families for more than a decade, focusing on personal storytelling, shaming, and other value-laden discursive practices that help to orient young children within a moral universe. One of our key findings is that Taiwanese families embrace a didactic orientation with unusual avidity and faith in the efficacy of explicit teaching. Compared to their American counterparts, Taiwanese youngsters from middle-class, urban-dwelling families routinely participate in narrative practices that resound loudly with didactic vibrations. They are exposed repeatedly to parental and sibling voices who invoke moral rules, shame the child for wrongdoing, distinguish sharply between right and wrong, remind and re-remind the child of misdeeds committed in the distant past, and link here-

and-now transgressions to previous lapses. From an American standpoint, this version of socialization may look rather monolithic and unilateral, with children offered little room to maneuver beyond either acceding to or defying parental authority.

This is a misreading, however, for it presumes that to be cast in the listener role is to be relegated to a position of passivity, weakness, and unquestioning submission. In this chapter we argue that a strikingly different version of listening lies at the heart of Taiwanese didacticism, a version that links listening to active sense making, reflectiveness, and moral agency.

Where does this version of listening come from? Traditional Chinese models of communication, inflected in a Confucian direction, are one likely source. We consider this possibility in the next section of the chapter, followed by a description of the complex mix of Western and neo-Confucian practices that characterize contemporary Taiwan. We then turn to a summary of our past findings pertaining to everyday narrative practices in families. This sets the stage for a close analysis of young children listening to stories in two extended examples. We conclude the chapter on a reflexive note. That is, we use this foray into Taiwanese storytelling to reflect on the study of narrative by Western researchers. We argue that the Taiwanese inclination to privilege the listener role challenges developmental researchers to re-think the contribution of listening to narrative development.

CONFUCIAN ROOTS OF CHINESE COMMUNICATION STYLE

Regardless of the particular language employed, human communication involves ambiguity, requiring that listeners make inferences in order to comprehend the speaker's intended meaning (Scollon & Scollon, 1995). Scholars have argued, however, that styles of communication in cultures that have been influenced by Confucianism are especially likely to exploit ambiguity as a communicative resource, thereby placing heavy demands on listeners (Clancy, 1986; Cook, 1999; Gao, 1998; Gao, Ting-Toomey, & Gudykunst, 1996; He, 2001; Young, 1994; Yum, 1991). The Confucian character of Chinese communication style is often discussed along two dimensions: an emphasis on hierarchical structure and role differentiation at the interpersonal level, and a distinctive view of language that emphasizes the individual's moral character.

Regarding the social aspect, Confucianism places a high value on proper human relationships (*yi*) and on propriety (*li*). The Chinese self is defined by its embedded multiple layers of interpersonal relationships, and each person is expected to be sensitive to his or her position in relation to others. It is one's role and status rather than the self alone that determine how one should act or talk. In ancient China, speaking was a privilege of the elite; the superior and the more knowledgeable spoke while the inferior and the less knowledgeable listened (Gao, 1998; Gao et al., 1996; Yum, 1991). Because children rank at the bottom of the hierarchical structure, "the ability to listen is, therefore, highly emphasized as a major mode of communication for children" (Gao, 1998, p. 173). In Chinese, a good child is literally a child who "listens to words (*tinghua*)."

Moreover, to harmoniously maintain and develop hierarchical interpersonal relationships and obligations defined by roles, implicit and indirect communication becomes highly desirable. Verbal expressions among Chinese are highly context dependent, rich in connotation and evasive in denotation. There are patterned verbal as well as nonverbal maneuvers to express degrees of politeness and to preserve one another's face. Hence, in contrast to the English-speakers' outcome-oriented view of communication in which the speaker is responsible for the clarity of the message, Chinese communication is much more process-oriented, involving an intricate interpretive process with a particular burden on the receiver's end (Yum, 1991).

In addition to the rules imposed on interpersonal relations, Confucianism embodied a particular view of language. When asked what makes a true scholar, Confucius presented three features in the following order: a sense of shame, being filial and fraternal, and sincerity in word and deed (Chang, 1997). Although Confucius had little faith in verbal expression and skills, he did not argue against people who are talented speakers, nor did he see language only as a tool for preaching. Nevertheless, since speech must correspond with one's inner state and reflect the cultivation of virtue, a gifted speaker should be sincere and truthful in what he says and trustworthy and circumspect in what he does. At the same time, he should demonstrate the flexibility and sensitivity that allows him to be attuned to different situations and different types of relationships.

A cautious speaker avoids making the mistake of speaking before the time to speak, not speaking when it is time to speak, and speaking without observing the superior man's countenance (Chang, 1997). The effectiveness of words, however, does not come from one's ability to articulate language or construct images, because if he is sincere and virtuous, the listener will accept, trust, and be moved by him regardless of the words chosen. As annotated by Soothill (1968) in his translation of *The Analects of Confucius,* "To hear and observe much is the widening of culture; to reserve the doubtful and risky is the essence of selection (discretion); to speak and act warily is the restraining advantage of self-control" (p. 168).

In sum, the Confucian perspective on interpersonal relationships and language implies an asymmetrical style of communication and an emphasis on attentive observing and listening. As Gao (1998) has said, "Chinese communication appears to be passive in speaking, but it emphasizes activeness in listening" (p. 174). Moreover, the model of communication embodied in ancient Confucian texts has modern reverberations, a claim that is developed further in the next sections of this chapter. For example, according to contemporary indigenous models of learning, Chinese learners are encouraged to observe and prioritize actions ahead of words (Li, 2001).

CONTEMPORARY TAIWAN: A CONFLUENCE OF NEO-CONFUCIAN AND WESTERN CURRENTS

Taiwan is a small island that lies off the southeastern coast of China. It has a population of 23 million, most of whom are descendants of different waves of Chinese migrants. In the past several decades, Taiwan has witnessed phenomenal economic growth, moving from an agrarian to a consumer economy, and drastic sociopolitical changes, transforming from a one-party dictatorship into a full democracy. In addition, with increasing globalization, advancement of technology and expanding Internet communities, dissemination of popular culture (particularly from Korea and Japan), flourishing tourism, and growing international migration, Taiwanese people are increasingly exposed to cultures other than Chinese. Children growing up today in Taiwan, and especially in Taipei, its capital city, inhabit a world significantly different from that of their parents and grandparents.

As Taiwanese society becomes much more pluralistic and individualistic, people are confronted with multiple and contesting cultural models and have to reconstruct, reinterpret, or redefine their beliefs and practices in creative ways. For instance, based on an analysis of recently published popular books in Taiwan, Chang (2001) discovered two countervailing trends: an ever-increasing number of translated books that purport to teach people how to communicate in a Western style, and re-valuing and elevation of Chinese cultural traditions. In response to challenges from the West, and in line with the need to use words to navigate a vibrant democratic society, books by local authors redefine Chinese cultural tradition as embracing eloquent speaking skills (rather than merely emphasizing listening and humility) and call for readers' appreciation of verbal skills employed by ancient Chinese philosophers and politicians. Chang (2001) noted that instead of adopting the step-by-step instruction characteristic of most translated Western books, local authors expect readers to look for the lessons in *stories* about how exactly ancient peoples' verbal skills led them to accomplish important tasks. Paradoxically, the act of redefining the tradition is also an act of revitalizing the historical past.

The Confucian past has also been re-envisioned by parents and educators. Parents of preschoolers often solicit child-rearing and educational advice from materials translated from Japanese or English sources and from professionals who are educated in foreign countries. Sending children to "all English" or "bilingual" kindergartens is an increasing trend, which makes the English teaching business, franchised or independently run, a thriving industry.

Parents' concern with how to make their youngsters globally competitive coexists with a pedagogical revival of classical primers in kindergartens and primary schools. Local advocates distribute free copies of classical primers to kindergartens and schools, offer workshops that train teachers in traditional pedagogy, and organize children's reciting contests island-wide. Children are encouraged to memorize and recite these texts in a manner that differs little from the pedagogical practice of hundreds of years ago. The rationale is phrased in both market and moral terms. The former includes stimulating the functioning of the brain, exploring the child's potentials, and improving intelligence and memory, whereas the latter includes purifying the child's mind and stabilizing his or her disposition, correcting the chaotic, disordered society, and continuing Confucian traditions.

One of the most popular classical primers adopted by Taiwanese parents and teachers is *The Rules of the Disciples,* a portion of which is quoted at the beginning of this chapter. This book was originally written by a scholar, Yu-xiu Li (1662–1722), in the Qing Dynasty and contains 90 four-line rhymed verses with three characters to each line (i.e., 1,080 characters in total). This primer offers concrete, extensive, and detailed instructions on how a young person should act and behave in daily life. These instructions were derived from a passage in *The Analects* of Confucius, which reads as follows:

> A young man should be a good son at home and an obedient young man abroad, sparing of speech but trustworthy in what he says, and should love the multitude at large but cultivate the friendship of his fellow men. If, after all these activities, he has any energy to spare, let him use it to making himself cultivated. (I, 6, translated by Lau, 1992, pp. 3–5).

Apparently, the revival of interest in ancient Confucian primers has spread to some Chinese American parents as well. A long-time friend of the first author, who is a mother of three children and a teacher at a Chinese heritage language school in Tennessee, reports that after acquiring a copy of *The Rules of the Disciples* from a teacher in Taiwan, their community school has decided to incorporate it into the curriculum, along with etiquette training. She explains that it is important for them, as teachers and parents, to not only pass on the Chinese language to their American-born children but to teach them how to be a proper Chinese person.

CONFUCIAN ECHOES IN EVERYDAY NARRATIVE PRACTICES

The foregoing discussion suggests that Confucian perspectives are discernible in the complex and shifting confluence of cultural currents that are reshaping Taiwanese understandings of communication and of classroom pedagogy. But what about the informal, taken-for-granted practices of everyday family life? This is the arena in which our research is situated (Fung, 1999; Fung & Chen, 2001; Miller, 1996; Miller, Mintz, Hoogstra, Fung, & Potts, 1992; Miller, Fung, & Mintz, 1996; Miller, Wiley, Fung, & Liang, 1997; Miller, Sandel, Liang, & Fung, 2001). The families in our study were relatively privileged: The parents were middle-class, highly educated, and owned their own apartments in Taipei. They spoke Mandarin Chinese with their children, and most had some Western ties (e.g., a relative living in the United States). Our approach involved ethnographic fieldwork, repeated video-recorded observations of ordinary family life, and interviews with the mothers. In one strand of this work, we have compared these families with their European-American counterparts in Longwood, a neighborhood in Chicago (Miller et al., 1992, 1996, 1997, 2001).

To greatly oversimplify our findings, we have found evidence that a strongly didactic and distinctively Confucian perspective informs the Taiwanese parents' avowed beliefs about childrearing and their childrearing practices, especially their narrative practices. In interviews, parents express their belief in "early training" and "opportunity education (*jihui jiaoyu*)" (Fung, 1999). The latter notion encompasses two interlinked ideas: it is more effective to situate a moral lesson in the child's concrete experience than to preach in the abstract, and parents should take every opportunity to provide such concrete lessons. In the observational data, parents assiduously enact their commitment to the moral education of children as young as 2;6 (Miller et al., 1996, 1997, 2001). This occurs both in co-narrations, in which the young child tells a story of his or her past experience in collaboration with one or more family members, and in stories that care givers tell about the child in the child's presence. In the latter practice, the child contributes little if anything to the narration but is present as a co-present other and possible listener. Interestingly, this participant structure accounts for more of the stories of personal experience for the Taipei children, compared with the Longwood children.

An important part of the Taiwanese parents' didactic practice involves pointing out to the child—again and again—where he or she went wrong. For instance, 35% (as opposed to 7% in the observed European-American families) of the spontaneously occurring family stories (involving both co-narrations and stories about the child) invoke a past misdeed committed by the focal child (Miller et al., 1997). These youngsters are exposed to a steady stream of stories, about one per hour on average, in which they are cast as transgressors in some past event.

Moreover, with regard to the structure and content of these stories, the children's transgressions are not handled with kid gloves (Miller et al., 1996, 2001). Their transgressions are talked of openly, publicly, and explicitly, often in strong language. Transgression stories are constructed so as to establish the child's transgression as the point of the story. Sometimes family members shame the child ("You made your mother lose face." "Aren't you ashamed of yourself?"). Sometimes they try to extract confessions from the child ("Tell me why did you go in there?" "Would you do it again?"), and sometimes they end the story with a didactic coda that draws out the moral of the story ("Now I don't cry at all." "Saying dirty words is no good."). Many of the transgression stories are occasioned by a misdeed in the here-and-now, suggesting that these are occasions when parents put into practice their beliefs about opportunity education. They treat the child's current misdeed as an opportunity to remind the child of a previous misdeed, thereby reinforcing and personalizing moral lessons through concrete exemplars. Thus, the child may hear particular misdeeds narrated again and again. In short, children repeatedly encounter and participate in descriptions of themselves as failed moral actors. Parents, for their part, cannot escape the burden of being alert to their children's misdeeds, of keeping account of past transgressions, and of remaining vigilant for opportunities to guide and correct, if they are to discharge their responsibilities as moral educators of their children.

YOUNG CHILDREN AS ATTENTIVE AND CREATIVE LISTENERS

Are these recurrent messages of failure overwhelming to 2-year-olds? As they rank at the bottom of the social hierarchical structure, do these young children have no choice but to listen? Will these practices create in the children an unthinking and docile obedience while undermining their faith in their ability to act? Is there room for young children to construct their own sense of moral rules and to engage in self-directed moral action? In this section we present two extended examples that illustrate that young children do, in fact, listen creatively and construct novel meanings within narrative discourses of moral scrutiny and may even turn the tables on their care givers, demonstrating just how well they have learned to exercise independent moral judgment.

Yoyo's Novel Response

This co-narration occurred when Yoyo was 2½ years old. Immediately before the co-narration, Yoyo's brother, age 6, recited the lion story from *Esop's Fables,* which his grandmother had read to him the previous day. The grandmother, who was sitting on the sofa, asked how smart Yoyo was compared to that "stupid" lion. She then initiated the following interaction as a way of demonstrating how smart he is. As she did so, she pulled him closer to her and held him in her arms.

Example 1

Grandmother (GM): Oh, yes, this morning, when Mom was spanking you, what did you say? You said, "Don't hit me," right? Then, what did Grandma tell you what to say?

Child (C): (quietly) "[I] won't push the screen down [again]." (GM lowers her head and puts her ear next to C's mouth)

GM: Oh right. What would you say to your mom?

C: I would say to Mom, "I won't push the screen down." (raises his head and speaks in a very low tone into GM's ear)

GM: Oh, you would say to Mom, "Mama, I won't push the screen down [again]," oh?

C: Hmn. (nods)

GM: So, Mom wouldn't hit you. Right, oh? If you asked Mom, "You don't hit me," Mom would have hit you, right?

C: Right. (nods)

GM: So you would directly say to Mom in this way, "Mom, I won't push the screen down." Then how would Mom have reacted?

C: Won't hit. (almost unintelligible)

GM: What? (lowers her head and expects C to speak louder)

C: Won't hit. (quietly)

GM: Then she wouldn't hit you, right? Oh. Next time when

	Mom is going to spank you, which sentence is better for you to say to her?
C:	Hmn. Hmn. Say, "I won't, I won't push the screen down." (raises his head up and talks into GM's ear)
GM:	Oh, yes, now you have choices. You say, "Mom, I won't push the screen down." In that way, Mom won't spank you. So next time when Mom is spanking you, you shouldn't say, "You don't hit me (raises her voice and stamps on the floor with her right foot). You don't hit me (raises her voice and stamps on the floor again)." You shouldn't talk that way.
Researcher (R):	(laughs)
GM:	[If] you say, "Don't hit me (raises her voice and stamps on the floor)," Mom would even hit more (gently hits C's butt). Right? Instead, [if] you say to Mom, "I won't push the screen down." What would mom do to you?
C:	(slightly bends forward) [Will give me] "a tender touch." (in Taiwanese dialect, almost unintelligible)
GM:	What?
C:	"A tender touch." (in Taiwanese dialect)
GM:	"A tender touch." Ah, she would give you "a tender touch." (both times in Taiwanese dialect) Ah. (laughs loudly, picks up Yoyo, sits him on her lap and holds him tightly)

In this example the grandmother invited the child to review an incident that happened earlier in the day in which his mother spanked him for playing with a screen (which divides the living room and the dining area). She focused her didactic efforts on the child's response to having committed the misdeed—namely, that he said, "Don't hit me!" to his mother—which itself constituted a misdeed from the mother's perspective. The grandmother patiently took the child through the incident, pointing out where he went wrong and rehearsing with him what he should have said, invoking hypothetical and future scenarios. Eventually, apparently satisfied that the child understood how to behave when his mother corrects him, the grandmother explained to him that now he has choices about how to act in the future.

This stretch of interaction involves true/false questions, either/or options, lengthy rehearsals, and a lesson that moves rapidly from the past, to the hypothetical, to the future. The logical connection that the grandmother is at pains to explain is presumably not easy for a 2-year-old to grasp: begging not to be punished ironically invites more punishment. Without explicitly directing the child to listen attentively, the grandmother seems to assume that Yoyo is able to follow a complex line of cognitive and moral reasoning on the spot. She seems to implicitly trust in his ability to exercise sound moral judgment in the future.

For our purposes what is most intriguing about this example is the way that Yoyo responds. Throughout this lengthy episode he is highly attentive to his grandmother. Most of his responses are of two sorts: he repeats words, preselected for him by his grandmother, or he nods verbally or nonverbally, indicating assent to what she is saying. If we focus only on Yoyo's initial responses, we might be tempted to think that he was, at best, merely parroting what his grandmother said. Toward the end of the episode, however, he comes up with his own novel contribution, one that surprises and delights the grandmother. When Yoyo forecasts that his mother will give him "a tender touch," he conveys his faith that next time he will make the right choice and that the right choice will restore his mother's love. In other words, as expected by his grandmother, Yoyo not only listens and comprehends but also joins her to reflect upon his own behavior and project a better self.

Another remarkable feature of Example 1 is that it is the last in a series of five thematically linked retellings of the "same" events. These retellings, which unfolded over the course of an hour and a half, pertained to two consecutive transgressions that Yoyo had committed earlier in the day: he played with a screen, imperiling a vase of flowers, and then he protested when his mother left for work.

While the first and third tellings focused on Yoyo's inappropriate crying and yelling in the "not letting the mother go" incident, the second telling, a *co-narration,* focused on the rules that were invoked in connection with the first transgression. In response to the grandmother's prompts—"What did Mom say? Don't touch the flowers, right?" "When did Mom say it?" "How many flowers did Mom hand over to you?"—Yoyo's brother reported, "This morning, Mom said, not even one bud of the roses (which were put in a vase and placed in front of the screen) should be missing. The screen should not be pushed down either." Yoyo then repeated after him, "The screen should not be pushed down either." The grandmother then brought up yet another transgression that occurred some days earlier in which the children knocked down the screen, and the brother added that the wooden pieces fell apart and later had to be glued together.

The fourth telling was a detailed depiction of what happened in both incidents. In this *story about the child,* Yoyo's grandmother and his older brother recounted, in Yoyo's presence, that while the mother was rushing off to work, Yoyo yelled at her fiercely from the balcony, "Come back, come back, I say Mommy be back. Come back to me." The grandmother then related that, in fact, just a brief while earlier, Yoyo had been spanked by his mother for playing with the screen. Yoyo's older brother explicated the rule: "Mom said we cannot play with the screen, because if the screen is knocked down, it will fall down onto these roses, and the roses will break and die. Therefore she spanked Yoyo." From the second telling, we realize that the mother's reprimand must have served to forestall a more serious transgression—knocking down and breaking the screen—which had happened on a previous occasion.

Thus, when Example 1 is examined in the context of the previous retellings, it is striking how much time and energy this family spent reviewing Yoyo's misdeeds. Equally striking, Yoyo accepted these critiques with patient forbearance, even when his older brother joined in. Yoyo listened attentively, admitted to his wrongdoing, rehearsed rules for appropriate conduct, and imagined doing better in the future. Notice too that the retellings varied in subtle ways, highlighting different facets of the past events, making links to other events, developing slightly different moral implications. This is typical of the way that children's transgressions are narrated in the Taiwanese families. Retellings differ in terms of the immediate contexts out of which they arise, what gets foregrounded as the main point, the perspectives that the care giver takes (e.g., in addition to invoking rules and judging the child, the care giver may also sympathetically mitigate or explain the event from the child's stance), how the child is portrayed in the narrated event, and the participant roles into which he is cast in the here-and-now narrative activity (e.g., co-present other, listener, co-narrator).

It is likely that the frequent but variable retelling of children's past transgressions promotes listening because the child is called upon to make different responses each time, even when the "same" event is recounted. Unlike the European-American children studied by our research team (Miller et al., 2001; Mintz, 1999), these children do not get off the hook with an admission of wrongdoing or a brief apology. Also, as Example 1 demonstrates, these narrative practices are embedded in and linked to other nondidactic practices, involving love, care, and affection. The intertwining of these sentiments with discourses of moral scrutiny and evaluation may allow the child to "hear" critiques without rebelling or becoming discouraged.

Angu Challenges Her Aunt

The next example illustrates that not speaking may reflect active listening and that a 4-year-old can be a formidable moral critic. Angu was a very bright, appealing, well-loved, and verbally precocious child, and she was the recipient of some of the longest and most intense shaming interactions among the observed families. The incident in question occurred toward the end of our longitudinal study; by this time the researcher and the family had known each other for 2 years.

When the researcher arrived at the door on this particular day, Angu's aunt was scolding her severely for spilling food and behaving inappropriately at the table. (The aunt was the primary care giver; Angu lived with her and addressed her as "mama.") Angu ceased misbehaving but the reprimand continued for almost 10 minutes. The researcher did not feel at ease and asked if she should leave and come again at another day. Apparently, the aunt was not in a good mood; she was in failing health and she was exhausted from taking care of both Angu and her newborn baby sister. As she listened to her aunt's reprimand, Angu made faces at the researcher, indicating her displeasure with her aunt. After several prompts by the aunt and the researcher, Angu cautiously and reluctantly recounted how she celebrated her birthday 2 days earlier, including that her aunt had spanked her for rushing into a pile of dishes. Throughout the first hour of the observational session, the aunt occasionally shouted at and harangued Angu and brought up her past misdeeds. Angu bore this long period of tense interaction in silence.

The really interesting part happened about an hour and a half later. When the aunt had become much more relaxed, Angu playfully argued with her as to whether Angu or her 5-month-old baby sister made more noise. Then Angu suddenly changed the topic and began to challenge her aunt's "mishandling" of her previous transgressions—rushing into dishes on her birthday and spilling food. Although the aunt never apologized, she recognized Angu's anger and allowed her to talk back and make her point.

Example 2

Child (C): (index finger pointing at Aunt) Mama, I'm asking you a question. When I kicked the dishes, kicked [them] far away, why were you unreasonable to me? Tell me. (holds up her chin with a scornful attitude) Hum!

Aunt (A): In what way was I unreasonable? You knocked over my dishes, "ping ping pang," to that far. You kicked it all the way, kicked "ping pang" to that far. What did you do? Early in the morning, you kicked dishes, from that. . . . How come you didn't walk carefully but instead rushed into all those dishes, which were all broken by your kick?

C: Because I fell! (very loudly)

A: Why did you fall? How come you didn't know how to walk? (looks down and talks to the baby sister who is drinking milk in her arms) Your sister is quarreling. Boy, isn't she mad. (laughs, looks up and talks to Angu again) Why did you [do that], you give me a reason for that.

C: Disgusting! (loudly)
A: Huh? Right? Why every day you cannot . . . (interrupted by C)
C: Not right! (loudly)
A: Why can't you ever sit properly when you eat? And then, whatever you eat [or drink], you spill. Whatever you eat, you spill.
C: (in a very serious tone) But why didn't you reason with me nicely? It's not that you didn't have Daddy and Mommy. You had Daddy and Mommy before. When you were young, didn't you ever spill?
A: Me? I was very well-behaved. I never spilt food.
C: Really?

Finding her aunt's claim of childhood perfection incredible, Angu decided to call her grandmother on the phone to get the real scoop on her aunt. Unfortunately, her grandmother was not at home and thus the conflicting claims about the aunt's unblemished childhood could not be resolved. Angu's arguments were well grounded from her perspective. Knocking down the dishes was not an intentional act but caused by tripping; besides, it was her birthday so her aunt should have been kinder. As for spilling food, since the aunt was once young, she should have been more sympathetic.

The timing of Angu's challenge is also of interest. Although she remained cautiously quiet during her aunt's prolonged reprimand and ensuing accusations, she attentively observed "the superior's countenance," and waited for an auspicious moment in which to upbraid her. Moreover, her protest seems to imply that if the aunt fails to reasonably discipline her on justifiable grounds, she may refuse to listen to her in the future.

In sum, these analyses illustrate a mode of interaction in which care givers and other family members assume the role of moral guide and critic, leading young children through the lessons inherent in their own past misdeeds, while young children assume the reciprocal role of attentive listener. These youngsters make substantial verbal contributions to the stories being narrated; in this sense, they are *co-narrating* stories with family members. However, the term co-narrator is something of a misnomer in this case, emphasizing narrating at the expense of listening. We suggest that *listening/learning* would better capture the local meaning of the child's part in this narrative activity. Care givers structure children's participation in a manner that casts the child in the role of listener/learner, treating all of the following as evidence that the child is listening: silent attentiveness, verbal and nonverbal gestures of assent, repetition of the caregiver's utterances, novel verbal responses, and even critiques of the care giver.

These and other routine moral discourses afford young Taiwanese children many opportunities to reflect on their own conduct. Although they engage in a kind of moral self-scrutiny that is modeled and structured in starkly black-and-white terms, they are also invited to make their own contributions to the discourse. Care givers hold young children to high standards of moral conduct and offer them numerous opportunities to listen carefully and to reflect upon their actions both before and after the fact. Within these didactic interactions, not speaking does not necessarily mean a lack of creativity or critical thinking, nor does listening necessarily imply passive submission or docile obedience. At a very young age, these children already demonstrate a highly reflective form of agency through attentive listening.

CONCLUSION: RETHINKING THE STUDY OF NARRATIVE DEVELOPMENT

The importance attributed to listening in Confucian traditions and in everyday narrative practices in Taiwanese families leads us to take a fresh look at the study of narrative. If developmentalists brought to their research projects the kinds of perspectives and inclinations that pervade the narrative practices of Yoyo and Angu's families, what kinds of research questions would they ask? Or to frame the question slightly differently, what would the study of narrative development look like if it assumed a didactic model of narrative that privileged the listener role?

We believe that researchers with these meta-theoretical biases would be keenly interested in children's development as *listeners*. They would regard listening as a moral/social/cognitive skill—an obligation to parents, a means of learning how to be a right and proper person, and a vital part of the child's emerging narrative competence. Researchers with these assumptions would chart children's narrative development in terms of their growing ability to listen. They might ask the following kinds of questions: Does the child adopt the appropriate listening demeanor? Is the child able to grasp complex sequences of events, detect subtle differences across stories, register nuances conveyed by the narrator's voice and face, and time his or her responses so that they will be heard? Does the child request certain stories or position himself or herself to be able to listen? What kinds of listening opportunities does the family routinely provide? How do these opportunities change with age? Are stories told to, about, and around the child? Are children encouraged to listen? If so, how are they encouraged? If they fail to listen, what are the consequences? Are children allowed to listen, as bystanders, overhearers, or eavesdroppers, to adult stories? The list could go on and on.

Privileging the Narrator Role

Although there has been a tremendous amount of interest in children's narrative development in the last two decades, very few studies address these kinds of questions. Instead, whether the focus is on the development of narrative itself or on narrative as a window into autobiographical memory, self-construction, or socioemotional processes, most studies implicitly privilege the child's role as narrator (Applebee, 1978; Bamberg, 1997; Berman & Slobin, 1994; Engel, 1995; Fivush, 1993; McCabe & Peterson, 1990; Miller, 1994; Miller et al., 1992). Conducted largely by American researchers, studying American children, these studies rely primarily on measures of narrative production or observations of children telling or co-telling stories. This bias toward the narrator role and away from the listener role may reflect hidden assumptions, rooted in American culture, that the narrator role is the only active role and thus the only role that really matters developmentally.

One major strand of research addresses the development of narrative per se, especially narrative structure (e.g., Applebee, 1978; Botvin & Sutton-Smith, 1977; McCabe & Peterson, 1990; Peterson & McCabe, 1983). These studies rely upon production tasks and usually involve story elicitations. The elicitation procedures range from open-ended to controlled. The researcher asks the child to tell a story (Applebee, 1978), to make up a story about something familiar (Bennett-Kastor, 1986), to tell a story of a past personal experience (Labov, 1972), or to tell a story based on wordless picture books (Bamberg, 1997; Berman & Slobin, 1994; Hickman & Hendriks, 1999; Wigglesworth, 1997).

Other strands of research investigate children's narratives in order to understand their social, emotional, or cognitive development (e.g. Fivush, 1993; Pitcher & Prelinger, 1963; Stern, 1985, 1989; Sutton-Smith, 1981). Again, most of these studies emphasize children's narrative productions. However, some of these studies treat children as *co-narrators* rather than solo narrators. For example, the child's mother (or a researcher) is asked to tell a story with the child about a particular event, such as going to the circus or what happened at school that day (Fenny, Eder, & Rescorla, 1996; Fivush, Hamond, Harsch, Singer, & Wolf, 1991; Fivush, Haden, & Adam, 1995; Haden & Fivush, 1996; Reese & Fivush, 1993). In other studies, the researcher provides a short prompting narrative (e.g., being stung by a bee) to induce children to tell similar stories (Ely & McCabe, 1993; Peterson & McCabe,

1983; Peterson, Jesso, & McCabe, 1999; Wang & Leichtman, 2000); or asks the child to complete story stems (e.g., using *MacArthur Story-Stem Battery,* Oppenheim, Emde, & Warren, 1997; Oppenheim, Nir, Warren, & Emde, 1997) or finish the stories with beginnings provided (e.g., Domino & Hannah, 1987; Oppenheim, Emde, & Warren, 1997; Wang & Leichtman, 2000).

Still another strand of work focuses on the role that storytelling plays in socializing children into the meaning systems of their culture (e.g., Bruner, 1990; Engel, 1995; Heath, 1983; Miller et al., 1990, 1992). As Bruner (1990) points out, narratives are a means by which children navigate meanings. When children's narrative skills advance, this not only represents "a mental achievement, but an achievement of social practice that lends stability to the child's social life" (p. 8). These researchers tend to adopt a more naturalistic approach, observing children's everyday narrative practices in classrooms (Michaels, 1981; Stone, 1992) and homes (e.g., Blum-Kulka & Snow, 1992; Burger & Miller, 1999; Mintz, 1995; Preece, 1987; Wiley, Rose, Burger, & Miller, 1998). Although the focus on everyday narrative activity allows researchers to cast a larger net, here too studies are more likely to focus on children co-narrating stories than on children listening to stories.

A Range of Participant Roles

However, informed by Goffman's (1974) notion of "participant framework" and by perspectives from the interdisciplinary field of language socialization (Ochs & Schieffelin, 1984), research on narrative socialization does recognize that a variety of participant roles are possible, beyond the narrator role (e.g., Miller & Moore, 1989; Miller, et al., 1990; Ochs & Capps, 1996, 2001; Ochs & Taylor, 1995; Sperry & Sperry, 1996; Taylor, 1995). For example, stories may be told directly *to* the child as the designated recipient or *about* the child, as a bystander, overhearer, or ratified recipient of the story.

In addition, some studies within this tradition have described communities in which listening to stories is an important part of everyday family life, with the listening role carved out somewhat differently in each instance. For example, Heath (1983) described a working-class African American community in which young narrators had to listen closely and act quickly in order to gain the floor. Miller (1994) described White working-class families in which young children were constantly exposed to adult stories of personal experience. The stories were told *around* young children, who were free to tune in or not, as they wished. Watson-Gegeo (1992) described a practice among the Kwara'ae of the Solomon Islands in which young children were included in evening gatherings in which everyone listened quietly as stories were told and conflicts resolved. Thus, these studies suggest that it is not just the Taiwanese who value listening and organize many opportunities for young children to listen to stories in the family context. They point to the need to learn more about how listening is culturally organized and elaborated in different cultural cases.

In sum, in contrast to Taiwanese traditions and narrative practices that valorize the listener role, much developmental research has privileged the narrator role. As a result, little is known about how children develop as listeners. By focusing on the flow of interaction between family members and young children and by following in the interpretive footsteps of the various participants (Briggs, 1998), it is possible to study listening from the perspective of both socialization and acquisition. The analyses presented in this chapter suggest that young children's achievements as listeners are best appreciated via prolonged observation and painstaking inspection across the boundary of each narration, across genres, and even across observational sessions. For instance, in Example 2, if the researcher had left Angu's home earlier, she would have missed Angu's challenge to her aunt and would have concluded that Angu had timidly listened without responding. Similarly, in Example 1, Yoyo's moral agency could be understood only within the context of repeated narrations of the same transgression with modified details, and in contrast to how competent his older brother was at reciting the rules and correcting Yoyo's misdeeds.

We are not suggesting that researchers should ignore or downplay the narrator role; our point is that the study of narrative development will benefit from a more balanced approach that encompasses the whole range of ways in which children and their families participate in narrative. Conversational narration is an interactive process accomplished jointly by participants who occupy a whole range of roles, including narrator, co-narrator, listener, bystander, and overhearer. Therefore, it is essential to treat all narrative practices as the collaborative and co-constructed work of these several participants and to chart children's development in terms of the full range of roles available to them. A more balanced perspective should also be cultivated in educational arenas. In the United States, where speaking is assumed to be conducive to active learning, Chinese learners are often seen by American teachers as passive or unwilling to participate (Li, 2003). Our work lends weight to Pang's (1996) advice that American teachers need to respect Asian students' "attentive silence" (pp. 188–189). They often remain silent because they perceive silence as respectful to the teacher and fellow students or because they are engrossed in active listening and observing.

REFERENCES

Applebee, A. N. (1978). *The child's concept of story.* Chicago: University of Chicago Press.

Bamberg, M. (1997). *Narrative development: Six approaches.* Hillsdale, NJ: Lawrence Erlbaum Associates.

Bennett-Kastor, T. (1986). Cohesion and predication in child narrative. *Journal of Child Language, 10,* 135–149.

Berman, R., & Slobin, D. (1994). *Relating events in narrative: A crosslinguistic developmental study.* Hillsdale, NJ: Lawrence Erlbaum Associates.

Blum-Kulka, S., & Snow, C. (1992). Developing autonomy for teller, tales, and telling in family narrative event. *Journal of Narrative & Life History, 2,* 187–217.

Botvin, G. J., & Sutton-Smith, B. (1977). The development of structural complexity in children's fantasy narratives. *Developmental Psychology, 13,* 377–388.

Briggs, J. (1998). *Inuit morality play: The emotional education of a three-year-old.* New Haven, CT: Yale University Press.

Bruner, J. S. (1983). *Child's talk.* New York: W. W. Norton.

Bruner, J. S. (1990). *Acts of meaning.* Cambridge, MA: Harvard University Press.

Burger, L., & Miller, P. (1999). Early talk about the past revisited: Affect in working class and middle class children's co-narrations. *Journal of Child Language, 26,* 133–162.

Chang, H. C. (1997). Language and words: Communication in the Analects of Confucius. *Journal of Language and Social Psychology, 16,* 107–131.

Chang, H. C. (2001). Learning speaking skills from our ancient philosophers: Transformation of Taiwanese culture as observed from popular books. *Journal of Asian Pacific Communication, 11,* 109–133.

Clancy, P. M. (1986). The acquisition of communicative style in Japanese. In B. B. Schieffelin & E. Ochs (Eds.), *Language socialization across cultures* (pp. 213–250). London: Cambridge University Press.

Cook, H. M. (1999). Language socialization in Japanese elementary schools: Attentive listening and reaction turns. *Journal of Pragmatics, 31,* 1443–1465.

Domino, G., & Hannah, M. T. (1987). A comparative analysis of social values of Chinese and American children. *Journal of Cross-Cultural Psychology, 18,* 55–77.

Ely, R., & McCabe, A. (1993). Remembered voices. *Journal of Child Language, 20,* 671–696.

Engel, S. (1995). *The stories children tell: Making sense of the narratives of childhood.* New York: W. H. Freeman.

Fenny, N. C., Eder, R. A., & Rescorla, L. (1996). Conversations with preschoolers: The feeling state content of children's narratives. *Early Education & Development, 7,* 79–94.

Fivush, R. (1993). Emotional content of parent-child conversations about the past. In C. A. Nelson (Ed.), *Memory and affect in development: Minnesota symposia on child psychology* (Vol. 26, pp. 39–77). Hillsdale, NJ: Lawrence Erlbaum Associates.

Fivush, R., Haden, C., & Adam, S. (1995). Structure and coherence of preschoolers' personal narratives over time: Implications for childhood Amnesia. *Journal of Experimental Child Psychology, 60,* 32–56.

Fivush, R., Hamond, N. R., Harsch, N., Singer, N., & Wolf, A. (1991). Content and consistency in young children's autobiographical recall. *Discourse Processes, 14,* 373–388.

Fung, H. (1999). Becoming a moral child: The socialization of shame among young Chinese children. *Ethos, 27,* 180–209.

Fung, H., & Chen, E. C. H. (2001). Across time and beyond skin: Self and transgression in the everyday socialization of shame among Taiwanese preschool children. *Social Development, 10,* 419–436.

Gao, G. (1998). "Don't take my word for it"—Understanding Chinese speaking practices. *International Journal of Intercultural Relations, 22,* 163–186.

Gao, G., Ting-Toomey, S., & Gudykunst, W. B. (1996). Chinese communication processes. In M. H. Bond (Ed.), *The handbook of Chinese psychology* (pp. 280–293). Hong Kong: Oxford University Press.

Goffman, E. (1974). *Frame analysis.* Cambridge, MA: Harvard University Press.

Haden, C. A., & Fivush, R. (1996). Contextual variation in maternal conversational styles. *Merrill-Palmer Quarterly, 42,* 200–227.

He, A. W. (2001). The language of ambiguity: Practices in Chinese heritage language classes. *Discourse Studies, 3,* 75–96.

Heath, S. B. (1983). *Ways with words: Language, life, and work in communities and classrooms.* Cambridge: Cambridge University Press.

Hickmann, M., & Hendriks, H. (1999). Cohesion and anaphora in children's narratives: A comparison of English, French, German, and Mandarin Chinese. *Journal of Child Language, 26,* 419–452.

Labov, W. (1972). *Language in the inner city.* Philadelphia: University of Pennsylvania Press.

Lau, D. C. (Trans.). (1992). *Confucius: The Analects.* Hong Kong: The Chinese University Press.

Li, J. (2001). Chinese conceptualization of learning. *Ethos, 29,* 111–137.

Li, J. (2003). The core of Confucian learning. *American Psychologist, 58,* 146–147.

McCabe, A., & Peterson, C. (Eds.) (1990). *Developing narrative structure.* Hillsdale, NJ: Lawrence Erlbaum Associates.

Michaels, S. (1981). "Sharing time": Children's narrative styles and differential access to literacy. *Language in Society, 10,* 423–442.

Miller, P. J. (1994). Narrative practices: Their role in socialization and self-construction. In U. Neisser & R. Fivush (Eds.), *The remembering self: Construction and accuracy in the self-narrative* (pp. 158–179). New York: Cambridge University Press.

Miller, P. J. (1996). Instantiating culture through discourse practices: Some personal reflections on socialization and how to study it. In R. Jessor, A. Colby, & R. A. Shweder (Eds.), *Ethnography and human development: Context and meaning in social inquiry* (pp. 183–204). Chicago: University of Chicago Press.

Miller, P. J., Fung, H., & Mintz, J. (1996). Self-construction through narratives practices: A Chinese and American comparison of early socialization. *Ethos, 24,* 1–44.

Miller, P. J., Mintz, J., Hoogstra, L., Fung, H., & Potts, R. (1992). The narrated self: Young children's construction if self in relation to others in conversational stories of personal experience. *Merrill-Palmer Quarterly, 38,* 45–67.

Miller, P. J., & Moore, B. B. (1989). Narrative conjunctions of caregiver and child: A comparative perspective on socialization through stories. *Ethos, 17,* 428–449.

Miller, P. J., Potts, R., Fung, H., Hoogstra, L., & Mintz, J. (1990). Narrative practices and the social construction of self in childhood. *American Ethnologist, 17,* 292–311.

Miller, P. J., Sandel, T. L., Liang, C. H., & Fung, H. (2001). Narrating transgressions in Longwood: The discourses, meanings, and paradoxes of an American socializing practice. *Ethos, 29,* 159–186.

Miller, P. J., Wiley, A. R., Fung, H., & Liang, C. H. (1997). Personal storytelling as a medium of socialization in Chinese and American families. *Child Development, 68,* 557–568.

Mintz, J. (1995). Self in relation to other: Preschoolers' verbal social comparisons within narrative discourse. *New Direction for Child Development, 69,* 61–73.

Mintz, J. (1999). Self-esteem as ideology and practice: A study of narrative discourse practices among parents and preschool children in a middle-class, European-American community (Doctoral dissertation, University of Chicago, 1999). *Dissertation Abstracts International, 60,* 856.

Ochs, E., & Capps, L. (1996). Narrating the self. *Annual Review of Anthropology, 25,* 19–43.

Ochs, E., & Capps, L. (2001). *Living narrative: Creating lives in everyday storytelling.* Cambridge, MA: Harvard University Press.

Ochs, E., & Schieffelin, B. (l984). Language acquisition and socialization: Three developmental stories and their implications. In R. Shweder & R. LeVine (Eds.), *Culture theory* (pp. 277–320). Cambridge: Cambridge University Press.

Ochs, E., & Taylor, C. E. (1995). The "father knows best" dynamic in dinnertime narratives. In K. Hall & M. Bucholtz (Eds.), *Gender articulated: Language and the socially constructed self* (pp. 97–120). New York: Routledge.

Oppenheim, D., Emde, R. N., & Warren, S. (1997). Children's narrative representations of mothers: Their development and associations with child and mother adaptation. *Child Development, 68,* 127–138.

Oppenheim, D., Nir, A., Warren, S., & Emde, R. N. (1997). Emotion regulation in mother-child narrative co-construction: Associations with children's narratives and adaptation. *Developmental Psychology, 33,* 284–294.

Pang, V. O. (1996). Intentional silence and communication in a democratic society: The view point of one Asian American. *High School Journal, 79,* 183–190.

Peterson, C., & McCabe, A. (1983). *Development psycholinguistics: Three ways of looking at a child's narrative.* New York: Plenum.

Peterson, C., Jesso, B., & McCabe, A. (1999). Encouraging narratives in preschoolers: An intervention study. *Journal of Child Language, 26,* 49–67.

Pitcher, E. G., & Prelinger, E. (1963). *Children tell stories: An analysis of fantasy.* New York: International University Press.

Preece, A. (1987). The range of narrative forms conversationally produced by young children. *Journal of Child Language, 14,* 353–373.

Reese, E., & Fivush, R. (1993). Parental styles of talking about the past. *Developmental Psychology, 29,* 596–606.

Scollon, R., & Scollon, S. W. (1995). *Intercultural communication: A discourse approach.* Oxford, UK: Blackwell.

Soothill, W. E. (Trans.). (1968). *The analects of Confucius.* New York: Paragon.

Sperry, L. L., & Sperry, D. E. (1996). Early development of narrative skills. *Cognitive Development, 11,* 443–465.

Stern, D. (1985). *The interpersonal world of the infant.* New York: Basic Books.

Stern, D. (1989). Crib monologues from a psychoanalytic perspective. In K. Nelson, (Ed.). *Narratives from the crib* (pp. 309–319). Cambridge, MA: Harvard University Press.

Stone, P. S. (1992). "You know what?" Conversational narratives of preschool children. *Early Childhood Research Quarterly, 7,* 367–382.

Sutton-Smith, B. (1981). *The folkstories of children.* Philadelphia: University of Pennsylvania Press.

Taylor, C. E. (1995). Child as apprentice-narrator: Socializing voice, face, identity, and self-esteem amid the narrative politics of family dinner (Doctoral Dissertation, University of Southern California, 1995). *Dissertation Abstracts International, 57,* Z0667.

Wang, Q., & Leichtman, M. D. (2000). Same beginnings, different stories: A comparison of American and Chinese children's narratives. *Child Development, 71,* 1329–1346.

Watson-Gegeo, K. (1992). Thick explanation in the ethnographic study of child socialization and development: A longitudinal study of the problem of schooling for Kwara'ae (Solomon Islands) children. In W. W. Corsaro & P. J. Miller (Eds.), Interpretive approaches to children's socialization. *New Directions in Child Development, 58,* 51–66.

Wigglesworth, G. (1997). Children's individual approaches to the organization of narrative. *Journal of Child Language, 24,* 279–309.

Wiley, A. R., Rose, A. J., Burger, L. K., & Miller, P. J. (1998). Constructing autonomous selves through narrative practices: A comparative study of working-class and middle-class families. *Child Development, 69,* 833–847.

Young, L. W. L. (1994). *Crosstalk and culture in Sino-American communication.* New York: Cambridge University Press.

Yum, J. O. (1991). The impact of Confucianism on interpersonal relationships and communication patterns in East Asia. In L. A. Samovar & R. E. Porter (Eds.), *Intercultural communication: A reader* (pp. 66–78). Belmont, CA: Wadsworth.

PART V

Aging and Grandparenthood in Narrative

14

Telling Stories and Getting Acquainted: How Age Matters

Odette Gould
Mount Allison University

Whether through sharing the minutiae of everyday life or making heart-felt disclosures, whether conversing with a spouse, a child or a grandchild, most family relationships could be described as the direct result of a life span's worth of dyadic exchanges. Particularly in late adulthood, many (if not most) conversations are carried out between only two people—spouses, children, grandchildren, care givers, friends, and acquaintances. Arguably, the well-being of family members across the generations is dependent upon how informative, and how pleasant, intergenerational talk is.

It is well established that old age is accompanied by declines in certain cognitive domains—but a question that remains, perhaps the most crucial one, is the effects of these cognitive changes on conversations and, by extension, on relationships. Do the cognitive deficits of normal aging affect our ability to participate fully in conversations with age peers or across generations? One interesting and theoretically useful (although admittedly incomplete) way of conceptualizing such conversations is by focusing on the information exchanged: what is said, how it is said, what is understood, and how it is remembered. Effective and pleasant informational exchanges are an integral part of close, long-lasting, and emotionally satisfying relationships with families, both within and between generations.

In this chapter, I discuss a series of exploratory studies using a primarily cognitive approach, specifically the study of the quantity and quality of information exchanged by older adults. This is not meant to be a thorough review of research on older adults' discourse. My much more modest goal is to discuss studies carried out by my colleagues and me over the last few years and to use these as a means of highlighting the exciting possibilities and questions that are raised when cognitive aging is considered in a collaborative context. With a few exceptions (e.g., Baltes & Staudinger, 1996; Strough & Margrett, 2002a), most cognitive aging research has been limited to measuring how older adults working alone fail to meet performance standards set by younger adults (Strough & Margrett, 2002b). However, there have been indications in the literature for quite some time that many aspects of communication skills do not decline in old age, at least not until very late in life (Ryan, Giles, Bartolucci, & Henwood, 1986). Thus, the studies I discuss herein focus on older adults' ability to communicate information to others.

First, I review a series of studies we have done to investigate how older adults collaborate on remembering information. Whether telling an adult child what the physician said, or sharing the latest family gossip, older couples, older siblings, and older friends often work together to recall as much information as possible. Our research begins to explore how effective this collaboration can be.

In the second part of this chapter, I discuss some work that explored how older adults work with others to co-create personal disclosures. Traditionally, older family members have often been seen as the keepers and sharers of family history, and the bearers of sage advice based on personal experiences. However, little is known of the manner (i.e., the conversational style) in which these personal experiences are shared with others. Moreover, the content and appeal of the experiences that older adults consider life changing (and presumably worthy of sharing with younger family members) is of interest.

Finally, I speculate on how certain social boundaries influence older adults' management of the task of exchanging information with others. How do older adults manage the difficult task of presenting and receiving information from individuals, even their own children and grandchildren, with whom they share neither an age cohort nor a shared social history?

REMEMBERING STORIES

Most researchers of cognitive aging find that performance on episodic memory tasks declines as we reach late adulthood (Zacks, Hasher, & Li, 2000). Episodic memory is the facet of memory that we use when we witness an event or read a story and attempt to recall the information at a later date. Although rarely presented in this context, these types of discourse memory tasks are arguably a form of storytelling, since they involve the creation and presentation of a coherent organization of facts (Dixon & Gould, 1996). One particularly fertile perspective offered by Craik and colleagues (e.g., Craik &

Jennings, 1992) has been that the performance levels attained by older adults are determined to a large extent by the amount of environmental support provided either when information is being learned or when it is being retrieved from memory. In our work, my colleagues and I have explored the possibility that collaboration may offer a special form of retrieval support that would allow older adults to maintain high levels of recall performance despite age-related memory losses. Thus, one possibility is that in a collaborative recall setting, compensatory mechanisms may come into play and older adults may not be at a performance disadvantage. Of course, a second possibility is that the collaborative context could be particularly detrimental to older adults' cognitive performance. Indeed, many aspects of collaborative recall involve substantial demands to working memory, and working memory performance is consistently found to decrease in late adulthood (Zacks et al., 2000). For example, the process of collaborating involves (a) monitoring partners' verbal productions at the same time as one is planning one's own production, (b) a constant updating of what one planned to say based on what the partner said, and (c) the ability to quickly switch one's attention between one's own thoughts and the partner's speech. Thus, one goal of our early research on collaborative recall was simply to establish whether older adults would be able to be effective collaborators, despite the presumably heavy working memory demands of this context.

In one study (Dixon & Gould, 1998) we simply compared recall performance of younger and older adults who recalled information as individuals, groups of two, and groups of four. Twelve units of participants were tested at each of the three group sizes and the two age levels. Results indicated that recall performance increased across group size, but younger adults consistently recalled more information than older adults. Groups of four older adults, although recalling more than both older dyads and older individuals, only attained levels of recall similar to that of younger individuals. These early results were important in our thinking about collaborative memory in many ways. First, we managed to establish that older adults are effective collaborators since they, like younger adults, performed better as groups than as individuals. Second, we established that the structure of stories recalled by groups is similar to the structure of stories recalled by individuals: most main ideas are recalled, and details of the story, as they decrease in importance to the gist of the story, are less likely to be recalled. Finally, we established that even when working as a group, older adults do not (always) recall as much information as younger groups.

The results just described focused exclusively on the amount of information (specifically the number of idea units) that was recalled. Of course, this is only a small part of the picture. My colleagues and I have also begun exploring collaboration by attempting to identify what else, other than restated (i.e., correctly recalled) ideas from the stimulus-story, was being produced by the groups during recall. This type of analysis is of interest because it allows us to begin addressing the process of collaboration (i.e., how it happens). One set of analyses focused on categorizing elaborations, defined as statements made during the recall sessions that were neither errors nor correctly recalled statements from the stimuli (Gould, Trevithick, & Dixon, 1991). We identified two main types of elaborations and labeled them *denotative* and *annotative* elaborations. Denotative elaborations are inferences that are based on the content of the stimulus story, and state information that was implied but not stated directly in the story. For example, if the original story stated that someone had "gone shopping," a participant could recall that the protagonist had "driven his car to the shopping mall." The participant is adding information to the original story, but this information is implied. Annotative elaborations are much less closely tied to the stimulus story and include statements where the speaker is evaluating and commenting on the story, its events, and its characters. For example, a participant might state that the stimulus story is unrealistic, that the protagonist is foolish, or that he has had a similar experience in his own life.

We found no age differences for the number of denotative elaborations produced, although their number tended to increase as the size of the group increased. In contrast, older adults produced more annotative elaborations than younger adults, and for older, but not younger adults, the number of annotative elaborations increased with every increase in group size. Finally, it was particularly intriguing that while the production of denotative elaborations correlated positively and significantly with recall performance, the production of annotative elaborations was unrelated, for both age groups, with recall. Thus, older adults, particularly when they work in groups, seem to be making the recall task not only a purely cognitive one, but a social one as well. By commenting on the stories and their protagonists, older adults are bringing in more of a subjective, or at least evaluative, component to the task than younger adults are. One possibility is that adding this subjective aspect to the task may be one way that older adults, particularly groups of older adults, compensate for age-related memory loss. Indeed, it may be that, by adding a subjective and evaluative component to the stimulus story, it becomes more memorable than it would otherwise be. Of course, this hypothesized compensatory process, if it does occur, is secondary at best, since (a) younger adult groups still remember more information than older groups, and (b) the production of annotative elaborations is not positively correlated with recall.

However, as stated in the original paper, compensatory processes could be improving older adults' performance from a hypothesized base rate, even if performance is not ultimately brought up to the level of younger groups (Gould et al., 1991).

A further question of great interest is whether or not the relationship between the collaborators affects the quality of the collaboration. Specifically, we, and others (e.g., Johannsson, Andersson, & Rönnberg, 2000; Sillars & Wilmot, 1989) have speculated that older married couples may be particularly effective collaborators for two main reasons. First, their years together would mean that they share a large background of experiences, such that they could easily and effectively cue each other's memories (Sillars & Wilmot, 1989). Second, through many years of practice at accomplishing tasks together, they would have become "experts" at managing the process of collaboration (Dixon, 1999).

Our early results supported the view that familiarity with one's partner improved collaboration performance. In the second study reported in Dixon and Gould (1998), a small number of younger and older married couples working together to recall stories were compared to a small sample of unacquainted (same-sex) dyads. Although the older unacquainted dyads recalled significantly less information than younger dyads, older married couples recalled just as much information from their stimulus stories as did younger couples. In a follow-up paper, we focused on the process (rather than the outcome) of such dyadic/couple collaborations (Gould, Kurzman, & Dixon, 1994). Basically, we looked at how familiar and unfamiliar dyads spent their time when collaborating. To do this, we categorized each statement uttered by a member of the dyad as falling into one of four categories: (a) individual story-related statements, where one person is recalling information from the stimulus, (b) collaborative story-related statements, where the two collaborators are querying each other about details from the stimuli, (c) task discussion, where the partners discuss strategies for performing the task, and (d) sociability/support statements, where the partners are encouraging each other, or making personal disclosures only tangentially related to the task at hand. Clearly, the first two categories can be described as task-related statements, and the latter two as process work.

One of our main hypotheses when we began this study was that older adults would be particularly aware of the need for effective collaboration, and thus would spend more time on group process than did younger groups. This prediction, at least in its simple form, was not supported. The overall proportion of group process statements was the same for all four types of dyads. However, further analyses offered interesting evidence that our hypothesis was not so much invalid as overly simplistic. Indeed, we found that for younger adults there was no relationship between recall performance and group process, but for older adults, the correlation between recall performance and task discussion was positive and significant, while the correlation between recall performance and sociability/support statements was negative and statistically significant. Furthermore, we found that one of the main distinctions between the groups was the fact that older unacquainted dyads produced more sociability/support statements than other types of dyads, particularly at the end of the recall conversations, and married couples (both young and old) increased their production of task discussion statements as the recall conversation progressed.

One interpretation of this pattern is that all types of dyads adopted a strategy where the first part of the recall conversation consisted mostly of having individuals recall what they could, and the end of the conversation consisted much more of group process. Seemingly, older unfamiliar dyads were getting acquainted as a prerequisite to strategizing, while the married couples could go directly to planning how to accomplish the task. The overarching assumption here is that for older adults, the task of remembering information is more likely to be considered challenging, and therefore "functional interdependence" is present. Functional interdependence is a term used by Steiner (1972) to describe a situation where group members believe that they are unable to accomplish a task without the help of other group members.

Recently, my students and I investigated the effects of group familiarity on performance levels in more depth (Gould, Osborn, Krein, & Mortenson, 2002). As already mentioned, the earlier study (Dixon & Gould, 1998) was problematic, particularly because the unfamiliar dyads and the married couples were not tested using the same stimuli, but also because there may be fundamental differences between the types of participants who come to a study as part of a married couple and those who come as individuals. Thus, in the Gould et al. (2002) study we proposed that the best way to carry out this comparison was to do a within-subject comparison of dyad type. We therefore tested two same-aged couples at the same time, so that each person carried out a series of cognitive tasks with his or her spouse, but also with an opposite-gender stranger. We asked our participants to carry out three main cognitive measures: word recall, story recall, and a referential naming task.

The two memory tests in the Gould et al. (2002) study yielded similar—and surprising—results. We asked our participants to predict their recall before the task began. They predicted (and so did we) that higher levels of performance would be obtained when participants worked with their spouses than when they worked with strangers. However, familiarity with the partner did not affect performance, for neither the young nor the older dyads! Moreover, there was a significant interaction between the age and the gender factors in both tasks: Older women remembered just as much information as the younger adults, but older men recalled significantly fewer words and fewer story ideas. Unfortunately, the design we used did not permit us to distinguish between a cognitive and a social process explanation for these findings. Specifically, it may be that older men (at least those of this cohort) show lower performance on episodic memory tests, or it may be that these older men were less likely to interrupt their female partners to insert their own recalled information. (Of course, older men may not have inserted their recall because they were too polite to interrupt their female partner, or because their older female partners resisted being interrupted, or both). The referential naming task used in Gould et al. (2002) is one where one partner must describe repeatedly a set of ambiguous images so that the partner can organize these images into the correct order. We had felt that in this task, in particular, familiarity with one's partner would be an advantage, since shared past experiences could be used to create referents. However, virtual strangers carried out the task just as well as long-married couples. Of course, our findings need to be interpreted in context: The tasks may have lacked ecological validity, and it is possible that if familiar and relevant stimuli were used, then familiarity effects would be obtained.

It is important to note that the research described here is only one aspect of the exciting work being carried out on the more general topic of collaborative cognition, including much recent work on collaborative everyday problem solving (e.g., Goodnow, Lawrence, Ryan, Karantzas, & King, 2002; Margrett & Marsiske, 2002; Meegan & Berg, 2002; Strough, Cheng & Swenson, 2002). Overall, the research on collaborative cognition is yielding exciting and provocative findings. Despite the presumptive cognitive demands of the collaborative setting itself, older adults seem to be very effective collaborators when recalling information together. Even more exciting is the possibility that the collaborative setting is differentially beneficial to older adults. The next step in this research is to establish exactly how older adults benefit from working in groups. Are older adults better than younger adults at cuing each other? Are older adults better at managing the collaborative process? Do older adults collaborate as well with younger partners? Does familiarity with the younger partner make a difference? These are the questions that we are addressing in the projects that we are undertaking presently.

In conclusion, the results described earlier can be seen as being fundamentally optimistic in two ways. First, we have found evidence that at least some older dyads can recall just as much information as younger dyads. Thus, friends and family members could potentially perform important functions in providing cognitive support (e.g., aiding in the recall of health-care information) as well as in providing the more often recognized functions of social and emotional support. Second, the fact that strangers perform as well as married couples means that highly effective collaboration partners are commonly available, and not limited to individuals with whom we've been familiar for many years. Thus, even if we lose long-term partners, new partnerships such as may occur in late-life romantic pairings could be very helpful to ensure our ability to remember the vital information of everyday life. This is particularly important because the cohort of older adults tested here is probably the first and the last for whom very long marriages are common (Mares & Fitzpatrick, 1995). Indeed, Baby Boomers and subsequent generations are not likely to marry as young, or to have marriages as stable, as did today's seniors. Few older adults in the future may be able to depend on romantic and cognitive partnerships that last from the teens to the late 80s.

TELLING STORIES

In the research described previously, the focus was on how dyads and small groups of peers worked together to remember a stimulus story that they had read or heard moments before. An equally interesting topic is investigating how older adults tell (rather than "re-tell") a story, particularly their own story. How adept are we at describing to friends and family members the events from our own life in interesting ways? And what events from our own life do we consider key to explaining who we have become?

There has been surprisingly little research focusing on the production of discourse by healthy, normally aging older adults (Kemper & Kemtes, 2000). Indeed, much of the recent work addresses the production of language by older adults with dementia (e.g., Forbes, Venneri, & Shanks, 2002), the comprehension of language given processing rate deficits (e.g., Tun, 1998; Wingfield, 1999), or the comprehension of intergenerational speech (e.g., Kemper, Othick, Warren, Gubarchuk, & Gerhing, 1996). Of the discourse production work that has been carried out, a distinctly multidirectional perspective is portrayed: some aspects of speech show age-related decline, some show improvement, and many show stability.

Many researchers have found age-related loss in the quality of speech produced when older adults are asked to describe pictures or scenes. Older adults are described as having less coherent speech (e.g., Ulatowska, Hayashi, Cannito, & Fleming, 1986), using syntactical forms that require less working memory processing (e.g., Kynette & Kemper, 1986), producing more referential errors and lexical ambiguity (e.g., Pratt, Boyes, Robins, & Manchester, 1989), producing speech that is disrupted by word retrieval problems (e.g., Kemper, 1992), and being overly loquacious (Obler, 1980) and verbose (Gold, Andres, Arbuckle, & Schwartzman, 1988). Moreover, when asked to provide a summary of a story, older adults create summaries that are less succinct, in that they contain a mixture of central and noncentral details (Byrd, 1985). Such losses have also been found across different linguistic groups (Juncos-Rabadan, 1996).

In contrast, many researchers have identified age-related improvements in speech production, or at the very least qualitative differences in how older adults describe scenes and events. For example, in Kemper, Kynette, Rash, O'Brien, and Sprott (1989), undergraduate and adult judges rated older adults' productions to be clearer and more interesting than those of younger speakers. Older adults' productions were also found to contain syntactically simple sentences, and the authors proposed that these simpler sentences may have been produced not only because of working memory deficits, but also because of stylistic concerns for producing interesting stories. Similarly, Kemper, Rash, Kynette, and Norman (1990) found that individuals in their seventh and eighth decades produced stories that were more structurally complex (i.e., containing multiple embedded episodes), even though individual sentences tended to be syntactically simple. Similar results were obtained by Kemper (1990) when she analyzed the diary entries of Kansas pioneers. The diary entries written when the diarists were in their 70s and 80s were judged by expert teachers to be more interesting and better written. Pratt and Robins (1991) also analyzed personal narratives produced in the laboratory and found that older adults were more likely to produce stories that followed the classic narrative form; again, these stories were judged as superior by listeners.

Finally, some studies find similarities in performance across age. Glosser and Deser (1992), for example, found no age differences on lexical cohesiveness or on many microlinguistic measures of discourse, and Ulatowska, Chapman, Highley, and Prince (1998) found that many global levels of processing were maintained when longitudinal analyses were carried out from the 80s to the 90s. Boden and Bielby (1983) found that getting-acquainted conversations did not differ structurally, although they did differ in terms of content. Finally, Obler et al. (1994) compared individuals in their 30s, 50s, 60s, and 70s and pointed out that there was a great deal of variability in performance at all age groups, and that statistically significant age differences were often not present. They also suggested that findings indicating stability of language performance across adulthood may be underrepresented in the field because of the difficulty of publishing nonsignificant findings. Finally, in Labov and Auger (1993), the same elderly individuals spontaneously produced the same narratives during conversations with the same experimenter, 17 years apart. These narratives were described as having lost no syntactic complexity over time, and the organization of the stories may have improved over time. Although practice at telling specific narratives may be a concern in this design, it does highlight the lack of longitudinal studies of older adults' discourse abilities.

Most studies described so far incorporate the relatively unnatural situation of asking someone to speak in response to a stimulus in a laboratory setting (Bower, 1997). In everyday life, most discourse occurs as part of a dialogue, or at the very least when speakers (optimally) take listeners into account. While this approach is common in sociolinguistic research, very few researchers using a cognitive/developmental paradigm have looked at the older person's ability and willingness to accommodate to the conversational needs of partners, especially age peers.

In our work, we have begun to investigate how older adults manage conversations with age peers when they are telling a story together (Gould & Dixon, 1993). We asked younger and older married couples to describe together a vacation or trip that they had taken together. We asked our participants to describe a trip for two reasons. First, the topic was felt to be age-neutral, since couples of all ages had taken at least a short trip together. Second, this topic could produce much latitude in the telling. Because there is no way to describe a trip without summarizing, it provides us with a glimpse of what details our participants believed worthy of telling. Thus, we were able to analyze (a) the structure of the stories told, (b) the content of the stories told, and (c) how the task of co-telling a story was shared across the two speakers.

The older couples tended to produce longer stories, longer grammatical clauses, and more elaborated idea units (Gould & Dixon, 1993). Their stories were more likely to order events chronologically using relative terms (e.g., the next day), while younger adults were more likely to provide absolute chronological statements (e.g., on June 5th). In terms of their content, older couples produced stories that were rated as more subjective overall, and where less emphasis was put on discussing the itinerary and specific events of the trip, and more time was spent on descriptions of places seen and people met. Similar results were obtained by Kemper (1990) when she analyzed the diary entries of Kansas pioneers. With increasing age, the content as well as the format of these diary entries differed. As they aged, the diarists were more likely to write about people who had affected their lives than about daily activities.

The third group of analyses in our study addressed how the two members of the couple shared the task of telling the story (Gould & Dixon, 1993). One variable of particular interest here was in looking at topics (i.e., sections of the story) where all content words were spoken by only one member of the couple. We found that older adults were more likely to produce sequences of these monologues, but that in older couples it was more likely that both spouses produced some monologues. In other words, for younger couples, when monologues were present, they were produced by mostly one speaker, whereas older spouses were more likely to share in the production of these monologues. Thus, the pattern of results suggests that younger and older couples were sharing the task of telling the story in fundamentally different ways. Younger couples shared the task at what we called a micro-level: Monologues were rare and most events (and often sentences) were spoken by both partners. In contrast, the older couples seemed to be sharing the task at a more macro-level. More monologues were produced overall by older couples, and some older couples even stated explicitly that they were taking turns at telling different parts of the story.

In the following excerpts, some of the age-related differences just listed are highlighted. The first excerpt is the very end of an older couple's description of a trip to Europe taken in the 1950s, when they were in their 20s. The partners are shown to take longer turns, and they are explicitly aware of the effect of their storytelling on the audience. (Many of the older couples also explicitly discussed how to make the story interesting to the listener.) The second excerpt presents the last few moments of a younger couple's description of a vacation taken in Germany a few years before.

Excerpt 1

(Brackets indicate overlap in speech.)

Male (M): . . . and then we came home by ship. Seven days from Liverpool to Montreal and that was the last sign of luxury that [we've seen].

Female (F): [We traveled first] class. They don't have classes any more on ships. I wanted my own bathroom and they wouldn't guarantee it if you [traveled second]

M: [I think it was second] class or tourist

F: Tourist yeah so anyway we [had a beautiful] . . .

M: [We had a table] of four there was an elderly, to us an elderly lady, and from Montreal and a young fellow who was a cipher clerk in the Canadian Embassy in India I think it was, and he was on his way home on leave. We hardly saw him because he had a girlfriend in the tourist section. {laugh} But the four of us, one waiter had nothing to do but look after us. I used to come down. I'd be the only one there for breakfast. He would shove me into my chair and . . .

F: OK dear that's enough I think.

M: OK alright, I won't go anymore, I can get into {laughter} . . .

F: We had some lovely, lovely trips in our life.

Experimenter (E): {laugh} It sounds like a wonderful trip.

Excerpt 2: Younger Couple

Male (M): . . . and we, we walked around Lahr one day shopping, remember through, through the stores and stuff like that?

Female (F): It rained.

M: Ya . . . yeah I think so.

F: And what did we do, that was what we did on our last day, wasn't it? We walked around Lahr.

M: Yeah, walked around Lahr.

F: And then we went hmm?

M: We went to the EuroPark.

F: We did, that wasn't very fun {laugh} no big fair, wasn't fun at all, it was a kiddie fair.

M: And then one night we went to see the Rhine? We couldn't really see, it was too dark out (laughter). And then we went to (*missing word*).

F: {laughter}

M: mmmmm . . .

F: Ya {laugh} . . . then you went to Cyprus and I went home.

M: Yeah that's about it {laugh}.

F: {laugh} Yeah, that's it.

E: I've never been to Germany, I'd love to go sometime.

It is interesting to speculate what is the reason for the different styles of sharing the storytelling task adopted by the younger and older married couples (Gould & Dixon, 1993). One possibility is that older adults have adapted to the working memory losses that make co-telling a story at a microlevel too difficult. (Memory difficulties could also explain the use of relative rather than absolute chronological markers.) A second and not necessarily incompatible explanation is the possibility that older adults have learned that stories are more interesting for the listener if each speaker produces certain parts of the story. Finally, these results could also be due to simple cohort differences: These older couples may have told stories together in this way during their entire married life. Indeed, strong cohort differences are consistently found when marriage relationships are studied (Mares & Fitzpatrick, 1995).

Most of the studies that have looked at how, or how well, older adults accommodate to the needs of their conversational partners have looked at intergenerational conversations. For example, Coupland and colleagues studied older women's production of painful self-disclosures (e.g., discussions of death, illness and loneliness) during conversations with younger and middle-aged women (Coupland, Coupland, Giles, & Weimann, 1988). Although the presentation of these negative and painful disclosures is thought to have face-saving and identity-maintenance functions for the older women (Coupland, Coupland, & Giles, 1991), they result in conversations that are uncomfortable and unpleasant for the younger partners. In contrast, Bower (1997) found that older American-Italian men used complex discourse strategies to avoid discussing emotionally painful topics. In our own work (Collins & Gould, 1994), we found that in simple getting-acquainted conversations, older women did not produce disclosures that were either more intimate or more negative than their younger partners. They did, however, produce slightly more self-disclosures about the past than did younger women, although the two age groups did not differ on the production of self-disclosures about their opinions, their present lives or their future plans. Boden and Bielby (1983) also found that older women were more likely to discuss their personal past during getting-acquainted conversations. Of course, it could simply be that by virtue of being older, they have more "past" to discuss than younger conversationalists. However, it may also be that, as suggested by Boden and Bielby, older adults are finding common ground with their partners, and thereby establishing a positive conversational identity. At any rate, it is important to note that at least with our healthy and relatively well-off sample of older women, getting-acquainted conversations were not dominated by older women's overly negative or intimate disclosures, as some stereotypes of the elderly would suggest (Collins & Gould, 1994).

Surprisingly, relatively little research in psychology has focused on the style and content of conversations that occur between older adults and their own children and grandchildren. One aspect of intergenerational conversation that is particularly fascinating is the question of what types of personal narratives people of different ages consider important in their own lives. Will family members share a recognition of what is an important autobiographical event and how these autobiographical memories should be recounted?

It is well established from the autobiographical memory literature that when people of all ages are asked to remember events from their past, they are likely to recall events that occurred when they were in late adolescence or early adulthood (Fitzgerald, 1996). We obtained similar results when we (Gould, Webster, Goreham, & Ulven, 2002) asked individuals from across the life span to describe a special memory that is an important turning point in their life. Our sample contained over 20 respondents for each decade from the teens to the 90s, with slightly fewer respondents (less than 15) in the 30s and the 90s. As mentioned previously, the reminiscence bump was clearly present: All of our age decades, from the teens to the 90s, described events that they later rated as having happened between the ages of 15 and 35. Perhaps more surprising is the lack of a significant age decade difference in how often participants reported reminiscing about this event. Given a seven-point scale ranging from 1 (less than once per year) to 7 (at least once per day), the range of the age decade averages was narrowly distributed around 4 (once per month) for all decades. Of course, this finding is consistent with results indicating that the total frequency of reminiscing is similar across the life span, even if the functions of reminiscence are different across age groups (e.g., Webster, 1997).

Although the content analysis of these memories is not yet complete, some interesting patterns are appearing. We began by rating the valence of these memories (using a similar system to that developed in Collins & Gould, 1994). Each memory was rated on a three-point scale for both positivity and negativity. Overall, there was no age effect when the age decade groups were compared on positivity. In contrast, both a significant linear and cubic age trend were statistically significant for negativity ratings. Basically, there was a steady decrease in negativity from the teens to the 80s, with both the 40s and the 90s standing out as having higher ratings on negativity than surrounding decades. Preliminary attempts to identify themes yielded two groupings. First, many of the memories can be categorized as involving a strong sense of loss—the loss of a loved one through death, the loss of innocence through close calls like automobile accidents, and in a few cases, a very powerful sense of loss of trust because of abandonment or personal violation. A second main theme that emerges strongly is one of having met a personal challenge, and being proud of one's achievement. Analyses continue to try to identify whether the themes and the ways these themes are expressed change across the decades. Our main goal with this study was to explore whether the type and content of individuals' landmark memories relate to their self-reported reminiscing behaviors. The range of topics was amazing, and the intimacy intrinsic in such revelations is powerfully felt by the reader (Thorsheim & Roberts, 1990). Of course, these data are very rich, and deserving of much more in-depth analyses of the themes and storytelling styles used. Obviously, more qualitative analysis techniques are necessary for a fuller understanding of how identity and self are defined through stories (e.g., Kenyon, 1996; Pasupathi, 2001). Initial results offer a fascinating glimpse into the process of intergenerational family exchanges of personal experiences. Older adults do not seem to tell stories that are more negative, or that deal with substantially different themes from those of their children and grandchildren. How such personal narratives are received, interpreted, and appreciated by other family members, however, is a topic that remains to be addressed in depth.

In conclusion, while some aspects of discourse production clearly reflect age-related deficits, some aspects show improvement, and many show stability. One valuable skill is the ability to take into account one's partner and one's audience during conversation. This process is even more challenging when conversations occur between individuals who belong (or are perceived to belong) to different social and age groups. The beliefs, attitudes, and stereotypes that each member of the dyad holds toward the other may then add another layer of complexity to the situation. While sociolinguists have begun to broach these issues, cognitive psychologists have, for the most part, ignored them.

EXCHANGING INFORMATION ACROSS BOUNDARIES

Communication Accommodation Theory (CAT) is a sociolinguistic model that studies how language, communication, and social psychology intersect during interindividual interactions (Giles, Coupland, & Coupland, 1991). The dimension of CAT that has received the most attention in the aging literature is attuning, which has been used as a conceptual model to study intergenerational interactions. Specifically, younger adults have often been observed to overaccommodate to older adults, such as when they underestimate the older person's sensory and cognitive abilities. Older adults have also been described as underaccommodative to younger adults, such as when they are seen as pursuing topics of conversation that are not of interest to the younger partner (e.g., Williams & Nussbaum, 2001). Both forms of counter-attuning are hypothesized to be due to the salience of age. Namely, both age groups are treating the partner as a member of an age group (with all attending ageist stereotypes) rather than as an individual.

When a speaker accommodates his or her speech to the needs of the recipient, this speech must meet the needs of the recipient along many dimensions, including the discourse needs (choice of topics, turn taking), interpretability (clarity and complexity of the speech), and interpersonal control needs (permitting a positive face in the recipient). An optimal situation is one where the two conversation partners work together to establish each other's level of knowledge, ability, and conversational needs. This process must occur in real time, be a co-creation of each member of the conversation, and be in constant flux as the conversation ranges across different topics. Obviously, this is an enormously complex process.

Most of the research carried out to investigate younger adults' satisfaction with intergenerational conversations has focused on their discourse needs: They report feeling that the topics discussed in conversations with older adults are not enjoyable (Williams & Nussbaum, 2001). Interestingly, there are suggestions that younger adults themselves may limit the topics addressed in intergenerational conversations (Williams & Giles, 1996). In contrast, younger adults' accommodation (or lack thereof) when communicating with others has often been investigated. Most of the research carried out to investigate older adults' satisfaction with intergenerational conversations has focused on their interpretability needs: They report that younger adults' speech is oversimplified and patronizing (Ryan, Hummert, & Boich, 1995). The term *elderspeak* is often used to describe this speaking style.

In most of the work investigating elderspeak, the main measure of interest has been the older person's subjective reaction to the younger person's elderspeak. In our work, we (Gould & Dixon, 1997) explored whether older adults benefit from elderspeak in a cognitive sense. Specifically, we investigated whether elderspeak has the intended purpose of increasing the older person's comprehension and memory for the information presented. Our participants watched a video of an actor presenting medication instructions in either a neutral speaking style or in elderspeak. Our results were unexpected: Some individuals did remember more information when a message was presented using elderspeak, but these same individuals rated the speaker and the speech negatively. What was particularly surprising was that the older individuals who benefitted from the oversimplified speech tended to be the ones with higher, rather than lower, working memory ability. We replicated and extended these findings in a subsequent study (Gould, Saum, & Belter, 2002). Again, we found that working memory ability was not correlated to recall when neutral speech was used. However, when elderspeak was used, positive and statistically significant correlations were present between working memory ability and recall performance for both younger and older adults.

We proposed a cognitive explanation for these findings. Specifically, superior working memory abilities may be necessary to take advantage of certain characteristics of elderspeak (e.g., reiteration of concepts). Ironically, while many individuals in caring professions naturally adopt this speaking style to help their most frail and cognitively deficient patients, these seem to be the individuals least likely to benefit from this speaking style. Moreover, even the individuals who do remember more information when this speaking style is used are going to react negatively to the speaker, and thereby may be less willing to follow that speaker's recommendations. Kemper and Harden (1999) have established that in experimental settings, it is possible to train speakers to use an optimal speaking style that retains the beneficial, but not the patronizing, dimensions of elderspeak. However, since elderspeak, like "motherese" with young children, is adopted without forethought or planning by most users, it is not clear whether widespread use of such an optimal speaking style is likely.

In the second elderspeak study (Gould, Saum, & Belter, 2002), we were also able to better establish the complexity of the affective reactions to the neutral and oversimplified speech. The latter was rated both more positively and more negatively by the younger and older listeners. Of particular interest was the finding, in both of the elderspeak studies, that there was a strong relationship between emotional reaction and recall performance for the older, but not the younger participants. It may very well be, as some theoretical models (e.g., Carstensen, 1992) have proposed, that subjectivity increases in salience in old age.

Very few studies have looked at older adults' ability to adapt their speech across multiple conversational settings. Some authors have suggested that old age is accompanied by a lack of flexibility in language processing. Indeed, when older adults were asked to give directions using a map or diagram, they did not adapt their speech (e.g., prosody and grammatical complexity) to the age and comprehension needs of the recipient (Kemper, Vandeputte, Rice, Cheung, & Gubarchuk, 1995; Kemper et al., 1996).

In contrast, older adults caring for a spouse with dementia have been found to adapt their speech to help their spouse with cognitive tasks (Cavanaugh et al., 1989; Cavanaugh, Kinney, Dunn, McGuire, & Nocera, 1994) and to repair communication breakdowns that occur when conversing with their spouse (e.g., Orange, Miller, Johnson, & Van Gennep, 1998). Although these care givers have had many months or years to learn to compensate for their spouse's communicative deficits, older adults have also been shown to adapt to unfamiliar conversational partners. For example, Coupland, Coupland, and Grainger (1991) present a case study of one older woman's successive conversations with two different partners. The authors highlight how the woman works with each partner to co-create a completely different persona. With the younger adult partner, she subscribes to the negative stereotypes of old age, and this portrayal is endorsed by the younger partner. When talking to an age peer, she portrays herself as an active and social person who copes well with the constraints in her life. What is most striking about this case study is the way it highlights this older woman's communicative flexibility.

In our own work, we (Gould & Shaleen, 1999) looked at older women's ability to adapt their speech by pairing them sequentially with two younger and unfamiliar partners that differed on cognitive ability. Each older woman participated in two interactions: one with a young university student, and the other with a person with mild mental retardation. The older woman collaborated on the same set of cognitive tasks with each partner: (a) a 3-minute getting-acquainted session, (b) menu planning, (c) collaborative block design, and (d) finding 20 things in common. Our results indicated that older women were very adept at adapting their speaking style to meet the needs of their partners, particularly the passiveness that characterizes the speech of individuals with mental retardation (Kuder & Bryen, 1991). Older women used different strategies across the different tasks to ensure the participation of their less talkative partners. They used significantly more questions with MR partners than with student partners in the menu and commonalities task, and significantly more direct commands with MR partners during the more difficult collaborative block design.

In the Gould and Shaleen (1999) study, it was particularly remarkable that although older participants were told nothing about their partners before the getting-acquainted task began, adaptive communicative styles began to appear very quickly (i.e., during the first 3 minutes of the testing session). For example, when older women asked a getting-acquainted question to a student partner, the partner tended to answer the question, and then ask one of her own. Thus, both interactants got the opportunity to disclose personal information. However, MR partners tended to answer questions, but not ask any. The older women quickly adopted an approach where they would ask a question, listen to the answer, and then spontaneously disclose information in response to the question that "should" have been asked but wasn't. For example, many of our older participants asked their MR partner where she'd grown up, and after a few seconds, would break the silence to make a comment, such as, "Well, I grew up here and have lived here all my life." It should be noted that these findings are not necessarily in disagreement with those of Kemper et al. (1995) and Kemper et al. (1996). Indeed, while the Kemper studies focused on older adults' ability to accommodate to the partner's comprehension abilities, we focused on their ability to accommodate to the partner's conversational (i.e., turn taking) abilities. In my view, we've established that at least on some very important aspects of conversation, older women were found to adapt very clearly to the needs of their partners.

A next step is to investigate whether older women and men are willing and able to accommodate to conversational partners in a variety of social contexts and cognitively demanding situations. If we can gain a better understanding of how flexible older adults are as conversationalists, we can begin to understand the delights and the frustrations of intergenerational conversations. Why do some grandchildren cherish conversations with grandparents, while others find them frustrating and boring? Are older adults unable to handle the cognitive load of speaking and at the same time monitoring recipient's reactions—especially when the recipient belongs to a different age or social cohort? Or do many grandparents consciously choose to transgress their grandchildren's discourse and interpersonal expectations?

DISCUSSION AND CONCLUSIONS

The main theme underlying most of the research discussed in this chapter is that cognitive factors play an important role in defining how intra- and intergenerational communication occurs. The stories we tell to describe our family to others and to describe ourselves to our own family are a fascinating mixture of memory and imagination, and of logic and emotion. For too long, cognitive developmentalists have looked at memory independently of why information is being recalled, and at language independently of who is being addressed. By the same token, social developmentalists have too often focused on relationships without considering the cognitive abilities of the people in these relationships.

A second theme in this chapter is that understanding communicative abilities of older adults is going to require both a multidirectional and a multidimensional perspective. In other words, simple decremental (or for that matter incremental) models are not sufficient. A much more complex and potentially useful perspective involves exploring the delicate equilibrium between abilities that improve with age, abilities that decline, abilities that are compensated for, and abilities that are abandoned (either willingly or otherwise).

In the present chapter, I have attempted to provide examples of ways that my colleagues and I have explored these ideas. One example is the interaction between the complex set of cognitive and social variables that are required for co-recalling, co-telling, and co-accommodating. The cognitive demands of coordinating, in real time, one's own verbal productions and those of someone else are substantial. Yet, despite well-established working memory losses, older adults manage, and sometimes excel at, collaboration and storytelling. A second example is the possibility that old age is accompanied by an increased salience of affect in cognitive functioning and in the processing of language. It may be that at least some of the time, older adults have different communicative goals that emphasize personal narrative and reminiscence. Many cognitive aging researchers have noted that older adults sometimes "personalize" laboratory settings. Even when we ask them to solve simple problems and answer trivia questions (e.g., Camp, 1989), or remember information from stories (e.g., Gould et al., 1991), they tend to link the stimuli to events in their own lives, to comment on them, and overall to transform the testing session into an interesting and pleasant social interaction. In many situations, this approach may be beneficial, and even optimal—it may be what makes older adults better storytellers. However, it's possible that in some settings, such as a physician's office, or a family reunion, that a narrativistic and subjective style of presenting information may be less effective. Indeed, it may be that this style of presenting information is particularly incompatible with the training, the speaking style, and the communicative needs of the physician (Smyth, Gould, & Slobin, 2000), or the topical and stylistic expectations of the adult child and grandchild. The physician may miss important diagnostic details because they are buried so deeply in the narratives, especially if he or she is concentrating on how to best shut off the flow of the narrative in order to "get back" to the task at hand. Similarly, the grandchild may wish for a swift presentation of information, rather than a drawn-out (even if entertaining) narrative.

Many young people feel that older adults, including members of their own extended family, do not adequately meet their conversational needs (e.g., Williams & Nussbaum, 2001). Stereotypes abound that older adults are boring, negative, repetitive, and judgmental. One possibility is that older adults are unable or unwilling to meet the conversational content and style needs of their younger interactants. Another possibility is that younger adults' perceptions are false, and based on stereotypical and incorrect views of older adults. Clearly, in-depth analyses of actual intergenerational same-family interactions are necessary for a better understanding of intergenerational conversations to emerge. For example, it would be useful to compare how the very same, shared event (e.g., a conversation, a dinner, a family reunion) is experienced, remembered and described by different family members. Moreover, it would be particularly illuminating if accurate representations of the cognitive abilities of the event participants were also obtained. Do older adults use long conversational turns to reduce the working memory demands of quick back-and-forth conversations? What determines the adoption of this compensatory strategy over others? Do adolescents use short conversational turns because they find longer turns too syntactically demanding? When individuals of different generations use different conversational styles, when do they perceive the other as entertaining rather than "ornery"? In my view, we will need both cognitive and social perspectives to answer such questions, and to understand how family narratives are created and used.

In conclusion, the main goal of this chapter has been to highlight many questions and possibilities that my colleagues and I find interesting and productive. Empirical research on many of these topics is sorely lacking. Even more important is work that integrates cognitive psychology with other theoretical and empirical traditions. If we want to understand the complex and fascinating phenomena reviewed here, discourse between scholars is as necessary as discourse between and by aging study participants.

REFERENCES

Baltes, P. B., & Staudinger, U. M. (Eds.). (1996). *Interactive minds: Life-span perspectives on the social foundation of cognition.* Cambridge: Cambridge University Press.

Boden, D., & Bielby, D. D. (1983). The past as resource. A conversational analysis of elderly talk. *Human Development, 26,* 308–319.

Bower, A. R. (1997). The role of narrative in the study of language and aging. *Journal of Narrative and Life History, 7,* 265–274.

Byrd, M. (1985). Age differences in the ability to recall and summarize textual information. *Experimental Aging Research, 11,* 375–388.

Camp, C. (1989). World-knowledge systems. In L. W. Poon, D. C. Rubin, & B. A. Wilson (Eds.), *Everyday cognition in adulthood and late life* (pp. 457–482). Cambridge: Cambridge University Press.

Carstensen, L. L. (1992). Social and emotional patterns in adulthood: Support for socioemotional selectivity theory. *Psychology and Aging, 7,* 331–338.

Cavanaugh, J. C., Dunn, N. J., Mowery, D., Feller, C., Niederehe, G., Fruge, E., & Volpendesta, D. (1989). Problem-solving strategies in dementia patient-caregiver dyads. *The Gerontologist, 29,* 156–158.

Cavanaugh, J. C., Kinney, J. M., Dunn, N. J., McGuire, L. C., & Nocera, R. (1994). Caregiver-patient dyads: Documenting the verbal instructions caregivers provide in joint cognitive tasks. *Journal of Adult Development, 1,* 27–36.

Collins, C. L., & Gould, O. N. (1994). Getting to know you: How own age and other's age relate to self-disclosure. *International Journal of Human Development and Aging, 39,* 55–66.

Coupland, N., Coupland, J., & Giles, H. (1991). *Language, society and the elderly.* Oxford, UK: Blackwell.

Coupland, J., Coupland, N., Giles, H., & Weimann, J. M. (1988). My life in your hands: Processes of self-disclosure in intergenerational talk. In N. Coupland (Ed.), *Styles of discourse* (pp. 201–253). London: Croom Helm.

Coupland, J., Coupland, N., & Grainger, K. (1991). Intergenerational discourse: Contextual versions of aging and elderliness. *Aging and Society, 11,* 189–208.

Craik, F. I. M., & Jennings, J. M. (1992). Human memory. In F. I. M. Craik & T. A. Salthouse

(Eds.), *The handbook of aging and cognition* (pp. 51–110). Hillsdale, NJ: Lawrence Erlbaum Associates.

Dixon, R. A. (1999). Exploring cognition in interactive situations: The aging of N+1 minds. In T. M. Hess & F. Blanchard-Fields (Eds.), *Social cognition and aging* (pp. 267–290). San Diego, CA: Academic.

Dixon, R. A., & Gould, O. N. (1996). Adults telling and retelling stories collaboratively. In P. B. Baltes & U. Staudinger (Eds.), *Interactive minds: Life-span perspectives on the social foundation of cognition* (pp. 221–241). New York: Cambridge University Press.

Dixon, R. A., & Gould, O. N. (1998). Younger and older adults collaborating on retelling everyday stories. *Applied Developmental Science, 2,* 160–171.

Fitzgerald, J. M. (1996). The distribution of self-narrative memories in younger and older adults: Elaborating the self-narrative hypothesis. *Aging, Neuropsychology and Cognition, 3,* 229–236.

Forbes, K. E., Venneri, A., & Shanks, M. F. (2002). Distinct patterns of spontaneous speech deterioration: An early predictor of Alzheimer's disease. *Brain & Cognition, 48,* 356–361.

Giles, H., Coupland, N., & Coupland, J. (1991). Accommodation theory: Communication, context, and consequence. In H. Giles, J. Coupland, & N. Coupland (Eds.), *Contexts of accommodation: Developments in applied sociolinguistics* (pp. 1–68). Cambridge: Cambridge University Press.

Glosser, G., & Deser, T. (1992). A comparison of changes in macrolinguistic and microlinguistic aspects of discourse production in normal aging. *Journal of Gerontology: Psychological Sciences, 47,* P266–272.

Gold, D., Andres, D., Arbuckle, T., & Schwartzman, A. (1988). Measurement and correlates of verbosity in elderly people. *Journals of Gerontology: Psychological Sciences, 43,* 27–33.

Goodnow, J. J., Lawrence, J. A., Ryan, J., Karantzas, G., & King, K. (2002). Extending studies of collaborative cognition by way of caregiving situations. *International Journal of Behavioral Development, 26,* 6–15.

Gould, O. N., & Dixon, R. A. (1993). How we spent our vacation: Collaborative storytelling by young and old adults. *Psychology and Aging, 8,* 10–17.

Gould, O. N., & Dixon, R. A. (1997). Recall of medication instructions by young and old adult women: Is overaccommodative speech helpful? *Journal of Language and Social Psychology, 16,* 50–69.

Gould, O. N., Kurzman, D., & Dixon, R. A. (1994). Communication during prose recall conversations by young and old dyads. *Discourse Processes, 17,* 149–165.

Gould, O. N., Osborn, C., Krein, H., & Mortenson, M. (2002). Collaborative recall in married and unaquainted dyads. *International Journal of Behavioral Development, 26,* 36–44.

Gould, O. N., Saum, C., & Belter, J. (2002). Recall and subjective reactions to speaking styles: Does age matter? *Experimental Aging Research, 28,* 199–213.

Gould, O. N., & Shaleen, L. (1999). Accommodative speech by older women. *Journal of Language and Social Psychology, 18,* 395–418.

Gould, O. N., Trevithick, L., & Dixon, R. A. (1991). Adult age differences in elaborations produced during prose recall. *Psychology and Aging, 6,* 93–99.

Gould, O. N., Webster, J., Goreham, K., & Ulven, J. (2002). *Exploring the links between reminiscence and landmark memories.* Manuscript in preparation.

Johansson, O., Andersson, J., & Rönnberg, J. (2000). Do elderly couples have a better prospective memory than other elderly people when they collaborate? *Applied Cognitive Psychology, 14,* 121–133.

Juncos-Rabadan, O. (1996). Narrative speech in the elderly. Effects of age and education on telling stories. *International Journal of Behavioral Development, 19,* 669–685.

Kemper, S. (1990). Adult diaries: Changes made to written narrative across the life span. *Discourse Processes, 13,* 207–223.

Kemper, S. (1992). Adults' sentence fragments: Who, what, when, where, and why. *Communication Research, 19,* 444–458.

Kemper, S., & Harden, T. (1999). Experimentally disentangling what's beneficial about elderspeak from what's not. *Psychology & Aging, 14,* 656–670.

Kemper, S., & Kemtes, K. (2000). Aging and message production and comprehension. In D. Park & N. Schwarz (Eds.), *Cognitive aging: A primer* (pp. 197–214). Philadelphia: Taylor and Francis.

Kemper, S., Kynette, D., Rash, S., O'Brien, K., & Sprott, R. (1989). Life-span changes to adults' language: Effects of memory and genre. *Applied Psycholinguistics, 10,* 49–66.

Kemper, S., Othick, M., Warren, J., Gubarchuk, J., & Gerhing, H. (1996). Facilitating older adults' performance on a referential communication task through speech accommodations. *Aging, Neuropsychology, and Cognition, 3,* 37–55.

Kemper, S., Rash, S., Kynette, D., & Norman, S. (1990). Telling stories: The structure of adults' narratives. *European Journal of Cognitive Psychology, 2,* 205–228.

Kemper, S., Vandeputte, D., Rice, K., Cheung, H., & Gubarchuk, J. (1995). Speech adjustments to aging during a referential communication task. *Journal of Language and Social Psychology, 14,* 40–59.

Kenyon, G. M. (1996). The meaning/value of personal storytelling. In J. E. Birren & G. M. Kenyon (Eds.)., *Aging and biography: Explorations in adult development* (pp. 21–38). New York: Springer.

Kuder, S. J., & Bryen, D. N. (1991). Communicative performance of persons with mental retardation in an institutional setting. *Journal of Education and Training in Mental Retardation, 26,* 325–332.

Kynette, D., & Kemper, S. (1986). Aging and the loss of grammatical forms: A cross-sectional study of language performance. *Language & Communication, 6,* 65–72.

Labov, W., & Auger, J. (1993). The effect of normal aging on discourse: A sociolinguistic approach. In H. Brownell & Y. Joanette (Eds.), *Discourse in neurologically impaired and normal aging adults* (pp. 115–133). San Diego, CA: Singular.

Mares, M., & Fitzpatrick, M. (1995). The aging couple. In J. F. Nussbaum & J. Coupland (Eds.), *Handbook of communication and aging research* (pp. 185–206). Mahwah, NJ: Lawrence Erlbaum Associates.

Margrett, J. A., & Marsiske, M. (2002). Gender differences in older adults' everyday cognitive collaboration. *International Journal of Behavioral Development, 26,* 45–59.

Meegan, S. P., & Berg, C. A. (2002). Contexts, functions, forms, and processes of collaborative everyday problem solving in older adulthood. *International Journal of Behavioral Development, 26,* 6–15.

Obler, L. K. (1980). Narrative discourse style in the elderly. In L. K. Obler & M. L. Albert (Eds.), *Language and communication in the elderly* (pp. 75–90). Lexington, MA: Heath.

Obler, L. K., Au, R., Kugler, J., Melvold, J., Tocco, M., & Albert, M. L. (1994). Intersubject variability in adult normal discourse. In R. L. Bloom, L. K. Obler, S. D. Santi, & J. S. Ehrlich (Eds.), *Discourse analysis and applications. Studies in adult clinical populations* (pp. 15–27). Hillsdale, NJ: Lawrence Erlbaum Associates.

Orange, J. B., Miller, L., Johnson, A. M., Van Gennep, K. M. (1998). Resolution of communication breakdown in dementia of the Alzheimer's type: A longitudinal study. *Journal of Applied Communication Research, 26,* 120–138.

Pasupathi, M. (2001). The social construction of the personal past and its implications for adult development. *Psychological Bulletin, 127,* 651–672.

Pratt, M. W., Boyes, C., Robins, S., & Manchester, J. (1989). Telling tales: Aging, working memory, and the narrative cohesion of story retellings. *Developmental Psychology, 25,* 628–635.

Pratt, M. W., & Robins, S. L. (1991). That's the way it was: Age differences in the structure and quality of adults' personal narratives. *Discourse Processes, 14,* 73–85.

Ryan, E. B., Giles, H., Bartolucci, G., & Henwood, K. (1986). Psycholinguistic and social psychological components of communication by and with the elderly. *Language and Communication, 6,* 1–24.

Ryan, E. B., Hummert, M. L., & Boich, L. H. (1995). Communication predicaments of aging: Patronizing behavior toward older adults. *Journal of Language & Social Psychology, 14,* 144–166.

Sillars, A. L., & Wilmot, W. W. (1989). Marital communication across the life-span. In J. F. Nussbaum (Ed.), *Life-span communication* (pp. 225–254). Hillsdale, NJ: Lawrence Erlbaum Associates.

Smyth, J., Gould, O., & Slobin, K. (2000). The role of narrative in medicine: A multitheoretical perspective. *Advances in Mind-Body Medicine, 16,* 186–193.

Steiner, I. D. (1972). *Group process and productivity.* New York: Academic.

Strough, J., Cheng, S., & Swenson, L. M. (2002). Preferences for collaborative and individual everyday problem solving in later adulthood. *International Journal of Behavioral Development, 26,* 26–35.

Strough, J., & Margrett, J. (Eds.). (2002a). Collaborative cognition in later adulthood [Special issue]. *International Journal of Behavioral Development, 26*(1).

Strough, J., & Margrett, J. (2002b). Overview of the special section on collaborative cognition in later adulthood. *International Journal of Behavioral Development, 26,* 2–5.

Thorsheim, H., & Roberts, B. (1990). Empowerment through storysharing: communication and reciprocal social support among older persons. In H. Giles, N. Coupland, & J. M. Weimann (Eds.), *Communication, health and the elderly* (pp. 115–125). Manchester, UK: Manchester University Press.

Tun, P. A. (1998). Fast noisy speech: Age differences in processing rapid speech with background noise. *Psychology and Aging, 13,* 424–434.

Ulatowska, H. K., Chapman, S. B., Highley, A. P., & Prince, J. (1998). Discourse in healthy old-elderly adults: A longitudinal study. *Aphasiology, 12,* 619–633

Ulatowska, H. K., Hayashi, M. M., Cannito, M. P., & Fleming, S. G. (1986). Disruption of reference in aging. *Brain & Language, 28,* 24–41.

Webster, J. D. (1997). The reminiscence functions scale: A replication. *International Journal of Aging and Human Development, 44,* 137–148.

Williams, A., & Giles, H. (1996). Intergenerational conversations: Young adults' retrospective accounts. *Human Communication Research, 23,* 220–250.

Williams, A., & Nussbaum, J. F. (2001). *Intergenerational communication across the lifespan.* Mahwah, NJ: Lawrence Erlbaum Associates.

Wingfield, A. (1999). Comprehending spoken questions: Effects of cognitive and sensory change in adult aging. In N. Schwarz, D. C. Park, B. Knäuper, & S. Sudman (Eds.), *Cognition, aging, and self-reports* (pp. 201–228). Philadelphia: Taylor & Francis.

Zacks, R. T., Hasher, L., & Li, K. Z. H. (2000). Human memory. In F. I. M. Craik & T. A. Salthouse (Eds.), *The handbook of aging and cognition,* (2nd ed., pp. 293–358). Mahwah, NJ: Lawrence Erlbaum Associates.

15

"As Long as They Go Back Down the Driveway at the End of the Day": Stories of the Satisfactions and Challenges of Grandparenthood

Joan E. Norris
Stephanie Kuiack
University of Guelph

Michael W. Pratt
Wilfrid Laurier University

> *When I became a grandmother, I said to myself that I wasn't going to be one of these grandmothers that's always talking about her grandchildren, but I found that I could only do that a certain length of time. Someone will come along and ask about your grandchildren and first thing you know you are in the grandmother class and you are kind of glad to be there. I used to think, well, it's just a child like your own, but it is different. You look at them and you think, well for one thing, you are not responsible for them. You just enjoy them and you look at them and you wonder how they are going to unfold and blossom, what their personality will be and who. It is quite an extra dimension that I didn't know was possible until I experienced it.*
>
> —Mrs. Sparks, grandmother of four (Norris & Tari, 1985)

In recent decades, we have seen a dramatic change in the age structure of families in the industrialized world. Thanks to increasing longevity and the verticalization of the family—more generations but fewer members of each generation—there are more grandparents than ever before and more *kinds* of grandparents than ever before. Most adults in their 30s have living grandparents, and many also have great-grandparents, step-grandparents, or grandparents who act as surrogate parents (Giarrusso, Feng, Silverstein, & Bengtson, 2001). The sheer availability of older adults within a family, then, makes it likely that children will have the opportunity to form a relationship with at least one grandparent well into their adult years.

But what kind of relationship will this be? A challenge for contemporary family scientists is to do justice to the remarkable diversity within and across families, and to understand how this diversity affects interactions and relationships. Nowhere is this challenge greater than if one considers the situation of grandparents. Not only do these adults differ in the generational place they may hold with the family, they also can vary widely in age, onset of grandparenthood, and the experience of life events such as work, divorce, and simultaneous care giving for multiple generations of older and younger family members. The situation of this 58-year-old grandfather of nine is not unusual: "We've still got two sons at home, so you don't miss children, if you know what I mean. Like other grandparents don't have any children at home so they really think it's a big deal to have kids around. Well at times Dora and I just wish they would all go away and leave us alone!" (Norris & Tari, 1985, p. 3).

In this chapter, we explore one method by which the variability in intergenerational interaction and relationship building may be examined: that is, through storytelling. By storytelling, we mean the narratives that grandparents weave into their interactions with others. These narratives include stories told *to grandchildren* about grandparents' personal history, that of the family, and of the world that they grew up in. They also include stories told *about grandchildren* to others in their family and larger social networks. When such narratives occur within an intergenerational context, they have at least four separate functions: building a relationship, education about personal and historical events, value transmission, and the expression of generativity. We examine research on these four functions and provide examples to demonstrate their role in building and maintaining relationships across the generations. Throughout the chapter, an intergenerational family systems approach guides our analysis, reminding us of the multiple times, relationships, and generations that influence the narrative of any family.

INTERGENERATIONAL FAMILY SYSTEMS

Despite acknowledging the variability inherent within and across grandparenting experiences, many researchers have been intent on identifying normative roles. As we have noted elsewhere, this approach has resulted in a proliferation of typologies developed in an effort to describe the experiences of all grandparents (Norris & Tindale, 1994; Norris, Pratt, & Kuiack, 2003). The 1960s version of this approach resulted in classifications like the one proposed by Neugarten and Weinstein (1964). According to authors such as these, the oldest generation of a family can be found sharing fun, a rocking chair, or wisdom with their grandchildren. More recently, researchers have acknowledged the difficulty in creating one typology to fit all grandparents, some even suggesting that the grandparent role is too ambiguous and lacking in normative prescriptions to be considered a role at all (Fischer & Silverman, 1982). Nevertheless, current work is still focused on classifying older family members, not by instrumental activities with correspondingly catchy names, but this time by extent of involvement in the family. Some grandparents are virtual strangers, rarely seeing their grandchildren—for example, because of a child's divorce (Gladstone, 1988); others may have custody of their grandchildren and are fully involved as surrogate parents—for example, when the middle generation has died or is incapacitated (Hayslip & Goldberg-Glen, 2000).

As Silverstein, Giarrusso, and Bengtson (1998) have pointed out, the attempt to identify classes of grandparents obscures the interaction and negotiation among family members that lead to particular styles of grandparenting. This focus also directs our attention away from examining the give-and-take between grandparents and their grandchildren as they work to establish relationships with one another. Consequently, we know relatively little about the nature and meaning of interaction between the generations. Is there a developmental purpose to that spirited argument over world affairs between a teen and her grandfather? Is there a systemic, family purpose, when other members good-naturedly fan the flames with their own views?

In order to answer these questions, it is important to consider both the unique developmental trajectory of each individual as well as the interacting influences of relationships among family members. Further, these developmental events and relationships must be considered in the larger context of the family's history and hopes for the future. To deal with such complexity, we have found it useful to conceptualize family roles such as grandparenthood, and dyadic relations such as grandparent-grandchild, within a wider systems framework. We developed our theory of intergenerational family systems (Norris et al., 2003) to help understand the continuity and discontinuity of key beliefs and behaviors within an adult family. In a three-generational family, individuals, separately and in subgroups, socialize one another to patterns of belief and behavior. These ongoing efforts at socialization are influenced by memories and beliefs about past generations as well as by hopes for future change or stability. Shadowy figures of the remembered past and anticipated future families have a significant but uneven influence on the thoughts, feelings, and actions of current members. Weaker reciprocal influences of extended kin who share, variably, some of the beliefs and behaviors of the target family are also present. Finally, the dynamic nature of the system is reinforced by considering the trajectory of the family through time. This temporal element focuses attention on the development of individual members, the impact of this development on the intergenerational system, and on the evolving nature of relationships within the system.

The individual elements of the Intergenerational Family Systems Model, and its focus on values, beliefs, and behaviors, provide an ideal framework within which to understand grandparents' narrative. As we discuss in the next sections, grandparents' motivation to tell stories, as well as the content of these stories, is strongly influenced by their experiences with their own parents and grandparents, their hopes for the future of the family, and their desire to provide a legacy of values and traditions for younger generations.

FUNCTIONS OF STORYTELLING IN THE GRANDPARENTAL RELATIONSHIP

"I think people have a natural-born tendency to tell stories. There's poetry inside each and every one of us. The job of any good listener is to simply get it out" (Terkel, 2002).

Traditionally, older adults have been considered the story tellers in a family (Obler, 1989). Nussbaum and Bettini (1994) have pointed out that when grandparents and grandchildren interact, they most often do so by sharing a story. These authors argue further that such storytelling occurs more frequently in the grandparent-grandchild relationship than it does in other family relationships. While other researchers might take issue with this conclusion, given the pervasiveness of family stories across the life span as illustrated in the present volume, it does lead us to consider what might be the special purpose of stories and storytelling in the context of grandparenting. Our analysis of the extant literature indicates that there are four primary functions to the telling of a story to grandchildren: relationship building, education about personal and historical events, values transmission, and, through these, expression of generativity. All of these functions appear linked to an overarching goal for grandparents: that of preserving and enhancing family relationships while making sense of their own unique life stories.

Building Intergenerational Relationships

"I like to take Susan by the hand for a walk down to the pond and I tell her stories and she listens to them. We have a little house out there in the woods and I tell her that is where the tree bears lived and she has a big imagination and she will ask me to take her out to see the bears. I take great pride in taking her for a walk up into the wood and showing her around" (65-year-old grandfather; Norris & Tari, 1985).

When a child asks for a bedtime story, she is probably not asking to be educated or socialized! All of us enjoy sharing a good story, one with coherence, a little excitement or complexity, and a satisfactory conclusion. Our research demonstrates that listeners of all ages recognize these qualities in the narratives they hear and read (Pratt & Robins, 1991). Studs Terkel (2002), that master weaver of other people's stories, tells us to "Find your Florence," the person in your family who can really tell the story well and delights in doing so. Not everyone enjoys this role, but according to many researchers, a family's storyteller is likely to be an older member (Nussbaum & Bettini, 1994). Perhaps, then, the main reason grandparents tell stories to their grandchildren is just for the pleasure of it. This function has been overlooked in the literature on grandparenting, and largely in the literature on narrative as well, yet it is vital.

Part of the pleasure of sharing a good story is, of course, the interconnection it can make between people. As Ryan, Pearce, Anas, and Norris's analyses of grandparents' writing in the next chapter reveal, telling a loved one a story creates a vital connection between two people. It builds on and adds to the shared experiences of the teller and listener. Telling a well-loved family anecdote engages both teller and listener in a ritual that can connect current and past generations (Norris et al., 2003). The grandfather quoted at the beginning of this subsection has obviously created an imaginative narrative for his granddaughter, but sharing the stories of others can also have its rewards, as this 77-year-old great-grandmother, interviewed about the meaning of grandparenthood, observed: "I've got to finish reading *The Old Man and the Sea* by Hemingway. It is so interesting. I promised Rob, my 16-year-old great-grandson, that I'd read it and help him put an essay together on it. . . . Will do my best to try and help him. I love to see all my grandchildren" (Norris & Tindale, 1994, p. 71).

Kennedy (1992) found that grandchildren of all ages sought out their grandparents for comfort, support, and advice, and argued that they did so even more than young people of several decades ago. If there is such an increase, it may be due in part to changes in family structure that encourage intergenerational requests for contact and assistance (Norris & Tindale, 1994). Kennedy and Kennedy (1993), for example, found that there were closer and more active relationships between grandparents and grandchildren in stepfamilies and single-parent families than between grandparents and grandchildren in intact first families. Although there is as yet no research on this subject, it is possible that in the face of recent difficult and frightening world events, children may be more likely to ask for the close connection and reassurance that a grandparent's presence and perspective can provide. Personal stories of challenge and survival are inspiring to those with worries about their own future and that of their generation.

Learning About Family and Social History

Ryan and colleagues (Ryan, Elliot, & Anas, 2000; Ryan, Elliot, & Meredith, 1999; Ryan et al., this volume) report that grandparents tell many stories to their grandchildren of their youth, the intergenerational history of their grandchild's family, and their personal perspectives on major historical events such as the Depression and World War II. Telling these stories appears to strengthen intergenerational connections as well as to educate other generations about the past (e.g., Putney & Bengtson, 2001). Older adults have a great deal of investment in the future of their families and usually view other family members as closer and more similar to them than do those members in return. Sharing personal histories may be one way to enhance these similarities. The work on storytelling among Holocaust survivors and their families, for example, indicates that grandparents intentionally try to reinforce family cohesiveness and unity—as well as a distrust of nonfamily members—through their reflections on that tragedy (Chaitin, 2002).

A positive relationship with grandparents encourages the incorporation of such values and attitudes into the personal stories of younger family members, and facilitates their identity development (Hayslip, Shore, & Henderson, 2000; see also Pratt & Fiese, this volume). Outwardly, a teenaged boy, concerned that he has the right brand of skateboard and properly spiked hair, might not seem concerned about maintaining Grandma's Sunday dinner tradition. Nevertheless, even he is likely to retain some vestige of her belief in family rituals (Kopera-Frye & Wiscott, 2000), more strongly if Grandma has managed to find a role for this dinner tradition in the overall family story that she is trying to preserve. Manoogian (2002) found that these family stories are an essential part of the legacy that grandmothers strive to provide for their grandchildren. For the Armenian Americans in this study, where there was virtually nothing tangible left to pass on to future generations, legacies were seen to play an essential role in adolescents' identity development. In Manoogian's research, cultural assimilation of grandchildren was acutely painful to these refugees because their stories, traditions, and values were all that they could provide to link these young people to their roots.

Some of our own research also underscores the importance of intergenerational connection in the lives and stories of older adults (Norris & Tari, 1985). This investigation focused on 33 grandmothers and grandfathers who were interviewed at least twice about the meaning of being a grandparent in the context of other important roles, activities, and events in their lives. One question of particular interest was the perception of intergenerational similarity in grandparenting styles through generations of the family. Thus, these older adults were asked to reflect on the kind of grandparents that their own parents and grandparents had been. Interestingly, most of these grandparents did not highlight past intergenerational similarity, but stressed that their approaches to their grandchildren were consistent with those used by their adult children. Modern child-rearing strategies, while perhaps not wholeheartedly endorsed, were at least respected. Their own grandparents, on the other hand, were frequently characterized as rigid disciplinarians who had little time for children. Consider this 65-year-old woman's reflection on previous generations of grandparents: "My mother was, well she didn't show too much affection [to my children]. She never showed much affection, even though I know that she loved them but she couldn't show it. I can kind of picture what I've seen of my mother's parents, and her parents were very, very strict, very, very strict."

Another grandmother in her early 60s provides a similar story of grandparental uninvolvement, in contrast to her own active pattern of relating to her grandchildren: "I can't really tell you, but they would sit in a chair and just—like I'm a grandparent and we don't sit in a chair when our kids come, we run around with them. They never ran around with us or played with us. They talked to us, yes. They talked to us and told us what was right and wrong. My grandfather sat in a chair and smoked his pipe while he met my husband-to-be and he was smoking and he said, 'I like that lad because he doesn't smoke,' and he was smoking all the time his pipe. But they were very religious Baptists just the same."

Seen from the perspective of intergenerational family systems, patterns of relating must be understood in the context of perceptions of the family's past and current traditions, values, and relationships, as well as hopes and beliefs for the future. Grandparents are in a critical generational position, balancing a need for closeness and similarity with their children and grandchildren with a need to remain anchored in the important values of the family's past. It is not surprising, then, that the grandparents in our research provide sympathetic stories about their own parents' and grandparents' approach to grandchildren, while making it clear that they have more up-to-date methods of relating and socializing with their own grandchildren. Modern grandparents see endorsement in the value of hard work in their own grandparents' stern approach to life, while presenting this value to their grandchildren through stories that have a gentler touch, ones that fit current social norms and child-rearing approaches.

Values Transmission

"While babysitting a while ago, I caught my granddaughter lying about a situation and blaming someone else for something she had done. I tried to stress upon her she would get into more trouble for lying than she would for the actual incident. She was punished for both, more severely for lying. To my knowledge, she has not lied to me since. I think I got through to her it is better to own up at the beginning" (DeForge, 2002).

One of the most common motives attributed to grandparents who tell stories to their grandchildren is that of teaching important personal and family values (e.g., Kandell, 1996). Bengtson has termed the intergenerational sharing of beliefs and values *consensual solidarity,* and notes that many social theorists have regarded the successful socialization of grandchildren by their grandparents to be evidence of social stability (Silverstein et al., 1998). Our own work within an intergenerational systems framework underscores the perceived importance of shared family values to all family members, but particularly to grandparents. In one study (Smith, Norris, Pratt, & Arnold, 1998), we asked 84 unrelated adults stratified into three age groups (18–30; 31–63; 65+) to select, from a list of ten core values (e.g., honesty, kindness, justice), three that they felt their grandparents and had tried to pass on to them, three that their parents had tried to instill, and three that they had tried (or would like to try) to transmit to their own children. Responses indicated more intergenerational consistency in the values picked by the oldest sample than in those selected by the young. It is, of course, possible that this generational difference in perception is due, in part, to cohort differences in the importance of certain "family values." Nevertheless, there was also evidence in our findings that values consistency can be linked at least as much to relationship quality and patterns of interaction. When individuals came from families with more frequent intergenerational contact and feelings of emotional closeness, they were more likely to report value similarity across generations.

In a second study (DeForge, 2002), we examined the shared intergenerational values of 35 families: grandparents, parents, and 8-year-old eldest children. In this study, we once again used the same list of ten core values, as well as following up by asking parents and grandparents to provide us with stories that illustrated their efforts at transmitting these values to the children. Using our values list, we found substantial similarity within families, including that between children and grandparents—much greater than would be expected by chance. In fact, intergenerational consistency was sometimes greater than that within generations (i.e., between mothers and fathers). Even more compelling, perhaps, were parents' and grandparents' stories. In the case of the Wilson family, for example, the child chose "honest and truthful" from our list of values. Independently, both parents and the maternal grandmother provided stories that illustrated their attempts to transmit this value:

Mother: "I said to her, 'You are still in big trouble, but I am glad that you told me the truth and you are going to get this punishment instead of this great big one because you didn't lie.' It had been years of telling her that if she tells the truth she will get in less trouble."

Father: "It is better to tell the truth and get punished, and one thing we did learn, she did learn that if she lied and then got caught the punishment would be far worse."

Grandmother: "I tried to stress upon my granddaughter that she would get into more trouble for lying than she would for the actual incident. She was punished for both, more severely for lying."

Other researchers have commented on the power of grandparents' stories to transmit or reinforce values that they feel are important for their grandchildren's moral socialization. Indeed, McAdoo and McWright (1994) found that many African American grandparents rely on a narrative short form—the proverb—in their efforts to teach important values. We know less about whether these children actually "receive" these moral messages, although our work on shared intergenerational values just described suggests that family level transmission and exchange may be occurring.

Generativity: A Moderator of Grandparents' Goals in Storytelling

Generativity, in Erikson's (1963) life span developmental framework, represents the period of midlife when adults are said to invest especially in the care of future generations as a legacy of the self. The prototype of this period is parenting, and indeed previous work has suggested that high levels of generativity in midlife are associated with more engaged and effective parenting of children and adolescents (McAdams, 2001; Peterson, Smirles, & Wentworth, 1997; Pratt, Danso, Arnold, Norris, & Filyer, 2001). However, it seems plausible that individual variations in generativity may remain an important predictor of different patterns of engagement in family roles into later adulthood as well (Norris et al., 2003). As already discussed, family stories can play an important role in socializing the young into both the family and its history and traditions, as well as into the wider culture and its values. Given this, how might variations in levels of generativity among older adults be related to the sorts of family stories that they tell? We conceive of generativity among grandparents as a moderator of the ways that storytelling goals are manifested. In this section, we describe two relevant studies, one with a general sample of older adults, and one including a family sample of grandparents.

In the initial study, we investigated how younger and older adults drew on their own personal life stories in the teaching of values to youngsters (Pratt, Norris, Arnold, & Filyer, 1999). In a previous study by McAdams, Diamond, de St. Aubin, and Mansfield (1997), midlife adults who were identified as very high on generativity by the nominations of others were likely to tell distinctive life stories in several ways, compared to a less generative group of adults. These differences often were expressed in optimistic themes among the highly generative. For example, generative adults focused on feelings of special opportunities ("early blessings") in their early family lives that they felt needed to be reciprocated or given back in later life, as well as on "redemptive" structures in their stories. Redemption structures are episodes that involve negative events that are followed by or transformed into an event or outcome that is positive. Such redemptively oriented stories are of course widely available, and popular, in our culture. One thinks of *A Christmas Carol* (Dickens, 1986) or the recent *A Beautiful Mind* (Nasar, 1998). McAdams et al.'s results suggest that generative people may appropriate such structures into their personal life narratives more readily than do others (e.g., McAdams & Bowman, 2001).

In a follow-up to the McAdams' study, we investigated the kinds of stories told by 130 younger (20–30), middle-aged (30–50), and older (60+) adults about the personal life experiences that they selected as appropriate for the purpose of teaching values to the younger generation (Pratt et al., 1999). People were asked to tell two life stories, one teaching about any value they wished to choose, and a second that was specific to teaching about the value of honesty. Here is the story of a 70-year-old woman, high on McAdams's standard measure of generativity, the Loyola Generativity Scale, about a personal experience that she would use to teach "honesty" (Pratt et al., 1999):

> I was a mediocre student and I used to absolutely hate geometry. One time we were given this homework assignment to do and I couldn't, and so the next day when I went to school, I didn't want to tell the teacher I hadn't done it because she was a real battle-axe and I was scared of her. So what I did was I selected one of the books from the girls who had handed their assignments in, and went to the washroom and I copied it into my book. I felt quite content, but then two days later I got my book back, and the teacher said on the bottom, "Please see me." So the girl I'd copied from also had a note and we went to see the teacher. And so of course I had to own up to the fact that I'd copied and it just happened to be the wrong book, because we both had these same silly answers to the question. So I was really scared, but the teacher sat down and had a good talk with me, and she said, "I'm going to help you understand." And from that moment on, I realized she wasn't so horrible, and she really helped me a lot. I was scared out of my wits, but as soon as I'd managed to explain what happened I felt as if a heavy burden had been lifted. . . . And so I told this story to my daughter, who was having problems in another subject, and she did this exact same thing. And I was able to help her realize it was the wrong thing to do with my example because I'd done it myself. (p. 422)

This story in fact clearly shows the elements of both generative themes (caring for the young) and redemptive structures that involve turning bad events into good. Several results from the study help to demonstrate the importance of variations in generativity for the stories of older adults. First, older adults in our sample were more likely to tell stories for children that had generative themes, and as likely to tell redemptively structured episodes, as were the two younger age groups (Pratt et al., 1999). Second, like the findings of McAdams et al. (1997), older adults who were higher on generative concern on a questionnaire (the standard Loyola Generativity Scale of McAdams and de St. Aubin, 1992) were more likely to tell personal stories that included these two key properties of generative themes and redemptive structures. Third, stories by those in all age groups, including the oldest, that had these two properties were judged by a panel of raters who read and rated the stories without any instructions to be more interesting and engaging overall. Presumably, then, they might be more meaningful and memorable as value messages as well, though we do not have direct evidence on this point. Finally, generative older adults were more likely than nongenerative adults to express motivation for teaching values to the younger generation (Pratt et al., 1999). These findings, then, suggested that generativity among older adults was linked to both greater investment in socialization processes and different styles of narrating the life story in the service of such socialization.

How might all this be relevant to the role of grandparenting specifically? As noted previously, a number of earlier studies have pointed to a range of "styles" of grandparenting that different adults in our culture adopt, including those with rather "distant" or "passive" patterns, for example, who have lower investment in actively socializing their grandchildren (Cherlin & Furstenberg, 1985; Neugarten & Weinstein, 1964). These types of grandparenting styles were contrasted with those who were more engaged and involved in socialization and disciplining ("authoritative" or "influential" types, according to Cherlin & Furstenberg, 1985). Our results for the mature adult sample above would suggest that generative grandparents might be engaged more actively in socialization roles than are others. In a second study, we explored this hypothesis through examining grandparents' stories of interactions with their own grandchildren (Pratt, Norris, Kelly, & Arnold, 2003).

In this research, we asked 78 grandparents, aged about 65–67 on average, to complete a questionnaire for us. These grandparents were drawn from a sample of 35 intact, middle-class families with an 8-year-old eldest child, and represented a sample of individuals drawn quite equally from all four grandparenting roles (maternal and paternal grandmothers and grandfathers). As part of their questionnaires, these grandparents were asked to fill out the standard Loyola Generativity Scale (LGS), as well as to write two brief stories about their own elementary-school-aged grandchild, a story about teaching a value to this child, as well as a story about a time when they were proud of the child. We examined the differences in the types of stories told by grandparents who were high on the LGS measure, versus those of grandparents who scored low. We were interested in whether differences in engagement in the grandparent role would be reflected in these stories, so we coded them for the specificity of their examples of socialization, with good reliability between two independent raters. We hypothesized that greater investment would be associated with more detailed and specific story episodes of teaching and pride.

Our findings indeed pointed to distinctive differences in the stories told by each of these groups. Generative grandparents (those above the overall sample median score on the LGS) were likely to recall stories of value teaching that stressed specific episodes or qualities of the child, whereas less generative grandparents often said they could not recall any such episode, or reported that they did not see this as their role. For example, here is the comment of a less generative grandfather regarding teaching a value to his granddaughter: "My granddaughter is too young to have done much." Another less generative grandfather wrote: "Let's face it. I have lots of grandchildren, and I love them all, but when we babysit them or visit them we know that they're going back to their parents, so it's not the same as your own kids. So most situations, I leave it up to the parents. I guess you could call it chickening out—ha-ha!"

These latter comments are hardly unusual among grandparents, who often seek to minimize the disciplinary aspects of their role, as we noted earlier. Then, too, issues of generational differences in discipline are often problematic, and this may be one way to limit friction around them (Smith, 1995). But contrast this view with the quite specific story written by a highly generative grandmother: "One day while my husband, Sandy and myself were at the park, we ran into a group of kids. Instead of playing nicely with each other, they were picking on one little boy, calling him names, and saying mean things. You could see the hurt on his face, in his eyes. When Sandy asked why they were being so mean, we explained that the names they were calling him had to do with where the boy's family was from. We explained to Sandy that it does not matter about where people come from, or the color of their skin. Everyone is the same."

Among the value teaching stories of grandparents, 82% of those above the median score on the LGS told a story that was judged concrete and specific, like the preceding example of Sandy, according to our coding system. For those who were low on the LGS, however, only 50% wrote a story about a specific episode of value teaching, a significant difference by chi-square ($p < .05$), suggesting evidence of more specific socialization engagement for more generative grandparents.

While most grandparents were enthusiastic when asked to tell of episodes of pride in their grandchildren, more generative grandparents differed from less generative grandparents in being better able to articulate specific qualities of the child that made them feel this way. For example, one highly generative grandmother said, "Last Christmas, Billy got a toy at the dinner table. His younger cousin did not like the toy he got and began to cry. Billy quickly offered to trade toys with Andy. I feel Billy is very sensitive and thoughtful, and I'm proud of him as a person." Less generative grandparents had trouble coming up with specific experiences; some said they could think of none, or simply said they were "always proud." Some, as in the example here from a grandmother who scored low on the LGS, talked more about how the child had been nice to, or proud of, them. "My story is about the pictures that Mary drew of my dog, and all the pictures she's sent me over the years. I've kept them in a box, so she'll have them, long after I'm gone. I also get lots of photos and when I phone her mom, she always says, 'Hi, Grandma.' This makes me feel really good."

Analysis of those grandparents scoring above the median on generativity on the LGS again showed that these individuals wrote stories of pride that were likely to be focused on specific positive qualities of the child in our coding system (77%), whereas those who were lower on generativity were less likely to write a story incorporating any such specific elements (47%). This again was a parallel trend in the chi-square analysis ($p < .06$) in the type of proud stories told about grandchildren by those grandparents differing in their relative level of generative concern.

As we had expected, then, more generative adults seemed more engaged in the socialization aspects of the grandparenting role, as reflected in the stories they told about the grandchild, both about a specific episode of value teaching and about a time when they were proud of the child. We infer this because generative grandparents seemed better able to recall concrete instances of these types of interactions with their grandchildren than were others. Our results with grandparents and grandchildren resemble those reported by McAdams (this volume) with regard to the recall of family stories in general among midlife adults, which was found to be more difficult for those low on generativity. We should also note that these patterns did not vary systematically by age or gender of the grandparent, gender of the grandchild, or amount of time reportedly spent with the grandchild (Pratt et al., 2003). These results suggest, then, that variations in engagement across the grandparenting styles reported in earlier literature (e.g., Cherlin & Furstenberg, 1985) might be linked to variations in levels of generativity among grandparents, though further evidence would be needed to test this directly.

As described earlier, grandparents are at a kind of intergenerational fulcrum within the family, spanning many generations in their own lives and personal experiences, and thus providing special opportunities for linking the generations in important ways through the stories they tell. The goal of encouraging such close intergenerational bonds may also be pursued more actively by generative grandparents. In earlier work, we found that older adults who were more generative reported feeling closer to their own parents and grandparents than did others (Norris et al., 2003). Peterson (2002) has reported similar findings regarding generative midlife women and their relations with their older parents. We suggest, then, that grandparents who are more generative, and thus perhaps more engaged with this role and concerned with family legacies, may be more likely to actively implement our three key goals of strengthening family bonds, conveying family history, and socializing values through the stories they tell to and about their grandchildren. In this specific sense, then, generativity in maturity may be a moderator of the vigor and effectiveness of these narrative functions in the family.

CONCLUSIONS

We have noted that with increasing longevity and the verticalization of the family, there are likely to be more living grandparents and a greater likelihood that younger members of any family will have the opportunity for a relationship with grandparents. Increased interest in the role of grandparents in the family has resulted in literature that attempts to create rather simplistic typologies for how grandparents behave. This approach has met with mixed success, and may actually obscure our understanding of the interaction between younger and older family members and the negotiation of relationships between them.

The theoretical framework of the Intergenerational Family Systems Model (Norris et al., 2003) permits an exploration of how relationships are negotiated between younger and older family members. This model directs researchers' attention to the bidirectional influences of each family member in socializing one another to patterns of belief and behaviors. Socialization is influenced by memories and beliefs about the past, as well as by hopes for the future. A family systems approach also encourages consideration of influences from extended kin (such as aunts or uncles), fictive kin, and step-relationships. Further, it acknowledges the dynamic nature of the family system—the time element directs our attention to development of individuals in the family and the effect of this development on the family system as a whole.

In this chapter, we have emphasized that one method by which intergenerational interaction and relationship building may be examined is through the study of storytelling. Our research indicates that there are at least four functions of storytelling within intergenerational relations: building the relationship, education about personal and historical events, value transmission, and the expression of generativity. This chapter has examined research on these four functions and provided examples to demonstrate their role in relationships across the generations. These functions of story*telling,* not surprisingly, overlap considerably with the themes identified in grandparents' *written* stories composed for grandchildren, as described in the chapter by Ryan et al. (this volume). For example, grandparents in this work point to the importance of narrative as a means of telling their own stories, bringing their experiences of world history alive, and offering advice. Grandchildren in the same studies express an appreciation of their grandparents' efforts to strengthen family relationships and to explain personal and family histories. As well, they note their own reciprocal efforts at providing advice and linking the culture of their own generation to that of their grandparents. Both generations underscore our argument that intergenerational storytelling fulfills important roles in building relationships and promoting a sense of history and shared values within families.

Relationships between younger and older family members may be built through storytelling. Storytelling can be entertaining, both for the listener and for the storyteller, and can create a connection between the two. Family history also can be transferred across generations in this manner and represents a way to make sense of where one has come from. Relationships may also be built specifically by the sharing of personal or historical events. Appreciating the events leading up to the present day in the form of familial history provides any family member with a sense of personal history, identity, and validation. Sharing important familial values through storytelling allows the older generation to impart the wisdom of their own experiences in a manner that younger family members may apply to their own lives. These concrete and personal stories may represent guideposts for how to behave in ambiguous or challenging situations, and adults often refer to such exemplars in their own life tales (Pratt & Norris, 1999). Finally, a sense of generativity on the part of the older family members, or an attempt to strength family ties across the generations, can be both accomplished and expressed through storytelling. As we have argued, the various functions of storytelling in the grandparent role may be especially salient and frequent among those who are more generative in their personal life tasks and roles. These findings suggest that generativity remains an important element within the family beyond the period of midlife and parenting (e.g., Pratt et al., 1999), well into the roles of later life, and serves as a moderator variable in guiding how these important functions of storytelling are expressed.

Our work suggests that intergenerational families would do well to follow the lead of Studs Terkel and put some effort into uncovering the personal narratives of older members. The increasing diversity and complexity of families make it less likely that some traditions and values will endure through generations. But one could argue that there was never a time when it was more important for children to feel rooted, secure, and confident about the future. If family storytelling were to be lost to mass-produced entertainment, then an important means of establishing intergenerational connections will have been lost as well. Those who are fortunate enough to have living grandparents do not need to rely on media portrayals of older people as embodiments of important values and models of successful aging. More relevant inspiration is closer at hand. Indeed, with the growing numbers of older adults who act as surrogate parents to their grandchildren, researchers have begun to suggest an even larger role for grandparents in shaping the lives of young people (Hayslip et al., 2000; Kopera-Frye & Wiscott, 2000).

A fruitful avenue for future research would be to consider how variations in grandparenting behavior—and specifically in storytelling behavior—provide information about the forms of grandparenting and likewise about interaction within the increasingly common multigenerational family. We submit that to understand the changing relationships within a family system, it is important to hear the stories of multiple generations of family members. The intergenerational family systems model directs attention to an analysis of the patterns of interaction that occur within family roles and relationships. This approach should afford us a better understanding of comments such as those of Mr. Sparks—husband of the grandmother who introduced our chapter—and the creator of this chapter's title: "We love our kids and our grandchildren but there is a limit to what time . . . when you are living your own life as we are here and we have commitments one way and another. Well, we are happy to see them as long as they go back down the driveway at the end of the day." Affection for one's grandchildren may well occur within the context of a need for some intergenerational distance as well. How this balance is struck and maintained is probably the result of the interaction of personal predilections, family tradition, and ongoing negotiation with a spouse, adult children, and the grandchildren themselves. As we have found in our own work (Beaton, Norris, & Pratt, 2003), seemingly straightforward questions about which grandparents to visit for the holidays are not at all simple for many young couples with children. Both husbands and wives may struggle with ambivalent feelings as they assert their own needs, while remaining mindful of their connections to parents and in-laws. Studies based in the complex and dynamic perspective afforded by a family systems model certainly seem worthwhile when investigating such intergenerational dynamics and the stories that reflect these family relations.

PUTTING STORYTELLING INTO PRACTICE

In this chapter, we have argued that storytelling is a vital part of rewarding intergenerational relationships. How, then, might we encourage this activity in busy modern families? Our research suggests that grandparents, parents, and grandchildren all have a part to play. In conclusion, we would like to offer a few suggestions as to how each of the authors in the intergenerational family story might add further chapters:

Grandparents:

- Take any opportunity for communication. If you wait for a cozy moment in a rocking chair, this may never come—especially as a young child grows older. Instead, explore your grandchild's interest in video games. How does a war game like "Medal of Honor" relate to your experiences as veteran?
- Write an e-mail and enroll in an online chat service. Kids love to get mail, but are not likely to write a letter in return. You can get a faster, more interactive response using their technology. This is true even if you live next door.
- If you live nearby, help your grandchildren with their homework. Children have many assignments that require a broad perspective on the world and provide an opportunity to explore your views and values.
- Expose your grandchildren to the activities about which you are passionate. Stories easily emerge as you explain why you love to cook, volunteer with the food bank, or are an active advocate for animal welfare.

Parents:

- Have an open-door policy. Whatever your relationship with your parents, remember that they are important to your children.
- Invite your parents to babysit. Most grandparents are happy for an opportunity to see and interact with their grandchildren—for a limited period.
- Keep your parents informed about the activities of your children. If your father knows that your son is an avid hockey player, it becomes much easier to talk about his experiences in the small town arena.

Grandchildren:

- Ask your grandparents for help with your homework, your naturalist badge for Scouts, or a ride to the ballet studio. They welcome some private time with you, and are often more patient than your parents.
- Get your grandparents to tell you about the time your mom or dad was a problem for them. Grandparents love to do this! And it provides for very entertaining stories for you.
- Share your knowledge of technology. If your grandparents can send you an e-mail, or you can send them your latest artwork as an attachment in your return message, you'll both feel a sense of accomplishment and have a special way of interacting.

ACKNOWLEDGMENTS

The research reported in this chapter was supported in part by Social Sciences and Humanities Research Council of Canada grants to authors Pratt, Norris, and to Mary Louise Arnold.

REFERENCES

Beaton, J., Norris, J. E., & Pratt, M. W. (2003). Unresolved issues in adult children's marital relationships involving intergenerational problems. *Family Relations, 52,* 143–153.

Chaitin, J. (2002). Issues and interpersonal values among three generations in families of Holocaust survivors. *Journal of Social and Personal Relationships, 19,* 379–402.

Cherlin, A., & Furstenberg, F. (1985). Styles and strategies of grandparenting. In V. L. Bengtson & J. Robertson (Eds.), *Grandparenthood* (pp. 97–116). Beverley Hills, CA: Sage.

DeForge, R. T. (2002). *Examining shared values, attitudes and beliefs across three generations of families.* Unpublished master's thesis, University of Guelph, Guelph, Ontario, Canada.

Dickens, C. (1986). *A Christmas carol.* New York: Bantam Books. (Original work published 1843)

Erikson, E. (1963). *Youth: Change and challenge.* New York: Basic Books.

Fischer, L. R., & Silverman, J. (1982, November). *Grandmothering as a tenuous role relationship.* Paper presented at the National Council on Family Relations, Portland, OR.

Giarrusso, R., Feng, D., Silverstein, M., & Bengtson, V. L. (2001). Grandparent-adult grandchild affection and consensus: Cross-generational and cross-ethnic comparisons. *Journal of Family Issues, 22,* 456–477.

Gladstone, J. W. (1988). Perceived changes in grandmother-grandchild relations following a child's separation or divorce. *Gerontologist, 28,* 66–72.

Hayslip, B., Jr., & Goldberg-Glen, R. (Eds.). (2000). *Grandparents raising grandchildren: Theoretical, empirical, and clinical perspectives.* New York: Springer.

Hayslip, B., Jr., Shore, J. R., & Henderson, C. E. (2000). Perceptions of grandparents' influence in the lives of their grandchildren. In B. Hayslip, Jr., & R. Goldberg-Glen (Eds.), *Grandparents raising grandchildren: Theoretical, empirical, and clinical perspectives* (pp. 35–46). New York: Springer.

Kandell, S. L. (1996). Grandparents tales: Stories our children need to hear. *Dissertation Abstracts International Section A: Humanities & Social Sciences, 57*(1-A), 0028 (UMI 9613924).

Kennedy, G. E. (1992). Shared activities of grandparents and grandchildren. *Psychological Reports, 70,* 211–227.

Kennedy, G. E., & Kennedy, C. E. (1993). Grandparents: A special resource for children in stepfamilies. *Journal of Divorce and Remarriage, 19,* 45–68.

Kopera-Frye, K., & Wiscott, R. (2000). Intergenerational continuity. Transmission of beliefs and culture. In B. Hayslip, Jr., & R. Goldberg-Glen (Eds.), *Grandparents raising grandchildren: Theoretical, empirical, and clinical perspectives* (pp. 65–84). New York: Springer.

Manoogian, M. M. (2002). Linking generations: The family legacies of older Armenian mothers. *Dissertation Abstracts International, Section A: The Humanities and Social Sciences, 62*(8), 2894-A.

McAdams, D. P. (2001). Generativity at midlife. In M. Lachman (Ed.), *Handbook of midlife development* (pp. 395–443). New York: Wiley.

McAdams, D. P., & Bowman, P. (2001). Narrating life's turning points: Redemption and contamination. In D. McAdams, R. Josselson, & A. Leiblich (Eds.), *Turns in the road: Narrative studies of lives in transition* (pp. 3–34). Washington, DC: APA Press.

McAdams, D. P., & de St. Aubin, E. (1992). A theory of generativity and its assessment through self-report, behavioral acts, and narrative themes in autobiography. *Journal of Personality and Social Psychology, 62,* 1003–1015.

McAdams, D. P., Diamond, A., de St. Aubin, E., & Mansfield, E. (1997). Stories of commitment: The psychosocial construction of generative lives. *Journal of Personality and Social Psychology, 72,* 678–694.

McAdoo, H. P., & McWright, L. A. (1994). The roles of grandparents: The use of proverbs in value transmission. *Activities, Adaptation & Aging, 19,* 27–38.

Nasar, S. (1998). *A beautiful mind: The life of mathematical genius and Nobel laureate John Nash.* New York: Touchstone.

Neugarten, B., & Weinstein, K. (1964). The changing American grandparent. *Journal of Marriage and the Family, 26,* 199–204.

Norris, J. E., Pratt, M. W., & Kuiack, S. (2003). Parent-child relations in adulthood: An intergenerational family systems perspective. In L. Kucznyski (Ed.), *Handbook of dynamics in parent-child relations* (pp. 325–344). Thousand Oaks, CA: Sage.

Norris, J. E., & Tari, A. J. (1985). [Grandparenting relations.] Unpublished raw data.

Norris, J. E., & Tindale, J. A. (1994). *Among generations: The cycle of adult relationships.* New York: Freeman.

Nussbaum, J. F., & Bettini, L. M. (1994). Shared stories of the grandparent-grandchild relationship. *International Journal of Aging and Human Development, 39,* 67–80.

Obler, L. (1989). Language beyond childhood. In J. B. Gleason (Ed.), *The development of language* (2nd ed., pp. 275–302). Columbus, OH: Merrill Publishing.

Peterson, B. (2002). A longitudinal analysis of midlife generativity, intergenerational roles and caregiving. *Psychology and Aging, 17,* 161–168.

Peterson, B., Smirles, K., & Wentworth, P. (1997). Generativity and authoritarianism: Implications for personality, political involvement and parenting. *Journal of Personality and Social Psychology, 72,* 1202–1216.

Pratt, M. W., Danso, H., Arnold, M. L., Norris, J., & Filyer, R. (2001). Adult generativity and the socialization of adolescents: Relations to mothers' and fathers' parenting beliefs, styles and practices. *Journal of Personality, 69,* 89–120.

Pratt, M. W., & Norris, J. (1999). Moral development in maturity: Lifespan perspectives on the processes of successful aging. In T. Hess & F. Blanchard-Fields (Eds.), *Social cognition and aging* (pp. 291–317). New York: Academic Press.

Pratt, M. W., Norris, J., Arnold, M. L., & Filyer, R. (1999). Generativity and moral development as predictors of value socialization narratives for young persons across the adult lifespan: From lessons learned to stories shared. *Psychology and Aging, 14,* 414–426.

Pratt, M. W., Norris, J. E., Kelly, A., & Arnold, M. L. (2003, April). *The apple of their eye: Older adults levels of Eriksonian generativity and the stories they tell about their grandchildren.* Poster presented at the biennial meetings of the Society for Research in Child Development, Tampa, FL.

Pratt, M. W., & Robins, S. (1991). That's the way it was: Age differences in the structure and quality of adults' personal narratives. *Discourse Processes, 14,* 73–85.

Putney, N., & Bengtson, V. (2001). Families, intergenerational relationships, and kinkeeping in midlife. In M. E. Lachman (Ed.), *Handbook of midlife development* (pp. 528–570). New York: Wiley.

Ryan, E. B., Elliot, G. M., & Anas, A. P. Eds. (2000). *Exchanges between us: More intergenerational connections.* Hamilton: McMaster Centre for Gerontological Studies.

Ryan, E. B., Elliot, G. M., & Meredith, S. D. (Eds.). (1999). *From me to you: Intergenerational connections through storytelling.* Hamilton: McMaster Centre for Gerontological Studies.

Silverstein, M., Giarrusso, R., & Bengtson, V. L (1998). Intergenerational solidarity and the grandparent role. In M. E. Szinovacz (Ed.), *Handbook on grandparenthood* (pp. 144–158). Westport, CT: Greenwood Press.

Smith, M., Norris, J. E., Pratt, M. W., & Arnold, M. L. (1998, October). *Examining the transmission of values between generations.* Paper presented at the annual meeting of the Canadian Association on Gerontology, Halifax, Nova Scotia, Canada.

Smith, P. K. (1995). Grandparenthood. In M. Bornstein (Ed.), *Handbook of parenting* (Vol. 3, pp. 89–112). Mahwah, NJ: Lawrence Erlbaum Associates.

Terkel, S. (2002). Tell it like it was: A Pulitzer-winning journalist's tips for preserving your family story. *Modern Maturity.* Retrieved August 30, 2002 from http://www.modernmaturity .org/dpartments/2002/lifestyle

16

Writing a Connection: Intergenerational Communication Through Stories

Ellen Bouchard Ryan
McMaster University

Kristine A. Pearce
University of Toronto

Ann P. Anas
McMaster University

Joan E. Norris
University of Guelph

> *Everyone needs to have access both to grandparents and grandchildren in order to be a full human being.*
>
> —Mead, 1972, p. 311

One of the most important relationships many people experience within their lifetime is that between grandparent and grandchild. The experience of having been a grandchild and then a grandparent gives one a true stake in humanity through connections back in time two generations and forward two generations (Norris, Pratt, & Kuiack, in press). These connections are forged through communication, including the sharing of stories.

SETTING THE CONTEXT

As people begin to live longer and healthier lives, greater numbers of people will be undertaking the role of the grandparent for longer periods (Giarrusso,

Silverstein, & Bengtson, 1996; Kennedy, 1990). This increase in grandparenting can significantly affect society, as both grandparents and their grandchildren have much to gain and contribute through this special family relationship. Yet, it is sometimes difficult for younger and older family members to communicate with each other because of different interests, stereotypes of aging, geographical distance, and the fast pace of contemporary life.

In this chapter, we explore story writing as a means of bridging the generations. First, we briefly review the literature concerning the relationships between grandparents and grandchildren and the role of storytelling within those relationships. Second, we present a narrative analysis of letters and stories written by grandparents for grandchildren and by grandchildren for their grandparents. Major themes from both grandparent and grandchild writings are described, in addition to specific benefits associated with intergenerational communication through writing. Finally, we discuss the implications of this study in terms of grandparent-grandchild relationships and the importance for older adults to record their life stories for family.

Communication Between Grandparents and Grandchildren

Scholars have described the many roles grandparents play in their grandchildren's lives. Grandparents give grandchildren love and affection, support, trust, connections to the past, family heritage, and moral values, and they act as role models (Brussoni & Boon, 1998; Kalliopuska, 1994, Kornhaber, 1996; Szinovacz, 1998). In return, grandchildren give grandparents joy, inspiration, love, and hope for the future (Kalliopuska, 1994).

The roles and meanings of grandparent-grandchild relationships are highly diverse in modern North American society (Silverstein, Giarrusso, & Bengtson, 1998; Strom et al., 1999; Tomlin, 1998; Williams & Nussbaum, 2001). Major sources of variability include cultural differences, gender of grandparent, parental divorce, and cases where the grandparent takes on the role of the parent. Moreover, roles and the relationship inevitably change as the grandparent and the grandchild traverse through the stages of life (Norris & Tindale, 1994; Roberto & Skoglund, 1996). For example, individual variability in the meaning of grandparenthood has been assessed by Kivnick (1983). Life-history interviews were carried out with grandparents aged 40 to 90 years, yielding five dimensions in the meaning of grandparenthood: centrality—grandparenthood central to an older person's life; valued elder—passing on tradition and being valued in the role; immortality through clan—commitment to the future of the family; reinvolvement with personal past—identification with own grandparents; indulgence—leniency towards grandchildren. It is problematic to apply this typology to all grandparents, because additional diversity is quite likely (Norris & Tindale, 1994). Nevertheless, the conceptualization does remind researchers of the underlying importance and richness of the grandparenting role to older adults.

It is often difficult for grandparents and grandchildren to maintain optimal relationships with each other (Harwood & Lin, 2000; Silverstein et al., 1998; Williams & Nussbaum, 2001). The increased pace of life associated with technological change can make it difficult for different generations to connect. Young people may be busy and have little contact in general with older people, whom they might consider slow and out of date. The relationship can be strained by the difficulties of some life stages such as adolescence for grandchildren and frailty of extreme old age for grandparents. Geographical distance may exacerbate the impact of these potential obstacles. Yet, level of satisfaction can remain high even with declining frequency of contact as grandchildren age, and the relationship can be enriched by efforts on the part of grandparents and/or grandchildren at any stage of their lives (Kornhaber, 1996; Tomlin, 1998). In most families, the generations adapt to changing circumstances to support and maintain cherished beliefs, values, and patterns of relating (Norris et al., in press).

Storytelling

Societies all over the world have especially valued the stories of their older members as a way of passing on the wisdom of experience from generation to generation (Kenyon, 1996, 2002; McAdams, Diamond, St. Aubin, & Mansfield, 1997; Mergler & Goldstein, 1983). Older persons can fulfill their call to generativity by transmitting cultural and family values through stories for their grandchildren (Norris, Kuiack, & Pratt, this volume). In contemporary North America, stories told by older adults are viewed as more effective than those told by young adults (Adams-Price, 1998; Pratt & Robins, 1991).

The act of sharing stories has long been associated with the grandparent's role, and is one of the most frequently recorded types of exchange between grandparents and grandchildren (Kornhaber, 1996; McKay & Caverly, 1995; Tomlin, 1998). Grandparents play a crucial role in passing on information about family members and historical events through storytelling. This activity facilitates identity formation and builds strong relationships between the grandchildren and all of their family members (see Norris, Kuiack, & Pratt, this volume; Pratt & Fiese, this volume). In addition, grandparents use stories to teach moral values even as they entertain and establish a sense of closeness.

Nussbaum and Bettini (1994) conducted a study in which college students shared stories reflecting the meaning of life with one of their grandparents. Gender differences occurred, in which grandfathers spoke more reticently and more about mastery, while grandmothers were more likely to emphasize the salience of family to their definition of self and to their happiness. Grandchildren rarely told stories, but rather offered lists of qualities or a set of points. The contrasting fluency of grandparent stories suggests that storytelling tends to be unidirectional from grandparent to grandchild in many families.

Story Writing

Although older adults have traditionally passed down valuable information to younger generations through storytelling in face-to-face situations, this intergenerational communication can also be done through writing. One can write letters and share written stories with grandchildren and one can write one's memoirs to share with the family.

Life stories can help preserve one's immortality. Grandparents may feel more satisfied in knowing that their memories and beliefs will carry on through their grandchildren. Writing the stories enables people to take an active approach to their lives by allowing them to express themselves and to explore their sense of identity and continuity. Moreover, exchanging written stories or letters can transcend geographical distances which limit opportunities for face-to-face encounters (Harwood, 2000).

Schuster (1998) investigated the effects of nursing home residents' writings on familial relationships and found that the perceived status of the older person was raised when the written works were shared with family members. While nursing home residents are often not viewed as contributors to society, this study found that the writing activities caused the younger generation to view the elders as more "complete," "accomplished" people, which transformed the way they related to their elders. The writing activities gave the residents a sense of control and raised self-esteem, since they actively created works, often for family occasions such as weddings and family reunions. Thus, both the older adults' views of themselves and the younger generations' perceptions were positively transformed, leading to more satisfying interactions.

THE PRESENT STUDY

Collecting Intergenerational Stories

Within this project designed to stimulate intergenerational communication, we invited older adults, young adults, and elementary school children to write stories. The older adults were asked to write a story, poem, or letter addressing a grandchild, or someone like a grandchild, on any subject matter they chose. It was suggested that the story be centered around a past memorable event, a lesson, or a moral that was of value to them, and that it could be something they might want to share with the younger person on a special occasion. Young adults and children were asked to write a story, letter, or poem for or about their grandparent or any other older adult whom they considered to be a grandparent figure in their lives.

The call for stories by the older adults (aged 60 years or older) was open to the public but focused on those affiliated with gerontological activities at McMaster University. The younger groups were university-aged students completing stories for a gerontology creative writing assignment and local elementary school children, ranging in age from 5 to 15 years old, who participated as part of a class project.

All of the submitted stories were rated by at least two evaluators on their publishability, relevance to intergenerational issues, and goodness of fit with the instructions. Those receiving the highest ratings were selected for analysis and publication in one of two collections entitled *From Me to You: Intergenerational Connections Through Storytelling* (Book I; Ryan, Elliot, & Meredith, 1999) and *Exchanges Between Us: More Intergenerational Connections* (Book II; Ryan, Elliot, & Anas, 2000). There were 62 older authors (53 females and 9 males), 38 university authors (36 females and 2 males), and 52 elementary school authors (41 females, and 11 males). Even though a few of the writers were not actually writing to their grandchild or grandparent, we refer to the older group as the "grandparent authors" throughout the chapter. Both the young adults and school children are referred to as the "grandchild authors."

Narrative Analysis

These stories were examined using a thematic analysis approach to describe what grandparents and grandchildren chose to convey, how this exemplified meaningful intergenerational communication, and the value of story writing in the grandparent-grandchild relationship. Thematic analysis has been identified as possessing many benefits, because it addresses the individual's point of view, experiences, life views, and beliefs (Luborsky, 1994). We used both approaches outlined by Luborsky (1994) to discover themes: searching for repeated or recurring statements, and examining statements marked by the author as being especially significant. This approach is well established in other research on narrative content, including studies of grandparenting (e.g., Roberto, Allen, & Blieszner, 2001). An open coding system was used to create a complete list of themes and patterns in the writing. During this process, input was obtained from two of the other chapter authors. Where there were disagreements about which themes were present or where themes overlapped, discussions were held to reach consensus. Each story quotation given throughout the remainder of this chapter is identified with a code corresponding to Book I or Book II and the number of the first page of the story.

Grandparent Themes

The most evident themes identified in the older adults' stories were: history, family, advice, and life story. Also, the stories provided a window into the various relationships that many grandparents share with their grandchildren.

History. One of the most common themes that emerged from the older adults' stories was the theme of history. The majority of references to history focused on the war, the Depression, and the conveniences that society now has acquired compared to those that were available in the past. Historical examples from the stories include:

> It may seem strange to you why anybody would run for 5 miles to get a popsicle, when in those days a popsicle was only worth 3 cents, but these were the days of the Great Depression and even 3 cents were hard to come by. (Book I, p. 52)

> The world of today has brought many wonderful changes. To hear from my Mother I had to wait three weeks for a letter to come by ship. My granddaughter talks to her Mother on the E-mail three times a week . . . I bless the technical world of today; it keeps her close to all of us. (Book I, p. 93)

> We grabbed a couple of blankets and Skipper . . . hurried down to Citadel Hill. From time to time the sky would light up with the glow from an explosion. I never did understand what all the minor explosions were about but they were definitely there throughout the night. (Halifax Explosion, December 1917; Book II, p. 28)

The use of specific historical examples in the older adults' stories supports the notion that grandparents undertake the role of the provider of history to the younger generation (Kornhaber, 1996; McKay & Caverly, 1995; Roberto & Skoglund, 1996). Through the use of concrete and personal experiences, as shared in the grandparents' stories, grandchildren may begin to interpret historical events as having had a personal impact on their own family. Since the younger generation has not been directly exposed to similar historical experiences such as the World Wars, grandparents may view their grandchildren as being "remote" to these particular experiences. This gap in historical knowledge between the generations may provide grandparents with the opportunity to enlighten their grandchildren about history through the act of writing. Similarly, grandchildren may become more interested in their grandparents' lives, and in historical events in general as they come to see their own personal, family connections to the past. Ultimately, understanding one's personal connection to the past may lead to the establishment of a new relationship between the two generations.

Family. Similar to the theme describing historical events, many older adults wrote to their grandchildren about their family history. Stories in which this theme emerged often described family members with whom the grandchild had not been acquainted. Examples of this theme include:

> You never knew your great grandparents, at least on your father's side, but I know you're interested. Since I love to tell stories, I thought I'd like to share with you a little walk down memory lane . . . My mother, Katie, your great Grandma, was the youngest of twelve children, born in 1884, pioneer times in the pioneer country of Grey County. (Book I, p. 22)

> [Grandpa] said that when he was a little boy, his grandfather, born in 1790 in a log cabin in our area, used to get up about four o'clock in the morning . . . This was the man whose portrait, darkened with age, hung in a heavy frame on the wall behind us. I had never had any idea that it represented a real person . . . I had heard almost nothing about our predecessors. (Book I, p. 62)

> I think that most of us during our lifetime wonder about our roots. We are curious about our ancestors, and from which set of parents we inherited certain traits, and set of values . . . my father, William Burton Allen, was a descendent of the Empire Loyalists . . . my other great-great-great-great-great-grandfather was one of the first Yorkshire settlers to emigrate to Canada, in 1772. (Book II, p. 132)

In these stories, the grandparents have used their writing as a means of communicating to the grandchild a portion of their family history. Within the descriptions of the family ancestors, older adults are able to describe to the grandchild where they see themselves as belonging within the larger family history. Writing about the family's history may thereby provide for some older adults the opportunity to develop a "coherent story about one's self." The older adult may also be able to use story writing as a means for evaluating one's life in relation to the larger family. As one author writes, "much of what I have preserved would otherwise have been lost forever. Knowledge of my forbearers' achievements has given me encouragement and strength when times were difficult" (Book I, p. 62). This writer appears to feel a sense of worth from being able to preserve and learn from the family history.

The stories discussing family history also provided the grandchildren with an opportunity to learn about people that they might not have personally known or whom they may have only "known" through hearing stories about them. Learning about one's family ethnic "roots," for example, appears to help grandchildren to establish their sense of identity—a common challenge encountered by young people (Giarrusso, Feng, Silverstein, & Bengtson, 2001). A sense of identity may be fostered as the grandchildren begin to see themselves in relation to the people described in the stories. Specifically, they may learn whom they resemble, or how they differ from their family, which thereby may help to solidify a sense of identity for the grandchild. This point is further discussed in the grandchildren section of the chapter.

Advice. Many of the stories contained advice that the older adults wanted to share with their grandchildren. These pieces of advice were typically life lessons they had learned and appeared to have the intention of trying to benefit the younger generation by expressing the knowledge they had gained. Examples from stories in which the theme of advice emerged include:

> Your entire life will be a path of choices . . . Don't be afraid to choose. Live the questions; that's the only way to the answers. (Book I, p. 79)

> I can honestly say that I have lived a richer life by engaging with my mistakes, I have come to realize that the one who never makes a mistake is likely someone who never takes a risk either . . . My story of mistakes is meant to help you avoid making the same ones. (Book I, p. 24)

> May you always shine and succeed in whatever you undertake. Also respect your teachers as they contribute so much to the moulding of your character, outlook, knowledge and progress of your life . . . (Book II, p. 79)

The grandparent literature suggests that grandchildren interpret one of the roles grandparents play as that of providing advice or wisdom to help them in their lives (Kornhaber, 1996). Based on the frequency of the theme of advice within the stories included in this study, it is evident that these older adults also saw their role as one in which they provide guidance and offer advice to the young. This sense of generativity or caring for the younger generation is an important developmental goal of later life, according to Erikson (Gatz & Zarit, 1999). Writing stories that offer advice is one method older adults may use to attain a sense of generativity (Norris et al., this volume).

In some of the stories containing advice, the grandparents attempted to describe the similarities between themselves and their grandchildren. Within their stories, the grandparents chose to write about life experiences or lessons that they felt their grandchildren would also encounter in their lifetime. By doing so, the older adults create a "common ground" where grandchildren and grandparents can potentially relate better to one another. Ultimately, the result of pointing out the similarities with the younger generation could be one of greater communication; that is, grandchildren may come to realize that their grandparents may have had similar life experiences and may be a valuable source of knowledge. For example, grandchildren may begin to see their grandparents as undertaking the role of the "teacher," where the grandparent provides advice to help the grandchild learn, and potentially to help them avoid making similar mistakes (McAdoo & McWright, 1994).

One technique for communicating the theme of advice was the use of figurative language. Life metaphors have been identified as helping to explain a difficult concept or to describe the grandparents' life experiences to the grandchild in a way that the grandchild can easily understand (Nussbaum & Bettini, 1994). Examples of life metaphors include:

> I see life as a cathedral—a personal cathedral with marvelous stained glass windows portraying a life story in all its many colours and with windows under construction . . . Your cathedral has a strong framework, because a loving family helps create the basic framework, but the design of the windows takes a lifetime, and that's the intensely personal part. The windows are constructed of your life's experience. (Book I, p. 79)

In this example, it is evident that the author is attempting to compare the qualities of a cathedral to life. Using this figurative device helps to emphasize to the grandchild that each person experiences different life events which contribute to the creation of one's individuality. Although the following quote comes from a story that was not selected for publication, it is given here as an example of an especially vivid metaphor:

> I would liken Life to learning alpine skiing, which I took up at 35 between children 3 or 4. With never a lesson I developed my own technique, not paral-

> lel exactly nor graceful, but I can dare the higher peaks and get down them unscathed. And so, my dear, I don't wish for you skiing without moguls. Else how . . . will you develop your technique to surmount life's problems.

In this example, the author uses the metaphor to explain to the grandchild the value of trying new experiences as well as the importance of developing one's own individual approach to life. The moguls are also used to represent life's challenges. Within this story, the grandparent is not only describing an event in her life that the grandchild may find interesting (i.e., that the grandparent learned to alpine ski at the age of 35), but is also providing advice or a life lesson to the grandchild at a more in-depth level. The use of metaphor is a creative writing technique that grandparents may use to capture their grandchild's attention, in order to transmit and share the information. Metaphor is one example of the complexity of language, which has been shown to increase in later adulthood (Adams-Price, 1998).

Life Story. Some of the older adults' stories described an event in their life that was significant to them. One example of a story that contained the theme of the life story began as follows: "It was a happy childhood in spite of the Depression of the early 1930's" (Book I, p. 85). As the story continues, the writer describes to her grandchild how she grew up in Ireland, later moved to Canada where she was married, and eventually raised the grandchild's mother. The grandmother concludes her story by writing:

> Telling you this little bit about the first 25 years or so of my life makes me wish . . . that I had asked my mother and father to tell me about their young lives and what their parents were like . . . Learn what you can from your parents and grandparents (Book I, p. 85).

The grandparent has described her life to her grandchild and, in so doing, has undertaken the process of reviewing her life as well. Writing this story has helped the grandparent realize the importance of knowing about one's family, and the grandchild is able to come to an understanding that there may be more to the grandparent's life than previously realized. This point is further exemplified in a story in which a grandmother describes an event in her younger life when she stole a lipstick from Mr. Brown's Variety Store and the life lesson she learned from doing so:

> To this day, as an adult, I am unable to examine any item in a store without an awareness of Mr. Brown standing beside me reminding me that no item is mine until I pay for it . . . My dear grandchild, you have your whole life ahead of you and you will face many challenges which will require you to make

choices. With the support of your loving family and community, I know you will make the right ones. (Book I, p. 58)

From this story, it is clear that the grandparent has learned from her mistakes and is using the medium of writing to relay a portion of her life story. Other research has confirmed the idea that values teaching is an important part of the grandparent role for many older adults (see Norris et al., this volume). The anecdote chosen by this grandparent is a clear example of an attempt to transmit a personally central value—honesty—in an intergenerational context. Many of the life stories we have discussed in this chapter contain such obvious values-teaching strategies, made palatable through entertaining or compelling narrative. The grandchild receiving the preceding story may especially benefit because the events took place when the grandparent was a child, helping the grandchild to relate to it, and because the tone of the story is light-hearted and engaging.

Two other examples of the life story are those in which the grandparent's experience in elementary school is described. One writer began his story describing how he was enrolled in school and the type of school he attended: "I was enrolled in the nearest school, the always reliable one-room schoolhouse with five full grades . . . All my early teachers were seventeen-year olds" (Book II, p. 139). The grandparent continues to describe his early experiences in school and concludes the story stating: "It was the end of my education as a child. From now on, I was a workingman earning his living, as many of my age, not quite thirteen" (Book II, p. 139). Another writer describes a similar topic. The writer begins the story stating, "I started to school when I was almost seven" (Book II, p. 85) and continues on to describe the school, her teacher, and her first experiences in a classroom environment. The grandparent concludes the story by describing how almost 50 years later she was reunited with her Grade one teacher when she then realized that her parents had been right about her teacher being one of the best. This quotation also exemplifies how new perspectives on one's life can be discovered through the recounting of experiences. Parenthetically, there is also here an implicit message to the grandchildren to listen to one's parents (advice).

Grandchildren Themes

A thematic analysis of the stories submitted by children and young adults was also conducted. The process was more difficult here than for the grandparents' and young adults' stories since the children tended to be descriptive rather than content-oriented in their writing. This supports Bamberg's claim

(1987; as cited in Juncos-Rabadan, 1996, p. 681) that descriptiveness is an "early stage in children's narrative development." The main themes that emerged within the stories are as follows: appreciation of what grandparents have done for them, family relationships, acknowledgment of losses in old age, and regard for grandparents never known or passed away.

Appreciation for What Grandparents Have Done. One common theme that emerged was that of the grandchild's appreciation for the support and encouragement grandparents offer them. For example, one grandchild wrote that her grandfather was "always there to support and to encourage . . . [her]" (Book I, p. 138). Similarly, in another example, one author wrote: "I want you to know that you have shaped my dreams for the future . . . I want you to know how much you have influenced my life . . . you will always be my hero" (Book II, p. 267). It is clear from these quotations that grandparents have a significant impact on their grandchildren's lives.

One recurring idea that appeared throughout some of the stories was that of appreciating grandparents for passing on knowledge, skills and values. It could be inferred that grandchildren may perceive grandparents as undertaking the role of "teacher," and see themselves as undertaking the role of "student" or "listener." For example, one grandchild wrote, "we both like old planes. A lot of what I know comes from Grandpa telling me facts and stories about World War II planes. Grandpa got me interested in planes" (Book II, p. 258). The grandchild in this example acknowledges the influence the grandfather has played in his developing interest in airplanes. This common interest in planes may serve to strengthen the grandparent-grandchild relationship as they may share stories with one another and learn from each other. A second example of the idea of grandparent as "teacher" is evident when a grandchild writes about her grandmother, "She taught me how to share, how to cook and many other things" (Book II, p. 233).

Another common role that grandchildren often attributed to their grandparents was that of providing a sense of fun and friendship. Examples of this idea can be seen in the following quotations:

> I decided to write about my Grandma. She was really cool. She loved to dance . . . Her favorite place to dance was on the coffee table (Book I, p. 116)

> Good to me/Really funny . . . Never yells . . . Make me laugh/Adores me (Book I, p. 118)

> I have learned that everyone has a story to tell, all you have to do is take time to listen and care . . . Thank you for not only being my Gran, but my friend as well (Book II, p. 248)

One example from a university-aged grandchild who also saw her grandparent in a "fun-loving" way was described in a story. She writes, "This is perhaps one of the best qualities of a relationship with a grandmother; namely the absence of the need to discipline" (Book I, p. 127). It is clear from these examples that many grandchildren associate their grandparents with "fun" and "friendship." Perhaps this fun-seeking/friendship role has contributed to the meaningful relationship that often develops between grandparents and grandchildren. Specifically, some grandchildren (as the university-aged grandchild points out) may recognize that grandparents and grandchildren can love one another in a similar manner that a parent loves a child but without the need to discipline, thereby contributing to the special relationship often shared between the two generations (see Norris et al., this volume, for a further discussion of the relationship-building role of intergenerational narrative).

Family Relationships. A second theme that emerged in some of the grandchildren's stories related to communicating the important role that grandparents play within the family unit. Examples include the following:

> Don't leave me here, all by myself, I love you too much, you know everyone needs you and myself.
>
> You can't go, we'll all be left in sorrow. (Book I, p. 101)
>
> She is the center of our family, the glue that keeps us all together and our moral leader . . . I do not know what would happen to our family if we ever lost her. (Book II, p. 303)

In these examples, the grandchild is emphasizing the significant influence that grandparents have within the family. Based on these quotations it would seem that the grandchildren see their grandparents as playing a central role in keeping the family unit together. Since grandparents also interpret one of their roles as being family oriented (Nussbaum & Bettini, 1994), it is clear that this message is being communicated to the grandchildren.

Some grandchildren recognized that their grandparents had helped provide them with a sense of identity and family history. This act of providing their grandchildren with a sense of who they are is a role that is consistent with past findings (see Kornhaber, 1996). In a letter addressed to her now deceased grandfather, the author explains the relief she feels at knowing where she has come from. She writes, "What matters now to me is that I know who you are and therefore to some extent who I am. I have a more complete image of myself and I like it" (Book I, p. 143). This quotation exemplifies the influence that grandparents can have on their grandchildren's lives. Knowing about the grandparent has helped this grandchild gain an understanding of who she is and of her family's past. Similarly, one of the younger children's stories reads:

> I wanted to write about my grandfather because I didn't know him and I wanted to know a little about him. I learned that even though my cousins and I didn't know him, we all have a piece of him in our own different way and that's better than any gift from a store! (Book II, p. 223)

In this example it is clear that through story writing, the grandchild has benefitted by the opportunity to learn about her grandfather, perhaps by asking other family members questions about him. By doing so, she has gained a sense of identity and connectedness to her grandfather as she is able to identify similarities between herself and her grandparent despite not knowing him personally. In addition to the connection the grandchild has made with her grandfather, she also may have inspired stories about him from other family members which has fostered a connection with the family as a whole.

Acknowledgment of Losses in Old Age. While research has suggested that grandchildren interpret the grandparent's role as one in which they provide advice to the young (Kornhaber, 1996), some of the university-aged grandchildren offered advice and support to their grandparents. Generally, this occurred because either the grandparent was ill or had lost his or her spouse. It is important to acknowledge that the grandparent/grandchild relationship is generally characterized by a reciprocal interaction, and therefore, providing advice is an act that can be performed by both generations (Norris & Tindale, 1994). Each generation holds the potential of learning and benefitting from one another. For example, one author points out some of the positive experiences that can emerge as one ages by writing qualities associated with the letters in the words "Growing Old": "I wish you would find some positive changes that come with getting older . . . G is for the experience of becoming a grandparent, R is for those that have earned our respect . . . W is for the wisdom acquired over the years" (Book I, p.157). Another example in which the grandchild tries to empathize with the grandparent occurs when one grandchild writes, "I know you are frustrated, but the process of aging is one that is confusing to everyone . . . I understand you have been through a lot of tough times during your life" (Book I, p. 138). Regardless of whether it is the grandparent or the grandchild who is offering the advice or support, the intentions seem to be well-meaning. Specifically, each generation, through writing, is attempting to express their concern for one another. In each case, story writing is an attempt to provide the other generation with support, guidance, and encouragement.

Regard for Grandparents Never Known or Passed Away. Throughout many of the stories, grandchildren expressed their feelings about grandparents who have passed away or who were never known. One university-aged grandchild has come to the realization that she does not "believe [that] people realize how much an influence grandparents can be, but until they don't have them anymore they will not appreciate the enormous contributions they make in their lives" (Book I, p. 143). This quotation exemplifies an appreciation of the extent to which grandparents affect their children's lives. Other examples include: "You're why I'm alive right now, But you died and I ask how? . . . but . . . you'll always be with me" (Book I, p. 117) and "Others think you're gone/but I know you are still here" (Book I, p. 140). These stories, that are written by the two different grandchild age groups, demonstrate how grandchildren may cope with the loss of a grandparent. Specifically, the grandchildren have come to the conclusion that despite the death of their grandparent, the grandparent will continue to live on. Perhaps this belief that the grandparent continues to live on even though others may not believe it (as one grandchild's story points out), demonstrates the special connection grandparents and grandchildren have with one another. Also, grandchildren may feel comforted in knowing that grandparents will live on in their memories because of the stories that have been shared between them or from stories told about their grandparents by other family members. For example:

> A lot of the things that I remember about my grandpa are stories that I hear and not vivid memories (Book II, p. 279)

> [T]he only things I know about Grandpa are the stories his children tell about him . . . Often when we go to visit Grandma, her sons and daughters stand around the kitchen telling stories about the old days. (Book II, p. 303)

In these two examples, the importance of telling stories is evident. Not only can stories connect grandparents and grandchildren in present-day life, but other family members can provide grandchildren with an opportunity to connect with grandparents they might not have known by sharing stories about them with the grandchildren. Other examples in which grandparents are associated with stories include:

> My grandpa likes to tell stories of when he was a kid and when he was working in the navy. (Book II, p. 234)

They tell you stories/While you fall asleep with them hugging you tight. (Book II, p. 250)

This association between grandparents and stories is seen often in the ways the grandchildren describe their grandparents as storytellers. Sharing the stories is one way that each generation can relate to one another, and reinforces the grandchildren's perception that their "memories" of the grandparent will live on. Perhaps the grandparent's stories serve as "memories" of the grandparent to the grandchild that can be kept and shared even after grandparents pass away.

Some of the younger grandchildren expressed their feelings regarding the absence of grandparents. One story illustrates how the lack of a relationship with grandparents can affect a grandchild: "As a child, I remember feeling a void created by the absence of an extended family . . . a grandparent with whom I could have contact . . . the geographical distance between us prevented the formation of an emotional closeness" (Book I, p. 127). In this example, the sadness that the grandchild feels at not knowing her grandparent is evident. On the other hand, one young grandchild wrote: "Doesn't it feel good knowing that they are always there? Whether they are next door or miles away, they are always there for you" (Book II, p. 235). In this example, the grandchild comments on the dependable relationship that grandparents and grandchildren can have with one another despite geographical distance. It is clear that the nature and quality of the grandparent-grandchild relationship can vary from family to family. However, it seems that while the grandparent-grandchild relationship can vary, the stories in this study commonly reflected the valuable influence that grandparents can have in their grandchildren's lives.

Benefits of Story Writing

The time-honored reason for writing letters to family members has been to overcome geographical distances separating authors and recipients. Although the authors in our project took this purpose for granted, grandparents and occasionally grandchildren did explicitly identify within their stories numerous benefits of exchanging written stories and letters (see Table 16.1). Some grandparents explicitly stated that the purpose of their stories was to preserve or pass down a legacy. Writing is an effective medium for preserving legacies because it is less likely that the story will be misconstrued or forgotten. Knowing that the legacy will continue to be passed on may serve to strengthen family relationships, as each generation understands and continues to pass on

TABLE 16.1
Benefits of Story Writing

Type	*Evidence from Stories*
Overcome Geographical Distance [Implicit acceptance of time-honored role of letter writing]	
Legacy	"I want you to know this [importance of Prayer] since you are now at the age that I was when my Mother left this legacy to me" (Book I, p. 74). "I want to be faithful to the legacy that was passed on to me, and I now pass on to you, which is your rightful heritage" (Book II, p. 132).
Create New Connections	"I can appreciate the confusion you feel about your future . . . Although more than fifty years separate me from a situation similar to yours, I can remember the feelings, if not all the details, that accompanied my path to independence from family life" (*Book I; p. 79*)—(attempts to identify with the grandchild which may lead to discussion as to how the grandparent reacted to similar situations currently being faced by the grandchild.) "You decide when my grandchild is old enough for my letter (Written to the unborn grandchild's parents; Book II, p. 32).
Express Unsaid Feelings	". . . feel that writing to each other has made us closer because I can write things to you that are hard to say in person. You make me feel special the way only you can" (Book I, p. 157). "The hardest part of dealing with your disease is that you no longer remember who I am. I guess that is why I am writing you this letter . . . this is the only way I can tell you how much I love you" (Book I, p. 138).
Future Opportunities to Converse	"I have quite a few [stories] compiled in a loose-leaf binder. I'll let you read them sometime, if you want to" (Book I, p. 85). "I would like you to think about this letter, and I will ask you later what you think of what I've said" (Book I, p. 10).
Opportunity to Express Self	"Your tenth birthday is almost here and it is a special milestone for us all and I think this is a good time to talk to you about WORDS" (Book I, p. 10) "I won't go into detail about what took place when. . . . I'll let my story speak for itself" (Book II, p. 20).
Surpass Time	(A letter written to be given to a grandchild in ten years when he is old enough to understand): "It must be hard for you to accept the fact that the Grandpa, whom you loved and had fun with, who read to you and played games and catch with you, has disappeared into an old man in a wheelchair who has difficulty remembering any one" (Book I, p. 54). "To my yet unborn grandchildren who will someday face the world with all its challenges" (Book I, p. 58).

family history. Story writing also serves as a means to create new connections and strengthen existing ones between the generations (Norris et al., this volume; Pratt & Fiese, this volume). For the participants in this study, writing provided the opportunity to express thoughts or feelings that might otherwise have been left unsaid. For some, writing may be a more comfortable form of communication, or may be perceived as the only means to convey one's message or have one's message "heard" by the receiver. Being able to express oneself can also have therapeutic value (Schuster, 1998). As well, story writing might lead to future opportunities for the writer and the reader to converse. For example, some stories pointed out a common interest between the generations; others created opportunities for the reader to take an active role in the relationship, as the story posed questions or invited later interaction based on the story. Finally, some grandparents transcended time in writing for the future to unborn, or very young grandchildren; some grandchildren wrote in memory of grandparents (sometimes never known).

Summary

Writing offers grandparents and grandchildren the opportunity to express themselves, as well as to establish a link with the other generation. Nussbaum and Bettini (1994) found that sharing stories in their study was primarily "unidirectional from grandparent to grandchild" (p. 78). In our study, however, both groups succeeded in connecting across the generations. The grandparents' stories focused on the themes of history, family, advice, and life story, while the grandchildren's stories expressed appreciation, family, acknowledgment of age-related losses, and regard for absent grandparents. Intergenerational writing can strengthen the grandparent-grandchild relationship by supplementing face-to-face communication and by overcoming obstacles of geography and time.

GENERAL DISCUSSION

Intergenerational Connections and Life Span Development

Intergenerational communication through writing enabled grandparents to pass on the lessons learned through their life experiences. Family stories serve to foster development and to regulate behavior and affect (Gatz & Zarit, 1999; McAdams et al., 1997; Pratt & Fiese, this volume). Through story-writing, grandparents were able to strive toward two important developmental life stage goals, those of generativity and wisdom (Erikson & Erikson, 1998). Conveying aspects of one's life story to a grandchild directs an older person's attention to the generative aspects of one's life and thereby strengthens a sense of contribution and connection with contemporary society. Pasupathi (2001) argues for the benefits of telling one's life story for different audiences and the role of the story recipient in shaping the sense of memory and self. Sharing life stories of who we are is one of the key strategies outlined by Kenyon (2002) for expressing ordinary wisdom; both teller and recipient grow from such expressions.

Young grandchildren reveal in their stories concerns with reliable and trusting relationships, while older grandchildren demonstrate interest in the identity issues of adolescence and early adulthood (Erikson & Erikson,1998). Committing their thoughts and concerns to paper and sharing them with grandparents may also facilitate psychosocial development in children moving from one life stage to another. As well, the grandparents' own identity can be strengthened by the written offerings of appreciation for the ways in which they have made a difference in their grandchildren's lives.

On a broader level, we would argue that fostering the grandparent-grandchild relationship through the exchange of letters and stories can contribute to improving understanding of aging issues in general. Many scholars have acknowledged the central role of relationships with grandparents in the development of positive aging attitudes (Kornhaber, 1996; Williams & Nussbaum, 2001). Improving this key intergenerational relationship can enhance intergenerational communication beyond the family for both young and old (Ryan, Meredith, MacLean, & Orange, 1995). The following story by a 9-year-old grandchild exemplifies this learning:

> My grandparents are wonderful. I have two grandmas and one grandpa. So three, but I did have four. I had one more grandpa. His name was Russel. He died when I was five. All I remember is that he used to call me his little Pixy Girl. I know he loved me just like I loved him. I love all my grandparents. My dad's mom Grams helps me very much. She's the one that taught me how to hold a fork and knife. Then there's my dad's dad. He is very nice, old, but wise and loving. You can't forget my mom's mom! She is very smart, old, but young in a way. I do not mind what they look like. I know I will always love them, it's just the way life goes. (Book II, p. 238)

Value of Intergenerational Writing

As compared to storytelling, story writing offers some key advantages. Sharing stories beyond the face-to-face situation extends the range of strategies for fostering the grandparent-grandchild relationship, which may be undermined in contemporary society by waning interest in traditions and heritage and by a fascination with what is new and modern. Reliance on the telephone for social connections across geographic distances emphasizes superficial communication as compared to traditional letter writing. The increasing availability of e-mail to all generations opens the way for a resurgence of intergenerational communication through the printed word—both the quick and spontaneous and the longer, more reflective message (Harwood, 2000). In cases where the parents are divorced, the written mode may be especially useful to grandparents and grandchildren because this type of communication relies much less on the parents for the arrangement of face-to-face meetings (Williams & Nussbaum, 2001).

The printed word can overcome the limitations of geography and time. As well, older adults with hearing impairments or other difficulties in oral communication can be expected to enjoy a special advantage in developing a writing relationship with grandchildren. In our study, participants wrote to family members far away or who lived only in their minds. Recorded family stories are important assets within families because of the changing interests associated with life span development. All too often, by the time we want to "hear" the stories, the tellers are no longer available to us. In addition, the writing of stories is a work of art, an accomplishment which contributes to an older person's sense of remaining active and productive and which fosters a young person's burgeoning sense of competence and participation in the world into which they are growing (Koch, 1977; Schuster, 1998). Moreover, Schuster (1998) underscored the way in which recognition beyond the family for older persons' writings transformed relationships within the family.

Facilitating Story Writing

The purpose of making our two collections of intergenerational stories available to the public is to inspire young and old with the feasibility and potential of exchanging stories with younger and older members of their own families. Grandparents might consider writing their life stories (memoirs) for the family in a series of short texts, sent to individual recipients or to all family members over a period of time. This option not only seems more manageable to a number of potential authors, but also can create a more receptive and responsive audience. Directly involving grandchildren in the preparation of a recorded family/life story can also enrich intergenerational connections. Likewise, grandchildren might be encouraged to consider their correspondence with a grandparent in terms of a series of letters/stories that might build into a larger work.

It is also important to consider facilitating the writing of stories for older adults who cannot undertake this task on their own. Many communities offer courses on memoir writing, and healthy seniors often form mutual support groups to encourage each other in this endeavor. Koch (1977), Schuster (1998), and John (1992) have shown the value of assisting nursing home residents to write their stories or to create poems. We have begun to explore the merit of writing down aspects of the life story of individuals with dementia to foster conversational remembering and to help caregiving staff become acquainted with them (Hagens, Beaman, & Ryan, 2003; Ryan, Schindel Martin, & Beaman, in press; Thorsheim & Roberts, 2000). Older adults with visual impairment would require some assistance to put their stories into writing, either through transcriptions of their tape recordings or accessible computer hardware/software. The written mode offers a special advantage for grandparents whose grandchildren no longer speak the family tongue, as illustrated in *The Bonesetter's Daughter* (Tan, 2001) by the fictional account of a translator being hired to make an older person's memoirs accessible to younger family members.

Future Research and Conclusion

Future research concerning individual differences in themes would be of interest, with attention to the role of age and gender among both grandparents and grandchildren, either as authors or as recipients (see Nussbaum & Bettini, 1994; Williams & Nussbaum, 2001). It should be remembered that the grandparents and grandchildren involved in our project were predominantly female, perhaps influencing the nature of our findings; "men are more likely to write about external things, while women are more likely to be personal and write about internal states" (Ray, 2000, p. 78). In addition, our participants, particularly the grandparents, were highly selected volunteers in keeping with our goal to analyze effective writing samples. To complement our procedure, greater variation in quality and content perhaps could be observed by collecting writing samples in a more controlled setting. Pratt and Norris (1999), for example, reported on the use of written narrative as a means of exploring a wide variety of themes in the moral and social reasoning of older adults. It would also be particularly valuable to recruit grandparent-grandchild pairs for a study in which they would write for each other over a period of time. With such a longitudinal design, it would be possible to track the development of themes across each pair over the evolution of their correspondence.

We conclude in the words of a grandchild author who demonstrates the value of storywriting between the generations:

> Memories are neatly stored and cherished;
> Then retrieved when apart
> To re-live the special moments.
> This bond between grandparent and grandchild—
> Forever sealed in love. (Book I, p. 9)

ACKNOWLEDGMENT

The authors express their appreciation for partial support for this research by Grant No. 410-2000-1358 from the Social Sciences and Humanities Research Council of Canada. We also gratefully acknowledge the assistance of Gail Elliot, Alan Bishop, Katie Allen, Miranda Beamer, Marie Savundranayagam, and Amanda Beaman.

REFERENCES

Adams-Price, C. (1998). Aging, writing, and creativity. In C. Adams-Price (Ed.), *Creativity and successful aging* (pp. 269–287). New York: Springer.

Brussoni, M. J., & Boon, S. D. (1998). Grandparental impact in young adults' relationships with their closest grandparents: The role of relationship strength and emotional closeness. *International Journal of Aging and Human Development, 46,* 267–286.

Erikson, E. H., & Erikson, J. M. (1998). *Life cycle completed.* New York: W. W. Norton.

Gatz, M., & Zarit, S. H. (1999). A good old age: Paradox or possibility? In V. L. Bengtson & K. W. Schaie (Eds.), *Handbook of theories of aging* (pp. 396–416). New York: Springer Publishing.

Giarrusso, R., Feng, D., Silverstein, M., & Bengtson, V. L. (2001). Grandparent-adult grandchild affection and consensus: Cross-generational and cross-ethnic comparisons. *Journal of Family Issues, 22,* 456–477.

Giarrusso, R., Silverstein, M., & Bengtson, V. L. (1996). Family complexity and the grandparent role. *Generations: Journal of the American Society on Aging, 20*(1), 17–23.

Hagens, C., Beaman, A., & Ryan, E. B. (in press). Reminiscing, poetry writing, and remembering boxes: Personhood-centered communication with cognitively impaired older adults. *Activities, Adaptation, and Aging.*

Harwood, J. (2000). Communication media use in the grandparent-grandchild relationship. *Journal of Communication, 50*(4), 56–78.

Harwood, J., & Lin, M.-C. (2000). Affiliation, pride, exchange, and distance in grandparents' accounts of relationships with their college-aged grandchildren. *Journal of Communication, 50*(3), 31–47.

John, M. T. (Ed.). (1992). *Story writing in a nursing home: A patchwork of memories.* Binghamton, NY: Haworth Press.

Juncos-Rabadan, O. (1996). Narrative speech in the elderly: Effects of age and education on telling stories. *International Journal of Behavioral Development, 19,* 669–685.

Kalliopuska, M. (1994). Relations of retired people and their grandchildren. *Psychological Reports, 75,* 1083–1088.

Kennedy, G. E. (1990). College students' expectations of grandparent and grandchild role behaviors. *The Gerontologist, 30,* 43–48.

Kenyon, G. M. (1996). The meaning/value of personal storytelling. In J. Birren, G. Kenyon, J. Ruth, J. Schroots, & T. Svensson (Eds.), *Aging and biography: Explorations in adult development* (pp. 25–37). New York: Springer Publishing Company.

Kenyon, G. M. (2002). Guided autobiography: In search of ordinary wisdom. In G. E. Rowles & N. E. Schoenberg (Eds.), *Qualitative gerontology: A contemporary perspective* (2nd ed., pp. 37–50). New York: Springer.

Kivnick, H. Q. (1983). Dimensions of grandparenthood meaning: Deductive conceptualization and empirical derivation. *Journal of Personality and Social Psychology, 44,* 1056–1068.

Koch, K. (1977). *I never told anybody: Teaching poetry writing in a nursing home.* New York: Random House.

Kornhaber, A. (1996). *Contemporary grandparenting.* Thousand Oaks, CA: Sage.

Luborsky, M. R. (1994). The identification and analysis of themes and patterns. In J. F. Gubrium & A. Sankar (Eds.), *Qualitative methods in aging research* (pp. 189–210). Thousand Oaks, CA: Sage.

Mead, M. (1972). *Blackberry winter: My earlier years.* New York: William Morrow & Company.

McAdams, D., Diamond, A., St. Aubin, E., & Mansfield, E. (1997). Stories of commitment: The psychosocial construction of generative lives. *Journal of Personality and Social Psychology, 72,* 678–694.

McAdoo, H. P., & McWright, L. A. (1994). The roles of grandparents: The use of proverbs in value transmission. *Activities, Adaptations and Aging, 19,* 27–38.

McKay, V., & Caverly, S. (1995). Relationships in later life: The nature of inter- and intragenerational ties among grandparents, grandchildren, and adult siblings. In J. Nussbaum & J. Coupland (Eds.), *Handbook of communication and aging research* (pp. 207–226). Mahwah, NJ: Lawrence Erlbaum Associates.

Mergler, N., & Goldstein, M. (1983). Why are there old people—Senescence as biological and cultural preparedness for the transmission of information. *Human Development, 26,* 72–90.

Norris, J. E., Pratt, M. W., & Kuiack, S. (in press). Parent-child relations in adulthood: An intergenerational family systems perspective. In L. Kucznyski (Ed.), *Handbook of dynamics in parent-child relations.* Thousand Oaks, CA: Sage.

Norris, J. E., & Tindale, J. A. (1994). *Among generations: The cycle of adult relationships.* San Francisco: Freeman.

Nussbaum, J., & Bettini, L. (1994). Shared stories of the grandparent-grandchild relationship. *International Journal of Aging and Human Development, 39,* 67–80.

Pasupathi, M. (2001). The social construction of the personal past and its implications for adult development. *Psychological Bulletin, 127,* 651–672.

Pratt, M. W., & Norris, J. E. (1999). Moral development in maturity: Life-span perspectives on the processes of successful aging. In T. M. Hess & F. Blanchard-Fields (Eds.), *Social cognition and aging* (pp. 291–317). San Diego, CA: Academic Press.

Pratt, M. W., & Robins, S. (1991). That's the way it was: Age differences in the structure and quality of adults' personal narratives. *Discourse Processes, 14,* 73–85.

Ray, R. E. (2000). *Beyond nostalgia: Aging and life story writing.* Charlottesville: University Press of Virginia.

Roberto, K. A., Allen, K. R., & Blieszner, R. (2001). Grandfathers' perceptions and expectations of relationships with their adult grandchildren. *Journal of Family Issues, 22,* 407–426.

Roberto, K. A., & Skoglund, R. R. (1996). Interactions with grandparents and great-grandparents: A comparison of activities, influences, and relationships. *International Journal of Aging and Human Development, 43,* 107–117.

Ryan, E. B., Elliot, G. M., & Anas, A. P. (Eds.). (2000). *Exchanges between us: More intergenerational connections.* Hamilton, ON: McMaster Centre for Gerontological Studies.

Ryan, E. B., Elliot, G. M., & Meredith, S. D. (Eds.). (1999). *From me to you: Intergenerational connections through storytelling.* Hamilton, ON: McMaster Centre for Gerontological Studies.

Ryan, E. B., Meredith, S. D., MacLean, M. J., & Orange, J. B. (1995). Changing the way we talk with elders: Promoting health using the communication enhancement model. *International Journal of Aging and Human Development, 41,* 89–107.

Ryan, E. B., Schindel Martin, L., & Beaman, A. (in press). Communication strategies to promote spiritual well-being among people with dementia. In A. Meier, P. VanKatwyk, & T. S. J. O'Connor (Eds.), *Spirituality, health and pastoral counselling.* Waterloo: Wilfrid Laurier University Press.

Schuster, E. (1998). A community bound by words: Reflections on a nursing home writing group. *Journal of Aging Studies, 12,* 137–147.

Silverstein, M., Giarrusso, R., & Bengtson, V. L. (1998). Intergenerational solidarity and the grandparent role. In M. E. Szinovacz (Ed.), *Handbook on grandparenthood* (pp. 144–158). Westport, CT: Greenwood Press.

Strom, R. D., Strom, S. K., Wang, C. M., Shen, Y. L., Griswold, D., Chan, H. S., & Yang, C. Y. (1999). Grandparents in the United States and the Republic of China: A comparison of generations and cultures. *International Journal of Aging and Human Development, 49,* 279–317.

Szinovacz, M. E. (Ed.). (1998). *Handbook on grandparenthood.* Westport, CT: Greenwood.

Tan, A. (2001). *The bonesetter's daughter.* New York: Ballantine.

Thorsheim, H., & Roberts, B. (2000). *I REMEMBER WHEN . . . Activity ideas to help people reminisce.* Forest Knolls, CA: Elder Books.

Tomlin, A. M. (1998). Grandparents' influences on grandchildren. In M. E. Szinovacz (Ed.), *Handbook of grandparenthood* (pp. 159–170). Westport, CT: Greenwood Press.

Williams, A., & Nussbaum, J. F. (2001). *Intergenerational communication across the life span.* Mahwah, NJ: Lawrence Erlbaum Associates.

PART VI

Conclusions and Future Directions

17

Metaphors and Meanings of Family Stories: Integrating Life Course and Systems Perspectives on Narrative

Barbara H. Fiese
Syracuse University

Michael W. Pratt
Wilfrid Laurier University

> *Wherever a story comes from, whether it is a familiar myth or a private memory, the retelling exemplifies the making of a connection from one pattern to another. . . . Our species thinks in metaphors and learns through stories.*
>
> —Mary Catherine Bateson, 1994, p. 11

Taken together, the chapters in this book weave a tale of connecting patterns of family influence across the life span. And a complex tale it is indeed. Family stories provide messages of expected conduct, lessons learned, and relationship formation. The thematic content of these stories covers a wide range of common experiences, such as visits to Grandma, what to do when rules are broken, how to repair hurt feelings, and responding to peer pressure. In this regard, the contents of family stories serve as metaphors of the challenges faced by families in raising children, becoming partners, and growing old. Family stories extend beyond the messages relayed, however. The act of engaging others in the storytelling process is a context in which culture is conveyed and cognitive development supported.

In this final chapter, we structure our summary of the issues raised by these excellent contributions around two key questions: What can family stories tell us about development? What can narratives tell us about families? In part purposely structured by the selection of chapters for this book, we present a life-span perspective on how this collection of stories reflects a developmental sequence revolving around the content and medium through which stories are conveyed and the interplay between coherence and the depiction of meaning and relationships.

WHAT CAN FAMILY STORIES TELL US ABOUT DEVELOPMENT?

Childhood Stories: Reminiscence and Everyday Relationships

The stories told between parents and young children typically involve retellings of shared experiences. The early construction of family stories is based, in part, on a recounting of memories that sets the stage, much later in adolescence, for creating meaningful life stories (McAdams, 2001). Peterson and McCabe (this volume) describe classic prototypes of what makes a good story. Much like a good piece of music, there is a building up of tension with a crescendo, followed sometimes by a sweet ending. Indeed, the rhythm of story telling is no doubt established prior to the time the child can become an active participant in recalling memories. The rising tone and quality of mothers' speech to young infants parallels the rise and fall of classic storylines (Stern, 2002).

Although engaging the child in recounting personal memories may be a universal experience, there are important variations by parent style and culture. Peterson and McCabe (this volume) demonstrate that the degree to which families are comfortable with storytelling varies considerably and that this variability is directly related to the child's developing narrative competence. Children who are exposed to narrative environments rich in elaborative details are more likely to become good storytellers, in comparison to peers whose parents tend to switch topics rather than encourage elaboration. Fivush and colleagues (this volume) also detail differences in parent and family narrative style that may be related not only to the child's linguistic competence, but also to his or her developing emotional resilience.

When we consider how children are enculturated into storytelling partnerships, cultural styles of engagement become even more prominent. Fung, Miller, and Lin (this volume) point to how the role of listener is often downplayed or ignored in Western cultures. Yet, in Confucian cultures, as studied by Fung, Miller, and Lin (this volume) and Wang (this volume), to be a good storyteller means that you must first be a good listener.

There are several meanings associated with these childhood reminiscence processes. First, relationships are built through these everyday exchanges that are regulated in part by gender and culture (e.g., Wang, this volume). Parents in more individualistic Western cultures, according to Wang, foster different kinds of reminiscence processes and content, highlighting the autonomous individual, than do parents in collectivistic, Confucian cultures, where the child's network of relations with others is emphasized instead. The types of stories told to daughters and sons may also differ under some circumstances. Inherent in the recollection of everyday memories is the opportunity for problem solving and learning the lessons of growing up. Much of the back-and-forth exchanges reported in these first few chapters of the book include engaging children around such themes as "How did you feel?" and "What would you do next time?" The metaphors of these stories fall along the lines of how to experience as well as behave and act in the culture in which you are raised.

Story coherence is somewhat of a background to the evolving partnerships that are created through active storytelling. There is no doubt a strong cognitive and developmental component to this phase. Benson (1996) has demonstrated that although children can piece together the elements of story structure (e.g., beginning, middle, and end) when as young as 4 years of age, the ability to create a complex plot with intentions and resolution of inconsistencies is not fully developed until later. This does not preclude, however, the possibility that exposure to coherent vs. incoherent accounts influences younger children. Scaffolding effects were mentioned throughout the early chapters in this book. For example, Peterson and McCabe (this volume) report that notions of causality are introduced by parents in conversations 5 months prior to children's own use of causal statements in their recounts. Fivush and colleagues (this volume) point out that there are individual differences in the ways in which parents and children enter into co-constructed narrative exchanges. Families who build the narrative together may model coherence through synthesizing ideas and taking into account different perspectives.

On the other hand, narratives characterized by disharmonious interactions disrupt the flow of the narrative and may ultimately provide inconsistent and incoherent models to their children. The developmental course of incoherence then may become cemented in attachment relationships between parent and child, as described by Sher-Censor and Oppenheim (this volume).

Children who establish secure relationships during infancy are more likely to organize their narratives in a way that supports resolution of conflicts in a coherent manner. Thus, the foundation of a secure and responsive parent-child relationship may influence the degree to which children are able to create coherent accounts of interpersonal relationships in their discourse. Similarly, Robinson and Eltz (this volume) show how some patterns of parent living arrangements and less functional caregiving in a vulnerable sample of poor families can be predictive of more aggressive and dysfunctional narratives that young children display in their discussions about standard relationship situations. This chapter also hints at the important but under-studied role that fathers may play in these families in shaping children's social narrative resources.

Adolescence: Dialogues and Identity

During adolescence, the medium of family storytelling is centered on dialogues between adolescent and adults. Over time, the dialogue becomes more internalized and lays the foundation for a personal life story. The content of these stories reflects the personal challenges experienced by contemporary adolescents, as well as adults' investment in forewarning adolescents of potential dangers ahead. This process is clearly illustrated in the chapter presented by Arnold and colleagues. The values and lessons expressed in family stories need to percolate. "Turning points" in life stories become such through personal reflection and evaluation. An essential feature of this process is how the earlier exchanges between parent and child become internally reconstructed or "owned" by the adolescent over time. As was the case in parent-child reminiscences, there are individual differences in how parents and adolescents engage in this process. Adolescents whose turning point episodes included active interest on the part of parents, either through providing "useful advice" or just being a sounding board, were more likely to internalize parental values. Adolescents, on the other hand, who felt their stories cut short by parents, were more likely to author personal stories of disappointment and unresolved tensions between parent and child. The parallels between these narrative processes and more traditional descriptions of parenting style are evident, and were supported by the data. Adolescents whose stories showed that they experienced their parents as responsive and authoritative were better adjusted 4 years later than adolescents who experienced their parents as dictatorial and unresponsive to their individual needs in the stories that they told.

Coherence is an essential regulating feature of this phase. The chapter presented by Dunbar and Grotevant (this volume) is a complex picture of how variability in coherence defines identity types. Adolescents who are able to synthesize different elements of their life into a coherent story have a more integrated sense of self. It is interesting to note that the story need not be completely resolved and in fact can be a work in progress. The essential feature is the process of pulling together and considering the different elements of the story to construct a coherent whole. Adolescents who create a short story, summarizing elements without considering different perspectives, have missed an opportunity to examine their lives and present a picture of an unexamined identity. As pointed out by Dunbar and Grotevant, there are parallels between the relative coherence of adolescent stories and more traditional measures of adolescent identity (Marcia, Waterman, Matteson, Archer, & Orlofsky, 1993). However, the metaphors are different. From a narrative perspective, the metaphors of adolescent identity revolve not around what they did, as much as how they have made sense of their experiences. In this regard, adolescent identity is considered an active process of digesting and interpreting experiences that take into account parent voice, peer influences, affect, and the relation among domains of identity. Putting together a life story is work! Accordingly, an adolescent's story of identity may be complex, multifaceted, and well integrated, or disjointed, one-sided, and disconnected.

The importance of perspective taking and building a repertoire of relationship experiences is evident in the work on parents' stories of their earlier drug involvement presented by Thorne and colleagues. The use of vignettes of possible storied scenarios presented the opportunity to consider hypothetical alternatives in this charged real-life situation, asking the question, "What if this message were relayed to you?" The fact that the stories involved an illegal (but believable) activity highlights the sensitive nature of topics exchanged between parents and children. In this example, adolescents are asked to consider their parents engaging in activities that they have been warned against themselves. Whereas during childhood, personal transgressions focus on the child's behavior, during adolescence there is a greater opportunity to examine transgressions of the older generation. Attention to how these stories could be potentially co-constructed in real dialogues within the family (as in the case of childhood reminiscences) may shed further light on whether the lesson is learned or rejected. Trust and security in the adolescent-parent relationship may very well affect how these revelations of personal transgressions are received.

The Thorne et al. chapter is especially interesting because it points up the challenges of actually formulating family stories, what we have referred to here as the practicing aspects of storytelling (e.g., Reiss, 1989). Some story content may be problematic or dangerous for either the teller or the listener, and may damage the participants if not presented appropriately, or even, perhaps, if presented at all. There is a need, in other words, to attune the story to both the teller and the listener and to their relationship, and this matter may become more salient in adolescence than childhood, when the listeners are all the more ready to re-interpret the story through their own lenses. Stories about parental transgressions such as drug use thus highlight the problematic role of storytelling within the developing family context.

Adulthood: Relationship Histories

The section of the book dedicated to adults as partners and parents, and the conveyance of family stories, centers largely around depicting close relationships. Many of these stories tend to be prosaic, reflecting everyday events and routines within the family and the task of building intimate relationships within the newly constituted family. Dickstein (this volume) describes how the stories told about marriage reflect how adults value relationships and recognize their influence on other areas of family functioning. Although this chapter is presented from an attachment perspective, there are clear overlaps with Erikson's proposition that this is the period of intimacy versus isolation (Erikson, 1950). Erikson proposes that during this period, adults seek mutual intimate relationships that accommodate cycles of work, procreation, and recreation.

Fiese and Bickham (this volume) report that the stories shared by parents with their children include themes of work, being close to others, and how families spend leisure time together. The meanings implicit in these stories appear to include not only how to behave (as in the case of personal reminiscences), but also the importance of building relationships over time. The kinship ties identified in the Fiese and Bickham chapter highlight how, through stories, children are exposed to genealogical as well as geographical references. Through narratives, a scrapbook of family relationships is created that serves as a reference for making sense of personal relationships. Implicit in Erikson's stage of intimacy is the notion that through creating close relationships, we avoid self-absorption and isolation. Thus, family stories may be used to convey what to expect in close relationships, how to value them as sources of support, and to consider how being in a family insures membership in a meaningful group. Not surprisingly, the next stage is directed toward how to continue this process and invest in the next generation.

McAdams (this volume) eloquently describes how stories of generativity include not only messages of suffering but also of human kindness. At the core of these stories, there appears to be a Rousseau-like message that concern for others is inherently human. This concern does not come without cost, however. Oftentimes these messages are ones of suffering and sacrifice. Yet, at the core is a message of human kindness and being able to rely on others in times of need, as well as the capacity for redemption and growth that comes out of these times of trial. In this regard, these tales of generativity extend the attachment theme to include expectations that even outside of intimate relationships, within the wider social world, there is a common good and there are expectations for satisfying relationships. It is greater use of this type of plot that was found to distinguish more generative adult storytellers. Perhaps this is good news, in that those who have a more optimistic and hopeful view of the world may be the most avid message carriers to the next generation (e.g., Pratt, Norris, Arnold, & Filyer, 1999).

Coherence comes into play in two different ways in this set of stories. First is narrative coherence and the structure of the stories being told. Clearly, the work reported by Dickstein (this volume) suggests that the manner in which close relationships are described is linked to how family members interact with each other. Similar to the results reported in childhood reminiscence and the adolescent identity literature, stories that are well organized, resolve contradictory information, and synthesize different elements are related to more positive relationships and functioning overall. The process of building a coherent story of family relationships potentially serves as background to the types of stories that are told and expectations for rewarding or disappointing interactions.

The second type of coherence evident in this collection of stories is biographical, as pointed out by McAdams (this volume). Typically considered as involving the synthesizing of experiences of one's own life in adolescence (e.g., Habermas & Bluck, 2000), biographical coherence may also include reflections on others' experiences that are close to you. Dickstein's (this volume) assessment of marital attachment includes an analysis of whether the stories of marital relationships include recognition that forming such relationships is an important aspect of the life story. Couples differed in the degree to which they viewed their relationship as a work in progress and evolving over time. For some couples there was the clear recognition that marriage is a journey involving intimacy and personal challenges. For others, marriage is seen as something that "just happened" and you "do your own thing," perhaps in spite of the relationship. Fiese and Bickham's (this volume) discussion of family stories includes an appreciation for how parental experiences may indirectly affect the socialization of children along gendered lines, and what it means to grow up as a boy or as a girl. Indeed, they found that the role of other family members' experiences in activities and rituals may be more central in the stories of the family that are told by mothers to daughters, perhaps one element in the process of socializing females as the "kin-keepers" within the family system (Putney & Bengtson, 2001).

As well, the creation of biographical coherence happens in cultural context. Fung, Miller, and Lin (this volume) remind us that the roles and domains inherent in the storytelling process contribute to our biographical stance. In Confucian cultures, a more central building block of biographical coherence is being a good listener. Fung, Miller and Lin point out that the Chinese self is defined by relationships to others. It is one's role to consider not only the path of one's own life but to consider it in relation to the journeys of others. A part of this biographical stance appears to be resolving tensions between strivings for autonomy and independence and responsiveness to others in society. In this regard, Erikson's (1950) overarching framework comes into play, as "societies create the only condition in which human growth is possible" (p. 277). In Western cultures, biographical coherence may be more likely to include features such as acting on one's own, as described in the stories collected by Fiese and Bickham, and as reported in the chapter by Wang (this volume). The medium in which biographical coherence is created may vary by culture as well as by individual differences in relationship formation.

Older Adults: Epochs and Family Preservation

The stories told and valued by older adults are often epochal in nature. By the term epochal, we refer to the fact that embedded within such stories is an appreciation for the sweep of history, and for individuals' and the family's place in generational time. Ryan and colleagues (this volume) detail accounts where historical events such as war are often background to stories of personal loss and survival. The authors speculate that when grandparents use such historical frames in their family reminiscences, grandchildren may develop a greater appreciation for history in general. Often, however, the accounts were not necessarily related to the history of the world as much as they were tales of family history. Grandparent stories were used as opportunities to introduce grandchildren to relatives and events that preceded the birth of the grandchild. The authors cite one grandparent who considers his forebears' achievements as a source of encouragement when faced with challenging situations. One could speculate that some adolescents (given the need to process and reflect over time on a sense of self) may eventually take these stories of grandparents as part of their own personal history (e.g., Hilbers, 1997). In many respects, the stories of older adults provide tangible evidence of family legacies.

The drive to preserve family history and share advice is clearly evident in the chapters by Ryan and colleagues, and by Norris, Kuiack, and Pratt (this volume). One gets the sense that grandparents feel obliged to share their wisdom in the hopes that the younger generation will benefit (and survive!). There are important stylistic differences, however, that moderate the potential force of these stories. Norris and colleagues report that more generative grandparents create more detailed and engaged stories about their grandchildren than do less generative grandparents. They suggest that generative grandparents may enact their goals for the family more effectively through storytelling. Gould (this volume) also reports individual differences in older adults' styles of recounting personal experiences, similar to stylistic differences noted in parent-child reminiscences. Overall, then, the stories of older adults are used as opportunities for personal reflection and to deal with the question of what one's life means for the next generation.

Surprisingly, there was less attention to the notion of coherence in the research reported here on the stories told by older adults. Gould attends to the potential for memory loss in later life to affect story content and structure. However, the chapters by Ryan and colleagues, and by Norris and colleagues, focus more on the content of stories told between generations. The focus appears to be on connections and collaborations between generations rather than on individual coherence and its implications. In this regard, the illocutionary force investigated so far seems aimed at drawing generations together in the hopes that values are transmitted. Future research may attend to whether the coherence of the narratives told by individual older adults is related to generativity, ego integrity and effective value transmission. Certainly previous research has indicated that more coherent life stories, as told by older versus younger adults, may be better appreciated by readers and listeners (Kemper, 1992; Pratt & Robins, 1991).

Family Stories Across the Life Span. Table 17.1 summarizes the ways in which stories are told during different periods across the life span and suggests something of their meanings. The narrative environment is rich with opportunities to engage others in family stories. Building blocks of storytelling are evident in early childhood, with a focus on reminiscences and recountings of shared experiences, largely guided by adult partners. This type of storytelling sends the message that sharing everyday memories is a part of relating to others and provides an opportunity for problem solving. This process of storytelling builds linguistic, cognitive, and social competence in the developing child (e.g., McAdams, 2001).

TABLE 17.1
Elements of Family Stories Across the Life Span

Lifespan Period	*Medium*	*Meaning*	*Metaphor*	*Coherence*
Childhood	Reminiscence	Sharing everyday memories is relational	How do I learn to behave?	Narrative and social competence
Adolescence	Dialogue	Synthesizing different experiences lays foundation for coherence	Who am I?	Coherence of personal identity
Adulthood	Prosaic	Relationship histories	What do others mean to me?	Coherence across immediate family relationships
Older Adult	Epochal	Family preservation	What does my life mean to others?	Continuity across family generations

During adolescence, the medium shifts to a more balanced dialogue, where the adolescent is actively engaged in evaluating and perhaps changing parts of the family story to fit with his or her own evolving identity (see Table 17.1). The everyday memories that came before must now be considered and integrated across multiple perspectives to create a coherent whole (e.g., McAdams, 2001). Adolescent identity develops through these processes, as highlighted in the chapters by Arnold and colleagues, Dunbar and Grotevant, and Thorne et al.

During adulthood there is a new level of social responsibility that is associated with family stories for new parents. Implicit in these stories are messages of both socialization and relationship values. As conveyors of culture, adults as parents must come to terms with the role of sending messages that are consistent (or perhaps deliberately inconsistent) with shared cultural and family values. These stories are commonly about everyday events, routines, and rituals in the life of the immediate family, and thus we characterize them as "prosaic" aspects of the broad tasks of family socialization (Table 17.1). Their larger role, however, is to convey information and emotion about the web of relationships and meanings within the family context for the developing child. Although the topic of the stories may appear relatively mundane, through repetitive tellings there is the opportunity to transform the momentary practice to a symbolic representation of family experiences. Furthermore, such storytelling may become less prosaic and more challenging as children grow into adolescence, as demonstrated in the chapter by Thorne and colleagues.

Older adults extend this charge, and seize the opportunity to reflect on the unique nature of their own family in the context of a broader historical moment. Indeed, they may be the most time-conscious members of the family, and often have the strongest investment in preserving family history for the next generations (Putney & Bengston, 2001). Bengtson's idea of "generational stake" stresses that the oldest generations have the most investment in preserving family harmony and tend to emphasize this in their views and activities. Our concept of the "epochal" nature of family stories for the oldest generation is meant to stress this idea of family intergenerational process in historical context (see Table 17.1).

As depicted in Table 17.1, then, this book is premised on the notion that Erikson's (1950) framework of life-span development is a useful organizing perspective for viewing the role of family stories across the individual's life course. Early in life, the young child acquires both a competence in narrative and a sense of social relationships through the medium of participation in family reminiscence activities. As Fiese and Bickham (this volume) show, parental story content even seems to vary somewhat in parallel with the stages of development in the child's personality, as outlined by Erikson. In adolescence, the issues of identity are addressed by the construction of a sense of coherence in the life story, with the family as a central context for this process (e.g., McAdams, this volume, 2001). In adulthood, the sense of self enlarges to encompass relationships with partners and others, and a concern with socializing the next generation, following the Eriksonian framework, and family stories reflect and illuminate these intimacy and generativity themes. Finally, in late adulthood, a concern with the self's legacy is reflected in family stories designed to pass on the family, its values and history across generational lines, perhaps as a way of coming to terms with the issues of "ego integrity" in the sense described by Erikson. As several of our chapters point out, however, and as Erikson (1950) himself clearly recognized, these broad life-span processes are situated within diverse cultural contexts that may shape their expression differently.

WHAT CAN NARRATIVES TEACH US ABOUT FAMILIES?

Our second topic reflects the fact that there are lessons to be learned about families in general from these chapters on family stories. For one, the content of these stories reinforces the importance of family interactions as a group. It is thus noteworthy that in many instances the stories relayed were situated within family routines and rituals. Fivush and colleagues (this volume) noted that 78% of the positive events that were recalled were about family vacations or holiday gatherings. Fiese and Bickham (this volume) found that close to 40% of the stories told by mothers made reference to family routines. Wang (this volume) highlights the importance of everyday uses of memory and their salience in social gatherings such as family dinners. Norris and colleagues (this volume) refer to the process of engaging grandparent and grandchildren in storytelling as a "ritual which can connect current and past generations." We make note of these features for two reasons. First, the content of family stories provides clues as to what it means to be a member of a family. Second, it highlights how family stories include both practicing and representational components, a distinction we discussed in chapter 1.

A persistent challenge in studying family relationships and the construct of "family systems" as described in chapter 1 is considering how whole family process influences individuals, and how individuals contribute to whole family process (Cowan, 1999; Parke & O'Neil, 1999). Part of the quandary may be due to how we go about accessing family relationships. Family stories provide a unique opportunity to consider how individuals interpret whole family process as well as how family dynamics may influence individual members. The recurring presence of routines and rituals in many of these stories speaks to what families actually do together, reinforcing the importance of understanding the "narrative ecology of family life" (McAdams, this volume).

By definition, family routines and rituals involve multiple family members and, in many instances, provide meaning to group activities (Fiese et al., 2002). When people are asked to tell stories about family events, it is then reasonable to expect that many of these stories will include descriptions of repetitive patterns of family interaction, such as those found during meals, vacations, and birthday celebrations. On the one hand, these settings may include a cultural script that allows for an easier telling of such tales (Nelson, 1999). The predictability and "scriptability" of these interactions over time may foster cognitive ease in recounting particular stories and events.

In addition to this role of cognitive facility, however, is the notion that family routines and rituals involve a core interpretive component. Family rituals are noted for affective involvement, symbolic communication, and endurance across generations (Fiese et al., 2002). When asked to reflect on such family experiences, there is an essential interpretive component of what it means to be a member of a family that may be revealed in the stories themselves. These meanings may be relatively unique to a particular family, as in the case of the family legacies recounted by older adults, or they may be more universal, as in the case of creating secure and trustworthy bonds between parent and child in the service of attachment. The stories depicted and analyzed in the chapters in this volume, then, may provide a window into this important meaning-making process that extends beyond dyadic relationships to the wider family unit.

As described in our introductory chapter (Pratt & Fiese, this volume), family process can be distinguished along the two intersecting dimensions of family practices and family representations. The act of engaging family members in storytelling extends across the life span, with variations in elaborative style, in how eagerly individuals take on the task, and in how emotion is regulated in the telling. These stylistic features evident in storytelling are oftentimes concordant with interactions observed outside of the specific narrative exchange (e.g., Dickstein, this volume; Fiese & Marjinsky, 1999; Sher-Censor and Oppenheim, this volume). Thus, there may be quite plausible cross-situational consistency between behaviors observed in a narrative context, and those observed during everyday routine interactions.

Partly because of this, family stories can serve as a *method* for investigating important dimensions of family life, as noted in chapter 1. This is so because such stories may reveal consistencies in their tellings with practices within the family, as well as across underlying representations of family models. In addition, coherence between narrative style and overall family style in practices may aid in cementing the images and messages portrayed in the story. As suggested in the introductory chapter, family stories are also important as a *medium* for conveying key information between individual members, and this role is influenced, perhaps interactively, both by stories' practicing and representing aspects. Finally, the act of storytelling may lead, or transact, with the meaning or representational model of the family implicit in the story told. Stories thus serve the key role of constructing *meaning* and a sense of identity, both for the individual and for the wider family. Stories, as depicted in these chapters, are thus all of these simultaneously—method, medium, and meaning—and future research should continue to explore all of these potential aspects of narrative within the family.

For example, when considering members' representations of family life and its meanings, it is clear that these are works in progress. Consistent with Bowlby's (Bowlby, 1969) notion that repetitive interactions between caregiver and child become internalized and re-evaluated over time, families create working models of relationships that become integrated into the individual's sense of self and belonging. An examination of the different topics conveyed in these chapters expands the realm of working models to include guides for behavior in multiple domains. In addition to feelings of felt security and reliance on others, family stories contribute to working models of moral behavior, gender roles, emotion regulation, social orientation, and identity. Thus, an examination of the topics of family stories can provide us with an insider's view of a wide range of elements of family life.

As noted previously, the acts of telling stories, and the representations inherent in them, do not operate in isolation. We consider that there is a transactional process between these two key dimensions that evolves over time. If we chart the life course of the stories conveyed in the chapters in this book, as well as in Table 17.1, we note several features that support this contention. During early childhood, adults create active partnerships with youngsters to foster the act of storytelling. Although varying in style, these dyadic interactions also lay a template for considering the messages about family worlds inherent in the story. Children who are encouraged to participate more fully in such narratives may also themselves create more complex representations of family life. During adolescence the opportunity to explore and consider the multifaceted nature of relationships and personal meaning making appears to be advanced through the experience of responsive family interactions. Adult family members who are good listeners may encourage a more fully explored identity in their adolescents. As parents, the act of telling stories is tempered within the context of who is listening, son or daughter, and who is telling, mother or father. The messages received may then lead to expectations for what is valued behavior for boys and girls within the family and the wider culture. Finally, the storytelling activities between grandparents and grandchildren as described in the Norris et al. and Ryan et al chapters, illustrate how characteristics of each partner may interact and contribute to the type of tale that is told, as well as to which aspects are attended in the representations that members construct.

In addition to these developmentally based aspects of the family as a system across the life course, much of the work in this book stresses the important feature that family processes are inherently mutual and interactive in nature. We have come to understand this better within the context of recent research on parent-child relationships; parents both influence and are influenced by their children (e.g., Bugenthal & Goodnow, 1998). In a parallel sense, while much narrative research has concentrated so far on story telling, story listening is just as fundamental a role, and one that is inherent in a systemic account of the family's use of narrative (e.g., Fung et al., this volume). The audience shapes the teller's expression of tales, just as these tales may influence the audience (e.g., adolescents' role in eliciting various versions of parents' tales of their personal past; see Thorne et al., this volume). These interactive models of narrative also parallel the sociocultural perspective on cognitive and communicative development, in which all utterances are seen as fundamentally dialogical in nature, part of an extended conversation between the voices of self and other (Wertsch, 1991). More work focused on these interactive communicative processes within the family is clearly needed, following on the important beginnings described in various chapters here.

In sum, family stories tell us about the ways in which the family system operates, both through their practicing and representational dimensions. Because these stories are often drawn from, and situated within, family-wide rituals and organizational elements, they inevitably reflect—and, in turn, influence and convey—essential aspects of the systemic nature of the wider family. A central message of this book, then, is that storytelling itself can be one of these key rituals within the bounds of the family system, one that fulfills a range of functions across the life course of family members. Family members tell and respond to and construct together, the stories that express how they interact in their lives through time, as well as signaling how they represent the underlying meaning of those lives in their sense of family worlds.

A NEW BEGINNING?

As developmental psychologists, we strongly believe that the present volume very much must be seen as a work in progress. Although family stories have no doubt been around as long as there have been families and the words to tell them, they have only recently become the subject of scientific investigation. The present collection of chapters, by a range of excellent scholars working within this new area, is meant to convey a sense of the excitement and possibilities of such scientific narrative research. Hopefully, this collection also represents a beginning that is worthy of follow-up, raising essential questions about what family stories may be able to tell us about both individual and family development across the life course.

Indeed, there are many unanswered questions that need to be addressed in future research. From a developmental perspective, the course of narrative content across the life span has only begun to be charted, as described in many of the chapters in this book, and continued work is needed here. However, it will be as important to begin to clarify the course of narrative competence and coherence across time as well. For example, are there transition points in developing narrative coherence that may be opportunities to effect changes in personal development, as well as furthering our understanding of how individuals respond to stressful situations (e.g., Pennebaker, 1997)?

From a family systems perspective, it will be interesting to investigate whether the creation of "a family story" is relatively unique to each family, or whether there are types of family stories that reflect differences in more general patterns of family style and functioning.

More generally, as illustrated in the chapters by Fung et al. and by Wang, there are many important questions about how cultural differences may shape and inform the content and process of family stories, questions that have only begun to be considered in research to date. Are there cultural differences in the content or coherence patterns of family stories? Only careful exploration and theorizing can help us examine this. Similarly, the sociohistorical context of family storytelling is also a topic that deserves to be addressed. For example, the rapid pace of technological change and development in modern societies might be seen as making some aspects of the family narrative transmission of skills and values from previous generations, as Ryan et al. explored in their work in the present book, less compelling for younger generations. Do adolescents watching Music Television find Granddad's stories about the war a total bore? How, if at all, might such historical and cultural changes be influencing the broader role of value transmission through the medium of family narratives?

Finally, research to date has tended to focus more extensively on the positive role that family narratives may play across individual and family growth and development. Yet it is undeniably the case that family as well as individual life narratives can be problematic and destructive as well, as McAdams notes in his chapter in this volume. In the chapter by Thorne et al. on parent stories of their drug use, for example, it is evident that certain kinds of information may be problematic to share within the context of parent-adolescent relationships, and perhaps damaging to the parties and their relationships if not formulated with care. More systematic attention to these negative aspects of family stories and their actual enactment will be important in future work.

We also believe that future work on the applications of family narrative research and theorizing is very important. At our request, the authors of the present chapters generally provided brief commentaries about the applied implications of their research. We found many of these discussions provocative and challenging, and we hope that considering these comments will encourage readers and future researchers to pursue systematic work on this topic. As in other areas of psychology and science more generally, we believe that an ongoing dialogue of basic and applied research is needed to inform our understanding of the role of family stories.

In closing, let us turn once again to Shakespeare, that "inventor of the human" according to Bloom (1998). Yet this time we choose a negative exemplar. How wrong indeed was Macbeth, in his bitter and despairing, though perhaps understandable, soliloquy on his wife's death: "Life's but a walking shadow, a poor player that struts and frets his hour upon the stage, and then is heard no more; it is a tale told by an idiot, full of sound and fury, signifying nothing." Instead, as the authors of the chapters in this book have shown, the tales of family life, told both by the wise and the foolish, often prosaic, can signify much about the processes and meaning of individual and family development. We look forward to learning more in the future about how the metaphors of daily personal experience, as revealed in stories shared, provide meanings and rhythms to family life across time and generations.

REFERENCES

Bateson, M. C. (1994). *Peripheral visions.* New York: Harper.

Benson, M. S. (1996). Structure, conflict, and psychological causation in the fictional narratives of 4- and 5-year olds. *Merrill Palmer Quarterly, 42*(2), 228–247.

Bloom, H. (1998). *Shakespeare: The invention of the human.* New York: Riverhead Books.

Bowlby, J. (1969). *Attachment and loss: Vol 1. Attachment.* New York: Basic Books.

Bugenthal, D., & Goodnow, J. (1998). Socialization processes. In W. Damon (Gen. Ed.), *Handbook of child psychology, 5th ed.* (Vol. 3, pp. 389–462). New York: Wiley.

Cowan, P. A. (1999). What we talk about when we talk about families. In B. H. Fiese, A. J. Sameroff, H. D. Grotevant, F. S. Wamboldt, S. Dickstein, & D. Fravel (Eds.), *The stories that families tell: Narrative coherence, narrative interaction, and relationship beliefs. Monographs of the Society for Research in Child Development, 64,* 163–176. Malden, MA: Blackwell.

Erikson, E. (1950). *Childhood and society.* New York: Norton.

Fiese, B. H., & Marjinsky, K. A. T. (1999). Dinnertime stories: Connecting relationship beliefs and child behavior. In B. H. Fiese, A. J. Sameroff, H. D. Grotevant, F. S. Wamboldt, S. Dickstein, & D. Fravel (Eds.), *The stories that families tell: Narrative coherence, narrative interaction, and relationship beliefs. Monographs of the Society for Research in Child Development, 64*(2, Serial No. 257, pp. 52–68). Malden, MA: Blackwell.

Fiese, B. H., Tomcho, T., Douglas, M., Josephs, K., Poltrock, S., & Baker, T. (2002). Fifty years of research on naturally occuring rituals: Cause for celebration? *Journal of Family Psychology, 16,* 381–390.

Habermas, T., & Bluck, S. (2000). Getting a life: The emergence of the life story in adolescence. *Psychological Bulletin, 126,* 748–769.

Hilbers, S. (1997, April). *Adolescents' narratives of parent and grandparent value socialization: Stories of kindness and care.* Poster presented at the biennial meeting of the Society for Research in Child Development, Washington DC.

Kemper, S. (1992). Language and aging. In F. Craik & T. Salthouse (Eds.), *The handbook of aging and cognition.* Hillsdale, NJ: Lawrence Erlbaum Associates.

Marcia, J. E., Waterman, A. S., Matteson, D. R., Archer, S. L., & Orlofsky, J. L. (1993). *Ego identity: A handbook for psychosocial research.* New York: Springer-Verlag.

McAdams, D. P. (2001). The psychology of life stories. *Review of General Psychology, 5,* 100–122.

Nelson, K. (1999). Event representations, narrative development, and internal working models. *Attachment and Human Development, 1*(3), 239–252.

Parke, R. D., & O'Neil, R. (1999). Social relationships across contexts. In W. A. Collins & B. Laursen (Eds.), *Relationships as developmental contexts. The Minnesota symposia on child psychology* (Vol. 30, pp. 211–239). Mahwah, NJ: Lawrence Erlbaum Associates.

Pennebaker, J. W. (1997). *Opening up: The healing power of expressing emotions.* New York: Guilford Press.

Pratt, M. W., Norris, J., Arnold, M. L., & Filyer, R. (1999). Generativity and moral development as predictors of value socialization narratives for young persons across the adult lifespan: From lessons learned to stories shared. *Psychology and Aging, 14,* 414–426.

Pratt, M. W., & Robins, S. (1991). That's the way it was: Age differences in the structure and quality of adults' personal narratives. *Discourse Processes, 14,* 73–85.

Putney, N., & Bengston, V. (2001). Families, intergenerational relationships, and kinkeeping in midlife. In M. E. Lachman (Ed.), *Handbook of midlife development* (pp. 528–570). New York: Wiley.

Reiss, D. (1989). The practicing and representing family. In A. J. Sameroff & R. Emde (Eds.), *Relationship disturbances in early childhood* (pp. 191–220). New York: Basic Books.

Stern, D. N. (2002). *The first relationship: Infant and mother.* Cambridge, MA: Harvard University Press.

Wertsch, J. (1991). *Voices of the mind.* Cambridge, UK: Cambridge University Press.

Author Index

C

I

J

K

L

M

Z

Subject Index

D

E

F

G

I

R

S